A Companion to
Chimamanda Ngozi Adichie

A Companion to
Chimamanda Ngozi Adichie

Edited by

ERNEST N. EMENYONU

JC JAMES CURREY

James Currey
an imprint of
Boydell & Brewer Ltd
PO Box 9, Woodbridge
Suffolk IP12 3DF (GB)
www.jamescurrey.com

and of

Boydell & Brewer Inc.
668 Mt Hope Avenue
Rochester, NY 14620-2731 (US)
www.boydellandbrewer.com

British Library Cataloguing in Publication Data
available on request

ISBN 978-1-84701-162-6 (James Currey Cloth)
ISBN 978-1-84701-163-3 (Africa-only paperback)
ISBN: 978-1-84701-241-8 (James Currey paperback)

This publication is printed on acid-free paper

Typeset in 11.5/13pt Garamond MT
by Avocet Typeset, Somerton, Somerset TA11 6RT

Contents

Notes on Contributors   viii
Acknowledgements   xii

Introduction   1
ERNEST N. EMENYONU

1. Narrating the Past
Orality, History & the Production of Knowledge
in the Works of Chimamanda Ngozi Adichie   15
LOUÍSA UCHUM EGBUNIKE

2. Deconstructing Binary Oppositions
of Gender in *Purple Hibiscus*
A Review of Religious/Traditional Superiority & Silence   31
JANET NDULA

3. Adichie & the West African Voice
Women & Power in *Purple Hibiscus*   45
JANE DURAN

4. Reconstructing Motherhood
A Mutative Reality in *Purple Hibiscus*   57
INIOBONG I. UKO

5. Ritualized Abuse in *Purple Hibiscus*   73
EDGAR FRED NABUTANYI

Contents

6. Dining Room & Kitchen
Food-Related Spaces & their Interfaces with the
Female Body in *Purple Hibiscus*   87
JESSICA HUME

7. The Paradox of Vulnerability
The Child Voice in *Purple Hibiscus*   101
OLUWOLE COKER

8. 'Fragile Negotiations'
Olanna's Melancholia in *Half of a Yellow Sun*   115
PAULINE DODGSON-KATIYO

9. The Biafran War & the Evolution
of Domestic Space in *Half of a Yellow Sun*   129
JANICE SPLETH

10. Corruption in Post-Independence Politics
Half of a Yellow Sun as a Reflection of *A Man of the People*   139
CHIKWENDU PASCHALKIZITO ANYANWU

11. Contrasting Gender Roles in Male-Crafted
Fiction with *Half of a Yellow Sun*   153
CAROL IJEOMA NJOKU

12. 'A Kind of Paradise'
Chimamanda Ngozi Adichie's Claim to Agency,
Responsibility & Writing   169
SILVANA CAROTENUTO

13. Dislocation, Cultural Memory
& Transcultural Identity in Select Stories
from *The Thing Around Your Neck*   185
MAITRAYEE MISRA & MANISH SHRIVASTAVA

14. 'Reverse Appropriations'
& Transplantation in *Americanah*   199
GICHINGIRI NDIGIRIGI

Contents

15. Revisiting Double Consciousness
& Relocating the Self in *Americanah*   213
ROSE A. SACKEYFIO

16. Adichie's *Americanah*
A Migrant Bildungsroman   229
MARY JANE ANDRONE

17. 'Hairitage' Matters
Transitioning & the Third Wave Hair
Movement in 'Hair', 'Imitation' & *Americanah*   245
CRISTINA CRUZ-GUTIERREZ

Appendix: The Works of Chimamanda Ngozi Adichie   263
Index   291

Notes on Contributors

Mary Jane Androne is Professor Emerita at Albright College where she served as Director of Women's Studies and Co-Director of Africana Studies. Her papers and publications include articles on African and African American women writers, Tsitsi Dangarembga, Julie Dash, Mariama Bâ, Miriam Tlali, Ama Ata Aidoo and Nawal el Saadawi.

Chikwendu PaschalKizito Anyanwu is a Catholic Priest of the Archdiocese of Owerri, Nigeria. He holds a Doctorate degree in Creative Writing from Middlesex University, London. He is a poet and playwright with a number of published poems and stage productions to his name. These include an anthology *I Dance Ala-Igbo* (Lumen Veritas, 2000); *Ikoro na Mgbirimgba: Ije Okwukwe* (Centenary drama for Owerri Catholic Province, 2012); *Kingdom of the Mask* (an adaptation of Chinua Achebe's *A Man of the People*, 2007) and *Nkemakolam* (the first Owerri Archdiocesan Day/Odenigbo drama, 1996). He is a creative writing prizewinner with University of North London (now London Metropolitan University). Founder of the Igbo Conference, London, Chikwendu is currently the creative artist for his Archdiocese and the Principal of Christ the King Secondary School, Obike in Imo State of Nigeria.

Silvana Carotenuto is Associate Professor at the University of Naples 'L'Orientale', Italy, where she teaches Deconstruction, Écriture feminine, Cultural and Postcolonial Studies. Her literary and theoretical focus on feminism has produced the translation into Italian of *Three Steps on the Ladder of Writing* by Hélène Cixous (Bulzoni, 2000), the writing of *La Lingua di Cleopatra: Traduzioni e sopravvivenze decostruttive* (Marietti, 2008), and the editing of 'Writing Exile: Women, the Arts, and Technologies', *Anglistica* 17, 1 (2013). Her recent publications include: *A Feminist Critique of Knowledge Production*, edited with R. Jambresic Kirin and B. Prienda (UPress, 2014), and '"Go Wonder": Plasticity, Dissemination and (the Mirage of) Revolution' in B. Bhandar and J. Goldberg-Hiller (eds), *Plastic Materialities: Politics, Legality, and Metamorphosis in the Work* *of Catherine Malabou* (Duke University Press, 2015). She is the Director of the European Research 'Performance in the Mediterranean Region', and has created, with her researchers, the digital archive 'Matriarchivio del Mediterrano' (www.matriarchiviomediterraneo.org/en).

Oluwole Coker is a Senior Lecturer in Literature-in-English at Obafemi Awolowo University, Ile-Ife, Nigeria. His interests lie in post-colonial African fiction and orature studies. Dr Coker is a 2014 Post-doctoral Fellow of the American Council of Learned Societies/African Humanities Program (ACLS/AHP); 2015 Laureate of Child and Youth Institute, Council for Development of Social Science Research in Africa (CODESRIA) and a Fellow of the Summer Program in Social Sciences, Institute of Advanced Studies, Princeton, New Jersey, USA. (2015-2017). His most recent publications include 'Develop-ment Imperatives and Transnationalism in Third-Generation Nige-rian Fiction' *Matatu* (45) (University of Giensen, Germany, 2015) and 'Vulgar Typologies, Social Equilibrium and Moral Ethics in Yoruba Proverbs' *Proverbium* (33) (University of Vermont, 2016).

Pauline Dodgson-Katiyo was formerly Head of English at Newman University, Birmingham, UK, and Dean of the School of Arts at Anglia Ruskin University, Cambridge, UK. Her research interests are in African literature, particularly Zimbabwean and Somali, and contemporary women's writing. She is co-editor (with Helen Cousins) of *Emerging Perspectives on Yvonne Vera* (Africa World Press, 2012); and guest editor (with Helen Cousins) of *ALT 34 Diaspora & Returns in Fiction* (James Currey, 2016).

Jane Duran is a Lecturer in Black Studies at the Gevirtz Graduate School of Education at the University of California at Santa Barbara, where she has also been a Visiting Fellow in the Department of Philos-ophy. Among her most recent books are *Eight Women Philosophers* (Univer-sity of Illinois Press, 2005), and *Women in Political Theory* (Ashgate, 2013).

Louisa Uchum Egbunike is a lecturer in English at Manchester Metro-politan University. She completed her PhD in African literature at SOAS, University of London, where she has also lectured in contemporary African literature. In 2016 she was selected as one of the BBC's New Generation Thinkers. Louisa has published papers in academic journals, including *African Literature Today* and *Matatu*, and she is one of the founders and conveners of the annual international Igbo Conference at SOAS.

Cristina Cruz-Gutiérrez graduated in English Studies at the Univer-sity of the Balearic Islands, where she also completed her Master's

Degree in Modern Languages and Literatures. Her research interests include Postcolonial Literatures and Gender Studies, specifically focusing on African Studies. She is currently pursuing a PhD in Postcolonial Studies at the University of the Balearic Islands.

Jessica C. Hume holds a Bachelor's Degree in English from Bellarmine University and a Master's Degree in Writing (with a focus on poetry) from Spalding University, in the United States. She is currently a doctoral candidate at the University of Louisville (Kentucky, USA) earning a PhD in Interdisciplinary Humanities with a focus on Health Humanities. Her areas of interest include the female body in culture, health, and health care; illness narratives, specifically those of breast cancer (mammographies); the history of medicine and anatomy in literature; and the body in fairy tales. Jessica is also a full-time Instructor in the Galileo Learning Community for students in the Health Sciences at Bellarmine University.

Maitrayee Misra, a PhD Scholar (JRF) at the Department of English and Foreign Languages, Guru Ghasidas Viswavidyalaya (A Central University), India, has five international and national publications to her credit. Her research interest includes the fictional narratives of Caryl Phillips, Chimamanda Ngozi Adichie, Jhumpa Lahiri and Amitav Ghosh. She is a life member of the Indian chapter of the Association for Commonwealth Literature and Language Studies and a regular member of Société Internationale d'Ethnologie et de Folklore.

Edgar Fred Nabutanyi holds a PhD in English from Stellenbosch University, South Africa. He is currently a Lecturer in the Department of Literature, Makerere University, Kampala, where he teaches both undergraduate and postgraduate courses on research methods, literary theory and practical criticism. His research focus as, reflected in his African Humanities Program (AHP) 2015/2016 Postdoc fellowship, is on representations of vulnerable subjectivities such as children in African contemporary discourses

Gĩchingiri Ndĩgĩrĩgĩ is an Associate Professor of English and Africana Studies at The University of Tennessee, Knoxville. He has published widely on *Ngũgĩ* wa Thiong'o's drama and fiction. His most recent work has been published in *Popular Music and Society* (2016), *Ufahamu* XXXVIII (2015), *Unmasking the African Dictator: Essays on Postcolonial African Literature* (University of Tennessee Press 2014), *African Theatre 13: Ngũgĩ wa Thiong'o and Wole Soyinka* (James Currey 2014), and the Modern Language Association's *Approaches to Teaching the Works of Ngũgĩ wa Thiong'o* (2012).

Janet N. Ndula is a Lecturer at the Department of African Literature and Civilizations in the University of Yaounde 1, Cameroon. She is passionate about her research interests in the area of gender and contemporary literary theories in African and African American Literature. Her PhD dissertation, currently under review for defence, interrogates inhibiting gender characterizations internalized in contemporary African and African American Literature, represented in several recent novels including Chimamanda Ngozi Adichie's *Purple Hibiscus*.

Carol Ijeoma Njoku holds a PhD in English and Literature from the University of Nigeria, Nsukka, and a Master's Degree in International Law and Jurisprudence from Enugu State University. She is currently a Lecturer in the University of Nigeria, Nsukka, where she teaches Nigerian Literature in Law and the Use of English respectively. Her several books include: *Shackles of the Oracle* (Chimavin Publishers, 2005) and *Together in God: A Critical Analysis of the Three Major Religious Sects in Nigeria* (Gostak Publishers, 2002). She is the founder and former director of *The Radiance Magazine* and *Across the Threshold*, respectively 2005 and 2009 (Chimavin Publishers). Her research focus is in international humanitarian law and the representation of women in African and American war narratives, which is reflected in her recent CODESRIA Fellowship (2015/16).

Rose A. Sackeyfio has taught in the Department of English at Winston Salem State University since 1993 after completing a PhD at Ahmadu Bello University, Nigeria where she taught for 10 years. Her research interest is interdisciplinary and includes the literature of African and African-Diaspora women, Women's and Cultural Studies and, recently, South Asian Women's Writing. She is the co-editor of a forthcoming collection of critical essays, *Emerging Perspectives on Akachi Adimora Ezeigbo* who is a leading Nigerian woman writer.

Manish Shrivastava obtained the degree of Doctor of Philosophy in 2000, working on Thomas Hardy. After serving for a brief span at D.P. Vipra College of Bilaspur as Lecturer, he was appointed as Assistant Professor in the Higher Education Department and later as Reader in English in Guru Ghasidas University. Since 2011 he has been Professor & Head, Department of English & Foreign Languages, Guru Ghasidas Vishwavidyalaya, (A Central University), and is also Dean, School of Studies in Arts, State Govt. His specialization and areas of interest are British Fiction and Modern Literary Theories respectively. Manish Shrivastava has published in various national/international peer-reviewed journals and is the author of two books.

Notes on Contributors

Janice Spleth is Professor of French and African Literature in the Department of World Languages, Literatures, and Linguistics at West Virginia University. She has published two volumes on Léopold Sédar Senghor and is co-editor of *Interdisciplinary Dimensions of African Literature* and *Cultural Dynamics of Globalization and African Literature*. Her articles have appeared in *The Literary Griot, Matatu, Research in African Literatures, Studies in Twentieth Century Literature*, the *Journal of African Cinema*, and the *Journal of the African Literature Association*. She has served as president of the African Literature Association and as chair of the Executive Committee of the African Literature Division of the Modern Language Association.

Iniobong I. Uko is a Professor of English in the Department of English, and the current Director of Pre-Degree Studies, University of Uyo, Uyo, Nigeria. Her area of research is African Literature, specifically women's writing, and a cross-cultural study of African and Diasporic women's writings. She is concerned about the diverse issues that confront black women daily in all spheres of life in different cultures. She has published extensively in learned journals and books in Nigeria, Ghana, Germany, the United States of America and the United Kingdom. She is the author of the seminal book *Gender and Identity in the Works of Osonye Tess Onwueme* (Africa World Press, 2004).

Acknowledgements

I am deeply grateful to Chimamanda Ngozi Adichie for accepting our invitation to visit the University of Michigan-Flint in September 2014. Her extraordinary presentations and interactions truly inspired the demand for and production of this book. I am also grateful to UM-Flint Graduate School particularly the Dean, Dr Vahid Lotfi, for a Graduate Student Research Assistantship (GSRA) that enabled the appointment of Jesutofunmi Omowumi who produced the index for the book. Thanks immensely to the UM-Flint Office of Research for an Undergraduate Research Opportunity Program (UROP) grant which facilitated the appointment of Tiffany Lopez who proof-read and helped in many ways in the successful preparation of the manuscript. I am thankful also to Jody Honkanen (Interim secretary, Africana Studies Department) who assiduously typed, organized and coordinated the production of the manuscript. The extensive and brilliant Bibliography at the end of the book is the handwork of Daria Tunca to whom I am most grateful.

Thank you all!

Ernest N. Emenyonu

Introduction

ERNEST N. EMENYONU

Easily the leading and most engaging voice of her era, Chimamanda Ngozi Adichie has bridged gaps and introduced new motifs and narrative varieties that have energized contemporary African fiction since her first novel, *Purple Hibiscus* (2003). With *Half of a Yellow Sun* (2007) and *The Thing Around Your Neck* short stories (2009a), she established herself as Africa's pre-eminent story teller who uses her tales to give meaning to the totality of the world as she perceives it, producing in effect, narratives that seek to shape a new world of understanding as they give expression to realities people know and human commitments and awareness they need to know. *Americanah* (2013) is the culmination of the dexterous fusion of ingenious craftsmanship blending intriguingly sensitive themes of passionate love, independence, freedom and moral responsibility with versatile narrative innovations. Through her writings, she has made herself relevant to people of all ages – across racial and linguistic boundaries – whose needs, dreams, peculiar circumstances, successes and failures, hopes and aspirations, she has come to represent. Her talks, blogs, musings on social media, essays and commentaries, workshop mentoring for budding young writers and lecture circuit discourses, enrich her as they expand and define her mission as a writer. 'We should all be feminists', she once proclaimed, providing an important perspective on conventional feminist theory.

This powerful proclamation given in a TED Talk on 29 April 2013, soon reverberated across the globe (reportedly viewed more than 2 million times), with two totally unexpected, amazing outcomes. In the United States, the world-acclaimed singer Beyoncé further popularized the speech all over the music world by incorporating part of it into her song 'Flawless', later in 2013. The speech, now also published in book form (Adichie, 2014), was selected in December 2015 (according to

1

their website (https://sweden.se) by the Swedish Government for free distribution 'to every 16-year-old student in the country' to validate and enhance 'gender equality as one of the cornerstones of the Swedish society'. Teachers were encouraged to integrate the ideas in the book into their courses to inspire classroom discussions and conversations between boys and girls. The desired effect was the belief that inculcating the social values advocated by Adichie in the book will help to achieve harmonious mutual relationships across genders which would carry into adult life and produce the type of gender equality that would make the world a better place to live in. The salient point in Adichie's virtually new perspective on feminism is revealed in her contention that

> [t]he problem with gender is that it prescribes how we should be rather than recognizing how we are. Imagine how much happier we would be, how much freer to be our true individual selves, if we didn't have the weight of gender expectations. (Adichie, 2014, 34)

Earlier in the speech, Adichie had distilled what looks like a *modus operandi*, a pedagogical approach for the realization of this gender harmony:

> Gender matters everywhere in the world. And I would like today to ask that we should begin to dream about and plan for a different world. A fairer world. A world of happier men and happier women who are truer to themselves. And this is how to start: we must raise our daughters differently. We must also raise our sons differently. (ibid., 25)

Throughout the 48-page booklet, *We Should All Be Feminists*, Adichie illustrates the pragmatic ways humanity can go about 'rais[ing] our daughters differently' and 'rais[ing] our sons differently' to achieve a fairer and happier world.

It must be recalled that prior to the 'We Should All Be Feminists' speech, Adichie had given an equally far-reaching speech titled 'The Danger of a Single Story' (2009b), which focused on stereotypes in both reality and fiction with one disastrous consequence: 'the perpetuation of social and cultural misunderstandings in the world'. 'The Danger of a Single Story' has, since its inception, become a popular topic for classroom discussions across disciplines in schools and colleges world-wide. Thus, in two seemingly simple speeches, Chimamanda Ngozi Adichie had almost distilled into the Academy and beyond, the ideologies behind her imaginative creativity. As escorts to creative writers, it has become necessary, therefore, for critics to engage her works and ideas in structured conversations. Her contributions to African, diasporic and world literatures demand compellingly from scholars, teachers and critics, intensive critical analysis, commentaries and interpretations as eloquent, exuberant and resourceful as Chimamanda Ngozi Adichie's vibrant artistic innovations and penetrating ideological articulations. To fill this gap is the major goal of this *Companion*.

Fortunately, at the University of Michigan–Flint, there had been in existence since 2003, a unique forum for dialogue with renowned and world-acclaimed African writers. Titled, 'Renowned African Writers/ African and African Diaspora Artists Visit Series', the establishment of the forum was a collaborative project of the Department of Africana Studies and the Flint Public Library, funded by the Ruth Mott Foundation, whereby a world-acclaimed African writer was annually invited to Flint for a period of time ranging from four days to a whole week for a variety of literary activities between 'town and gown'.

Chimamanda Ngozi Adichie was invited in 2014 as the eighth visitor. Prior to her visit, the University of Michigan–Flint had hosted the Nobel Laureate Wole Soyinka, Buchi Emecheta, Dennis Brutus, Ngũgĩ wa Thiong'o, Nawal El Saadawi, Femi Osofisan and Chris Abani. (Chinua Achebe, originally scheduled as the first visitor could not make it due to ill health, and Sindiwe Magona and Niyi Osundare came after Adichie). Adichie arrived in Flint on 24 September 2014. Part of the letter inviting her read:

> [T]he visiting writer would interact with students (high school and college), public school teachers, the university community, friends and patrons of the Flint Public Library, and the community at large ... We will distribute freely hundreds of copies of the writer's selected work to high school students (as many as 350), public school teachers, and members of Flint Public Library Fiction-Only Book Club, who were required to read the book several weeks in advance ... We will choose *Purple Hibiscus* as the primary text for the Teen Forum, Educators' Workshop, and events at the University. *Americanah* would be selected for the Book Club. At each forum you will be asked general questions about your writing as well as specific questions about the book read by the audience. Your one-hour presentation on the campus will be on a topic of your choice but central to your writing or personal experience ... 'The Danger of a Single Story' is a favorite here.

Videos of 'The Danger of a Single Story' and 'We Should All Be Feminists' were shown at some of the events and, as was expected, they generated many questions from faculty, teachers, students, and the general public. In answering the questions posed, especially from participants at the Educators' Workshop (a free workshop organized for public school teachers, teacher trainees, educators and instructors at tertiary levels) on the general topic of 'Teaching African Literature and Cultures in non-African classrooms', with particular focus on the visiting author and his/her selected work/s, Adichie dwelt at length on her social background and how the values she advocates in her works, were things she imbibed as part of her upbringing in a remarkably stable and loving household. Drawing from her personal background in a lecture titled, 'The House on Cartwright Avenue' (the house in which Chimamanda grew up on the University of Nigeria, Nsukka Campus, where her father had been a professor and her mother an administrator, which by coincidence was also the house in which Chinua Achebe lived when he was a professor at the University), Adichie revealed how some intimate experiences in the social environments of her childhood shaped her ethical concepts of the world, and her human relationships. She has stood for these values ever since, and naturally reflects them in her fiction and non-fiction writings. Her ideas in 'We Should All Be Feminists' took centre-stage in audience questions, comments and reactions. The discussions at the all-day Educators' Workshop became so animated that Adichie joyfully left the podium and interacted one-on-one with the participants – explaining various points, chatting, taking photographs and signing autographs.

This *Companion* is an answer to the passionate pleas, requests and desires of the participants at the Educators' Workshop, as well as an attempt to complete the 'unfinished conversations' between Chimamanda Ngozi Adichie and the highly animated audiences at several venues in Flint, Michigan, 24–26 September 2014. A 'Call for Papers' was circulated to literary scholars, teachers, critics and interested others to contribute to 'a classic anthology' that would examine, explore, and analyse the ramifications of Adichie's creative outputs from a variety of perspectives that demonstrate a thorough understanding of her art, ideology, and vision as a writer. A few of the contributions in the *Companion* were by invitation. But in general, responses were wide-spread and overwhelming – from the United Kingdom, United States, Malaysia, South Africa, Italy, Nigeria, Uganda, Cameroon, India, Spain, etc. More than thirty submissions were received out of which seventeen were selected for inclusion after several levels of intensive blind peer reviews and assessments.

The scope and depth of the discourse in individual chapters underscore how intensely committed the authors were to the background researches that produced their submissions. The chapters are organized on each of Adichie's works in the chronological order of their publication beginning with *Purple Hibiscus* and ending with *Americanah*. There are six chapters on *Purple Hibiscus* (2003), four on *Half of a Yellow Sun* (2007), two on *The Thing Around Your Neck* (2009a), and four on *Americanah* (2013). These are all preceded by an opening chapter which provides an insightful theoretical base of Adichie's writings, including her use of Igbo oral elements and local sources, as well as an analysis of the significance of the university setting of much of her fiction, in terms of epistemologies and narrative forms.

In the opening chapter, 'Narrating the Past: Orality, History & the Production of Knowledge in the works of Chimamanda Ngozi Adichie', Louisa Uchum Egbunike provides a pertinent foundation for a better understanding of the Igbo worldview and the literary backgrounds of Adichie's fiction in general. She identifies significant aspects of the Igbo oral tradition and history from which Adichie draws her vision and inspiration. This background helps to authenticate the originality of Adichie's narrative forms and techniques.

The six chapters on *Purple Hibiscus* focus on various critical perspectives of Adichie's debut novel. In 'Deconstructing Binary Oppositions of Gender in *Purple Hibiscus*: A Review of Religious/Traditional Superiority & Silence', Janet Ndula works from the premise that *Purple Hibiscus* 'is a fresh contribution to the new generation of novels which carry implications that endorse individual effort over gender disposition, demonstrating that sex difference does not presuppose subordination'. Jane Duran, in 'Adichie and the West African Voice: Women and Power in *Purple Hibiscus*', focuses on characterization in *Purple Hibiscus* as Adichie's spectacular achievement, contending that, 'Adichie achieves the difficult by giving us female characters in whom we can believe … the author refuses to indulge in platitudes; rather, she provides us with characters whose credibility is underscored by both their strengths and weaknesses.' Extending as it were the discourse on characterization, in 'Reconstructing Motherhood: A Mutative Reality in *Purple Hibiscus*', Ini Uko links the sadistic nature of protagonist Eugene, to his tragic demise at the end of the novel – poisoned by his own long-suffering wife. Uko interprets this as victory for African womanhood, which for decades had suffered from mental torture, physical abuse and other forms of dehumanization at the hands of obdurate patriarchy and unbending cruel masculinity. Uko sees the poisoning as the ultimate feminist victory. She declares: 'Thus, Mama in *Purple Hibiscus* can be described as an African woman of the future, because of her ability to mutate reality, reconstruct motherhood, and modify her primary nurturing role as convenient. By violating the traditional female image and roles, Mama reacts to what threatens her and her children's welfare.'

In 'Ritualized Abuse in *Purple Hibiscus*', Edgar Nabutanyi, makes a clear case for linking child abuse to respectability and ritualized violence rather than conflict or poverty, through the figure of the testifying child, thus differentiating the book from existing studies of child abuse. It also makes a cogent case for reading child abuse as just that, rather than as a metaphor for postcolonial state. He declares:

> I argue that fiction deconstructs the veneer of comfort and safety that such homes [African middle-class homes] project to unearth how children are abused because of their parents' obsession with propriety and respectability ... *Purple Hibiscus* unmasks Eugene's ritualized abuse of his family in instances where he feels they have deviated from his (distorted) version of religious piety and its attendant rituals.

Shifting the discourse to another equally exciting direction, Jessica Hume, in 'Dining Room and Kitchen: Food-Related Spaces and their Interfaces with the Female Body in *Purple Hibiscus*', explores the possibilities of using theoretical approaches to space in the analysis of the book. The goal is to apply theories of space to kitchens and dining rooms in the novel towards a better understanding of the ways in which the female body interfaces with domestic and public spaces. According to the author,

> A brief overview of the cultural history of women living in Igboland will demonstrate that their identity has, in pre-colonial, colonial and post-colonial times, revolved around the production, provision, and marketing of food for their families and communities. Adichie's novel reflects this phenomenon, as dozens of revealing or important moments in the text occur around the kitchen dinner table or other places that revolve around food. So, I will present two interrelated spaces – kitchens and dining rooms – which will enable what Mills [Sarah Mills, 2003] might call a spatial archaeological dig, and give further insight into the interfaces between a city space and the female body in *Purple Hibiscus*.

Oluwole Coker, in 'The Paradox of Vulnerability: The Child Voice in *Purple Hibiscus*', while focusing on the characteristics of the child-narrator, seems to take umbrage at Uko's ultra-feminist position. '[I]t is doubtful', he maintains, 'whether murder is the solution to Eugene's domestic tyranny. This is because the poisoning of Eugene eventually shatters the home. It leaves Eugene dead, Jaja behind bars, and Beatrice a psychological wreck.' Quoting Ogaga Okuyade, Coker affirms the view that Adichie's 'intention [is] bold and uncompromising, though, it is only an invocation of pre-existing stasis, and it is an emphatic statement of resistance to the dominant group' (2009, 287). This type of internal dialogue, if nothing else, enhances the integrity of this classic *Companion* as it presents diverse and contrasting critical views with the fullest of objectivity.

The chapters on *Half of a Yellow Sun* examine a tragic landmark in Nigerian history, which Adichie recalls for Nigeria, Africa, and the world in this epochal novel. The Nigerian Civil War (6 July 1967 – 14 January 1970) introduced a new category of writing that hitherto was relatively unknown in Nigerian (indeed African) literature. The war attracted many works of fiction and non-fiction by Nigerians on the subject of human conflict and conflict resolution. Most of the writings were by writers from the former secessionist 'Republic of Biafra', particularly writers of Igbo origin. The works in various genres depicted the human condition at a time of war as each writer handled the dilemma of the choice between political commitment and dedication to art as a sacred entity.

There is a sense in which it could be said that the great Nigerian war novel did not exist until Adichie's *Half of a Yellow Sun*. Shortly after the war and the decades following it, there was an influx of writings based on or generated by the war or the experiences of particular writers who were active participants in the war either as combatants or as people who nurtured the embers of the conflagration. In those circumstances, the writers were hardly able to detach themselves enough to bring their imaginative visions to bear on a most complicated and unprecedented event in Nigerian history. They were too close to the events and the historical figures involved to be transparently objective. Chimamanda did not witness the war. She was born on 15 September 1977, seven years after the war. She credits the writing of her novel to the reading and regurgitation of the accounts of the war in thirty-one books listed at the end of *Half of a Yellow Sun*, aided in no small measure by the fruits of her parents' memories. She acknowledged her parents' influence in these words:

> However, I could not have written this book without my parents. My wise and wonderful father, Professor Nwoye James Adichie, *Odelu Ora Abba*, ended many stories with the words *agha ajoka*, which in my literal translation is 'war is very ugly.' He and my defending and devoted mother, Mrs. Ifeoma Grace Adichie, have always wanted me to know, I think, that what matters is not what they went through but that they survived. I am grateful to them for their stories and for so much more.' (Adichie, 2007, 542)

Adichie brought tremendous impetus to bear on the integrity of the Nigerian Civil War writing – its content, narrative, and historical relevance – depicted as never before. This is what makes the book *the great* Nigerian Civil War novel.

The authors of the four chapters in the *Companion* have examined the novel from four major perspectives. In 'Fragile Negotiations: Olanna's Melancholia in *Half of a Yellow Sun*', Pauline Dodgson-Katiyo examines the story through the framework of melancholia and the psychoanalytic theory with Olanna, a dominant character, as its pivot; linking moreover, the novel to the death of the legendary poet, Christopher Okigbo, in the Biafran war. In 'The Biafran War & the Evolution of Domestic Space in *Half of a Yellow Sun*', Janice Spleth discusses Igbo ideologies of domestic space giving prominence to Adichie's incomparable attention to innocent civilians fatally caught in the cross-fires of war, and the 'ifs' of history. Chikwendu PaschalKizito Anyanwu, writing on 'Corruption in Post-Independence Politics: *Half of a Yellow Sun* as a Reflection of *A Man of the People*', examines the resonances of Achebe's novel, *A Man of the People* (1966) in Adichie's writing. In 'Contrasting Gender Roles in Male-Crafted Fiction with *Half of a Yellow Sun*', Carol Ijeoma Njoku compares Adichie's representation of gender and war with male-authored war narratives. In previous critical writings on the Nigerian Civil War, these perspectives have hardly been paid as much focused attention as these chapters have done. Anyanwu in particular, spells out the historical importance of Adichie's contribution to Nigerian war literature. He postulates:

> Adichie emerges as one of those great reminders in a Nigeria where collective amnesia has become a major malaise, with History pushed aside as a subject in secondary schools; and, like a faithful disciple in adherence to the master's voice or, rather, a literary offspring who grew up in the same house her forebear lived in at the University of Nigeria, Nsukka, Adichie dubs *Half of a Yellow Sun* 'my refusal to forget'.

Anyanwu acknowledges Hewett (2005), agreeing that: 'Adichie does not only rewrite Achebe, she also challenges him', as she also updates him and makes his imagery more accessible. On 'Art' specifically, Anyanwu's articulation of Adichie's debt to Chinua Achebe is in itself philosophically intriguing. His theoretical equation seems to suggest that if genealogy or chronology were different or reversible, one would proclaim Adichie, Achebe's forerunner; one who came before with the mission of heralding the coming of a legend; but it was Achebe who saw Adichie and heard her voice (as one crying in the wilderness) and named her 'One who came fully made'. Identification of Adichie with Achebe has quite often dwelt on superficial interpretations and perceptions until Adichie begins *Purple Hibiscus* with 'Things began to fall apart at home when …'. Seen in the context of Anyanwu's biblical philosophical dimension, the reader must pause and ask, 'Is this mere intertextuality or more?'

The two chapters that focus on Adichie's collection of short stories, *The Thing Around Your Neck* (2009a), celebrate Adichie's eminent success as a story teller. In '"A Kind of Paradise": Chimamanda Ngozi Adichie's Claim to Agency, Responsibility & Writing', Silvana Carotenuto starts off with a panoramic discussion of the uniqueness of Adichie's artistic prowess. In her opening statement she declares: 'The creative singularity of the work of Chimamanda Ngozi Adichie seems resistant to theoretical interpretation, being always already informed by the translation of complex thoughts in a language and a form of writing whose goal is to communicate to her public, a vast audience, a global readership.' Citing a variety of sources and theories, Carotenuto affirms that 'the voices of some postcolonial authors share the same intellectual vocation as Adichie'. The premise of her focus on the twelve stories in *The Thing Around Your Neck,* is that 'Adichie finds the right and just language to utter and narrate stories of difficult realities, scenes of migratory experiences, and new utopias of future salvation.' The twelve stories in the collection are then discussed in the context of the three categories above. 'Stories matter. Many stories matter' (Adichie 2009a). This is the context in which Carotenuto perceives Adichie's short stories as the best manifestations of her claim to 'agency, responsibility and writing'. In all three entities, Adichie has unparalleled success. Carotenuto declares: 'Adichie is an organic writer. She goes to the "roots" of writing, where her vocation finds a specific dialectic: writing must keep memory of what substantiates it, witnessing its legacy for the coming of the future.' This articulates succinctly not only Adichie's vision and mission as a creative artist, but also her mastery of the medium by which she projects her thematic concerns.

The second chapter on Adichie's short stories focuses on the complex topical issue of migration and individual/national identity, using three stories for illustration, namely 'Imitation', 'The Arrangers of Marriage', and 'The Thing Around Your Neck'. In 'Dislocation, Cultural Memory & Transcultural Identity in Select Stories from *The Thing Around Your Neck*', Maitrayee Misra and Manish Shrivastava use a variety of theories of the ethnography of migration and return in fiction depicted by some pioneer African writers of the mid-twentieth century as rooted in the disastrous consequences of Colonialism in Africa, e.g., Achebe's *No Longer at Ease* (1960), to eloquently examine the vicissitudes of the migrant protagonist who returns to his/her place of origin in Africa after trying challenges and experiences abroad. The authors cohesively analyse the effects of 'dislocation' and 'return' on the lives of three female characters – Nkem, Chinaza and Akumma in the selected stories. They argue: 'At the point where two different cultures meet, a third space is generated and it creates in them [the characters] a conscious urge to develop a new identity for better social adaptability.' They conclude, after interpreting the pros and cons of various actions and reactions in specific events and situations, that the

> dislocated fictional characters of Adichie's short stories realize that it is beyond their ability to erase the differences between the cultures of their country of origin and their country of residence, but they can at least mould themselves to such a level of flexibility that it becomes easier for them to acculturate in any sort of cultural space.

The adherence, or lack thereof, of this pragmatic strategy manifests itself in the fates of characters elsewhere in African fiction where 'exile and return' is the dominant issue of conflict.

The last four chapters of the *Companion* focus on Adichie's latest novel, *Americanah*. In 'Reverse Appropriations & Transplantation in *Americanah*', Gĩchingiri Ndĩgĩrĩgĩ interrogates the issue of mobility in the novel arguing incisively that deterritorialized female travellers with 'flexible citizenship', like Ifemelu, unhitched from (male) spouses and partners, ultimately emerge as autonomous selves, able to live, negotiate and thrive in between traditional cultures and borders. Similarly, Rose A. Sackeyfio, in 'Revisiting Double Consciousness & Relocating the Self in *Americanah*', carefully applies the notion of double consciousness to the book, weaving the theoretical concept together with related ideas such as doubleness and difference. She postulates that

> *Americanah* is a masterfully crafted web of Nigerian immigrant experiences that spans Nigeria, the United States and the United Kingdom. Adichie displays penetrating insight and multiple perspectives through the skilful use of point of view to convey the complexities and contradictions in the lives of new African diaspora subjects, marginalized by their *difference*. [...] In telling the immigrant story, Adichie has interwoven the diverse, lucid and carefully nuanced perceptions of race, class

and gender dynamics, and relationships among African Americans and African immigrants.

In 'Adichie's *Americanah*: A Migrant Bildungsroman', Mary Jane Androne makes a vigorous case about how *Americanah* subverts typical expectations of achievement and affiliation in the bildungsroman. She highlights, among other things, that

> [o]ne aspect of Adichie's structure in *Americanah* is the juxtaposition of Ifemelu's stressful but productive years in America with Obinze's disastrous experience as an illegal immigrant in London, which ends with his deportation. In narrating this novel through time shifts in both of their lives, Adichie is able to record the consciousness of both Ifemelu and Obinze at various points in their experiences as immigrants and returnees in order to suggest the tumultuous psychological shifts they both go through before going home to Nigeria, as well as when they finally are there. … What Adichie creates in these opposing narratives of Ifemelu in America and Obinze in England is a diptych where the mirrored portraits reflect the dissatisfaction both characters come to feel in foreign environments, which becomes the basis for the 'growing up' they both experience.

In the last chapter in the *Companion,* '"Hairitage" Matters: Transitioning & the Third Wave Hair Movement in "Hair," "Imitation," and *Americanah*', Cristina Cruz-Gutiérrez deftly contextualizes theoretically and historically the hair politics of Adichie's works, focusing on the short stories 'Hair' and 'Imitation', and the novel, *Americanah*. The chapter examines how the transition from relaxed to natural hair – the big chop – changes personal and social identity, self-perception, body image, and personal development. Gutiérrez concludes, after several explications of symbolic and political imageries signified by hair formations: 'Altogether, the notion of controlling one's hair and body as a metonymic representation of being in control of one's identity suggests that transitioning can be read as the ultimate sign of Black women rejecting previously internalized discourses of normalized femininity and appearance.'

These authors have, in their intrinsically versatile and diverse discourses, given full meaning and critical attention to Adichie's *art and ideology* as a creative writer. In their studies, individually and collectively, they have shown that in Adichie's writings art and ideology complement each other and are never in conflict or contradiction. They are instead like inseparable twins. Art informs ideology as ideology defines and validates art. 'The Danger of a Single Story' and 'We Should All be

Feminists' are illuminating declarations of definitive ideological stance and narrative methodology clearly discernible in Adichie's fictional and non-fictional works. Her commitment as a writer lies in her vision of the writer as a harbinger of social awareness, truth, and empowerment; with responsibilities to educate as well as challenge human actions and reactions at a point in time. As a writer, Adichie is perceived playing these multiple roles in her works. Her art and ideology are embedded in these roles as she seeks through her stories to shape a new world of understanding, a better world, a world of inherent belief in one's self in relation to others and a benevolent socio-political and cultural environment. With Chimamanda Ngozi Adichie, art is a messenger, a carrier of tradition, and a translator of human ideas and beliefs for the benefit and enrichment of posterity. The foundation and inspiration of her art are situated in her Igbo heritage and oral tradition from which she generously harvests narrative forms, techniques, concepts of beauty, aesthetics, worldview, Igbo wit and wisdom, replete in her fiction. Her vocation as a modern African writer recalls for the reader the roles of the artist in traditional Igbo society:

> The Igbo traditional narrator was, for his audience, the educator, entertainer, philosopher, and counsellor. He entertained as he instructed and endeavored to make the values and beliefs portrayed in the tales come alive ... He had a clear conception of his immediate society, its problems and its needs, and when he performed for his audience, he reflected these needs and addressed himself to specific human problems, projecting through the ethical formulas in his tale a direction for his society and the individuals caught in the dilemmas of humanity. (Emenyonu, 1978: 2–3)

The authors in this collection have defined and demonstrated with ample evidence the things that make Adichie a unique story teller with an inimitable artistic integrity ostensibly rooted in solid ideological foundations.

In conclusion, the reader will find in *A Companion to Chimamanda Ngozi Adichie*, similar and variant views on Adichie's artistic vision, ideology and craftsmanship, all enriching and well informed. All the authors of the chapters that follow are, however, unequivocally in agreement on one thing: for Chimamanda Ngozi Adichie, story telling in whatever genre, is not just art; it is art with a purpose, art with social responsibility. In her works indeed, art and ideology inform, complement and affirm each other.

Works Cited

Adichie, Chimamanda Ngozi. *Purple Hibiscus*. New York: Anchor Books, 2003.

—. *Half of a Yellow Sun*. New York: Anchor Books, 2007

—. *The Thing Around Your Neck*. New York: Anchor Books, 2009a

—. 'The Danger of a Single Story'. TEDGlobal, 2009b.

—. *Americanah*. New York: Alfred A. Knopf, 2013

—. *We Should All Be Feminists*. New York: Anchor Books, 2014

Emenyonu, Ernest. *The Rise of the Igbo Novel*. Oxford: Oxford University Press, 1978.

Mills, Sarah. 'Gender and Colonial Space', in Reina Lewis and Sarah Mills (Eds), *Feminist Post-Colonial Theory: A Reader* (pp. 692–719). New York: Routledge, 2003.

Okuyade, Ogaga. 'Changing Borders and Creating Voices: Silence as Character in Chimamanda Adichie's *Purple Hibiscus*'. *The Journal of Pan African Studies* 2.9 (2009): 245–59.

1

Narrating the Past
Orality, History & the Production of Knowledge in the Works of Chimamanda Ngozi Adichie

LOUISA UCHUM EGBUNIKE

In an article entitled 'The Role of Literature in Modern Africa', Chimamanda Ngozi Adichie articulates the experience of many formerly colonized people, stating:

> we are a people conditioned by our history and by our place in the modern world to look towards 'somewhere else' for validation, to see ourselves as inhabitants of the periphery. I am not merely referring to political expressions like 'Third World', but to the phenomenon of being outside the centre in ways more subtle than mere politics, in ways metaphysical and psychological. (2010, 96)

The historical processes that ordered Africa as peripheral to Europe's centre and Africans as 'other' to Europeans were exacted in part by colonialist literature, which was then taught to children across the continent through the missionary school system. The disjuncture, brought about by the abrasion of African ontologies and an educational system that socialized individuals away from their cultures, led to a rupture in the conceptual location of African people in the world within which they inhabited. Consequently, they were relocated to the margins while Europe occupied the centre. The imposing nature of colonial rule and its associated institutions undermined indigenous epistemologies, dismissing African institutions of power, spiritualism and learning as inferior to those of Europe. In describing the process and impact of colonialism on the colonized as one marked by dispossession, Chinua Achebe notes in *Home and Exile* that 'what is both unfortunate and unjust is the pain the person dispossessed is forced to bear in the act of dispossession itself and subsequently in the trauma of a diminished existence' (Achebe, 2003, 70). The act of dispossession, Achebe

15

argues, was completed through the employment of 'storytellers', whose purpose was to rationalise and sanitise the colonial enterprise. Achebe and Adichie both cite the writings of the sixteenth-century London merchant, John Lok as inaugural in the development of a tradition that would continue to depict Africa in an unfavourable light.[1] Lok's pejorative representation of Africans as subhuman would be replicated in the colonialist tradition of writing that developed over the next three centuries. In this way, colonialist literature served a dual purpose of affirming the moral and evolutionary right for European imperialism, while also establishing the enduring dialectic of the colonizer and the colonized. This chapter will consider the representation of Igbo oral culture in the works of Chimamanda Ngozi Adichie with reference to the utilization of Igbo oral narrative in the decolonisation project during the independence era vis-à-vis the University locale. This discussion is prefaced with an examination of colonialist ideology and its impact upon Igbo epistemology.

It has been suggested that the environment created by the expansion of empire, provided the conditions for the introspection and individualism essential to the birth of the novel. Citing the 1719 publication of Daniel Defoe's *Robinson Crusoe* as an important moment in the development of the novel, Brett C. McInelly puts forward the compelling argument that '*Robinson Crusoe* indicates ways in which British colonial history made the genre of the novel possible'(2003, 2) as the 'entire process of isolating the personal, religious, political, and even economic facets of a fictional subject's life within an imagined colonial setting contributed directly to the features we now associate with the early novel' (ibid., 19). McInelly suggests that the development of the early novel is indebted to the colonial project. He identifies the writing and publication of *Robinson Crusoe* as marking not only the inception of a new literary form, but argues that the text 'indicates ways in which British colonial history made the genre of the novel possible' (ibid,.

[1] In Chinua Achebe's *Home and Exile* he states, 'Captain John Lok's voyage to West Africa in 1561 provided an early model of what would become a powerful and enduring tradition. One of his men had described the Negroes as 'a people of beastly living, without a God, laws, religion' (2003, 46). Similarly, in her 2009 TED talk, Chimamanda Ngozi Adichie references the influence of John Lok in the establishment of a European tradition of writing about Africa: 'This single story of Africa ultimately comes, I think, from Western literature. Now, here is a quote from the writing of a London merchant called John Lok, who sailed to West Africa in 1561 and kept a fascinating account of his voyage. After referring to the black Africans as 'beasts who have no houses', he writes: 'They are also people without heads, having their mouth and eyes in their breasts' (Adichie 2015).

2). In his monograph, *Dreams of Adventure, Deeds of Empire*, Martin Green identifies *Robinson Crusoe* as the 'prototype of literary imperialism' (1980, 5),[2] noting how colonialist 'adventure tales' advanced the construction of a totalising logic of imperialism, inspiring future generations. As Green aptly remarks, these tales which 'formed the light reading of Englishmen for two hundred years and more after *Robinson Crusoe* were, in fact, the energizing myth of English imperialism' (ibid,. xi). This body of literature affirmed the colonial enterprise; as 'they were, collectively, the story England told itself as it went to sleep at night; and, in the form of its dreams, they charged England's will with the energy to go out into the world and explore, conquer, and rule.' (ibid., 3)

British imperialism's moralising discourse identified the 'white man's burden' in his quest to 'civilize' the world's 'primitive' people, revealing Britain's epistemic terms of engagement with its colonies, according to which African people were only considered recipients rather than active producers of knowledge. This lay in contradistinction to the process of knowledge production within many African societies in which the oral transmission of knowledge allowed for the orator and the audience's creative contributions to the cultural capital of the community. Oral literature was thus not solely an inheritance passed on from one generation to the next, but the site for revision and ownership of the narrative, imbibing the creative licence of the orator in each retelling. Storytelling was an interactive endeavour, with built in devices for audience participation. In this way, many forms of knowledge were communal in their production, centred the community in their narration and belonged to the community at large. In the process of retelling oral histories, the multiple narrative accounts in circulation created a sense of plurality to the history. In each rearticulation of the past, adjustments could be made, and word choices altered. History was not singular or immutable; the past was not fixed or perpetual, but instead subject to a constant reimagining that characterized the act of retelling. The comparative flexibility of oral cultures permitted the possibility of change in the context of the past as well as the present and future, in that the negotiation of heterogeneous ideas was a composite feature in the dissemination, reception and modification of the oral story. The Igbo philosophy of duality[3] recognized the

---

[2] Here, Brett C. McInelly echoes James Joyce's description of *Robinson Crusoe* as the 'true prototype of the British colonist' (Joyce 1911).

[3] Igbo proverbs of duality include the following: 'Wherever something stands, something stands beside it' and: 'Let the kite perch, let the eagle perch too. If one says the other should not perch, let his wing break'.

existence of more than one 'truth' and this anti-essentialist worldview encountered the rigidity of early twentieth century print culture, in which concepts of 'eternal truths' were rooted in the seeming permanence of the written text. The church and the colonial administration's dogmatic and uncompromising stance was informed by the illusion of truth as singular, static and everlasting, existing on the pages of historical, legal and religious (Christian) texts.

Against this background, the development of the Igbo novel provided the opportunity to contest distorted representations of the Igbo specifically and Africa more generally, using the medium in which the distortions originated. The novel form provided fertile ground for experimentation, drawing upon an oral system of knowledge to inform the written text. Pita Nwana's 1933 publication *Omenụkọ* marked the beginnings of a written Igbo language literary tradition.[4] Part fiction, part biography, *Omenụkọ* tells the story of Chief Igwegbe Odum, a wealthy Aro warrant chief who was appointed to his position by the colonial government.[5] The text's focus on a prominent historical figure, and its incorporation of stylistic devices employed in oral narratives, reveals that 'the attributes of the traditional artist became legacies for the writer at the stage of Igbo written literature' (Emenyonu 2003, 234).[6] Within the oral tradition, narratives comprise both creative and informative components. Art serves both an imaginative and socio-political function and so a conceptual divide was not drawn between literary and historical oral texts. Helen Chukwuma's study of Igbo oral literature references the aesthetic and operational value of Igbo oral texts as 'the art of commemoration' (1994, 66), while Abiola Irele, speaking more generally on precolonial African societies, similarly describes the dialogue between historical account and fiction, as an 'imaginative commemoration of a common past' (1993, 160).

---

[4] Prior to the publication of Pita Nwana's *Omenụkọ*, the only other book published in Igbo was a translation of the Bible.

[5] Nwana's largely favourable account of the life of his fellow Aro, Chief Igwegbe Odum, on whom *Omenụkọ* is based, has been contested by Igbo Historian Adiele Afigbo, in his article 'Chief Igwegbe Odum: The Omenuko of History' (1966). This reminds us of the divergent oral histories that exist, but also how a creative writer and a historian draw upon oral narratives to write their respective works.

[6] Ernest Emenyonu notes that 'Proverbs, sayings, and anecdotes in the novel as well as peculiar expressions of the hero Omenuko, became part of the Igbo speech repertoire, which the young adult was expected to acquire and use.' (2003, 235) This presents a picture of exchange and influence, which is not solely the oral tradition's influence on the emerging Igbo literature, but in fact demonstrates the capacity for the written text to influence and contribute to oral cultures.

Drawing on the significance of historical figures in the Igbo oral and written traditions, the Igbo-Nigerian novel[7] has sought to weave historical 'truth' with fictional accounts. As a continuation of the oral tradition's approach to narrative, the Igbo written literary tradition stood in direct opposition to Britain's conceptualization of literature and history as two distinct traditions during the late colonial era. From the early nineteenth century, European historians took a 'common-sense view of history' in which it was regarded as 'a corpus of ascertained facts'(Carr 2001, 3). The shift in categorizing history from that of a 'literary art' to that of a science, was born out of the perceived 'excesses and failures' of the French Revolution, brought about by the prevalence of 'mythic thinking' (White 1978, 123–4). This marked the beginnings of a convention,

> at least among historians, to identify truth with fact and to regard fiction as the opposite of truth, hence a hindrance to the understanding of reality rather than as a way of apprehending it … Typically, the nineteenth-century historian's aim was to expunge every hint of the fictive, or merely imaginable, from his discourse, to eschew the techniques of the poet and orator, and to forego what were regarded as the intuitive procedures of the maker of fictions in his apprehension of reality. (ibid., 123)

As Nana Wilson-Tagoe aptly remarks, 'the contemporary African novel of history struggles against nineteenth-century European historicism with its view of history as objective and scientific, its separation of historical and fictional discourse and its unitary chronology for representing all histories' (1999, 156).

While the colonial period witnessed the epistemological dispossession of the Igbo, in the era of independence, sites of learning were central to the decolonisation process. As Emmanuel Obiechina notes, 'the founding of the University of Nigeria coincided with the accession of Nigeria to national independence' (1986, xv). This convergence of historical events birthed a University setting that followed many of the traditions of the British University system, but at the same time served as an important site in the development of the newly independent nation. 'The kind of education offered to Nigerians before the establishment of the University of Nigeria' B. I. C. Ijomah avows, 'was such as could effectively nourish the colonial apparatus' (1986, 2). The establishing of the University of Nigeria marked the assertion that independence would be incomplete if it did not extend beyond the realm of

---

[7] I use the term 'Igbo-Nigerian novel' to describe novels written by Igbo writers that examine the Igbo experience, but are expressed in Nigeria's official language, English.

self-governance, to include institutions of knowledge production. This act of self-determination, instigated by the University's founder and first president of Nigeria Nnamdi Azikiwe, sought to 'free the African intellect' from the imprisonment of colonial education' (ibid., 3). This not only marked a movement away from Eurocentric epistemologies, it also signalled an educational reorientation for the emerging middle classes towards the types of knowledge and expertise that were deemed useful in an independent Nigeria.

Obiechina presents the dual function of the University as 'an instrument of nation building' through its capacity to promote 'skills, ideas and outlooks that would transform Nigeria into a modern state while conserving and refining the people's authentic cultures and values' (1986, xv). During the period of transition from colonized to independent state, the University provided an important space for reflection, not only on colonial and precolonial histories, but also on the objectives of institutions of knowledge production in the newly independent nation. Colonialist education had sought to affirm the colonizers, and so education in an independent Nigeria had a restorative function. The University environment provided an important site for decolonisation, enacted in part through the incorporation of indigenous knowledge into its various fields of study. The aspirations for this institution to provide a liberatory pedagogy and to contribute to the wider decolonising agenda is articulated in the University's motto: *To Restore the Dignity of Man*. Adichie's recognition of the University as a site of transformative politics is evident in her depiction of the University of Nigeria, Nsukka in each of her novels as a locale for the radical politics or subversive actions of its academics and students.

Adichie, who grew up on the Nsukka campus, portrays the early years of the University in *Half of a Yellow Sun* [2006], as a space for nurturing a Pan-African consciousness that intersected with the ideals and aspirations of independence. *Purple Hibiscus* (first pubished 2004) and *Americanah* (first pubished 2013) provide a portrait of the University of Nigeria, Nsukka as a locale for civil disobediences, dissent and resistance to the military dictatorships of the 1990s. The University is embroiled in the particular battles of the day and Adichie demonstrates how its academics draw on and reproduce oral histories as a source of strength in their struggles. In the opening chapter of *Half of a Yellow Sun*, we are introduced to Odenigbo, a radical Pan-Africanist mathematician from the University of Nigeria Nsukka, whom we encounter through the narrative perspective of his new houseboy Ugwu. Odenigbo is representative of a new wave of academics in Nigeria, and his declaration 'Education is a priority!' is born out of a deep sense of patriotism and collective destiny. Education proves to be of primary importance for Odenigbo as he asks: 'How can we resist exploitation if we don't have the tools to understand exploitation?' (2007, 11). The paradox of learning in a system that is still undergoing the process of decolonisation presents the student with a challenge; they must reproduce colonialist accounts of history, while contesting these accounts through reaffirming indigenous oral histories outside the classroom. The situation that students in the newly independent state find themselves in could be likened to what W. E. B. Du Bois termed 'double consciousness', as they are forced to see themselves and their histories through the eyes of the empire, while maintaining their own truths in rearticulating their collective past. Ugwu is informed by Odenigbo of the politics of knowledge production and reproduction in the recently independent nation, as he must repeat inaccurate colonialist accounts before he will be afforded the space to oppose them. During this historical moment, colonialist texts have not been fully displaced from their authoritative position and histories of Nigeria produced by Nigerians are still emerging. Odenigbo explains to Ugwu:

> 'There are two answers to the things they will teach you about our land: the real answer and the answer you give in school to pass. You must read books and learn both answers. I will give you books, excellent books.' Master stopped to sip his tea. 'They will teach you that a white man called Mungo Park discovered River Niger. That is rubbish. Our people fished in the Niger long before Mungo Park's grandfather was born. But in your exam, write that it was Mungo Park.' (Adichie 2007, 11)

The framing of Mungo Park as explorer extraordinaire and discoverer of the Niger legitimises the colonial presence as it depicts Africa – in this case the area around the River Niger – as uninhabited, uncharted and, as such, unclaimed. The figure of Park, an ideological or imperial successor to the early explorers represented in *Robinson Crusoe*, occupied a central position in the narrative of the nation, while its inhabitants remained at the peripheries of the 'official' histories. Odenigbo's counter-discursive presentation of the past utilises the oral literary tradition to contest the presumed 'truisms' of the written text. Complicating British curricula and its elevation and centralizing of the written form, Odenigbo's validation of indigenous oral-based knowledge in the quest for an Igbo or Nigeria-centred historiography is of particular significance given his position within the University system. His decolonising agenda signals a new era in the politics of knowledge production in Nigerian institutions of higher education, and this impact is apparent most clearly in the figure of Ugwu; a point on which I will elaborate shortly.

Chimamanda Ngozi Adichie's engagement with the historical representation of the Igbo people enters into a dialogue with the writings of Chinua Achebe, particularly his pioneering novel *Things Fall Apart* (1958). Achebe's multi-layered narrative presents a literary account of how the Igbo people became subjects in Western anthropological and historical discourse. This novel presents a complex society prior to and at the moment of colonization. The abrasive presence of the colonial government disrupts the rhythm of life for the people of Umuofia, and *Things Fall Apart* depicts the early stages in the process of the dismantling of a particular way of life. Towards the later part of the novel the narrative voice shifts to that of the District Commissioner, a senior member of the colonial government, and the novel ends with a twist. The District Commissioner proclaims that he will write an account of Okonkwo, the protagonist of *Things Fall Apart*, deciding quite dismissively that Okonkwo's story requires no more space than a mere paragraph. This paragraph, or footnote in history, will feature in a book entitled 'The Pacification of the Primitive Tribes of the Lower Niger'. The narrative structure of *Things Fall Apart* pre-empts and undermines this conclusion, as the reader is privy to a preceding detailed account of Okonkwo and his society. The novel also provides a commentary on the affirmation that can be found in a people's image of themselves, and demonstrates how, for the Igbo, their depiction in colonialist literature is both reductive and partial, written by those whose default position is one of superiority. *Things Fall Apart* opens with an allusion to an oral historical account of Okonkwo's fame and success, described by the elders of the land. In contrast, the closing chapter captures the beginnings of a colonialist written history of the Igbo in which Okonkwo features, written by an agent of the colonial regime. In presenting the history of dispossession through the medium of the written text, Achebe is engaged in the repossession of the narrative; his ideological project is described by fellow Nigerian writer Ben Okri as one that intends to 'redream the world' (1990, 23).

Half of a Yellow Sun continues the conversation concerning the authorship of African histories, centring the importance of Africans as agents and not solely subjects of history. The narrative is told from three perspectives, Ugwu the houseboy, Richard the British writer, and Olanna who is a university lecturer and partner to Odenigbo. The narrative shifts among these three viewpoints and moves backwards and forwards in time, alternating between the period leading up to the outbreak of the Nigeria-Biafra war, and then to the period of war itself.

Richard's character is depicted as searching for a sense of belonging, and he believes that given his presence at the birth of Biafra and his contributions to the win-the-war effort, he can belong in Biafra in a way that he hasn't belonged anywhere else. Prior to the war, Richard makes multiple abortive efforts to write a book, but his overriding self-doubt always obstructs the completion of his manuscripts. His patriotism to Biafra ignites a sense of purpose, which is expressed through his intention to write Biafra's story, *The World Was Silent When We Died*. There are segments of a historical text with this title that punctuate the narrative, leading the reader to believe that it has been penned by Richard, when in fact Ugwu is the author. Evoking the twist at the end of *Things Fall Apart*, Adichie's revelation of the authorial voice behind *The World Was Silent When We Died* is indicative of a shift in representation of the Igbo people in historical texts, demonstrating an act of repossession of the narrative both intratextually and extratextually.

Intertextual references to *Things Fall Apart* are overtly made in the collection of short stories, *The Thing Around Your Neck* (2009), in which Adichie sustains her engagement with the politics of historiography and the production of knowledge in colonial Nigeria. The opening section of the short story, 'The Headstrong Historian',[8] is located within the world of precolonial Igboland, the image of which bears a striking resemblance to that of *Things Fall Apart*.[9] The story's intergen-

---

[8] 'The Headstrong Historian's historical continuities and sustained conversation with *Things Fall Apart* identifies the short story as homage to Chinua Achebe specifically, and his generation of writers and scholars more generally, for their pioneering work in the contestation of Eurocentric images of Africa. Many of the fictional biographical details of Afamefuna's life intersect with the Achebe's real life story; they were both the children of converts to Christianity but maintained a deep connection to and interest in indigenous Igbo belief systems and practices; they studied at University College, Ibadan in its early days, each enrolling in a science subject before eventually transferring to a subject in the humanities. This shift in discipline was motivated by a desire to contribute to the production of knowledge in the postcolonial nation whilst centring their communities. They both produced books that contest colonialist accounts, having come to the realization in earlier life that colonialist depictions of 'savages' were intended as representation of their communities. Their work became highly acclaimed within their respective fields, helping to lay the foundations for the writers and scholars that followed them and their ideological stances led them to drop their English names in favour of their Igbo names.

[9] There are multiple intertextual references to *Things Fall Apart* in this short story which include character names (Obierika and Okonkwo), recreational activities (the playing of the flute, wrestling matches), indigenous institutions of power (the Ozo titled men), and a slight variation in the title of a colonialist text which features at the end of *Things Fall Apart*.

erational focus illustrates the changing socio-political landscape, resultant of the combined colonial and missionary influences. The shift in ideology among some individuals, engendered by these external forces, impacts upon the existing modes of identification in this community. Across the three generations[10] depicted in this story we see shifting social, cultural and religious points of reference, out of which identities are forged. We are introduced to the world of Nwamgba, a widow, who decides to send her only child to a mission school at a time when access to the English language increases proximity to the new institutions of power. Anikwenwa, Nwamgba's son, is baptised and given the name Michael, marking the first step in his socialization away from his people. The mission school education brings about the psychological displacement of Anikwenwa from his community, so that 'Nwamgba knew that her son now inhabited a mental space that was foreign to her' (Adichie 2009, 211). As an adult, Anikwenwa's ideological difference manifests in the creation of physical distance as he and his wife 'treated non-Christians as if they had smallpox' (ibid., 213). This self-styled segregation creates a rupture between Anikwenwa and his community, but this rupture is later traversed by Anikwenwa's daughter Grace who is able to successfully negotiate these two worlds. Grace is a member of the third generation to have come into contact with colonial rule, and is positioned 'at the crossroads of cultures' (Achebe 1988, 34), in close propinquity to both the traditions of her grandmother's generation and the colonialist worldview.

Grace is given the name Afamefuna[11] by her grandmother Nwamgba, which translates as 'My Name Will Not Be Lost' (Adichie 2009, 214).[12]

---

[10] Chinua Achebe also undertook the intergenerational mapping of the colonial and missionary influence across three generations of the same family in *Things Fall Apart* through the characters of Okonkwo and his son Nwoye (later known as Isaac after converting to Christianity) and, in *No Longer at Ease*, we follow the narrative of Isaac Okonkwo and his son Obi Okonkwo.

[11] The names 'Grace' and 'Afamefuna' are both used in the story, the usage varying depending on the context. For the sake of continuity, from this point onwards I have used the name 'Afamefuna' when referring to this character.

[12] At the end of the short story we are told that she 'officially changed her name from Grace to Afamefuna' (Adichie 2009, 218), signalling an acknowledgement and embracing of her task to keep the name of her people alive. It is particularly significant that a female is given the name 'Afamefuna', considering the patrilineal nature of Igbo society (bar a few exceptions). At this important juncture in history, Adichie foregrounds the contribution of women in the reclamation of history. This is particularly pertinent given the marginalisation women experienced under colonial rule, so that this act of reclamation can also be read in light of the challenge to colonialist patriarchy.

Within Igbo culture, an individual's name serves as a form of incantation or prayer which is repeated each time that person is called. The importance of naming is entwined with the belief in the power of the spoken word, as to repeatedly enunciate an intention is to conceivably usher it into being. Within the context of a rapidly changing society, the central principle expressed in the name 'Afamefuna' reveals Nwamgba's entreaty for her people, which extends beyond the immediacy of her family to include the wider community. Nwamgba identifies a role for her granddaughter in the ideological project of recording the traditions and histories of their people, and this aspiration is later realized through Afamefuna's work as a historian in her adult life. At birth, Nwamgba recognizes in Afamefuna 'the spirit' of her late husband, 'Obierika that had returned' (ibid., 214), presenting a sense of continuity between Afamefuna's existence in this world and the world of the ancestors. The reincarnation of Obierika further demonstrates the temporal possibilities that exist within oral cultures, as the 'past' is very much alive and active within the 'present'. From the early stages of her life, Afamefuna straddles multiple worlds: the spiritual ties to both her grandparents and her 'solemn interest' in Nwamgba's poetry and stories (ibid.) identify in her a deep connection to an older way of life.

As an adult, Afamefuna pioneers as 'one of the few women at the University College in Ibadan in 1950' (ibid., 216). Studying at the first and only university in Nigeria at the time, she takes the decision to change her degree programme from Chemistry to History in recognition of the 'clear link between education and dignity, between the hard, obvious things that are printed in books and the soft, subtle things that lodge themselves into the soul' (ibid.). Having identified the processes that brought about the dispossession of the peoples of Nigeria during the colonial era, Afamefuna subverts colonialist epistemologies through utilizing the printed book, an instrument of colonial authority, as the medium through which she repossesses the narrative of her nation. During her secondary school days Afamefuna encounters a 'textbook with a chapter called "The Pacification of the Primitive Tribes of Southern Nigeria," by an administrator from Worcestershire who had lived among them for seven years' (ibid., 215) The point of realization that this text is supposed to constitute a history of her people brings about an awakening in her that fuels the ambition to contest this account. The textbook chapter's title parodies the District Commissioner's archetypal colonialist text in *Things Fall Apart*, in which the story of Okonkwo's life and death is only afforded a paragraph. Adichie demonstrates the shift in power that accompanies the act of repossessing the narrative, as she invoked the District Commissioner's book in order to reduce it to a solitary chapter. This power shift is reiterated in Afamefuna's writing of the historical text *Pacifying with Bullets: A Reclaimed History of Southern Nigeria*, which responds to colonialist histories through foregrounding the prevalence of colonial violence in the 'pacification' process, asserting the author's agency in contesting and reclaiming the writing of her history. *Pacifying with Bullets* is inspired by the community's framing of the past which has hitherto been silenced in colonialist literature. The people of Agueke recount to Afamefuna the 'stories of destruction of their village years before by the white man's guns' (ibid., 216) so that she 'would become haunted by the image of a destroyed village and would go to London and to Paris and to Onicha, sifting through moldy files in archives, reimagining the lives and smells of her grandmother's world' (ibid., 217). Drawing on the memory bank of the oral tradition, Afamefuna's production of a revisionist history of Southern Nigeria serves as her contributing to the anti-colonial and decolonisation movements which champion self-determination and the restoration of dignity.

In the writing of 'The Headstrong Historian', Adichie returned to an exploration of familial intergenerational experiences, with which she first grappled in her debut novel *Purple Hibiscus* (2004). Set during the military dictatorships of the 1990s, *Purple Hibiscus* presents the family unit as a microcosm of the nation, examining themes of oppression and liberation in the late-twentieth century Nigerian context. The novel's inclusion of important historical figures who were embroiled in anti-slavery and anti-colonial movements, such as Olaudah Equiano,[13] provides a long view of resistance struggles in the region, allowing for parallels to be drawn between past liberation struggles in the precolonial and colonial contexts. In a passage in *Purple Hibiscus*, Adichie examines the intersections of the public and the private in an exploration of the permeation of state-sponsored oppression and violence into the family sphere during a period of intense military rule. Jaja is the older of two children growing up in a repressive household ruled by his dictatorial father, Eugene. While visiting his paternal aunt, Ifeoma, a lecturer at the University of Nigeria, Nsukka, his cousin Obiora enquires into the origins of his name to which Jaja responds:

[13] There is reference to the biography of Olaudah Equiano, *Equiano's Travels, or the Life of Gustavus Vassa the African* (1789). Equiano was captured in what is now Southeastern Nigeria, transported to the Americas and enslaved. As an adult, Equiano secured his freedom and was a prominent activist in the abolitionist movement.

'My name is actually Chukwuemeka. Jaja is a childhood nickname that stuck.' ... 'When he was a baby, all he could say was Ja-Ja. So everybody called him Jaja,' Aunty Ifeoma said. She turned to Jaja and added, 'I told your mother that it was an appropriate nickname, that you would take after Jaja of Opobo.' 'Jaja of Opobo? The stubborn king?' Obiora asked. 'Defiant,' Aunt Ifeoma said. 'He was a defiant king.' ... 'He was king of the Opobo people,' Aunty Ifeoma said, 'and when the British came, he refused to let them control all the trade. He did not sell his soul for a bit of gunpowder like the other kings did, so the British exiled him to the West Indies. He never returned to Opobo.' ... 'That's sad. Maybe he should not have been defiant,' Chima said. ... 'Being defiant can be a good thing sometimes, Aunty Ifeoma said. 'Defiance is like marijuana – it is not a bad thing when used right.' ... Her conversation was with Chima and Obiora, but she was looking at Jaja. Obiora smiled and pushed his glasses up. 'Jaja of Opobo was no saint, anyway. He sold his people into slavery, and besides, the British won in the end. So much for defiance.' 'The British won the war, but they lost many battles,' Jaja said'. (Adichie 2008, 143–5)

Adichie presents two oral historical accounts with somewhat opposing views on Jaja of Opobo. Jaja's response to the actions of his namesake identifies what he regards as the importance of defiance, in spite of any eventualities. For Jaja, resistance is necessary, and in coming to this realization, he demonstrates an understanding that in any liberation movement there will be casualties. He suggests that defiance in the face of oppression is central to maintaining our humanity. The evocation of Jaja of Opobo inserts Jaja into a historical framework of resistance with their shared name bridging a sense of shared experience, and as such, creates a sense of foreboding in the novel. *Purple Hibiscus* opens with Jaja resisting his father's brutal authority and, as the narrative unfolds, the reader encounters multiple moments of defiance enacted by Jaja in addition to those enacted by other members of his household. The subversive act of slowly poisoning Eugene, which is undertaken by Jaja's mother Beatrice, leaves Beatrice, who has endured years of emotional and physical abuse, at risk of imprisonment. Jaja confesses to his mother's crime and his banishment takes the form of incarceration, echoing the expulsion of Jaja of Opobo to the West Indies.

In linking this narrative of resistance to British colonial domination, there are parallels drawn between colonial oppression and the oppression felt in both the private and public spaces under Nigerian military rule. We are again reminded that the past and the present are not separate entities, but instead are part of a continual, unfolding human experience, in which oppression and resistance exist. Within these cycles of oppression, strength and direction can be drawn from oral accounts of these historical figures, but Adichie also presents a sense of rebirth and renewal, as Jaja of Opobo is reborn in the character of Jaja in *Purple Hibiscus*. Adichie draws parallels between British colonial rule and Nigerian military rule, creating a metanarrative of history in which an underlying human struggle is set against a series of cycles of power. In centring the oral tradition Adichie decentres Western historiography, reminding us of the existing indigenous modes of engaging with the past. Across Adichie's writing, there is a constant engagement with Igbo epistemologies, which reiterates the continued importance and influence of the past in our contemporary lives. In evoking the oral tradition, Adichie locates her literature within a long tradition of Igbo literary cultural production. The significance of this literary and cultural inheritance to Adichie is apparent in her pronouncement that 'Our histories cling to us. We are shaped by where we come from. Our art is shaped by where we come from' (Adichie 2012).

Works Cited

Achebe, Chinua. *Things Fall Apart*. London: Heinemann, 1958.

—. *Hopes and Impediments: Selected Essays 1965–1987*. Oxford: Heinemann International, 1988.

—. *Home and Exile*. Edinburgh: Canongate, 2003.

Adichie, Chimamanda Ngozi. *Half of a Yellow Sun*. London: Harper Perennial, 2007 [2006].

—. *Purple Hibiscus*. London: Harper Perennial, 2008 [2004].

—. *The Thing Around Your Neck*. London: Harper Perennial, 2009.

—. 'The Role of Literature in Modern Africa'. *New African*, Nov. 2010: 96.

—. 'To Instruct and Delight: A Case for Realist Literature'. Commonwealth Lecture. London: Commonwealth Foundation, 2012.

—. 'The Danger of a Single Story'. TEDGlobal, 2009. Retrieved 9 October 2015 from www.ted.com/talks/chimamanda_adichie_the_danger_of_a_single_story.

Afigbo, A. E. 'Chief Igwegbe Odum: The Omenuko of history'. *Nigeria* 90, September 1966, 222–31.

Carr, Edward Hallett. *What is History?* Basingstoke: Palgrave, 2001.

Chukwuma, Helen. *Igbo Oral Literature: Theory and Tradition*. Abak: Belpot (Nig.), 1994.

Emenyonu, Ernest. 'Igbo Literature'. *Encyclopedia of African Literature*. Ed. Simon Gikandi. London and New York: Routledge, 2003: 234–6.

Green, Martin. *Dreams of Adventure, Deeds of Empire*. London and Henley: Routledge & Kegan Paul, 1980.

Ijomah, B. I. C. 'The Origin and Philosophy of the University'. *The University of Nigeria,1960–1985: An Experiment in Higher Education*. Ed. Emmanuel N. Obiechina, Vincent Chukwuemeka Ike & John Anenechukwu Umeh. Nsukka: University of Nigeria Press, 1986: 1–11.

Irele, Abiola. 'Narrative, History, and the African Imagination.' *Narrative* 1.2 (1993): 156–72

Joyce, James. 'Daniel Defoe (1911)'. Ed. & trans. By Joseph Prescott. *Buffalo Studies* 1.1 (1964): 24–5.

McInelly, Brett C. 'Expanding Empires, Expanding Selves: Colonialism, the Novel, and Robinson Crusoe'. *Studies in the Novel* 35.1 (2003): 1.

Nwana, Pita. *Omenụkọ*. London: Longman, Green & Co, 1933.

Obiechina, Emmanuel. 'Introduction'. *The University of Nigeria, 1960–1985: An Experiment in Higher Education*. Ed. Emmanuel N. Obiechina, Vincent Chukwuemeka Ike & John Anenechukwu Umeh. Nsukka, Nigeria: University of Nigeria Press, 1986: xv–xviii.

Okri, Ben. 'Redreaming the World: An Essay for Chinua Achebe.' *The Guardian* 9 August 1990: 23.

White, Hayden. *Tropics of Discourse: Essays in Cultural Criticism*. Baltimore; London: Johns Hopkins University Press, 1978.

Wilson-Tagoe, Nana. 'Narrative, History, Novel: Intertextuality in the Historical Novels of Ayi Kwei Armah and Yvonne Vera." *Journal of African Cultural Studies* 12.2 (1999): 155–66.

2

Deconstructing Binary Oppositions of Gender in *Purple Hibiscus*
A Review of Religious/Traditional Superiority & Silence

JANET NDULA

Purple Hibiscus is an illuminating example of how Chimamanda Ngozi Adichie prolifically blends art and ideology with great social significance to contemporary gender representation. Literary history of theories presents Deconstruction as an extension of Structuralism implying that by origins and material the theory is language-based. However, Deconstruction parts ways with Structuralism in its ideological foregrounding. What such a premise means is that Deconstruction proficiently accommodates not just what the writer says but also the manner in which the writer conveys his/her content. Adichie demonstrates a mastery of ambiguous and oppositional language and a staunch dedication to content, intently delivering critical social issues through overt and implied meanings. A deconstructive examination of binary oppositions that divide characters into hierarchical classes of religious or traditional superiority and silence in *Purple Hibiscus* (hereafter referred to as *Hibiscus*) attests to Adichie's creativity. More importantly, the exercise produces critical implications that are fundamental to emancipation, social understanding and future characterization in African literature.

Our self-conceptualizations in terms of gender and binary oppositions which have been internalized in our writings (as represented in this study of *Hibiscus*) are influenced by the human tendency to define each other in inclusionary/exclusionary terms. When this happens, certain individuals are bestowed with unearned power and opportunities while others are restricted and dispossessed of their dignity as human beings. The consequent representation of such persons in literature becomes problematic. As Molara Ogundipe-Leslie (1994) observes, if literature, though imaginative, can be used for a systematic study of society, then the nature of representations within literary

31

traditions are certainly issues of great relevance. The roles that men and women occupy within the general body of literature are a reflection of societal attitudes. Such roles, assigned principally in binary classifications in literature, are increasingly relevant in ensuring that men and women receive equal opportunities to participate and advance in all aspects of life.

Meanwhile, there is need to understand, as many scholars have proven, that gender behaviour is learned cultural behaviour and there is no such thing as original gender identity, but rather, constructed notions of gender that are purely cultural products (de Beauvoir 2009; Butler 1996). So, it is important to know that biological differences on their own do not restrict men or women. The challenge is to prevent socially constructed, gender-based, assumptions from inhibiting the full participation of men and women in all professions (Carnes 2010). So, the interest in deconstructing oppositional binaries of gender in *Hibiscus* is in order to contribute to contemporary universal debates on gender, not least, to see the unprecedented effects of examined literary gender designations, and if lessons can be drawn to enhance gender equality and the participation of especially the often slighted women.

The study is based on the premise that, in *Hibiscus,* Adichie presents major oppositions, contradictions and ambiguities that a deconstructive interpretation would describe to reveal subverted gender hierarchies. On this premise, the study posits that the novel is a fresh contribution to the new generation of novels that carry implications endorsing individual effort over gender disposition, demonstrating that sex difference does not presuppose subordination. To that effect Adichie presents women (usually represented in the underprivileged side) in unprecedented positions in the power dynamics of the binary oppositions by the close of the novel.

The social background into which the novel *Hibiscus* was published, included below, provides allowance for a better understanding of the factors that influence Adichie's conscious or unconscious choice of binary dichotomies throughout the novel.

Titi Salaam describes the year 2003, when the novel was published, as the year of the election in which for the first time two women were in the run for the presidency in Nigeria (Salaam 2003). She goes on to describe Nigeria in that year as a 'capitalist society in which a woman is doubly oppressed, first as a worker whose employer must maximize profit by exploiting her labour power and secondly as a woman in a patriarchal society'. It is the same decade in which Damilola Taiye Agbalajobi published the results of her study, 'Women's Participation and the Political Process in Nigeria: Problems and Prospects'. In the paper, she exposes women's contribution to the political cause in Nigeria, and also the social factors which guarantee or impede that. In her opinion, 'men dominate most public offices till date' and 'the greatest psychological weapon available to man is the length of time they have enjoyed dominance over women' (Agbalajobi 2010, 78). Agbalajobi traces this dominance to the continual socialization of children to 'expect and accept different roles in life' which has 'created a social mechanism for the development of values that engender the several forms of discrimination against the female sex' (ibid.). Not unexpectedly, Agbalajobi, like the Nigerian critic, Nkiru Uwechia Nzegwu, makes reference to the ungendered Yoruba society of precolonial Nigeria, when 'women held high political offices like the *Iyalode, Iyaloja, Iyalaje* and even the office of the *Oba*' (ibid., 75) – high power structures of traditional Yoruba society. With the prevailing socio-economic crises in Nigeria as a result of the IMF/World Bank dictating neo-liberal policies, Agbalajobi adds that jobs are lost at an increasing rate and, as may be expected, women are the worse hit. Sadly, in some cases, women can keep their jobs if they accept to become the objects of sexual satisfaction of their employers. Religion and tradition still remain major instruments of women's oppression in Nigeria. The resulting silencing of women constitutes among others the ideology of the society. The above reference to when things were better for Nigerian women puts into perspective the prevailing hard times and the hope of returning to the time before the 'rain began to beat' them, to use Achebe's famous phrase.

Hibiscus seems to place religious/traditional paradigms and the resulting silencing of women at the roots of what divide men and women on the archetype/stereotype oppositional binaries. Such division based on gender gives impetus to the consuming ideologies of women as 'the inessential', 'the incidental', 'the Other' as opposed to 'the essential,' 'the Subject,' or the 'Absolute', to use Simone de Beauvoir's words from her *Introduction to The Second Sex* (2009). Even though *Hibiscus* is narrated through the eyes of Kambili, it is basically a story about the overwhelming control and tyranny of her father, Eugene Achike, over his wife and children. Eugene, familiarly referred to in the novel as Papa, is a religious fanatic. His spiritual misconceptions combine with the entrenched traditional constructs of his home culture of Enugu to bestow him with unexamined and distorted ideologies of male supremacy. Such perversion breeds life into the multiple temperaments he exhibits as he ruthlessly consolidates his domestic powers.

Before delving into the hidden meanings conveyed in Adichie's choice of binaries it is important to present the overt meanings as the reader deduces at a superficial level. That is done below through an exhaustive restatement in the novel situating characters into different hierarchical classes. An ordinary or cursory reading of *Hibiscus* gives the impression that religion and tradition are normalizing social constructs applicable to certain characters without consideration to their devastating effects. Straight away the reader wonders if he/she is faced with yet another chronicle of a female character whose story will leave them searching for more answers to unresolved issues about the development of female characterization. Nzegwu points out that, while past novels show a range of women, both empowered and limited, no complementing resolutions are reached at the end (2001). Her submission prompts one to draw comparisons between the more-recent novel *Purple Hibiscus* (2003) and Tsitsi Dangarembga's *Nervous Conditions* (1988). It is such unclear resolutions, as for example in *Nervous Conditions*, that lead Nzegwu to predict (for future female characterizations) that 'challenges lie ahead for the heroine and the discerning leaders' (2001, 62). Tracing Nzegwu's prophesy to twenty-first century female representation in *Hibiscus* necessitates an answer to the pending question whether the promise of the escaped female, chronicled in the characterization of Dangarembga's protagonist, Tambudzai, is realized in Adichie's Kambili. An attempt at this question is useful here in locating how questioned and examined binary oppositions of gender are affecting the growth of female characterizations in twenty-first century African literature represented here in *Hibiscus*.

In the course of the narration, Kambili's mother, Beatrice, referred to as Mama, is presented as an ideal African woman, a quiet motherly figure for most of the novel. She is the typical stereotyped African woman depicted as 'subordinate, dependent and passive', to use Ogundipe-Leslie's words (1994, 51). In the novel, she presents a softer, warmer and motherly presence in the Achike home, guided by a powerful construct, to which she clings, that 'a husband crowns a woman's life' (Adichie 2006, 83). Her language is made up of more signs than words, marked with nodding and shaking the head (ibid., 18), speaking in a 'low voice which barely carried upstairs even with the door open' (ibid.,29). Though Kambili is painfully shy and reserved, she is depicted as an exemplary daughter of whom the parents should be proud: 'Kambili is intelligent beyond her years, quiet and responsible ... A brilliant obedient student and a daughter to be proud of' (46). When Papa's publisher, Ade Coker, remarks that Kambili and her older brother, Jaja 'are always so quiet ... So quiet' (65), Papa proudly contrasts them to 'the loud children people are raising these days with no home training and no fear of God' (66). However, Adichie empowers the character of Kambili with a close-to-perfect imaginative mind that paints the silence and other issues of her life, and other characters, in a remarkable way. She recalls 'the years when Jaja and Mama and I [herself] spoke more with our spirits than with our lips' (23–4), actions whose significance is transformed into an art represented in a full chapter in the novel entitled 'Speaking with our Spirits' (25). Describing their routine Sunday afternoons after Mass, Kambili summarizes the physical silence that ruled the life Papa imposed on them in a long passage interspersed with the words 'silence' and 'quiet'.

> Our steps on the stairs were as measured and as silent as our Sundays: the silence of waiting until Papa was done with his siesta so we could have lunch; the silence of reflection time, when Papa gave us a scripture passage or a book by one of the early church fathers to read and meditate on; the silence of evening rosary; the silence of driving to the church for benediction afterwards. Even our family time on Sunday was quiet, without chess games or newspaper discussions, more in tune with the Day of Rest. (Adichie 2006, 39)

One time during another lunch period she also remarks that 'silence hung over the table like the blue-black clouds in the middle of the rainy season' (ibid., 40). When Terry Eagleton (1996) talks about what women mean when they speak of being silenced, he states that 'they don't mean they are incapable of adequately speaking a language, rather they are referring to social and cultural pressures, which undermine their confidence and make them hesitant about speaking' (1996, 16–17). The silence of the Achike household is all of that and more; it physically manifests itself and actually impairs the act of speaking.

As a victim of physical violence at the hands of her father, Kambili is psychologically damaged. Even when she speaks, her speech is tainted by great fear, so that she translates everything she wants to say into what she should say, always wanting to say something, but ending up saying something else, or nothing at all. For instance, Kambili is scared to blame Papa for Mama's broken figurines though everyone is there when Papa breaks them. She says 'I meant to say I am sorry that Papa broke your figurines, but the words that came out were, "I'm sorry your figurines broke, Mama"' (Adichie 2006, 18). At some other time, she says 'I wanted to tell the girl that it was all my hair … but the words would not come … I wanted to talk with them, to laugh with them so much that I would start to jump up and down in one place the way they did, but my lips held stubbornly together' (ibid., 149). At another time she says 'I mumbled to my plate, then started to cough as if real sensible words would have come out of my mouth but for the coughing' (105). Kambili's artificial routines and ingrained quietness have rendered her factually mute. Her subjugation manifests itself in a loss of words and she is unable to speak more than imparted phrases accompanied by awkward stuttering or coughing (149). Cullen Roop comments that if she were not the narrator of the novel, Kambili's true feelings would not be understood (2014).

It is not only the women in *Hibiscus* who fall victim to the silence that permeates the novel. Papa's staunch adherence to Catholicism victimizes and silences even his own father, Papa-Nnukku, whom he has condemned to the negative side of the good/bad oppositional binary. Frequently referring to him as 'heathen' Papa has severed all family ties with him, including forbidding his children from interacting with him. Kambili and Jaja give two perspectives to Papa-Nnukwu's acceptance and resignation to his son's neglect: Kambili says 'He takes it well' and Jaja chooses to say 'He hides it well' (Adichie 2006, 76). Jaja's own silence translates into defiance which finally orchestrates the events leading to Papa's overthrow and the breakage of the silence. But before that, necessity becomes the mother of invention and he and Kambili devise an interesting means of communicating without the use of words, what Kambili refers to as an 'asusu anya', translated as a 'language of the eyes' (ibid., 308).

Meanwhile, Papa is at the centre of almost all the preordained archetypes re-established in the novel. He is the main source of oppression, silencing people and placing them, in opposition to the positive versions of the binary oppositions, mostly as victims for most of the novel. Papa has it all – power and wealth. He controls almost every aspect of his family life, including imposing a schedule upon the lives of Kambili and her older brother, Jaja, so that every minute of the day is mapped out for them. He frequently breaks out violently, subjecting his wife and children to serious corporal punishment. When Mama does not want to visit Father Benedict after Mass because she is ill, Papa beats her and she miscarries. In fact, Mama has suffered two miscarriages on account of his beatings. After the second she says to her children:

You know that small table where we keep the family Bible, nne? Your father broke it on my belly ... My blood finished on that floor even before he took me to St. Agnes. My doctor said there was nothing he could do to save it ... I was six weeks gone. (Adichie 2006, 248)

When Kambili and Jaja share a home with their grandfather whom Papa rejects, boiling water is poured on their feet for walking into sin.

For owning a painting of Papa-Nnukwu, Kambili is kicked until she is hospitalized. Yet Adichie also complicates her characterization of Papa as a violent patriarch. He is placed on the abusive side of the oppressor/victim dichotomy, but he is also a generous man who donates his wealth to worthy causes and runs a newspaper that resists the oppressive Nigerian regime, earning him the better position on the good/bad oppositional pair. In this way, Adichie represents the connection of fundamentalist Christianity and patriarchal oppression as an unfortunate quality of someone who otherwise is commendable.

However, the story begins on a deconstructive note as a recollection of what Papa used to be; of the time when his tyranny knew no bounds, leading to the day 'before Palm Sunday' when everything changed – some sort of recollection on the part of Kambili of when Papa exclusively possessed power and speech and everyone else was condemned to passivity and silence on the power/passivity, speech/silence binary oppositions. This means that as much as it is a story about Papa's power it is also a story about his downfall. The opening phrase reminds one of Chinua Achebe's famous allusion to colonization as the source of Africa's problems, but this time in reference to when 'the rain began to beat' Papa Eugene. The story actually begins with some of Achebe's words: 'Things started to fall apart at home when my brother, Jaja, did not go to communion and Papa flung his heavy missal across the room and broke the figurines on the étagère' (11). The rest of the novel details the events that culminate in Jaja's rebellion represented by his skipping communion on Palm Sunday.

Adichie's creative representation of the good and bad in Papa is not accidental. It is interpreted within the theoretical basis of this study to mean that she places Papa on both sides of the good/bad binary opposition. Delicately framed, the character of Papa is both evil and loving. He loves his wife and children and wants the best for them, but because it must be on his own terms, he uses extreme oppression to make sure of that. He therefore comes across as a compassionate protector and at the same time a dreaded tyrant. As the proprietor of a popular local newspaper, *The Standard*, he courageously defends freedom of speech against the military oppression of his country while, at the same time, he is the main cause of the silence that engulfs the members of his family, whom he rules with an iron fist.

Silence in itself might not be a bad or negative disposition but the silence of the characters in *Hibiscus* is overwhelming and so enslaving that it is just that – bad and negative. It knows no gender as everybody (men and women) are subjected to it. The liberating effect of speech as evidenced through the characterization of Aunty Ifeoma's household is therefore a welcome relief to the burning silence of the Achike family. Aunty Ifeoma is Papa Eugene's only sister and a lecturer at the University of Nigeria, Nsukka. Her introduction in the novel immediately suggests that she will not conform to the 'virtuous' silence of her tradition or religion (Adichie 2006, 79); it even suggests what her character may do or not do. Not surprisingly, the breaking of the silence of the Achikes begins in her house in Nsukka (ibid., 24) where things start to fall apart and Papa's centre can no longer hold, as Achebe would put it. It is when the tables of the binary oppositions that designate the characters to different gender categories begin to turn. Aunty Ifeoma is described throughout the novel as 'fearless' (84), 'flippant' (85), 'laughed so easily so often' (93), 'taller, even more fearless' (97), 'loud' (100), 'fiercer and louder' (103). All these qualities speak to the way she parts with the social constructs of her society for her gender. She does not conform to silence, being assertive and independent, displaying determination and hard work in bringing up her children without a husband. She reveals to her father, Papa-Nnukwu (custodian of some of the traditional constructs in the novel), that what she needs in life is career advancement. Her revelation is in response to her father's entrenched traditional idea that she needs 'a good man' to take care of her and her children' (91). She suggests what she would rather have him pray about: 'Let your spirit ask *Chukwu* to hasten my promotion to senior lecturer' (91).

At the same time, Aunty Ifeoma tries to exonerate Papa-Nnukwu of his son's condemnation. Exposing the lapses in Papa's religiousness, she downgrades his exclusive right to religious superiority by implying that there are other matching equals to the Christian things Papa holds in high esteem, like saying the rosary. She explains that: 'Papa-Nnukwu was not a heathen but a traditionalist, that sometimes what was different was just as good as what was familiar, that when Papa-Nnukwu did his *itu-nzu*, his declaration of innocence, in the morning, it was the same as our saying the rosary' (Adichie 2006, 173). Aunty Ifeoma therefore places Papa and Papa-Nnukwu as different sides of the same coin. Through her explanation of the similarity in the Christian belief to the traditional belief, another belief centre, other than Papa, is created in Papa-Nnukwu, dislodging the former's superficial belief superiority.

Aunty Ifeoma declares to Mama that 'sometimes, life begins when marriage ends' (ibid., 83), and the reason is because Mama seems to be helplessly stuck in an abusive marriage to Papa, confirming, as Abdou Sarr suggests that, 'a woman may be unable to consider herself as oppressed, because she believes that tradition is the source of her responsibilities and problems' (1991, 289). Aunty Ifeoma's suggestion is a destabilization to the construct of the 'forever' attribute to the institution of marriage in religion. Such a disruption is significant because the seemingly fixed stereotype about married people leaves matrimonial victims with no other choice but to remain in an abusive and enslaving relationship. Supportively, Jonathan Culler validates the importance of deconstruction in the dismantling of tradition and traditional modes of thought in *The Encyclopaedia Britannica* (Duignan 2016, 1276). At the same time, Aunty Ifeoma's outspokenness is as liberating to the whole experience of silence in *Hibiscus* as it is surprisingly also caging, introducing the free/caged opposition. It becomes the very source of her victimization, culminating in her dismissal and self-exile to the United States of America. In that is a demonstration of what happens when a balance between the delicate binary opposition of silence/speech is not struck.

In her paper entitled 'Women, Gender and Colonialism: Rethinking the History of the British Cape Colony and its Frontier Zones' Helen Bradford refers to the creation of the presence/absence binary in the mental maps in which woman and man are proclaimed by Christianity to become one, with that one being man (1996, 353). Mama's stereotyped response that 'a husband crowns a woman's life', quoted above (Adichie 2006, 83), registers the central/peripheral, man/woman positions in marriage. However, her next sentence in reference to men is ambiguous, allowing for a clashing interpretation of her dedication to social constructs such as she earlier states. She says: 'It is what they want' (ibid.), contradicting her seeming docility. It suggests that she knows more than she is presenting. It also dismisses the idea about the man crowning the woman's life as a construct suggesting that it is what men want, probably, for their convenience, as opposed to what is realistic.

It is thanks to the highly contrasting free atmosphere of Aunty Ifeoma's house in Nsukka to the Achikes that the narrator submits: 'Perhaps we all changed after Nsukka – even Papa – and things were destined not to be the same, not to be in their original order' (ibid., 215). The 'original order', which is apparently only original to tradition and religion, is subsequently put to question and destabilized. It is in Nsukka that Kambili and Jaja learn to be expressive. They get to know that there exists a freer world unlike the only one they know with Papa's rigid schedules and unrealistic religious rules. Aunty Ifeoma's children, Amaka and Obiora, are allowed to question authority and make decisions for themselves. Such awakening prompts Jaja to reconsider his entrenched commitments which do not in any way reflect his personal preferences. His resolve for a new beginning is symbolized in the stalk of the purple hibiscus, which he takes back home along with the lessons from Nsukka. He plants the stalk in their garden and as it blooms, so too does Jaja, denoted in his revolution against Papa.

At the end, Papa's gradual emotional downfall even translates to his physical looks. The narrator observes him

> crumpled on a sofa in the living room, sobbing. He seemed so small. Papa who was so tall that he sometimes lowered his head to get through door-ways, that his tailor always used extra fabric to sew his trousers. Now he seemed small; he looked like a rumpled roll of fabric. (Adichie 2006, 213)

In a deflating technique quoted above, Adichie demonstrates how, if re-examined, inhibiting, entrenched and seemingly unchangeable social, religious and traditional constructs can diminish someone like Papa and switch him from the strong to the weak option on the strong/weak binary pair.

The last section of the novel tellingly titled 'A Different Silence: The Present' appeals most to the theme of silence in this paper. It is the time following Papa's death by Mama's poisoning, but there is hope in the future. By the same act, Papa is silenced this time for good and the silence/speech opposition is disrupted with Mama as the new silencer. That is why Kambili describes the present silence that still survives around them as 'a different kind of silence, one that lets me breathe' (Adichie 2006, 309). Contrasting the present silence to the former she adds that she has 'nightmares about the other kind, the silence of when Papa was alive' (ibid., 309). Even laughter has been freed, as Kambili observes: 'I laughed. It seemed so easy now, laughter. So many things seemed easy now' (310).

Mama now maintains a deliberate silence which is not painful this time because it is voluntary. For example, since Jaja has taken the blame and is in jail, no one believes it when she confesses to killing Papa. She now remains silent because she possesses the power to silence. When David Lurie in J. M. Coetzee's *Disgrace* defends his decision not to give any details after pleading guilty of sexually harassing Melanie, he refers to the kind of deliberate silence similarly observed in Mama as 'freedom of speech. Freedom to remain silent' (Coetzee 1999, 188). Mama speaks now in ways of her own. Jaja no longer speaks with his eyes. Kambili takes her own freedom of speech to other liberating levels. She now dares to listen to the music of the controversial Fela Kuti. To crown everything up, the painfully shy and initially silenced Kambili, can 'talk about the future now' (ibid., 310). Hence, equating speech to hope; in binary oppositional terms that would translate silence into hopelessness.

The switching pattern of power centres between characters (Papa, Mama, Jaja, Kambili and Papa-Nnukwu) and the disruption of seemingly fixed power structures, enhanced here in the rereading of binary oppositions in *Hibiscus*, is indicative of the existence of many power centres in the novel. Not even the trend of stereotypical male characterization in women's fiction, what Florence Stratton refers to as 'a reversal of the manichean allegory of gender' (1994, 155) which is subversive, has been able to solve the problem of gender. Common sense teaches us that the movement or existence of many centres implies no centre at all. The ultimate take-home message from these power switches is that anyone, man or woman, can assume any position on any designating binary opposition (weak/strong, active/docile, victor/victim, good/bad, silent/speech) depending on their individual efforts and not necessarily gender disposition. The important thing is how any assumed position affects the individual and others. Papa Eugene's power position was obviously overbearingly oppressive, especially to his family members. However, in an attempt to dismantle Papa's religious and domestic superiority and power, Aunty Ifeoma creates yet another unstable traditional power base in Papa-Nnukwu, as stated earlier.

The going back and forth between power centres validates the disturbing implication of hierarchies created in binary oppositions, that the rise of one means the subjugation of the other, and, while one tries to maintain its position, the other strives to change it. Jacques Derrida described this concern more metaphorically when he observes that 'to close oneself in feminism is to reproduce the very thing one is struggling against' (1976, 55). Mama has been depicted on the weak and victim sides of binaries for most of the novel but she ends up plotting and killing Papa, making an unprecedented power turn that is neither associable to her initial characterization nor commendable. Jaja's defiant characterization has literally crumbled Papa's destructive authority but he is in jail for no just reasons. We could go on and on with demonstrating the power shifts between the characters implied in the binary dichotomies in which they are classified, but one thing stands out, and it is, as the American critic Whitney Mitchell has stated, that gender classifications in life and literature whether represented in binary oppositions or not are nothing more than abstract and conceptual (2002). They tell nothing concrete about people or characters apart from how different they are. Adichie's either conscious or unconscious reiteration of seemingly fixed gender-based centres is betrayed in the process of deconstruction and its validation of the instability of meanings which end up dislodging constructed hierarchies. The flexibility of deconstruction has provided the possibility in this paper for inhibiting binary oppositions embodied in *Hibiscus* to be exposed for what they are – products of societal constructs or mind-sets which are mostly phallocentric and inefficient for identifying people.

Eugenia Piza-Lopez admits that the transformation of unequal structures that discriminate against certain people, for example, women represents a difficult task, sometimes painful, sometimes rewarding (1991, 117). The propensity of deconstruction in establishing the instabilities inherent in binary oppositions, in interpreting and reinterpreting the meanings created by them, over which Adichie obviously has no control, has made it incredibly rewarding in this study.

Works Cited

Achebe, Chinua. *Things Fall Apart*. London: Heinemann, 1958.

Adichie, Chimamanda N. *Purple Hibiscus*. Lagos: Kachifo, 2006 [2003].

Agbalajobi, Damilola T. 'Women's Participation and the Political Process in Nigeria: Problem and Prospects', *African Journal of Political Science and International Relations*, 4,2 (2010): 75–82

Bradford, Helen. 'Women, Gender and Colonialism: Rethinking the History of the British Cape Colony and its Frontier Zones, c. 1806–70'. *Journal of African History*, 35.3 (1996): 1–70.

Butler, Judith. 'Variations on Sex and Gender: Beauvoir, Wittig and Foucault'. In Philip Rice & Patricia Waugh (eds), *Modern Literary Theory: A Reader* (3rd edn), London & New York: Arnold, 1996: 145–59.

Carnes, Molly. 'Commentary: Deconstructing Gender Difference'. *Journal of the Association of American Medical Colleges* 85.4 (2010): 575–7.

Coetzee, J. M. *Disgrace*. London: Vintage/Random House, 1999.

Culler, Jonathan. *On Deconstruction: Theory and Criticism after Structuralism*. Ithaca, NY: Cornell University Press, 1982.

Dangarembga, Tsitsi. *Nervous Conditions*. Seattle: Seal Press, 1988.

de Beauvoir, Simone. 'Introduction to *The Second Sex*'. In Elaine Marks and Isabelle de Courtivron (eds), *New French Feminisms: An Anthology*. New York: Schocken Books, 2009 [1949].

Derrida, Jacques. 'Linguistics and Grammatology' in *Of Grammatology* (2nd edn). Baltimore: Johns Hopkins UP, 1976.

Duignan, Brian. "Deconstruction". In *Encyclopaedia Britannica*. Encyclopaedia Britannica, 2016. Retrieved 4 November 2016 from www.britannica.com/topic/deconstruction/Deconstruction-in-literary-studies, accessed 4 November 2016.

Eagleton, Terry. *Feminist Criticism*. London/New York: Blackwell, 1996.

Mitchell, Whitney. 'Deconstructing Gender, Sex, and Sexuality as Applied to Identity' in *The Humanist* (2002).

Nzegwu, Nkiru U. 'Gender Equality in Dual-Sex System: The Case of Onitsha'. In Dillard Mary (ed.) *JENdA: A Journal of Culture and African Women Studies* 1.1 (2001).

—. *Family Matters: Feminist Concepts in African Philosophy of Culture*. New York: State University of New York Press, 2006.

Ogundipe-Leslie, M. *Recreating Ourselves: African Women and Critical Transformations*. Trenton, NJ: Africa World Press, 1994.

Piza-Lopez, Eugenia. 'Overcoming the Barriers: Women and Participation in Public Life'. In Tina Wallace & Candida March (eds), *Changing Perceptions: Writings on Gender and Development*. Oxford: Oxfam, 1991: 111–17.

Roop, Cullen. The 'Good Father': Deconstructing the Patriarch in Chimamanda Ngozi Adichie's *Purple Hibiscus*. Oral Paper. 27th Annual Student Research Conference, 2014. Retrieved 21 October 2016 from http://src.truman.edu/browse/display.asp?abs_id=3647&year=2014.

Sarr Abdou. 'Strategy for the Liberation of African Women: The View of a Feminist Man'. In Tina Wallace & Candida March (eds.) *Changing Perceptions: Writings on Gender and Development*. Oxford: Oxfam, 1991. 289–294

Stratton, Florence. *Contemporary African Literature and the Politics of Gender*. London and New York: Routledge, 1994.

Titi, Salaam. 'A Brief Analysis on the Situation of Women in Nigeria Today'. Democratic Socialist Movement (Nigeria), 2003. Retrieved 3rd July 2002 from www.socialistnigeria.org/women/1-3-03.html.

3

Adichie & the West African Voice
Women & Power in *Purple Hibiscus*

JANE DURAN

Chimamanda Adichie's *Purple Hibiscus* is now a staple of university courses, and is regarded as one of the most successful of recent African novels (Adichie 2003). But, if Adichie is thought of primarily as a stylist, there is much that is missed in an appreciation of her work, considering especially her construction of her female characters. From Kambili to her mother, to Aunty Ifeoma and other, more minor, characters, each of the women in the novel exhibits a remarkable complexity. It will be the argument of this paper that that complexity helps us to understand gender relations in at least certain parts of West Africa today.

Work on the cultures of Western Africa has frequently emphasized the constructs of trade and the importance of the roles of women – more contemporary writing has frequently tried to show that the roles of women are significantly different from female roles in the West. A great deal of the writing on the topic has underscored the matrilineal and female-empowered constructions of those societies, and the extent to which such constructions affected diasporic cultures across the globe.[1] But many have some difficulty imagining the lives of women of the various cultures to which advertence might be made – Igbo, Yoruba, Hausa – and the various permutations for women in those cultures. Adichie does a noteworthy job of providing us with characters that exemplify both the strength of the past and the fortitude of today. Yesterday's women traders exhibited particular characteristics that allow us to read into their societies. In *Purple Hibiscus*, Adichie achieves the difficult by giving us female characters in whom we can believe. This feat is all the more noteworthy since the author refuses

---

[1] See Duran 2009; also Blassingame 1977, for work on the extent to which the Diasporic groups exhibit cultural traits taken from the continent.

45

to indulge in platitudes; rather, she provides us with characters whose credibility is underscored by both their strengths and weaknesses. There is no romanticism or even attenuated essentialism in Adichie – we encounter strong individuals whose lives tell us about the urbanised West Africa of today.

* * *

Kambili, from the outset of the novel, is a quiet girl who is herself the rare purple hibiscus in a crowd of flowers of other colours. Part of what makes the novel so intriguing is that we experience not only the growth of Kambili, but a sense that whatever is inside her has been there from the outset. The author makes extensive use of metonymic linking, yoking flowers, growth and individual paths together to make her overall points. In Kambili's interactions with her family, she displays a purpose and determination far beyond her years – although much of the novel centres around her interactions with her father, Eugene, and his obsessive interest in religion, it is in Kambili's response to these issues that we see the makeup of her personality. Always the observer, she is moved on many occasions toward an internal dialogue that presents her with a variety of overviews. When visiting Papa-Nnukwu, the grandfather regarded as a pagan, and whose food she is forbidden to touch, she notes:

> I stared at the fufu on the enamel plate, which was chipped of its leaf-green colour at the edges. I imagined the fufu, dried to crusts by the harmattan winds, scratching the inside of Papa-Nnukwu's throat as he swallowed. (Adichie 2003, 51)

Kambili is the artist and intellectual – she is someone who stands apart, and her ruminations on what goes on around her provide us with a great deal of insight into the structure of her Igbo society. But, like any other young woman her age, she is also vulnerable to interpersonal attraction and, in the depiction of her relationship with Father Amadi, we see still other aspects of her personality. Again, careful use of metaphor is of the utmost importance here. Both her relationship with the priest and her interactions with her schoolmates indicate that Kambili, although outwardly hesitant, has a strong sense of self that will eventually assert itself. Insofar as school is concerned, she is an outstanding student, and like many students who fall into that category, also somewhat withdrawn and apart from what goes on around her. But because of her powers of vision, she can see much of the social life of her school for what it is. The superficially oriented youngsters around her are anathema to her – and her interior self has much to say in that regard. As Adichie writes, in depicting Kambili's frustration at school:

'Chinwe just wants you to talk to her first,' Ezinne whispered. 'You know, she started calling you backyard snob because you don't talk to anybody. She said just because your father owns a newspaper and all those factories does not mean you have to feel too big, because her father is rich, too.'

'I don't feel too big.' (ibid., 51)

Kambili is not the sort of individual who is given to rankings in social relations, or to attempts to make herself bigger. One of the features of Kambili's observant personality that plays the largest role in the novel's structure has to do with her ability to simultaneously distance herself from what she sees around her, yet play at least some kind of role. Because Kambili is a natural critic of the Igbo society that she sees manifested in the behaviour of her abusive father, Eugene, and her compliant mother, she is able to form a consistently internal set of observations that she can use to good purpose. When she finally meets Father Amadi, she is more ready than most to immediately identify with the priest who has made it his life task to serve others.

From the start, Kambili notices the differences between the Father and those around him. His unconventionality matches hers, and she is eager to learn more about him. She wants to be in his presence, and he makes an impression on her that she cannot readily shake. The force of Kambili's thoughts here, and her overall conceptualization pattern, have a great deal to do with the interiority with which she addresses various issues, including those having to do with Father Amadi. She is not one to discuss her feelings with others – unlike her cousin Amaka, or her schoolmates, she will not broadcast the depth of her feelings. Instead, this world of interiority will turn into something valuable that she can use for others. Although we often think of the participant-observer distinction as one that adheres to more-empirical thinking, the author makes wonderful use of this trope as a way of categorizing Kambili and her interactions. Adichie characterizes some of the activity between the priest and the young girl when they first meet in the following way.

'Nsukka has its charms,' Father Amadi said, smiling. He had a singer's voice, a voice that had the same effect on my ears that Mama working Pears baby oil into my hair had on my scalp. I did not fully comprehend his English-laced Igbo sentences at dinner because my ears followed the sound and not the sense of his speech. (ibid., 135)

Kambili is about to be placed in a position where the strengths that she has as a young, intellectually oriented woman will be put to the test by her attraction to Father Amadi. It is not so much any action in which she engages as her overall thought patterns that reveal to us that this remarkable young woman will use the opportunity of first love as a way to make something of herself. In other words, Kambili could choose to try to push her relationship with the Father further than it will go (and, indeed, on at least one occasion she seems to attempt this). But by the later portion of the book, she has noticed that love is really an internal relation – the important part of the relation is between the lover and her internal self. This allows for the patterns of growth that are the hallmark of her maturation. Once again, the notion of a love relationship becomes a metaphor for individual change.

If a strength of the Igbo woman, as portrayed by Kambili, has to do with this ability to forge ahead even under adverse circumstances, the fact that she is later exposed in the work to two other figures – Aunty Ifeoma and the woman in the marketplace who does her hair, who are themselves unconventional women and sources of fortitude – shows us how sensitive Adichie is as an author to the various sorts of situations that a young woman might encounter. After the humiliation of growing up in a home where her mother lets Eugene abuse her and her brother over a long period of time, it is crucial that Kambili begins to see that there are other ways of living. She will immediately notice the differences in the home managed by Aunty Ifeoma, for example, for it is here that she encounters the Father, and it is also here that she meets a new type of child – the children of the free-spirited and iconoclastic. Kambili is a quick learner, and the lessons to be had from the new family are readily taken in.

Toward the end of the work, describing her new attitude toward her love for Father Amadi – which she now sees as something internal to herself, and to be guarded – Kambili's voice notes:

I always carry his latest letter with me until a new one comes. When I told Amaka that I do this, she teased me in her reply ... But I don't carry his letters around because of anything lovey-dovey; there is very little lovey-dovey, anyway. (Adichie 2003, 303)

She carries them around because, in her new way of thinking, they remind her of her past.

The West African Voice: Women & Power in *Purple Hibiscus*

* * *

Aunty Ifeoma is, in a sense, the most free-spirited and unconventional woman in the novel, but she is simply a representative of what Adichie takes to be the strength of West African women. Her tirelessness in raising her children on a slender academic salary, her clear-sightedness, and her failure to conform to a number of traditional views, especially when those views might be demarcated as anti-woman, all mark her as someone who cannot be ignored. When Kambili first goes to stay with Ifeoma, she is struck by the laughter in her house, especially in comparison to the silence in her own home. That laughter in and of itself marks a way of going that will be revelatory for the young girl. Some of the new experiences for her in Ifeoma's home are set out in the text when Adichie tries to indicate that respect for at least the oral tradition within the Igbo culture is something that has been denied to Kambili. She writes that

> Amaka broke into song at the end of each decade, uplifting Igbo songs that made Aunty Ifeoma sing in echoes, like an opera singer drawing the words from the pit of her stomach. After the rosary, Aunty Ifeoma asked if we knew any of the songs. 'We don't sing at home,' Jaja answered. 'We do here,' Aunty Ifeoma said, and I wondered if it was irritation that made her lower her eyebrows.(ibid., 125)

The presence of singing signals a new degree of freedom, one to which Kambili is not accustomed.

If part of what Adichie intends to convey with the notion of hibiscus flowers of varying colours having to do with the artist or intellectual who stands outside the group – metonymy for the lives of more than one of the characters – much of the impact of what she is trying to articulate is brought home to the reader in having Kambili interact with a woman like Ifeoma, who becomes a model for her of everything that she wants to achieve. Where her own home is concerned with formality and whether or not the fufu has been cooked properly, Ifeoma is concerned with free expression and the exchange of ideas. Her father Eugene and her mother have a rule for everything, and if Kambili or her brother break these rules they are immediately punished. By contrast, it is almost as if Ifeoma has no rules – at least not rules worth bothering about. This characterization is remarkable for its force. Noise, dust and commentary are all a regular part of the scene, and what Kambili begins to learn is that there is another way of living. Some of the initial impression made on Kambili and her brother by their Aunty is given in the following description.

> Aunty Ifeoma came the next day, in the evening... Her laughter floated upstairs into the living room, where I sat reading. I had not heard it in two years, but I would know that cackling, hearty sound anywhere. Aunty Ifeoma was as tall as Papa, with a well-proportioned body. She walked fast, like one who knew just where she was going and what she was going to do there. And she spoke the way she walked, as if to get as many words out of her mouth in the shortest time. (ibid., 71)[2]

In contrast to the inhibited lives around her, Ifeoma's life seems like some kind of mystery or miracle. In general, we are tempted to think of the power of African women, especially in traditionally dominant groups such as the Igbo, as having to do with the marketplace or with tasks accomplished, but in the case of Ifeoma it has to do with attitudinal strength and style of nurturing. Unlike Eugene, who seems not to be able to interact with anyone on the basis of equality, and who possesses no skills in understanding his fellow human beings, Ifeoma's freespiritedness leads her to be able to rear her children to think for themselves and, most important for Kambili, to treat a visitor to the family as if she were her own child. When Amaka, Ifeoma's daughter, raises her voice at Kambili, Ifeoma tells her to answer back. She laughs at her children's faults, and does not hesitate to invite them to inquire further into a variety of matters. She is not rule-bound.

The abuse that Eugene heaps on his family, at least tacitly condoned by Kambili's mother, is partly physical abuse, but is also largely mental abuse. The atmosphere of mindless repetition of rules, the sense that one is not free to question, and the overshadowing presence of Eugene, even when he is physically absent from the home, all have a great deal to do with the difficulties that Kambili and her brother Jaja have. Theirs is a form of confinement that goes beyond the physical – they fear for the safety and health of the unborn baby that their mother carries even before they know anything about the situation. Adichie drives home the notion of imprisonment in scene after scene. Eugene's small-mindedness and tendency to tyrannize are legendary among those who have had contact with him and, when he visits his ancestral village, an elder shouts at him: 'You are like a fly blindly following a corpse into the grave!' (ibid., p.70). Even other traditionalists among the Igbo know that Eugene has gone too far in his desire to keep the rules.

---

[2] Stylistically, Adichie is similar in many of her descriptive passages to Buchi Emecheta (1974).

One facet of Ifeoma's family life that impresses Kambili – and that makes a difference for her in her own life – has to do with the ways in which Ifeoma encourages her children, both in terms of overall growth and day-to-day affection. Speaking about the problems at the local university, where Ifeoma teaches, her son begins the following exchange.

> 'If some Big Man in Abuja has stolen the money, is the V.C. supposed to vomit money for Nsukka?' Obiora asked. I turned to watch him, imagining myself at fourteen, imagining myself now. I wouldn't mind somebody vomiting some money for me right now, Aunty Ifeoma said, laughing in that proud-coach-watching-the-team way. 'We'll go into town to see if there is any decently priced ube in the market. I know Father Amadi likes ube, and we have some corn at home to go with it.' (ibid., 132)

The uninhibited nature of the dialogue in the family signals not only the family's various strengths, but the fact that Ifeoma, at least, is not afraid to show the family style to outsiders. Part of her own personal resilience is that she can see that Kambili and her brother are in need of assistance, and that a form of assistance to them would be to model a more healthful style. She is also unafraid of criticism; it is inevitable that outsiders will not like or will be put off to some extent by some of what they see, and yet this does not trouble Ifeoma. Her magnanimity of character is such that she moves on, fearless, and determined to show Kambili that there are other ways of living; and also comparatively unmoved by the notion that Eugene, for one, will probably disagree with her.

* * *

Kambili is a woman of the Igbo; so is Aunty Ifeoma. But toward the end of the novel, Adichie gives us some minor characters who are, in their own way, just as important. It is as if the details of everyday life make a great deal of difference for Adichie, and she is determined to try to present the mundane activities of the urban West African woman in full strokes.

One such woman is the hairdresser who, toward the end of the work, dresses Kambili's hair near the basket of snails (a treat in the Nigerian diet) that Kambili keeps remarking on in her interior voice while she is having her hair braided. This taking of a young girl to have her hair done – something that is done for her by Father Amadi – yields a rich commentary on the part of the market women, the hairdresser in particular. This passage is one of the most poignant in the novel; it fills in the details on urban life.

> She reached out to straighten a cornrow that did not need to be straightened. 'A man does not bring a young girl to dress her hair unless he loves that young girl, I am telling you. It does not happen,' she said. And I nodded because again I did not know what to say. 'It doesn't happen,' Mama Joe said again, as if I had disagreed. (Adichie 2003, 238)

Mama Joe is one of those whose forceful personality will carry the day in most situations – and Kambili knows this. But part of the poignancy here has to do with what it is that she says. Mama Joe can see something that perhaps Kambili does not want to see.

If Ifeoma represents an intellectualised trope of the Igbo woman, and if Kambili herself is the rare 'purple hibiscus', as the text implies, Mama Joe and her counterparts in the marketplace are the everyday, traditional women who hold the urban society together. Because of their ability to work under difficult conditions, they are able to make judgements and pass on information in a way that their perhaps more sophisticated sisters cannot. Kambili would, in some sense, like to believe that Father Amadi feels the same way about her that she feels about him, but in another sense it is too dangerous to hold that belief. For these reasons, the plain fact that Mama Joe feels called upon to give her opinion of the situation marks her as one who is unafraid. The entire atmosphere of the marketplace as depicted in the scene – from the snails crawling out of the basket to the multitudes of shoppers and those waiting to have their hair done – signals that, in composing this scene, Adichie wants to talk of the reality of the life of the average urban Nigerian.

There is, then, a large difference between Kambili's comparatively idealized inner life and the lives of the women around her. Although she might aspire to be like Ifeoma, or even Amaka, this will take time. But there is another mode, and Mama Joe represents that way of being. This mode is also the mode of the past – it is the way of being of generations of women who were the forebears of both Kambili and Ifeoma, even if this is not recognized. The ability to function on one's own, in the day-to-day reality of marketplace West Africa, is one that has gone on for generations, and is signalled, indeed, in the work of those who have written of gender constructs in Igbo and Yoruba society.[3] The

[3] See Oyewumi (1997). See also, again, for general work on those who led lives in the Diaspora, Blassingame (1977). Anne Moody's, *Coming of Age in Mississippi* (1968) is noteworthy for its latter-day descriptions of work under post-slavery conditions.

marketplace has traditionally been the site of catalytic energy for the West African woman, and Adichie signals this to us.

In order to introduce this brief but poignant episode, we are given a nicely-detailed description of the market where Mama Joe and the others do their work, and of the conditions there. The opening passages note:

> Mama Joe's shed in Ogige market just barely fit the high stool where she sat and the smaller stool in front of her. I sat on the smaller stool. Father Amadi stood outside, beside the wheelbarrows and pigs and people and chickens that went past, because his broad-shouldered form could not fit in the shed. Mama Joe wore a wool hat even though sweat had made yellow patches under the sleeves of her blouse. Women and children worked in the neighboring sheds, twisting hair, weaving hair... (Adichie 2003, 236)

This focus on the working conditions within the marketplace makes two points simultaneously. It not only tells us much more about the daily lives of most urban women – Mama Joe being an average worker, with her own work stall – but it also, implicitly, contrasts these lives to the lives with which we have already been acquainted in the novel. Mama Joe's life has nothing in common with the pristine, overdone sort of upper middle-class life that Kambili knows at home, but neither does it have anything in common with the free-spirited, university-oriented way of living that she has seen at Ifeoma's house. Here, three sorts of modes of living are contrasted, and it is easy for the reader to see that, although the hardscrabble life has its merits, and although owning nice furniture can make one more physically comfortable, the intellectual and inquiring life of Ifeoma and her family is one in which many would desire to participate.

Why is it important that the Mama Joe episode forms a crucial part of the last segment of the book? Mama Joe's take on the relationship between Father Amadi and Kambili is particularly important, for without it we have no real way of gauging the depth and extent of the commitment. Mama Joe provides us with a critical insight – she is making the point that the Father does, indeed, have feelings for Kambili. It is simply the case that those feelings cannot be manifested in the obvious straightforward sort of way, both because he is a priest, and also because he is old enough, mature enough – and cares enough – not to take advantage of her youth. The insight that we glean from this is that the Father actually cares more for Kambili than most would – more than the members of her immediate family, who have caused her such trouble, and more than the average young man who might have no scruples where she is concerned. And it is important that this epiphanic thought come to us from the dialogue, not of someone like Ifeoma who represents the university community, but of a market woman.

The juxtaposition of these three important female characters – Kambili, Ifeoma and Mama Joe – in one novel gives us a new take on the lives of West African women and girls. If the alleged helplessness and caricatured femininity of the young girl provide a backdrop for many a Western novel, particularly in the earlier parts of the twentieth century, the force of the woman in West African cultures has been a staple of commentary.[14] But that strength and force can be displayed in a number of ways. It is a signature of Adichie's style that she chooses a variety of characters to make her point, and that each character does so in a very distinctive fashion.

* * *

I have been arguing that the force of the West African woman is shown in Adichie's characters in *Purple Hibiscus*, but in ways that might surprise the unwary. A more-conventional sort of strength is shown by Kambili and Ifeoma – although even there, it is perhaps not what one would expect – but an entirely new sort of maturity and wisdom is shown by the marketplace women, for instance Mama Joe. What makes the novel so remarkable is that Adichie is aware of the fact that the matrilineality of the West African tradition is a trope for many, but she exploits it in a variety of ways. If others are inclined to argue that that particular forcefulness is part of what drove the African-derived cultures of the New World, then Adichie has the task of assembling a variety of characters and personalities who exhibit the force in new ways.

In Kambili's case, we see her change from a shy fourteen-year-old who can barely hold her own in conversation to a mature young woman who understands that she is entitled to feel as she does about Father Amadi, and that in a very real and genuine sense her feelings for him have more to do with her and her interior than they have to do with him or anyone else. We also see her learn to speak her mind, and to be able to interact with Amaka and others without falsity. She is the one who is responsible for the aftermath of what happens to Eugene.

In the case of Ifeoma, although we can argue that her personality is perhaps not so surprising for an intellectually oriented woman who teaches at a university, it is unexpected. Her resilience is all the more remarkable because she is faced with raising children on her own, and because she shows virtually no interest in conventional matters. She is determined, like her automobile, to go on without much of what might be thought by others to constitute the essentials.

Although her role is small, it is perhaps Mama Joe who is the most surprising of these female characters, unless one wants to count the hardly sketched personality of Kambili's mother. On the one hand, the bluntness that characterizes her speech might be thought all too commonplace – but Mama Joe uses this candour to good effect. She is the one who makes Kambili believe that Father Amadi loves her, because she understands that love is shown in a variety of ways. This particular move – along with the appearance of her stall in the market, and many other details – provides the backdrop and the focus of the major change in the story, Kambili's acceptance of the Father's type of love.

One could argue that although she might be more celebrated for work that came later, this first novel by Adichie remains one to be prized and admired because of the resonance that it has, particularly for the younger reader. The scope of the emotions, the focus on interpersonal interaction that is the sort of meeting likely to occur for adolescents and, of course, the focus on young love make this work one that will be read for some time to come. We can celebrate the fact that we can teach and work with *Purple Hibiscus*.

Works Cited

Adichie, Chimamanda, *Purple Hibiscus*, New York: Anchor books, 2003.

Blassingame, John, *Slave Testimony*, Baton Rouge: Louisiana State University Press, 1977.

Duran, Jane, 'African NGOs and Womanism: Microcredit and Self-Help', *Journal of African-American Studies*, 14.2 (2009), 171–80.

Emecheta, Buchi, *The Bride Price*, New York: George Braziller, 1974.

Moody, Anne, *Coming of Age in Mississippi*, New York: Bantam Dell, 1968.

Oyewumi, Oyeronke, *The Invention of Women*, Minneapolis: University of Minnesota Press, 1997.

4

Reconstructing Motherhood
A Mutative Reality in *Purple Hibiscus*

INIOBONG I. UKO

Maternity is viewed as sacred in the traditions of all African societies. In all of them, the earth's fertility is traditionally linked to women's maternal powers. Hence the centrality of women as producers and providers, and the reverence in which they are held (Amadiume 1987, 191).

The above assertion captures the essence of the concept of motherhood in African cosmology. A woman has to be a mother to enjoy the benefits and recognition that the society provides. Our focus in this paper is on the human family and the human mother. She is typically known and/or required to be caring and supportive of her husband and the children in the family. The concept of motherhood, which involves bearing and nurturing children, is a global phenomenon that assumes varying implications and levels of significance in different cultures. In many cultures, motherhood is revered as the status by which the human race is preserved and genealogy is perpetuated. This means that motherhood is closely linked with life, and the life-giving essence.

However, a twist in the above equation arises where the mother destroys life directly and consciously. In Chimamanda Adichie's *Purple Hibiscus*, Beatrice, Eugene Achike's wife and mother of Kambili and Jaja, suffers indignation and torture from her autocratic husband, and she ultimately murders him by poisoning his tea. This study examines the factors that reverse the course of nature, and make a mother, the bearer and nurturer of life, to be the one that terminates life. This twist in the role of the mother is the mutation, the alteration that opens up a vista of issues with which this paper is concerned. In the African context, the mother is also required to bear male children so as to ensure the perpetuity of the lineage, and care for the family –

her immediate/nuclear family and the extended family. She is always expected to be in a family context, which a man will always head – as her husband or her father or her uncle or her brother. That motherhood should be effective under assumed male protection easily derives from the image of the woman whose position is naturally 'under' the man. Lauretta Ngcobo asserts that in Africa, 'every woman is encouraged to marry and get children in order to express her womanhood to the full. The basis of marriage among Africans implies the transfer of a woman's fertility to the husband's family group' (1988, 144). These are some of the cultural notions of motherhood.

Motherhood, according to Remi Akujobi,

> is often defined as an automatic set of feelings and behaviours that is switched on by pregnancy and the birth of a baby. It is an experience that is said to be profoundly shaped by social context and culture. Motherhood is also seen as a moral transformation whereby a woman comes to terms with being different in that she ceases to be an autonomous individual because she is one way or the other attached to another – her baby. (Akujobi 2011, 2)

Significantly, motherhood assumes different meanings in different cultures and religions. The cultural meanings entail how motherhood is perceived, the expectations of mothers and the roles evolved by that culture for mothers to perform. The religious meanings may be the spiritual implications attached to motherhood.

As a spiritual concept, motherhood is couched in the fact that the woman produces the connection between the present and the future, through the birth of (possibly) sons. Within this framework, motherhood in Africa is viewed as a fundamental and critical phenomenon, and a woman is not likely to suffer a worse misfortune than to be childless. John S. Mbiti describes a barren woman as the 'dead end of human life, not only for genealogical level but also for herself' (1970, 124), and Courtney Smith notes a Senegalese woman's opinion that 'if women have money, and have everything, they are still nobody without a husband and children. To be a real [African] woman you have to bear children' (2010, 35). Motherhood is a revered spiritual status in Africa because it involves self-sacrifice and giving. While mothers are regarded as creators and nurturers, they are also viewed as endowed with powers to create and to serve as goddesses. Motherhood is seen as a

> symbol of the nation-state. So nationalists ... deploy the nation-as-mother symbolism to mobilize patriotic sentiments. Camara Laye and [Léopold

Sédar] Senghor express their love for African [*sic*] in terms of the love for mother, and [Adrian] Roscoe echoes this idea in his book *Mother is Gold*. [David] Diop glories mother in his poems and [Christopher] Okigbo recognizes the power of his mother 'Idoto'. In many texts written in Africa both by male and female, writers refer to the mother Africa trope and it has remained a prominent subject in African discourse. Love of mother and love of nation have been taken as one and the same (Akujobi 2011, 2).

A quick survey of how motherhood is portrayed in African literature reveals that this concept is more-prominently and more-effectively explored by women. Their early writings show that motherhood is a prerequisite for social acceptance and relevance. On the contrary, non-mothering women are faced with humiliation, rejection, frustration and low self-esteem.

In Flora Nwapa's *Efuru* (1966), the title character is frustrated by her inability to procreate and so she becomes a priestess. In Nwapa's *One is Enough* (1995), Amaka's barrenness causes such tremendous tension in her marriage with Obiora, until she leaves the marriage for the city where she does everything possible to survive and be accepted. She eventually gets pregnant by a Catholic Priest, and attains honour and acceptability. Zulu Sofola's *Wedlock of the Gods* (1972) depicts that Ogwoma's childlessness, even though caused by her husband's infertility, gets Ogwoma exasperated and driven into reactions that lead to her death. Nnu Ego in Buchi Emecheta's *The Joys of Motherhood* (1979) never considers herself a woman until she starts giving birth. In general, motherhood confers enormous power on the woman. In fact, through the mother's roles of bringing new life into the family and society, perpetuating the family and lineage, ensuring that the family's values are not extinguished, she is often revered, and regarded as very close to or a representative of God in the process of creation. Yet, conversely, motherhood in Africa is dangerous to women because it continues the structure within which they are denied the privilege of subjectivity and a world that is open and free.

Chikwenye Ogunyemi's analysis of women in Nigeria portrays four categories of motherhood: 'The Sweet Mother, the Bitter Wife, the Sour Widow, the Salt of the Earth' (1996, 74). 'The Sweet Mother' phenomenon was popularized in 1976 when the Cameroonian-born Prince Nico Mbarga released the hit tune 'Sweet Mother' with the lyrics 'I no go forget you, for dey suffer we you suffer for me'. The stereotype of motherhood being synonymous with suffering became significant as an African reality. It translated to a blackmail that the woman as a bitter wife must pretend to be happy and display good conduct for the sake of the marriage, her children and herself. Molara Ogundipe-Leslie questions this stereotype with its insistent conformism to bearing children to secure the woman in the family. She thus condemns 'the figure of the sweet mother, the all-accepting creature of fecundity and self-sacrifice' (1996, 75–6).

There are specific issues in *Purple Hibiscus* that portray Adichie's conception of motherhood as an evolving phenomenon, and modulated by such factors as the attitude of the husband, the welfare of the children and the woman's safety. The novel depicts the family of Eugene and Beatrice Achike, with their two children, Kambili as the daughter, and Jaja as the son. Set in postcolonial Nigeria, and told through the perspective of the fifteen-year-old Kambili, *Purple Hibiscus* espouses the story of the disintegration of the Achike family as led by the oppressively dominating but devout Catholic father, Eugene.

The central contradiction in the story is that Kambili's father, Eugene Achike (Papa) a wealthy businessman and a very strict Catholic who dominates his family, is also very harsh, near-tyrannical and violent towards his wife and two children. Even though Eugene is an important figure in the society and the church, and he donates generously to the less privileged and other worthy causes, he often displays violence within the family, making his wife, Beatrice (Mama), and the two children to live in fear, lose self-esteem and suffer tremendous physical pain. According to Ranti Williams, Papa was

> a complex picture of a man struggling with his own demons, taking out his struggles on those he loves: his wife, Beatrice, son, Jaja, and Kambili herself ... [He] beats his pregnant wife, and after deploring the soldiers' torture of his editor with lighted cigarettes, pours boiling water over the bare feet of his adored daughter as a punishment for coming second in class. And yet Eugene, self-made and ultimately self-hating, is the book's loneliest character; his misunderstanding of Christianity has led him to reject the animist beliefs of his own ageing father and to repudiate the old man himself, perversely hating the sinner more than the sin. (Williams 2004)

The metaphor of the colour purple is a significant motif in Adichie's *Purple Hibiscus*. It is emblematic of freedom and rebellion, a duality that is a major human characteristic. The two combine as a spirit to propel Beatrice (Mama), Kambili and Jaja to react against Eugene's tyranny. When Simone de Beauvoir wrote in her 1949 treatise *The Second Sex* that a wife's function in a marriage is to satisfy a male's sexual needs and to take care of his household in exchange for his protection (de Beauvoir 1970, 442), she did not imagine that Mama in Adichie's 2003 *Purple Hibiscus* is a mother of two teenage children, and a wife of a modern entrepreneur and ardent Christian who does everything, but not protect her. This lack of care brings about the reversal in the course of nature, whereby the mother, the bearer and nurturer of life becomes the one that terminates life.

In this novel, Adichie evolves a cause-and-effect template which clearly pitches the tyrannical, yet pious Papa on one side, and his children and Mama on the other. Running parallel to that template is the perception that Papa is powerful, influential and revered in the church and society, while the children and Mama are powerless, often intimidated by Papa's towering physical, economic and spiritual stature, and constantly in search of empowerment, as shown in the table.

Event no.	Cause	Effect
1.	Jaja fails to go to communion during the Palm Sunday Mass. According to him, 'the wafer gives me bad breath … And the priest keeps touching my mouth and it nauseates me' (6).	Papa furiously grabs the missal and throws it across the room, toward Jaja. It misses Jaja, but strikes the glass étagère, shattering the dainty ceramic figurines of ballet dancers. Mama comes into the room, stares at the figurine pieces on the floor and then without complaining, kneels and collects them with her bare hands (7).
2.	Afterwards, Mama recounts to Kambili her experiences of miscarriages after she had had Kambili. She reflects on the gossips among the villagers and family members, and the pressure on Papa to marry another woman or have children outside the marriage. But Papa refuses. Unfortunately, Mama loses yet another pregnancy.	Conditions Kambili's mind and personality to explore human personalities, especially Father Amadi's in Nsukka. Her pursuit of freedom is a vital category in the process of casting off the cloak that beclouds her mother, Mama, and keeps her in obsequious servility to Papa.

3.	On Christmas day, the Igwe visits the Achike family, and Mama greets him the traditional way for women – bending low and offering him her back so that he pats it with his fan (94).	Later at home that night, Papa tells Mama the sinfulness and ungodliness in bowing to another human being, as she did to the Igwe (94).
4.	Recognizing that, a few days later, when Papa and family visit the bishop at Awka, Kambili does not kneel to kiss the bishop's ring, trying to impress Papa.	But back in the car, Papa yanks her ear and complains that she lacked the spirit of discernment, she should know that while the Igwe is merely a traditional ruler, the bishop is a man of God (94).
5.	On the Sunday after Christmas day, Kambili experiences menstrual pains for which she needs to take some Panadol tablets. Mama and Jaja assist in getting her some cereal to eat so that she can take the tablets. Kambili, thus, violates the Eucharist fast.	Papa is angry about Kambili's act of profanity, and feels that Mama and the children are serving the devil, and that the devil may have been living in his (Papa's) house. In a practical response, he unbuckles his big, heavy leather belt, and beats Jaja first, across his shoulder, then lashes Mama's upper arm, and then strikes Kambili's back. He is 'like a Fulani nomad' – even though he is of a heavy and imposing stature. And as he beats, he declares that the devil would not succeed (102).

The above captures the close connectivity and intricate synergy that exists between the ostensibly diverse actions of some characters in the story. Adrienne Rich (1995) notes that besides the very ancient resentment of woman's power to create new life, there is a fear of her apparent power to affect the male genitals. Woman as elemental force, and as sexual temptress and consumer of his sexual energies, thus becomes, for man, a figure that generates anxiety. A woman is a mysterious being who communicates with spirits and thus has magical powers that she can use to hurt the male. He must therefore protect himself against her powers by keeping her subjugated (Adichie 2003, 114). The veracity of

Adrienne Rich's analysis above describes Papa's brutality, which seems to border on an intrinsic fear: largely, fear of what Mama can do that he cannot, fear that he is not an effective head of family. This fear seems to constantly drive him into violence.

The essential trait of Mama's which catalogues Papa's evil is her silence. She watches all of the following acts in silence.

- Papa beats up Jaja, and injures the small finger in his left hand because Jaja, at ten years old, misses two questions in his catechism test and is not named the best in his first Holy Communion class (ibid., 145).
- Papa pours hot water over Kambili's feet in the bathtub as punishment for acquiescing to stay in the same house with his heathen father, Papa-Nnukwu, in Nsukka with their paternal aunt, Ifeoma, where she (Kambili) and Jaja spent some of their holidays (ibid., 194–5).
- Papa batters her (Beatrice) while Kambili and Jaja are away on holidays in Nsukka with Aunty Ifeoma. On their return to Enugu, they find that her face is swollen and the area around her right eye is the black-purple shade of an overripe avocado (ibid., 190).
- Papa, in his fury, tears up the painting of Papa-Nnukwu, which Kambili and Jaja bring back from Aunty Ifeoma's house (ibid., 120).
- Papa severely kicks and rigorously whips Kambili to unconsciousness as she holds onto the pieces of the picture that he tries to shred. She wakes to find herself at St. Agnes Hospital where she spends some weeks; then on discharge, goes with Jaja to Nsukka to recuperate (ibid., 211).
- Papa again batters Mama while the children are away in Nsukka. He breaks a small wooden table on her belly, which causes her to bleed so profusely that by the time he takes her to St. Agnes Hospital, her pregnancy cannot be salvaged (ibid., 245). She loses a six-week-old foetus.

Mama watches helplessly all of these acts of brutality in silence because, in Papa's worldview, no other person can and should know anything to say or do about what he does, no person can dare to be opposed to what he does or says. Mama lacks the courage to cry audibly while Papa unleashes tyranny on the family. Often times, she cries, or tears merely roll down her cheeks. The more Papa displays brutality on his family, the more resentment gnaws at Mama's heart. Papa's continued cruelty on his wife and children is symptomatic of maternal envy, which is a cardinal feature of post-Freudian psychology. It explains that men's attitudes and actions are aimed at compensating for male lack of the one fundamental, elemental, creative power of motherhood, which belongs exclusively to women. This development causes a turn-around in Mama's psyche, and this is symbolized in the following.

> Everything came tumbling down after Palm Sunday. Howling winds came with an angry rain, uprooting frangipani trees in the front yard. They lay on the lawn, their pink and white flowers grazing the grass, their roots waving lumpy soil in the air. The satellite dish on top of the garage came crashing down, and lounged on the driveway like a visiting alien space-ship. The door of my wardrobe dislodged completely. Sisi broke a full set of Mama's china. (Adichie 2003, 257)

The significance of the catastrophic scenario above foreshadows the events that take place in Papa's family as Mama becomes changed as a result of the inhuman treatment that Papa unleashes on her and the children, and the agonizing, painful and humiliating experiences that constitute her reality as a wife and mother.

Mama's perception of motherhood becomes transformed just as the different devastating changes that occur in her environment: the howling winds, the angry rain, the uprooting of trees, the destruction of the lovely flowers, the crashing of the satellite dish, the dislodging of the wardrobe door, the breaking of Mama's china, etc. This symbol of abnormal, unexpected and violent changes from the usual trend informs Mama's new image in Enugu from the time she returns with Kambili and Jaja from Nsukka. There seems to be something new in the ambience in the Achike home, and Kambili describes that 'it was too new, too foreign, and I did not know what to be or how to be' (Adichie 2003, 258). Prominently, the new aura in the family seems to propel a fresh release that makes Mama to find her voice and use it, as Kambili explains.

> When Mama asked Sisi to wipe the floor of the living room, to make sure no dangerous pieces of figurines were left lying somewhere, *she did not lower her voice to a whisper. She did not hide the tiny smile that drew lines at the edge of her mouth. She did not sneak Jaja's food to his room,* wrapped in cloth so it would appear that she had simply brought his laundry in. *She took him his food on a white tray, with a matching plate* (ibid., 257, emphasis added).

The same new ambience in the family encourages Jaja to deny Papa's entry into his room by pushing his study desk against the room door.

Papa keeps the key to Jaja's room and refuses to release to him even after Jaja has asked to come out. Jaja stays in his room and defies Papa's directive that he should come out to join the family for dinner.

It is apparent that Mama and the children attain a status of self-expression. They have surmounted the muteness and intimidation that Papa imposed on them up to then. That is why Jaja's proposal to Papa for himself and Kambili to spend the Easter holidays in Nsukka again is approved: 'We are going to Nsukka, Kambili and I ... We are going to Nsukka today, not tomorrow. If Kevin [the driver] will not take us, we will still go. We will walk if we have to' (ibid., 261). They return from that trip at the event of Papa's death, to which Mama confesses to Kambili and Jaja: 'I started putting the poison in his tea before I came to Nsukka. Sisi got it for me; her uncle is a powerful witch doctor' (ibid., 290). Obioma Nnaemeka's opinion below serves to justify Mama's action.

> Extreme pain and suffering push women victims to the brink of madness ... Women appropriate and refashion oppressive spaces through friendship, sisterhood and solidarity and in the process reinvent themselves ... Women's solidarity [is] an issue of survival; solidarity among women offers a safety net and a breath of fresh air in a suffocating, constraining environment ... [in] relationships, solidarity and friendship among women mitigate pain and suffering. (Nnaemeka 1997, 19)

Mama's solidarity with Sisi is essential within this principle. An autopsy confirms that Papa died of poisoning. Actually, Mama began the process of eliminating Papa by the time she watched him pour hot water over Kambili's feet in the bathtub, and by the time he hit Mama's stomach with the table, causing her to lose her six-weeks pregnancy. Mama's act is self-deprecating, and she deals decisively with the problem that threatens her life and the lives of Kambili and Jaja. She surmounts her innate fear of Papa re-marrying or having children (sons) outside their marriage, and smashes the usual 'women's complicity in maintaining the status quo, a point dramatized in Emecheta's *The Joys of Motherhood* (1979),' as noted by Chikwenye Ogunyemi (1996) when she recounts 'Nnu Ego's readjusting of Nnaife's falling lappa in that crucial moment of his final emasculation, threatening to expose further his nakedness and powerlessness as he climbs into the police van, is epiphanic' (11).

Even though Jaja claims responsibility for the act of Papa's murder to save Mama from the consequences, it is significant that Mama murders Papa deliberately. Herein lies the essence of motherhood that is reconstructed: the nurturer of life becomes the destroyer of life. The central relevance of Mama's effort at reconstructing her notion of mother-hood derives from the proverb expressed by Aunty Ifeoma that 'when a house is on fire, you run out before the roof collapses on your head' (Adichie 2003, 213). This indicates the need for Mama to act in a way that ensures her safety. Unlike many women who would have opted to leave the marriage to escape the danger of being killed by Papa during one of his feats of anger, Mama stays on and is determined to stay, but plans for Papa to be the one to go somehow. Though Mama is a typical traditional African woman, unsophisticated and satisfied with the economic security that her husband provides, though she is silent about Papa's over-bearing, tyrannical attitude and obeys him unques-tioningly, she is, however, able to conquer her fractured, enervating, oppressed and muffled psyche, and to provide for herself and her chil-dren a lifetime of liberty.

The implication of mutation in Mama's motherhood principle is in the reversal of mothering/nurturing to murdering/termination of life. Obviously, the termination of Papa's sadistic life essentially symbolizes the perpetuation of the lives of Mama, Kambili and Jaja. By extension, Jaja's assumption of guilt demonstrates the credibility of Mama's act of murder. Thus, rather than save life, Mama destroys it, and conse-quently transcends to a life of freedom, full of mirth, warmth, laughter and love.

Generally, this paper proposes that the ways and manners that moth-erhood is conceptualized in contemporary Africa have changed. The modified reality of womanhood manifests in the process that woman-hood has transformed from being synonymous with irredeemable enslavement and extreme victimhood and self-sacrifice. The authen-ticity of contemporary motherhood derives in a methodology to live, a striving to be self-expressive and happy, an effort to escape exploita-tion and muteness and a drive to protect and preserve the children. These are visibly demonstrated by Mama in Adichie's *Purple Hibiscus*. The stages of her reconstruction of motherhood are clear.

- She has no voice.
- She watches Papa's oppressive dominance and dictatorship over the family.
- She endures his physical brutality on her and the children. He does not only beat Mama with a belt, he slaps, kicks and mistreats Kambili, their daughter.
- Mama is helpless.
- In misery, she loses two pregnancies. The loss implies two essential facts:

- she loses two potential children who would have cared for her later in life;
- she feels desperate about the possibility of Papa's succumbing to the pressure of marrying another wife to have more children.

Mama's pain and helplessness are obvious in her reactions after she loses the second pregnancy because of Papa's beatings: she travels all the way from Enugu to Nsukka wearing slippers; and then:

> She cried for a long time, she cried until my [Kambili's] hand, clasped in hers, felt stiff. She cried until Aunty Ifeoma finished cooking the rotten meat in a spicy stew. She cried until she fell asleep, her head against the seat of the chair. Jaja laid her on a mattress on the living room floor. (Adichie 2003, 249)

Mama's sleep is a metaphorical rite of passage. Her resolve to obliterate the source of her misery and painful loss of her pregnancies crystallizes after she wakes and returns to Enugu, and she begins the process of eliminating the one life that constitutes a threat to several lives – thus making good Aunty Ifeoma's caution that 'when a house is on fire, you run out before the roof collapses on your head' (ibid., 252). By eliminating Papa, Mama confirms that she cannot leave Papa's house, but can do very well without Papa, thereby controverting her earlier worry: 'where would I go if I leave Eugene's house? Tell me where would I go?' (ibid., 250).

The legitimacy of the powerlessness and invisibility of African women as wives is emphasized by Ifi Amadiume in *Male Daughters, Female Husbands* when she analyses that 'as Christianity introduced a male deity, religious beliefs and practices no longer focused on the female deity, but on a male God, his son, his bishops and priests' (1987, 134). This new pattern of the male heading and leading the female permeated all aspects of life and generated various forms of male domination over women. Consequently, as an ardent Christian, Papa does everything he can to rescue his family from going to Hell, and Kambili recounts a painful incident.

> I stepped out of my room just as Jaja came out of his. We stood at the landing and watched Papa descend. Mama was slung over his shoulder like the jute sack of rice his factory workers brought in bulk at the Seme Border ... 'There's blood on the floor', Jaja said. 'I'll get the brush from the bathroom'. We cleaned up the trickle of blood. (Adichie 2004, 33)

Kambili and Jaja are traumatized by Papa's ruthless high-handedness. Mama returns from the hospital the next afternoon and discloses that 'there was an accident, the baby is gone' (ibid., 34). Significantly, women's blood is different from the blood of men or animals. Rich asserts that women's blood:

> is associated not only with the 'curse' and mysteries of the menstrual taboo, but with the mana of defloration, the transformation mystery of birth, and with fertility itself. There is thus a complex fusion of associations derived from the several aspects of the female, which might be visualized as a cluster like the one below:

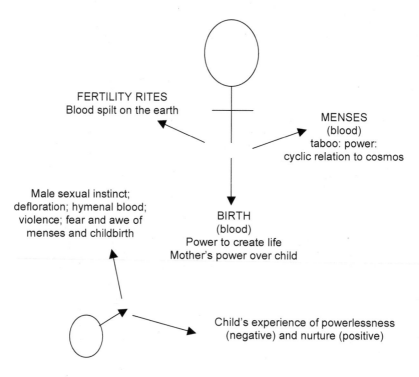

(From Rich 1995, p. 117)

Recognizing the power in the woman's blood and the exclusive creative qualities that it possesses, for Papa to cause the wastage, its untimely spill, its humiliating trail on the floor to be viewed by children, he must pay, and pay dearly. It is within this framework that Papa's murder has to happen, and to be implemented by Mama, while Jaja becomes the carrier. This re-enacts the reality of the Christian cosmology that has the innocent Son of God, Jesus Christ, who served as the sacrificial lamb for sinners – a perfect personality who died willingly to atone for the sins of other people. The essence of Jaja's character is situated in this principle.

Indeed, Adichie's *Purple Hibiscus* indexes under strict scrutiny the pains of the female desire for freedom, the reversal of the myth of the home as a place of safety and protection from the violence outside, the ability of women to respond to violence with violence. It highlights female striving to escape invisibility and dehumanization, or the objectification to the point of committing suicide. In the novel, Mama's act of murder provides a context for examining the relationship of madness, murder, and knowledge. Obioma Nnaemeka observes that what is usually radical in the female characters' violent acts is not so much what they did (the murder) but how it was done (intentionally). What is interesting is not so much the fact that the female characters are mad but how they use their madness. Here, the question of agency is linked to *intentionality* (1997, 19).

In conclusion, this study on reconstructing motherhood reveals a viable option to the helpless mother image often portrayed in African literature. It contributes to the corpus of literature on survival strategies for modern women in contemporary Africa, and argues that the way out for any woman is largely within herself. However, transcendence can occur only after the woman has resolved to be resolute and weather through all the challenges that she is bound to encounter. For Mama in Adichie's *Purple Hibiscus*, it is symbolized in the 'howling winds that came with an angry rain', ripping up trees, destroying beautiful and delicate flowers, pulling out the satellite dish from the rooftop and smashing it down across the driveway, hauling off the wardrobe door, and causing Sisi to break Mama's dishes (Adichie 2004, 257). This chain of violent incidents is emblematic of something drastic that is waiting to occur; it constitutes a premonition of tragedy and actually prefigures Papa's death.

In telling the story of Mama's murder of Papa, Adichie actually tells the story of Papa's murder of Mama, Kambili and Jaja. Her violence is symptomatic of Papa's. The pursuit of freedom and survival is the real impetus for her actions; for her, the end justifies the means, extreme situation demands extreme response. The fact that Mama administers the poison, and has been doing so for a while, and perhaps it was hitherto ineffective, is highly significant in the evaluation of women's roles in contemporary African family contexts. This is a graphic trope for women's complicitous cover-up of male weaknesses, a privilege that they would not enjoy in the same situation. Mama in *Purple Hibiscus* reverses this trend and makes Papa suffer for all the years of his tyranny and despotism towards her and the children. This is Mama's methodology in reconstructing motherhood; she evolves a means of changing women's perennial struggles against the eruptions of masculinism, which manifest as debilitating and oppressive phenomena in the family and the society.

Essentially, Mama's free admission of guilt even though it is generally disregarded by the society, highlights her satisfaction with, and justification for her action, and her courage and readiness to bear the consequences, which Jaja opts to bear instead. However, Mama's reaction to her detestable marriage and her oppressive husband is a clear departure from Ogunyemi's 1996 observation in *African Wo/man Palava* that, since Nigerians frown at divorce, the fact that women have to tolerate the intolerable in marriage has created, on the negative side, frustrated and pretentious wives. These women have grown into a nation of tough women who have no other place to go, so they remain in their homes, intent on rebuilding them instead of absconding and letting everything they have worked for come to naught (Ogunyemi 1996, 292). Mama initially endures the battering, indignation and oppression from Papa. Then she decides to not just end the marriage or go anywhere, but to end her husband's life, so that he will go away permanently from her and the children. Thus, Mama in *Purple Hibiscus* can be described as an African woman of the future, because of her ability to mutate reality, reconstruct motherhood and modify her primary nurturing role as convenient. By violating the traditional female image and roles, Mama reacts to what threatens her and her children's welfare.

It is within this purview that motherhood in Africa is reconstructed: as the woman does not end up the victim as depicted in much of African literature, as she is not just the survivor or a helpless, hapless victim of her husband, but she is in control of the family's wealth, as she is driven by the same family's interests. Mama's action stresses that being a good (or sweet) mother means taking care of ourselves first and learning to let others' needs come second (Crittenden 2000, 121). This is the thrust of the new reality of motherhood in Africa.

Works Cited

Amadiume, Ifi. *Male Daughters, Female Husbands: Gender and Sex in an African Society*. (London: Zed Books, 1987).

Adichie, Chimamanda Ngozi. *Purple Hibiscus*. (New York: Anchor Books, 2004 edn).

Akujobi, Remi, 'Motherhood in African Literature and Culture', *CLCWeb: Comparative Literature and Culture* 13.1 (2011). Retrieved from http://docs.lib.purdue.edu/clcweb/vol13/iss1/2 (accessed January 2, 2016).

Crittenden, Danielle. *What Our Mothers Didn't Tell Us: Why Happiness Eludes the Modern Woman*. (New York: Touchstone, 2000).

de Beauvoir, Simone. *The Second Sex*. (New York: Bantam Books, 1970)

Emecheta, Buchi. *The Joys of Motherhood*. (Oxford: Heinemann, 1979 [1949]).

Ngcobo, Lauretta. 'African Motherhood: Myth and Reality', in *Criticism and Ideology*. Ed. Kirsten Holst Petersen. (Uppsala: Scandinavian Institute of African Studies, 1988): 140–9.

Nnaemeka, Obioma. 'Introduction: Imag(in)ing Knowledge, Power, and Subversion in the Margins', *The Politics of (M)Othering: Womanhood, Identity, and Resistance in African Literature*. Ed. Obioma Nnaemeka. (New York: Routledge, 1997): 1–25.

Mbiti, John S. *African Religions and Philosophy*. (New York: Doubleday Anchor, 1970).

Ogundipe-Leslie, Molara. 'The Female Writer and her Commitment'. *Women in African Literature Today*, 15. Eds Eldred D. Jones, Eustace Palmer and Marjorie Jones. (Trenton, N. J: Africa World Press; London: James Currey, 1987): 5–23.

Ogunyemi, Chikwenye Okonjo. 'Firing Can(n)ons: Salvos by African Women Writers', *Africa Wo/Man Palava: The Nigerian Novel by Women*. (Chicago: University of Chicago Press, 1996): 1–16.

Rich, Adrienne. *Of Woman Born: Motherhood as Experience and Institution*. (New York: Norton, 1995 edn.)

Smith, Courtney. 'Who Defines 'Mutilation'? Challenging Imperialism in the Discourse of Female Genital Cutting', *Feminist Formations* 23.1 (2010).

Nwapa, Flora. *Efuru*. (London: Heinemann, 1966).

—. *One is Enough*. (Trenton, NJ: Africa World Press, 1995 edn).

Sofola, Zulu. *Wedlock of the Gods*. (Ibadan: Evans, 1972).

Williams, R. 'Review of *Purple Hibiscus*', *Times Literary Supplement* Retrieved 11 November 2016 from www.powells.com/review/2004_05_23.html.

5

Ritualized Abuse in *Purple Hibiscus*

EDGAR FRED NABUTANYI

Chimamanda Ngozi Adichie's *Purple Hibiscus* is one of the more recent African literary texts that deploy a testifying child to provide insightful comments on ritualized abuse of some children living in seemingly stable African middle-class homes. Her text builds on the huge scholarly archive that explores child physical abuse as one of the commonest forms of trauma to which many African children are exposed. While recent socio-anthropological scholarship of this African phenomenon attributes it to extreme poverty, civil wars, genocide and disintegrating families, Adichie's text eloquently establishes a link between performativity of respectability and propriety within some African middle-class homes and child abuse. I argue that fiction deconstructs the veneer of comfort and safety that such homes project to unearth how children are abused because of their parents' obsession with propriety and respectability. My reading extends scholarship of Adichie's fiction by exploring an aspect (cruel parenting) of her writing that many Adichie scholars read as a metaphor of postcolonial African state oppression and dictatorship. This tangent of her work illuminates a rarely interrogated facet of postcolonial African reality – cruel parenting practices. Thus, I argue that Adichie's *Purple Hibiscus* unmasks Eugene's ritualized abuse of his family in instances where he feels they have deviated from his (distorted) version of religious piety and its attendant rituals.

Among contemporary Nigerian writers, Chimamanda Ngozi Adichie has attracted a great deal of critical attention, especially with regard to her debut novel – *Purple Hibiscus* (2003). Most of this criticism reads the text as either a bildungsroman or a symbol of Nigerian post-independence reality of dictatorship, religious fanaticism, gender inequity, censorship and brain drain. While Jane Bryce (2008) and Madeleine Hron (2008) argue that Adichie's text is a postcolonial bildungsroman because of the fact that Kambili matures during the course of the narrative, Debra Beilke (2006) and Ogaga Okuyade (2009) establish a connection between the violence in Eugene Achike's household and the atmosphere of fear in the Nigerian society under military dictatorship. Other critics like Heather Hewett (2005), Elleke Boehmer (2009), Brenda Cooper (2008) and Roger J. Kurtz (2012) focus on the intertextual connections between Adichie's text and the corpus of canonical Nigerian writing to argue that Adichie 'is directly engaged with the Nigerian literary canon and is furthermore making a case for her inclusion in it' (Hewett 2005, 78). The above-mentioned critical readings that foreground public sphere tyranny and intertextuality as central concerns in Adichie's fiction are valid and persuasive.

However, I argue that it is possible to read Adichie's narrative as a personalised record of domestic abuse and its impact on children in some African middle-class families. This is because Adichie deploys a muted testifying child to spotlight ritualized abuse that children are exposed to in such families. My reading takes note of Akin Adesokan's (2012) argument that the recurrence of expressions such as 'communion', 'missal', 'figurines', 'palm fronds', and 'holy water' in *Purple Hibiscus* give 'us an intimation of the ritual[s]' associated with Catholicism. I agree with Adesokan that Catholic rituals are central in any reading of Adichie's text. However, I argue that Adichie deploys these rituals in order to highlight how Eugene perverts Catholic rituals to inflict pain, not as 'solemn festivit[ies] associated with the … church' as Adesokan claims (2012, 8). My use of the term 'ritualized abuse' takes cognisance of J. Barry Lyons' (2005) comments on the interface between ritual, corporal punishment and discipline among the Chimborazo of Ecuador and Christopher Bennett's (2008) postulations about apology in modern society.

Lyons argues that whipping among the Chimborazo community was not perceived as 'punishment, but rather as a purification of sin and a means of transforming one's internal moral disposition; the elder lashing the whip was perceived as a mediator of God himself and thus worthy of respect, even thanks from the penitent' (2005, 97). Bennett notes that one apologizes when 'motivated to do [so] spontaneously were she is appropriately sorry for her offense' (ibid., 152). The main argument that the two scholars advance is that, in the context of ritualized physical abuse, the 'victims' often read the pain inflicted on them as deserving and redeeming. For example, Bennett argues that punishment is meaningful and acceptable when the wrongdoer acknowledges his/her transgression. Similarly, Lyons notes that when the 'offender' is convinced of his wrongdoing, then the physical pain that is inflicted onto him is interpreted as a form of purification, and the 'perpetrator' of the pain is equated to a divine personage who deserves thanks from the victim. The conceptualization of pain as an avenue of moral purification and administrators of this pain as God's earthly representative that Bennett and Lyons underscore, is comparable to Eugene's ritualized abuse of his family in *Purple Hibiscus*. This is perhaps best captured in his question: 'why do you walk into sin?' ... Why do you like sin?' (Adichie 2003, 102).

This passage not only shows that Eugene believes that his wife, son and daughter are sinners who must be punished in order to redeem them, but also that he blindly believes in his divine responsibility to rigidly uphold God's law in his home by ensuring that any transgression from his notion of absolute piety is punished. Paradoxically, his abusive actions in the novel suggest a twisted, unquestioning conviction about the appropriateness of his actions and the painful, even loving 'duty' of administering violent punishment, much like the unquestioning conviction that often attends ritual acts. For example, when his wife declines to take Holy Communion on account of early pregnancy nausea, his son fails to correctly answer two questions during his catechism examination or his daughter breaks the Eucharist fast because of her menstrual cramps, Eugene reads these actions as inexcusable sins for which the three must be punished. It is perhaps because Eugene constructs himself as an enforcer of God's command – God's servant who is tasked with reforming the sinners in his family – that his infliction of pain is ritualized. While Eugene enacts several ritualized scenes of abuse in *Purple Hibiscus* such as the beating that results in Beatrice's miscarriage and the punishment that results in the deformation of Jaja's finger, in this chapter I concentrate on the physical abuse received by Kambili.

Here, it can be argued that Adichie uses her abused and fearful protagonist to unmask this family's ironic subversion of the supposedly benevolent qualities of Catholic rituals as idealized and affirming concepts. Whereas Catholic rituals carry connotations of sacrifice, selflessness, moral conduct and tolerance, their subversion by Eugene underscores how these values can be instrumentized with catastrophic consequence when focus is placed on dramatized decorum, the idea of a 'well-behaved' child and punishing the sinners.[1] The ironical use of Catholic rituals to foreground domestic abuse draws our attention to Adichie's insightfully creative way of using a cowed child to articu-

---

[1] I use the concept 'well-behaved child' to refer to the belief among some African middle-class families that a good child is one who is seen and not heard, one who does as s/he is told.

late the horrific mistreatment of children in some African middle-class homes.

In *Purple Hibiscus*, Chimamanda Ngozi Adichie allows her silenced, precocious fifteen-year-old protagonist a form of articulation to disclose the violent 'disciplining' in her middle-class home without invalidating her depiction as a traumatized child. By granting Kambili a double persona – as a a cowed, silenced and simultaneously an articulate child – Adichie creates for her a convincing grammar to speak about domestic abuse. Narrated through Kambili's first-person perspective, the novel depicts Eugene's violent 'disciplining' of his family when they transgress his distorted interpretation of ideal religious conduct.[2] Adichie's novel would seem to suggest that Eugene's violently heavy handed parenting style can partly be read as a re-enactment of his own upbringing. If, as Jeremiah Schumm and Ana Maria Vranceanu argue, 'loss initiated in childhood can snowball into resource loss spirals later in life, leaving individuals ill-equipped to handle [new] challenges' (2004, 42), then it is striking to note the similarities between Eugene's abuse as a child, and his current enactment of similar patterns and rituals of abuse on his children. As a student at the Catholic school, St. Gregory's, Eugene was 'cured' of masturbation by a priest who poured boiling water on his hands. Years later, the adult Eugene, now a father to two children, administers the same boiling-water punishment to his daughter's feet and legs as punishment for staying under the same roof as a 'heathen' – her own grandfather (Eugene's 'unchristian' father) – against Eugene's wishes.

> [Papa] lowered the kettle into the tub, tilted it toward my feet. He poured the hot water on my feet, slowly, as if he were conducting an experiment and wanted to see what would happen. He was crying now, tears streaming down his face. I saw the moist stream before I saw the water. I watched the water leave the kettle, flowing almost in slow motion in an arc to my feet. The pain of contact was so pure, so scalding, I felt nothing for a second. And then I screamed. (Adichie 2003, 194)

Eugene's mimicry of this form of punishment in disciplining his own family by targeting the offending parts of the body indicates how his childhood abuse resurfaces and is re-enacted in his adulthood. It also echoes the Gospel in John 13:1–17 when Jesus washes the feet of his disciples after the Last Supper. The feet washing ritual simulta-

---

[2] See St. Augustine's argument for authoritarian parental practice, that 'children should be punished for their sins' (quoted in Lampinen & Sexton-Radek 2010, 4).

neously underlines both betrayal and the cleansing of the sinner. As Jesus washes his disciples' feet to purify them because one – Judas – has betrayed him, Eugene's act of pouring hot water on Kambili's feet perversely underlines his belief that she has sinned and betrayed him by sleeping in the same house as a heathen.

The sombre manner in which he dispenses this punishment is particularly striking, both in this example and similar instances across the novel. To a large extent, Eugene's manner brings to mind a ritual act; in some ways mirroring the religious rituals that govern his household, and whose transgression often precedes the punishment of his wife and children. It is in view of this that I read Eugene's abuse of his children (and wife) as a form of ritualized violence. What I describe as Eugene's ritualized violence is evident in his targeting Kambili's legs, because they are the part of the body that allows her 'walk' into sin (Adichie 2003, 194), in a twisted enactment of Biblical dictum: to punish the offending body part.[3]

Eugene's double obsession with religious ritual and equally ritualized 'punishment' of what he sees as transgressions from his distorted notion of religious piety also mirrors Christ's uncompromising stance against sinners as portrayed in his violent confrontation with traders in the Temple. This is enacted in another scene in the novel when he assaults his daughter for breaking the Eucharist fast. Here, we are reminded of Kambili's perceptive observation that Father Benedict 'usually referred to the Pope, Papa and Jesus – in that order' (ibid., 4). If the previous passage showed how Eugene's ritualized abuse of his family is a re-enactment of his St. Gregory punishment and the mimicry of the Biblical dictum of punishing the offending parts of the body, then it is plausible to argue that his deification by the church and society, as suggested by Kambili's observation, deludes him into believing that his actions uphold God's law. Thus, *Purple Hibiscus* 'force[s] the [reader into] the role of [a] witness' (Socolovsky 2003, 189) to Eugene's enforcement of what he believes to be divine law.

This is poignantly depicted when he beats Kambili for breaking the Eucharist fast because of the pains of her first menstrual period, and Beatrice and Jaja for helping her to 'sin'. It is ironic that the essence of the Christian ritual of fasting as a form of cleansing, and the home as a nurturing and safe environment, are tainted by a father who feels his authority (and God's) has been undermined by his family's breaking the

---

[3] See the proclamation in Matthew 5:27–30 that if one's right eye causes him or her to sin, he or she must 'gouge it out and throw it away' because it is "better for [someone] to lose one part of [his or her] body than for [one's] whole body to be thrown into hell".

Eucharist fast. Adichie uses the symbolism associated with menstruation, which in many cultures is an occasion for celebration that marks a transition from girlhood to womanhood (flowering), to demonstrate that Eugene is not interested in the spiritual welfare of his family, but rather in the performance of publicly visible religious uprightness. We can also read Kambili's menstruation and her transition into adulthood as a threat to Eugene's authority. Eugene is unconsciously aware that Kambili will eventually break free of his control.

Here, his reason for abusing Kambili mirrors his beating of Beatrice that leads to her miscarriage. In both cases, the women are abused because they are seen to 'transgress' and 'challenge' Eugene's control over them, and his flawed ideal of maintaining publicly visible religious piety. What is important in both cases is that what Eugene reads as transgression is no such thing. Whereas Kambili's 'transgression' is because of her menstrual period, Beatrice's is caused by early pregnancy nausea. It is possible to read Eugene's furious punishment of his daughter and wife as induced by his threatened patriarchal pride through manifestations of femininity, which lie outside his rigid Catholic practice's frame of reference – the kind that does not make allowance for normal bodily function. It can also be plausibly argued that his punitive actions underline his primitively misogynist hatred for femininity.

Ironically, the enactment of violence to enforce publicly visible religious piety devalues one of the core aspects of Catholicism: the centrality of a happy family. The unhappiness of this family because of Eugene's seriously unbalanced personality is poignantly depicted in yet another instance of Eugene's 'disciplining' of his family, this time with his belt.

> It was a heavy belt made of layers of brown leather with a sedate leather-covered buckle. It landed on Jaja first, across his shoulder. Then Mama raised her hands as it landed on her upper arm, which was covered by the puffy sequined sleeve of her church blouse. I put the bowl down just as the belt landed on my back. Sometimes I watched the Fulani nomads, white jellabas flapping against their legs in the wind, making clucking sounds as they herded their cows across the roads in Enugu with a switch, each smack of the switch swift and precise. Papa was like a Fulani nomad – although he did not have their spare, tall body – as he swung his belt at Mama, Jaja and me, muttering that the devil would not win. We did not move more than two steps away from the leather belt that swished through the air. (Adichie 2003, 102)

Although the diction in the passage paints a vivid picture of the victims' agony, Adichie uses it to unmask the façade of this digni-fied middle-class home. Our empathy for Kambili, Jaja and Beatrice on the one hand, and contempt for Eugene on the other hand, can be enhanced by the repetition of the verb 'landed' in the passage. Whereas the adjective 'sedate' that describes the buckle on Eugene's heavy belt and Beatrice's evidently expensive 'puffy sequined sleeved church blouse' are displays of respectability and piety (decently covering the bodies) and the prosperity Eugene believes was earned by his pious practices, the repetition of the term 'landed' shows the powerful blows that Eugene inflicts on his family with dispropor-tionate rapidity and regularity. The violent connotation of the verb 'landed' has the power to imaginatively transport us into the sitting room as eyewitnesses to the intense pain to which Jaja, Beatrice and Kambili are subjected – especially when it is clear that their 'trans-gression' does not warrant such punishment.

Furthermore, it could be argued that the parallel yet contrasting image of a Fulani nomad can arouse readers' empathy for the victims of domestic violence. Whereas both Eugene and the herdsman are expected to play protective roles, Eugene subverts the positive care-taking parental role into abuse. Unsurprisingly, the only similarity between Eugene and the herdsman is the whip/belt, which symbolizes and reinforces Eugene's power over his family, while underscoring the dehumanizing power of domestic abuse in the implied comparison of his victims to a herd. This demonstrates how the African middle-class concept of a good child/good wife silences and dehumanizes victims of abuse. It is ironical that Eugene's rigid observation of Catholic ritual desecrates the expected safety of the home as a comforting and nurturing environment.

Eugene's ritualized abuse of his daughter is however not restricted to acts of punishment.[4] It is seen in an equally disturbing subversion of an apparently loving family ritual of regularly inviting his children to have a sip of his hot tea, oblivious of the children's cowed inability to protest that it scalds their tongues:

> [Papa] poured his tea, and then … told Jaja and me to take sips. Jaja took a sip, placed the cup back on the saucer. Papa picked it up and gave it to me. I held it with both hands, took a sip of the Lipton tea with sugar and milk

[4] It is ironic that, in his enactment of religious piety, Eugene is oblivious to Christ's declaration in Matthew 16:8 that 'whoso shall offend one of these little ones which believe in me, it were better for him that a millstone were hanged about his neck, and that he were drowned in the depth of the sea'.

and placed it back on the saucer. 'Thank you Papa,' I said, feeling the love burn my tongue. (Adichie 2003, 31)

This passage underscores the characteristics of a ritual – unquestioning obedience and repetitive performance – as executed by Eugene in ordering Jaja to take a sip and then picking the cup and giving it to Kambili for a sip. Here, Eugene's act of raising the cup and handing it to the children mirrors Christ's loving and sacrificial action with his disciples during the Last Supper. Eugene's required 'scalding sips of tea' periodically (or pervertedly) evoke the ritual of Holy Communion as usually administered by the priest (Father) through the symbolic sip of holy wine in commemoration of Christ's fathomless sacrificial love – his shedding of his blood for Christians' salvation.

If we take our reading of the scalding sips of tea as reminiscent of the Catholic ritual of Holy Communion, which symbolizes Christ's – and by extension, God the Father's – sacrificial love and suffering for His children's salvation, then Eugene's baffling blend of New Testament scriptures and violent anger as well as his deification by society signal a perverse distortion of religious ritual. Here, we are reminded of Kambili's observation that at church her father 'led the way out of the hall smiling at the many hands that reached out to grasp his white tunic as if touching him would heal them of an illness' (Adichie 2003, 90–91). His delusion of divine power, supported by society's adulation, gives him carte blanche to enforce his perversely distorted interpretation of religious rituals. Eugene's public dramatization of religious piety further manipulates his abused children and wife into silence, creating an impermeable and unchallengeable false front of the impeccable Catholic paterfamilias and patron to the needy.[5]

If, in both contexts of punishment and affection, Eugene resorts to ritualized violence, we are forced to wonder: who can protect Jaja and Kambili from their father's distorted application of religious piety? His wife, Beatrice, is disqualified because she is an abused housewife whose constant polishing of her figurines symbolizes her own vulnerability in an abusive marriage.[6] Brenda Cooper (2008) argues that Beatrice's ritual of polishing the figurines after every beating is her way of coping with her abuse. Rather than reading the ritualized cleaning of the figurines as a coping mechanism, I focus on the point

[5] See Cathy Caruth's (1995), Anne Whitehead's (2004) and Geoffrey Hartman's (1998) emphasis on the difficulty of narrating traumatic events.
[6] See the arguments of Brenda Cooper (2008), Daria Tunca (2009), Jane Bryce (2008), John C. Hawley (2008), Heather Hewett (2005) and Madelaine Hron (2008) on this topic.

that it indicates her failure and inability to protect her family. She takes better care of these miniature humanoid figures than of her own children. This is glaringly revealed in one instance when she sends Kambili to Eugene's bedroom well aware of what was going to happen; given that she has been a victim of 'bedroom-based' violence on several occasions herself. Furthermore, her inadequacy as a parent is evident when she lets her son go to prison for the crime she commits, that of poisoning her husband. Her fetishistic figurines which are broken during one of Eugene's ritualized violent outbursts, symbolize how her children are 'broken' by their father without her intervention. Here, we are reminded of Aunty Ifeoma's advice to Beatrice while visiting Kambili in hospital: 'This cannot go on, nwunye m ... When a house is on fire, you run out before the roof collapses on your head' (Adichie 2003, 213). The proverb and the image of a burning house show that by staying in an abusive marriage, Beatrice is complicit in her children's abuse. Furthermore, it is valid to argue that Kambili's lack of agency and 'muteness' are caused by Beatrice's apathy and compliance that normalize silent endurance of abuse to her daughter by always yielding to Eugene's dominance.

Can a child broken and silenced by abuse reclaim her agency and resist? The answer to this question is in the affirmative in this novel because Kambili, like Jaja did earlier, eventually stands up to her abusive father.[7] Whereas Jaja's refusal to attend Holy Communion (Adichie 2003, 6) that results in Eugene's flinging his heavy missal across the room and breaking the figurines (ibid., 3) is a verbalised rejection of his father's abusive authority, Kambili's standing up to Eugene's abuse is more subtle and nuanced. Her 'carelessness' with the half-finished painting of her grandfather after Eugene had poured boiling hot water on her feet, like her mother's decision to stop the self-comforting process of cleaning the figurines or her brother's refusal to attend Holy Communion, articulates her rejection of paternal abuse. The violence in the following passage epitomizes the clash that follows a daughter's rejection of the tyrannical legitimacy of her father's authority.

He started to kick me. The metal buckles on his slippers stung like bites from giant mosquitoes. He talked nonstop, out of control, in a mix of Igbo

---

[7] It is plausible to read Jaja's revolt as an inverted archetypal succession trope where a younger male ousts the old leader. Comparable to the earth's change of seasons, this motif is built on the idea that ousting the old leader is necessary for the rebirth and rejuvenation of the sick society. In some sense Jaja's rebellion against Eugene promises the healing of this family, especially when the symbol of evil is pruned from it.

and English, like soft meat and thorny bones … the kicking increased in tempo, and I thought of Amaka's music, her culturally conscious music … I curled around myself tighter, around the pieces of the painting; they were soft, feathery. (Adichie 2003, 210–11)

The intensity of the beating in this episode reminds us of Elaine Scarry's description of torture as the totality of pain (quoted in Harpham 2001, 206). To survive this kind of excessive pain, Kambili constructs an inviolable space in her mind that neither Eugene nor the pain can penetrate. Her description of Eugene talking 'nonstop' in a mixture of 'Igbo and English' and the increasing tempo of his blows signal his loss of control over her and her success in constructing a mentally inviolable space. If we read Eugene's crying when he abuses his family as a perversion of pained paternal love – much like God's painful loving sacrifice of Christ so that 'the devil would not win' – then this scene signals Kambili's rejection of this perverse 'love'. Her use of her imagination to tame the pain takes away Eugene's diabolic agency and control over her. In addition to severing that control, Kambili's inviolable mental space helps her to shut out the physical pain inflicted on her body by finding comforting thoughts. The images she uses to describe the beating and her embrace of the warm and loving spirituality of her grandfather, symbolized by the torn pieces of his painting and her cousin Amaka's culturally conscious indigenous music help her endure the beating and denote her symbolic embrace of an alternative cultural and ethical sphere to that which her father seeks to inculcate.

Unlike her earlier failure to name Eugene as the one who breaks her mother's figurines because she lacks an appropriate register to do so, here her silence and imagery eloquently communicate her rejection of her father's abuse. Her images imaginatively domesticate the pain by making it bearable and comprehensible. The comparison of the beating to 'giant mosquito bites' tames the pain she is subjected to. In her mind, if the beating becomes bites from giant mosquitoes, which she can easily slap off, and not blows from a strong man delivered in anger, she is able to withstand it. Similarly, if her father's mixture of 'Igbo and English' becomes the 'soft meat' in the 'thorny bones,' she is able to decipher the grammar of abuse, which helps her demystify and reject the awe he previously inspired. Her attachment to the feathery softness of the torn pieces of the painting signals her devotion to and respect for the loving and comforting spirituality of her grandfather. By coupling her grandfather's affirming spirituality with her cousin's culturally grounded music, she is mentally able to escape the world of her father's violent corruption of Catholic spirituality.

Kambili's rejection of Eugene's viciousness due to his misguided appropriation of Catholicism is contrasted with her healing relationship with Father Amadi. In a simple question of whether Kambili has ever worn lipstick, Father Amadi manages to bring a smile on the face of the girl whose laughter sounds strange to her because she rarely laughs. 'I laughed. It sounded strange, as if I were listening to the recorded laughter of a stranger being played back. I was not sure I had ever heard myself laugh' (Adichie 2003, 179). Her laughing voice is unknown to her because laughter and happiness are banished from her home. The above example coupled with Father Amadi's use of Igbo songs during Mass (ibid., 136) show up Eugene's heathenising everything Igbo as a distorted interpretation of Catholic spirituality. The contrast between Eugene's religious violence and Father Amadi's life-giving Catholicism arise out of Eugene's association with Father Benedict and the St. Gregory's priest's brand of Catholicism that not only demands blind obedience but also endorses violence as a way of disciplining and raising children.

In conclusion, it is plausible to argue that in the very act of writing *Purple Hibiscus* and granting her child protagonist the role of first-person child narrator, Adichie grants Kambili a voice – albeit as a simultaneously cowed/muted, yet articulately precocious narrator – to convincingly expose ritualized abuse in her middle-class family. Notably, Kambili's measured description of the gory details of domestic abuse in the text signals Adichie's authorial sensitivity to the risk of inadvertently vulgarising, sensationalising or cheapening the victim's pain in the process of drawing attention to it. At the same time, Kambili's visual and acoustic attention to detail is a credible grammar for the disclosure of domestic abuse through the eyes of a child that allows her talk therapeutically about her abuse as a means to her recovery. This is analogous to her intention to transplant freedom into a space previously devoid of it, as suggested by her plans to 'plant purple hibiscus' in Enugu after Jaja is released from prison (Adichie 2003, 306–7).

However, the juxtaposition of the 'ghost' of an abusive father with the planting of purple hibiscuses – whose colour resembles that of her mother's bruised eye – signals the lingering effects of abuse. As Ewald Mengel argues in another context, societies will always '[struggle] with the memory of their traumatic past' (2010, vii), which is also true for individual victims of abuse. The similarity between the bruises and the purple flowers as symbols of freedom shows the struggle both to achieve healing from abuse and to cope with the indelible memories of cruel and horrible experiences. Here, we are reminded of Lyons' argument that ritualized punishment simultaneously symbolizes 'the moral order as well as affirming the authority behind it' (2005, 120). The deeply ingrained belief that Eugene was right and had the power to punish her for her 'sinning' complicates Kambili's recovery. Although it is tempting to argue that Eugene's death and the blooming of the purple hibiscuses offer the possibility of a trauma-free future for the rest of the family, Adichie stresses the ambivalent aspects of survival of those permanently maimed by the experience of domestic abuse. Nevertheless, she privileges 'talking about' the abuse in her construction of Kambili's post-traumatic existence.

This reminds us of Kambili's cousin Amaka's observation that Kambili lowers her voice whenever she speaks and 'talk[s] in whispers' (Adichie 2003, 117). This clearly shows that Kambili has been muted by the violence in her home. However, in the course of the narrative, she not only survives physical abuse by her father, but also regains her voice and agency in order to tell 'Her Story'. The fact that she is mesmerized by her cousin's ease with language (ibid., 99) gestures to her need to retrieve her tongue – symbolically muted by repeated abuse – in order to voice the abuse she, her mother and brother Jaja suffered at the hands of their father. In a way, *Purple Hibiscus* uses Kambili's regaining of her ability to speak as a metaphor of post-traumatic recovery and survival.

Works Cited

Adesokan, Akin. 'New Writing and the Question of Audience.' *Research in African Literatures* 43.3 (2012): 1–20.

Adichie, Chimamanda Ngozi. *Purple Hibiscus*. London: HarperCollins, 2003.

Beilke, Debra. '"Blue Tongues on Fire": Suppressing the Mother(s) Tongue in Chimamanda Ngozi Adichie's *Purple Hibiscus*'. Conference of the African Literature Association. 'Pan-Africanism in the 21st Century: Generations in Creative Dialogue'. Accra, Ghana 17–21 May 2006.

Bennett, Christopher. *The Apology Ritual: A Philosophical Theory of Punishment*. Cambridge: Cambridge University Press, 2008.

Boehmer, Elleke. 'Achebe and his Influence in Some Contemporary African Writing'. *Interventions* 11.2 (2009): 141–53.

Bryce, Jane. '"Half and Half Children": Third-Generation Women Writers and the New Nigerian Novel'. *Research in African Literatures* 39.2 (2008): 49–67.

Caruth, Cathy. *Trauma: Explorations in Memory*. Baltimore, MD: Johns Hopkins University Press, 1995.

Cooper, Brenda. *A New Generation of African Writers: Migration, Material Culture & Language.* Woodbridge: James Currey, 2008.

Harpham, Geoffrey. 'Elaine Scarry and the Dream of Pain'. *Salmagundi* 130/131 (2001): 202–34.

Hartman, Geoffrey. 'Shoah and Intellectual Witness'. *Partisan Review* 65.1 (1998): 37–48.

Hawley, John. C. 'Biafra as Heritage and Symbol: Adichie, Mbachu, and Iweala'. *Research in African Literatures* 39.2 (2008): 15–26.

Hewett, Heather. 'Coming of Age: Chimamanda Ngozi Adichie and the Voice of the Third Generation'. *English in Africa* 32.1 (2005): 73–97.

Hron, Madelaine. '*Ora na-aẓu nwa*: The Figure of the Child in Third-Generation Nigerian Novels'. *Research in African Literatures* 39.2 (2008): 27–48.

Kurtz J. Roger. 'The Intertextual Imagination in *Purple Hibiscus*'. *ARIEL: A Review of International English Literature* 42.2 (2012): 23–42.

Lampinen, James Michael and Kathy Sexton-Radek. *Protecting Children from Violence: Evidence-Based Interventions.* New York: Psychology Press, 2010.

Lyons, Barry J. 'Discipline and the Arts of Domination: Ritual of Respect in Chimborazo, Ecuador'. *Cultural Anthropology* 20.1 (2005): 97–127.

Mengel, Ewald. Introduction. *Trauma, Memory and Narrative in South Africa: Interviews.* Eds. Ewald Mengel, Michela Borzaga and Karin Orantes. Amsterdam: Rodopi, 2010: vii–xii.

Okuyade, Ogaga. 'Changing Borders and Creating Voices: Silence as Character in Chimamanda Adichie's *Purple Hibiscus*'. *Journal of Pan African Studies* 2.9 (2009): 245–59.

Schumm, Jeremiah and Ana Maria Vranceanu. 'The Ties that Bind: Resource Caravans and Losses among Traumatized Families'. *Handbook of Stress, Trauma and the Family.* Ed. Don R Catherall New York: Brunner-Routledge, 2004: 33-51.

Socolovsky, Maya. 'Narrative and Traumatic Memory in Denise Chávez's *Face of an Angel*'. *Melus* 28. 4 (2003): 187–205.

Tunca, Daria. 'An Ambiguous "Freedom Song": Mind-Style in Chimamanda Ngozi's *Purple Hibiscus*'. *Postcolonial Text* 5.1 (2009): 1–18.

Whitehead, Anne. *Trauma Fiction.* Edinburgh: Edinburgh University Press, 2004.

6

Dining Room & Kitchen
Food-Related Spaces & their Interfaces with the Female Body in *Purple Hibiscus*

JESSICA HUME

In her piece, 'Gender and Colonial Space', Sarah Mills argues against viewing the concept of gender and colonial space strictly through the lens of confinement, or through what she identifies as binary of public versus private. She claims that a materialist feminist framework, which she offers, allows the possibility of 'making general statements about the gendered nature of colonial space, at the same time being aware of the material specificity of different colonial contexts' (2003, 693). She encourages us to produce what she calls (drawing on Foucault) an 'archaeology of space' in which we examine postcolonial spaces as ones which have been influenced by colonialism but which also include what Shohat and Stam (1994) call 'vestigial thinking' of precolonial times (cited in Mills 2003, 696). In other words, the meaning of post-colonial space is shaped by the actions which occur and have occurred in that space and the meaning behind those actions: 'What is inscribed in the organization of space is not the actuality of past actions, but their meaning' (Moore 1986, cited in Mills 2003, 697). Therefore, in order to conduct an analysis of postcolonial space, we need to be aware of the meanings of actions from the colonial perspective and the precolonial perspectives, lest we risk duplicating the viewpoint of the colonizers by reducing gendered space into simple public versus private binaries.

Elizabeth Grosz, too, in her piece 'Bodies/Cities,' is careful to note the flaws inherent in oversimplified views of the interactions between bodies and space; in this case, she is examining the specific space of the city. She notes two primary views: causal, in which the body is seen to have constructed the city and the city is a product of the body; and representational, the idea of the body politic, in which the city repre-sents the people. She discusses the problems with these two models at length, but the key concerns she wishes to bring to light are the fact that the first model effectively supports the mind versus body binary, giving precedence to the mind, and that the second model is a phallocentric one which effectively encourages the nature versus culture binary. Grosz suggests a third model instead, a model which asks those who apply it to consider the body and city interactions as a series of complex interfaces, claiming that 'their interrelations involve a fundamentally disunified series of systems, a series of disparate flows, energies, events of entities, bringing together or drawing apart their more or less temporary alignments' (Grosz 1999, 385). Also, she would have us avoid the application of spatial theories, specifically with regard to cities and bodies, in a way that enforces binaries; instead, she seeks to pluralise our notions of space in a way conducive to feminist theory. She asks that when we analyse cities and bodies, we bear in mind four basic ways in which the city interfaces with bodies: it orients sensory information and helps produce spatiality; it orients and organises social relations; it organises circulation of and access to goods and services; and it 'provides context in which social rules and expectations are internalized or habituated' (ibid., 386).

   Taken together, these theories suggest that analyses of space in postcolonial literature that are inclusive of these feminist theories offer a richer and more complex understanding of the meaning of space generally. A framework which takes into account Mills' archaeology of space and Grosz' emphasis on the ways in which bodies interface with spaces should also produce a clearer and more thorough understanding of the ways in which feminine space is constructed. Chimamanda Ngozi Adichie's novel, *Purple Hibiscus*, recounts the story of a young woman struggling to navigate life in late-twentieth-century postcolonial Nigeria. While it may seem a challenge to apply the work of Grosz and Mills (since they are Western feminists), it's helpful to note that both scholars are working specifically at the intersection of feminism with postcolonialism, and careful application of the theory offers and may prove valuable and provide fresh insight. For example, Sudarkasa notes that previous analysis of African women, which attempts to evaluate their status in relation to men, or to view the relationships between men and women in an egalitarian light, is mistakenly myopic, failing to take into account the 'social and ideological reality of the people's concerned' (1986, 93). Sudarkasa also notes the problems with the oversimplified view that West African men primarily occupy the public sphere and West African women, the private or 'domestic' sphere: 'many African societies … recognize two domains, one occupied by men and another by women, both of which were internally ordered in a hierarchical fashion, and both of which provided 'personnel' for domestic and extra domestic activities' (ibid., 94). Mills concurs, observing that adopting binary views reproduces the thinking of the colonizers. Application of Grosz' and Mills' theories about interaction of the body with space will allow us to avoid the problems Sudarkasa has noted and to view the relationships between Igbo men and women, and the occupation by both genders of one aspect of what may be considered a private, domestic space, with more complexity and nuance. The purpose of the current discussion is to apply Grosz' and Mills' theories of the construction of space to Adichie's novel, in order more fully to understand the ways in which the female body interfaces with space in postcolonial Igbo literature. A brief overview of the cultural history of women living in Igboland will demonstrate that their identity has, in precolonial, colonial, and postcolonial times, related to the production, provision, and marketing of food for their families and communities. Adichie's novel reflects this phenomenon, as dozens of revealing or important moments in the text occur around the kitchen dinner table, or other places that revolve around food. So, I will present two interrelated spaces – kitchens and dining rooms – which will enable what Mills might call a spatial archaeological dig, and give further insight into the interfaces between a city space and the female body in *Purple Hibiscus*.

Prior to colonization, the people of Igboland (a section of south-eastern Nigeria) comprised several hundred indigenous groups, each of which had its own organization and customs. There was no centralized government of the Igbo. Generalizing broadly about women across these diverse groups, it should be acknowledged, risks inflicting upon them the same types of oversimplifying perspectives that Sudarkasa has noted as problematic; however, there are some broad trends which can be observed in many Igbo (many of which Sudarkasa notes in her work), and the remnants of those trends and their effects is evident in *Purple Hibiscus* and therefore worth establishing here. In precolonial Igboland, the social and familial positions of women, while different from those of men, and differing by group, were generally perceived as complementary to those of men (Sudarkasa 1986, 91; Rojas 1990). Seniority was based on various levels of kinship and lineage rather than gender (Sudarkasa 2016, 95; Rojas 1990) and, culturally, more emphasis was placed on the overall community rather than individuals and the nuclear family structure (Modupe n.d., 2; Rojas 1990). Women were also encouraged to be involved with farming and crafting pursuits which offered them some engagement in the economic well-being of the family and the community (Sudarkasa; Rojas). The importance of women's involvement in agriculture to their cultural identity should not be underestimated: 'their very reason for being [was to] oversee the health of the nation' (Achebe 2010, 794). Traditionally, because of their involvement in these economic pursuits, women were in charge of the local markets which, according to Achebe, were a critical part of the lives of Igbo women: '"Affia" (market) traditionally is the formidable sacred space where women peacefully exchange life-giving properties of food and money' (ibid.). A young woman's informal education, in precolonial southern and Western Igboland, consisted of learning to manage the marketplace (Modupe n.d., 7). So, women had some level of economic freedom, and their role in food production and market sale was critical to identity within families and communities.

When Africa became colonized, European countries sought to exploit the continent for its natural resources (Rojas), and Igboland, part of the country which became known as Nigeria, was no exception. They began to encourage men to focus on large-scale cash crops, so they became involved in the influential European-based economic structure, while women's possibilities for involvement in financially lucrative agriculture dwindled (Rojas 1990). Additionally, the Europeans brought their beliefs about the subordinate roles of women to bear on Igbo societies; they insisted that the role of women was exclusively in the home, raising children, not involved in financial pursuits outside the home (ibid.). The emphasis on large-scale cash crops for exploitation resulted not only in dwindling opportunities for women financially, but also in the reduction of market activity (ibid.; Modupe n.d., 2). The European belief that women belonged exclusively at home and were subordinate to men in this way (not complementary to them) meant that women's domestic roles were considered a servant-like duty, and those roles lost their traditional value (Rojas 1990), and Sudarkasa concurs: 'the changes that occurred with the onset of colonialism (and capitalism, its economic correlate) were ones that created hierarchical relations between the sexes' (1986, 102). Colonial times took from women their financial independence, their sacred identity as food-providers and market women, subjugated them to the power of men, and marginalized them as women and citizens.

After Nigeria became free from colonization in 1960, Igbo women were able, to some extent, to return to small-scale agriculture and marketing, because men were working in larger export industries, and the civil war (1967–70, also known as the Biafran War) resulted in food shortages in the Biafran area (southern Nigeria) (Achebe 2010, 794). Igbo took the food shortage as an affront to their personal and cultural identity and took action to protect it: they worked to energize the land army effort and keep the markets open (ibid., 793). In some cases, women became desperate to fulfil their identity as providers of food and guardians of the health of the nation: 'This was a war of survival that was making a mockery of the women's self-worth and integrity and was threatening to strip them of their status in society. They had to modify their role to fit the new emergency' (ibid., 794). Some Igbo women attempted to regain some control of their role through engaging in 'affia attack', a process by which they would disguise themselves and cross the border from the Republic of Biafra (which had seceded) into Nigeria to procure food and other necessary items (ibid.). Affia attack was a dangerous venture and many women died in the effort, but they managed to provide some level of relief to starving Biafran citizens in their communities (ibid., 795). Some women also engaged in cross-border farming, a process in which they would cross the incredibly dangerous border into Nigeria and sow on abandoned farms, returning later to harvest the produce and either trade it in the Nigerian markets (while passing as Nigerian) or return with it to the Biafran markets for sale (ibid.). In post-war Igboland, women have regained some of their position in sustenance farming and basic marketplace work and trade but their domestic roles and economic contributions are not always considered especially valuable by men (Rojas 1990).

If, as Mills draws on Moore to claim, past and present actions are essential in the construction and understanding of space, the information above presents the legacy of actions which constructs space for women in Nigerian society. Thus, if we construct a combined application of Mills' archaeology of space and Grosz' interfaces between bodies and cities, we can use food-related spaces in *Purple Hibiscus* as a vehicle through which to examine how critical negotiations between space and the female body are established in the novel. By contrasting the way in which one space inscribes itself on women (Eugene's dining room) against another in which women inscribe themselves upon the social space (Ifeoma's kitchen) we see Kambili growing to understand and manoeuvre within space as a woman; she has finally worked out how to make her creation of space an exchange in which she can construct and be constructed by these spaces.

Before we can delve into the precise nature by which food spaces interface with the body in the novel, we must establish the definition of the body we plan to use. Grosz tells us in 'Bodies/Cities' that 'corporeality can be seen as the condition of embodied subjectivity' (1999, 381) and that her theoretical framework involves 'exploring how the subject's exterior is physically constructed; and, conversely, how the process of social inscription on the body's surface construct a physical interior' (ibid.). She asks us to avoid the mind versus body binary and instead examine the ways in which the two elements influence and construct one another. She claims that, as part of this analysis, we need to examine how the body is 'physically, socially, sexually, and representationally produced' (ibid.). While Mills does not specifically offer a definition of 'body' (since her examination is based specifically on gender) she does echo Grosz' sentiments that the ways in which the body is socially constructed are critical to understanding space, claiming that she hopes to develop 'a materialist-feminist analysis of representational space which will be aware that women and men, colonized and colonizer, negotiate their positions in space through their interrogations with respective social positions' (Mills 2003, 694). So, for the purposes of this discussion, the female body will be considered, through the lens of an archaeology of space, and interface with the space around it in the ways it is physically, sexually and representationally produced, and the way in which it is produced through social position.

Mills claims that 'colonized space troubles some of the binary opposition between public and private spheres' (ibid., 699) and Eugene's authority over the dining room in his household serves as an example of the way in which the binary of public versus private can be complicated and should be reconsidered. The standard public versus private binary which Mill and Sudarkasa oppose would indicate that the domestic and private realms are those of women. However, with Eugene's household, that is not the case: the dining room is his purview. Using analytical strategies that take into account the cultural archaeology of food-related spaces in Igbo culture, however, we see that Eugene's dominance over the dining room has specific cultural implications with regard to the way in which it interacts with concepts of female space and the way the female body negotiates space. It should be noted that those familiar with the work of Mills or Sudarkasa might argue that any attempt to equate women's value singularly with domestic space (as they might perceive I am doing below) also reinforces the binary of private belonging to female and public belonging to male. I would argue that that is not the case. First, we will also see the way in which the private is a male space. Second, the above discussion of Igbo culture tells us that the provision of food for the family is historically critical to female identity, but that that provision is not only private, but also very public, because of women's association with markets. In fact, I would argue that Nigerian women's association of themselves with food culture and food-related space amounts to a political act whereby they assert themselves in their cultural and historical heritage as women. Thus, the analysation below supports Mills' point that 'much of women's work cannot be fitted into this binary divide' (2003, 698).

From the very beginning of the novel, the dining room of the family's house in Enugu is constructed as a space which inscribes its influence, physically and emotionally, on the women who enter the space through the man who oversees it. It is dominated by Eugene, his temperament, and his religious formalities: 'I reached out and clasped [Jaja's] hand shortly before we went into the dining room ... Papa was washing his hands in the bowl of water Sisi held before him ... and started the grace' (Adichie 2003, 11). Kambili feels the need to physically and emotionally gird herself before entering the room, for she senses the potential for (literal and figurative) assault. The presence of women in the dining room is tolerated only insofar as they are subjugated to Eugene and when their attendance is required at mealtimes. For the most part, women are relegated to the kitchen: Beatrice sits on an armchair near the kitchen door to plait Kambili's hair (ibid., 10); Mama and Sisi work together in the kitchen to prepare the meals (ibid., 11). However, Kambili is never involved in meal preparation and readers never get a description of what happens in the kitchen of the family home. Given the history of Igbo women and the provision of food for the family, this physical exclusion of the women from the dining room in any genuine, engaged way, and the lack of acknowledgement of their work in preparing the meal in the kitchen amounts to a form of representational erasure on the part of Eugene, as readers see through one of Kambili's observations of a meal: 'Lunch was jollof rice, fist size chunks of azu fried until the bones were crisp, and ngwo-ngwo. Papa ate most of the ngwo-ngwo, his spoon swooping through the spicy broth in the glass bowl. Silence hung over the table like the blue-black clouds in the middle of the rainy season' (ibid., 32). Kambili is clearly attentive to and engaged with the menu, but it is Eugene's body, his 'spoon swooping', that dominates the space of the dining room such that the women who prepared the food (or might be interested in eating it) are erased.

Ifeoma, when she visits, attempts to resist this erasure by asserting herself regarding Eugene's eating habits. '"Did you want the rice to get cold, Eugene?" she muttered. Papa continued to unfold his napkin, as though he had not heard her. The sound of forks meeting plates, or serving spoons meeting platters, filled the dining room. Sisi had drawn the curtains and turned the chandelier on, even though it was afternoon' (ibid., 96). Eugene literally refuses to acknowledge his sister's existence, but not only in that specific moment; because he refuses to acknowledge her concern for the food, which has a powerful cultural connotation for women, he has refused to acknowledge her identity and her position and cultural legacy. His behaviour again amounts to erasure: in Eugene's dining room, the female body simply does not exist, as readers see through Kambili's commentary about the space: 'Although our spacious dining room gave way to an even wider living room, I felt suffocated. The off-white walls with the framed photos of Grandfather were narrowing, bearing down on me. Even the glass dining table was moving toward me' (ibid., 7). Eugene's dining room is a space in which she feels her existence shrinking to voicelessness, to nothing. While women may be physically present, they are representationally invisible in that space.

Eugene's dining room is a space in which female sexuality is not ignored but penalised. Readers see this when Kambili, who has menstrual cramps early one Sunday morning before Mass, needs to eat something in order to take a Panadol: 'We never broke the Eucharistic fast; the table was set for breakfast with teacups and cereal bowls side by side, but we would not eat until we came home' (ibid., 101). When her mother and brother insist that she eat something so she can take the pill, Eugene catches them, all complicit in violating the sanctity of his dining room and his rules, and he does not even acknowledge Beatrice's protest: 'Her period started and she has cramps' (ibid., 101). Instead, he takes off his leather belt and beats them all, holding them all responsible for the exposure of the reality of female sexuality in his male-dominated space. The fact that this beating takes place in the dining room, a space which culturally signifies the ways in which Igbo women care for their families, and that the beating took place for reasons related to Kambili's female sexual organs, is doubly cruel. The space becomes physically inscribed on her body, mind and sexuality. Through this space, Kambili and her mother are rendered non-people, non-women, and non-Igbo.

Socially, Eugene is viewed as a leader, an important man. While this aspect of Eugene may seem public, rather than related to the private element of his dining room space, it is related through Eugene's vision of himself as a Christ-like figure. His local priest, Father Benedict, regards him in front of the congregation as emblematic of Christ: 'How many of us have stood up for the truth? How many of us have reflected the Triumphant Entry?' (ibid., 5). An examination of Eugene's actions in his dining room reveal that he views himself in the same way: when he makes his tea, he offers Kambili and Jaja a 'love sip' before he drinks it, an action oddly reminiscent of Christ sharing his blood with his disciples (ibid., 8). Through Beatrice and Ifeoma's dialogue, readers also know that Eugene is esteemed by the community because he has remained committed to Beatrice as his one and only wife even when she, ostensibly, has not been able to give him more children, and cultural expectations would dictate that he should take on more wives in order to have more children (ibid., 250). Part of his social representation of himself in the community relies on the perception that he is a martyr to his marriage. His use of the Eucharist-like tea ritual, combined with his creation of the dining room as a space that erases women physically and figuratively, indicate that he relies on this space to reinforce his beliefs about his own social standing and martyrdom. Therefore, Eugene's dining room inscribes on its female characters a lowered social value, one which makes them even more dependent on him to establish their worth.

For most of the novel, Eugene's dining room remains a vacuum in which women are physically restricted and abused, representationally silenced and erased from cultural existence, and sexually repressed. This phenomenon may leave readers to wonder about what ways, if any, women inscribe themselves upon the dining room space in the house at Enugu. Eugene's control is so complete that these moments are few if any, that is, until the end of the novel, when the story reaches its climax with Beatrice poisoning Eugene's tea. The fact that she poisons his tea, his precious, ritualized, Eucharist-like dining room experience, demonstrates that she has empowered herself to be acknowledged as an Igbo woman, that she has created a way in which this space is now and forever constructed by her.

The space of Ifeoma's kitchen supports Mills' claim that the public and private spheres are 'more interconnected than has previously been recognized' (2003, 698); Ifeoma constructs her kitchen as a female space she uses to provide food for her family, thus asserting herself in the role of a traditional woman and citizen of her community, which amounts to a political act and therefore a public act. So, once again, the analysis of women to food spaces in *Purple Hibiscus* has supported Mills' theories that the public versus private binary is a misleading one, and that an archaeology of space is necessary to understand the ways in which women interface with their space.

While Eugene's dining room primarily demonstrates one space which inscribes itself upon the female body in a number of ways, Ifeoma's kitchen offers an example of the ways in which the female body inscribes itself on space. Readers see this phenomenon when Ifeoma seeks to define herself to her brother by what is eaten (or not eaten) in her home: 'A week, Eugene, they will stay a week. I do not have a monster that eats human heads in my house!' (Adichie 2003, 99). While the remark is made in the heat of the moment, Ifeoma's choice of language is nonetheless significant. The fact that she, in an argument with her brother, who uses the dining room as a space of female erasure and lowered social value, characterizes her home in such a way indicates that she defines herself partly by what is eaten in her house. Her remark also creates irony for the audience: the monster that destroys people by consuming them is not in her dining room; it is in Eugene's. In fact, it is Eugene himself.

From the time Kambili first enters Ifeoma's home, she draws a contrast between the effect the space has on her and the effect which she feels in her own home: 'I noticed the ceiling at first, how low it was. I felt I could reach out and touch it; it was so unlike home, where the high ceilings gave our rooms an airy stillness. The pungent fumes of kerosene smoke mixed with the aroma of curry and nutmeg from the kitchen' (ibid., 113). This comment is markedly different from Kambili's observation of her own dining room, which she identifies as suffocating; here, Kambili can breathe enough to smell the food smells from the kitchen.

The kitchen itself becomes the critical space for women in Ifeoma's home. Physically, it is a place where women are often present, as we see from the first night of Jaja and Kambili's visit, when Ifeoma greets them and then rushes back to the kitchen to help the family complete meal preparation. Kambili follows her female cousin, Amaka, back to the kitchen, where Amaka resumes cooking the plantains. She observes her aunt cooking the rest of the meal: 'Aunty Ifeoma chattered as she put the rice back on the stove and chopped two purple onions, her stream of sentences punctuated by her cackling laughter. She seemed to be laughing and crying at the same time because she reached up often to brush away the onion tears with the back of her hand,' (ibid., 115). The women's physical presence in the room creates a space that acknowledges and embraces the importance of food culture; the fact that Ifeoma and her children chatter and laugh throughout meal preparation creates a stark contrast to the dining room in Kambili's home. Here, in Ifeoma's kitchen, the powerful presence of the female voices constructs a space in which women are not only acknowledged but empowered culturally. Kambili notes this empowerment, and it is at first so foreign to her that she has trouble positioning herself in the new space: '"Kambili, is something wrong with the food?" Aunty Ifeoma asked, startling me. I had felt as if I were not there, that I was just observing a table where you could say anything at any time to anyone, where the air was free for you to breathe as you wished' (ibid., 120). Because she has been living in the vacuum of Eugene's dining room, Kambili does not even not how to interact with a space she can negotiate and construct freely as a woman.

Ifeoma's kitchen is the also the space in which Kambili begins to explore her sexuality as a woman, because it is the space in which she first interacts with Father Amadi: 'He nodded as he chewed his yam and greens, and he did not speak until he had swallowed a mouthful and sipped some water. He was at home in Aunty Ifeoma's house' (ibid., 135). In Ifeoma's kitchen, she is safely allowed to pay affectionate attention to Father Amadi's mannerisms in a way that interests her sexually, as readers see later when the family shares a snack while watching television: 'We put our rosaries away and sat ... eating corn and ube ... I looked up to find father Amadi's eyes on me, and suddenly I could not lick the ube flesh from the seed. I could not move my tongue, could not swallow. I was too aware of his eyes, too aware that he was looking at me, watching me' (ibid., 139). Kambili is paralysed with nervousness at the realization that Father Amadi is watching her, but her use of sensual description regarding eating the fruit indicates the sexual freedom she begins to feel in a space which acknowledges women, and allows her to begin to understand her own sexuality.

Social position in Ifeoma's kitchen is constructed through knowledge which, as Mills tells us, is critical to the construction of power and thus the production of space (2003, 704). Mills, drawing on Pratt (1992), claims that while imperial knowledge is often considered masculine, women have the opportunity to create other types of knowledge which may offer power (ibid., 705). In the case of Ifeoma's kitchen, the knowledge constructed by women to represent power, is food knowledge. Kambili, when she first enters the house, watches Amaka cut and fry the plantains (Adichie 2003, 119). Later, Amaka demonstrates her knowledge (in comparison with Kambili's lack thereof) regarding the peeling of a yam, a task which Kambili fails to do properly and relinquishes to Amaka: 'She picked up the knife and started to peel a slice, letting only the brown skin go. I watched the measured movement of her hand and the increasing length of the peel ... wishing I knew how to do it right. She did it so well that the peel did not break, a continuous twirling soil-studded ribbon' (ibid., 133). Ifeoma's kitchen is a place in which the power of the female body is constructed through the frugality and skill with which the woman can provide her family with food, a remnant of Shohat and Stam's 'vestigial thinking' (as cited in Mills 2003, 697). Kambili finally learns to raise her social position through the acquisition of such knowledge when she asks her cousin to teach her how to make orah: 'You don't have to shout, Amaka ... I don't know how to do the orah leaves, but you can show me' (Adichie

2003, 170). By acquiring the type of food knowledge that has long been a point of pride for the women in her culture, Kambili inscribes herself on the space of the kitchen and establishes a social position for herself.

A framework for analysation of female space, which takes into account Mills' archaeology of space and Grosz' emphasis on the ways in which bodies interface with city space produces a feminist view of Adichie's *Purple Hibiscus* that, without these theories, might fail to take into account the cultural and historical complexity of the meaning of space, and instead reproduce the reductive viewpoint of the colonizers. Through cultural history, we know that food is a critical motif in establishing the identity, self-worth, sexuality, and social position of Igbo women in all eras, so food-related spaces, either domestic or public, indicate moments in which they have been erased, silenced, empowered, constructed the space, or had the space construct them. Examining food spaces from the perspective of an archaeology of space, and the model of the body as a surface for many interfaces, shows readers the rich and complex way in which postcolonial Igbo women create and are created by the room, the city, the country around them.

Works Cited

Achebe, Christie. 'Igbo Women in the Nigerian-Biafran War, 1967–1970: An Interplay of Control', *Journal of Black Studies*. 40.5 (2010): 785–811.

Adichie, Chimamanda Ngozi. Purple Hibiscus, Chapel Hill, NC: Algonquin Books, 2003.

Grosz, Elizabeth. 'Bodies/Cities', in *Feminist Theory and the Body: A Reader*. Eds. Janet Price and Margrit Shildrick. New York: Routledge, 1999: 381–7.

Mills, Sarah. 'Gender and Colonial Space', in *Feminist Post-Colonial Theory: A Reader*. Ed. Reina Lewis and Sarah Mills. New York: Routledge, 2003: 692–719.

Modupe, Abdulraheem Nimah. 'Rights of Women in the Pre-Colonial and Post-Colonial Era: Prospects and Challenges,' University of Ilorin. n.d. Retrieved April 2015 from https://unilorin.edu.ng/publications/abdulraheemnm/RIGHTS_OF_WOMEN_IN_THE_PRE_COLONIAL_AND_POST_COLONIAL_ERA.pdf.

Moore, H. L. *Space, Text, and Gender: An Anthropological Study of the Marakwet of Kenya*. Cambridge: Cambridge University Press, 1986.

Pratt, M. L. *Imperial Eyes: Travel Writing and Transculturation.* London: Routledge, 1992.

Rojas, Maria. *African Post-Colonial Literature in English in the Post-Colonial,* 1990. Retrieved April 2015 from www.postcolonialweb.org/nigeria/nigeriaov.html.

Shohat, E. and Stam, R. *Unthinking Eurocentrism: Multiculturalism and the Media.* London: Routledge, 1994.

Sudarkasa, Naria. "The Status of Women' in Indigenous African Societies,' *Feminist Studies.* 12.1 (1986): 91–103.

Works Consulted

Nwapa, Flora. *Wives at War and Other Stories.* Trenton, NJ: Africa World Press, 1980.

Adichie, Chimamanda Ngozi. *We Should All Be Feminists,* New York: Anchor Books, 2015.

7

The Paradox of Vulnerability
The Child Voice in *Purple Hibiscus*

OLUWOLE COKER

This essay focuses on child narration in *Purple Hibiscus* (2013) as a device deployed by Chimamanda Adichie to convey thematic messages that demonstrate the drama of underdevelopment and post-independence pains prevalent in the enabling society. Through a close reading of the novel, the paper draws insights from psychoanalytic and gender theorizing to fully situate the emergence of child narration as a vehicle for transmitting the post-independence angst in the enabling milieu of contemporary Nigerian fiction. The child hero instantiates a paradox of vulnerability, through the will power she exhibits in the narrative. This becomes a metaphor which is foregrounded in the use of child narration that empowers the child figure, ultimately deepening the thematic directions of the text, while also conferring unique narrative qualities that help to engage the socio-historical context of the works. In this sense, the peculiar omniscience of the child hero, which enables her to navigate the intricacies of the world, comes across as a key feature in turning a disadvantage to an advantage – in the sense that her presumed innocence makes her a powerful and harmless vessel of domestic and societal vicissitudes.

African literary discourse is replete with childhood narratives. As a matter of fact, concerns of childhood especially within the precincts of family have been a recurring trope in African fictional narratives, for example in Camara Laye's *The African Child* (1959); Mongo Beti's *Mission to Kala* (1970) and, more recently, Ben Okri's *The Famished Road* (1991). One can infer that childhood as a concept has consistently featured and developed over generations of African writings. The attendant dynamism associated with the childhood trope explains why, in twenty-first century literary imagination, it continuously begs for critical exploration.

It should be stated that the prevalence of representation of child-hood in early written African literature is associated with the Negritude movement. One agrees with M. Okolie (1988, 29) that the preoccupa-tion of Francophone African writers during the 1950s and 1960s on the need to negotiate issues of Black identity may have been respon-sible for this. This was a reaction to the French policy of Assimilation, which necessarily encouraged the re-symbolism of the Black essence through a collective unconsciousness of the repositioning of self in Francophone African creative imagination. In this connection, works like Laye's *The African Child* (1959) and Ferdinand Oyono's *Houseboy* (1966) exemplify a Negritude conception of childhood, while Mongo Beti's *Mission to Kala* (1970) and *The Poor Christ of Bomba* (1971) introduce gender dimensions to the discourse and acknowledge the reality of dual cultures as represented in the downplayed indigenous essence of the African identities, on the one hand, and the Francophone burden, on the other.

In essence, childhood in early Francophone African literature reveals the tensions of innocence and conflict, but shows cultural retrieval as a dominant motif. Hence, childhood as a trope is a direct response to the Negritudists' consciousness of a racial African identity which symbolizes a collective angst by virtue of it being a means of retrieving a collective pastoral psyche that was believed to be 'African'. In effect, innocence, cultural consciousness and nostalgic longings in Franco-phone African literature are associated with the concept of childhood and the portraiture of child heroes in the various narratives.

Representations of the child thus become a matter of cultural and historical dialectic, centring on a recurring tension in the cultural milieu. This explains why, for instance, Laye's *The African Child* depicts innocence and purity through the child protagonist who undergoes an acculturation process courtesy of colonial education (1959). This evolution leaves the family in despair over the thought of sending their children to school. In other words, the concept of childhood in African fiction presents the dilemma that confronts the child, and the difficult path of navigation between tradition and modernity. Given the centrality of childhood to the overall subject of identity, it is worth-while locating and exploring its treatment within contemporary post-colonial theorizing.

The point is, to borrow Mudimbe's (1994) 'idea of Africa', childhood has assumed a central place in the discourse of African postcolonial identity construction. Post-independence African fictions generally allow a broad perspective of the bizarre metamorphosis in the conti-nent's polity as manifested in the political landscape. Generally, in third-generation Nigerian novels, the authors attempt to narrate the post-independence woes by illuminating the pangs of pain inflicted on the country's landscape. This explains why most writers of this period engage the issues of socio-historical decadence by evolving strategies aimed at creatively explicating the issues, and ultimately seeking to offer pragmatic alternatives.

A critical examination of the childhood trope exploits the paradox of innocence, and shows that the child is a complex being; in fact, as S. K. Desai notes, child narrators are 'often more complex than the adult, subjected to an unpredictable process of growth'. Desai further argues that the African child in these narratives is in fact, 'no romantic angel' but 'a bundle of impulses ... trying to piece together his fragmentary experiences' (1981, 45). Childhood is therefore a complex phenomenon that enables literary imagination to negotiate a variety of contestations, for example, the deconstruction of masculinity or father figures, among other things.

To focus on the depictions of childhood in early Nigerian literature, one recognizes that, the depiction of family scenario in Chinua Achebe's *Things Fall Apart* typified by Okonkwo's family evinces diversities in childhood representations of household members. This is adequately represented in Ikemefuna, Ezinma and Nwoye (1958). Specifically, to use M. Wright's definition of the black diaspora, exemplified as 'other-from-within, Ezinma occupying both a terrestrial and extra-terrestrial world and Nwoye's childhood contested by Okonkwo using the social construct of gender' (2004, 8). These descriptions confirm Hall's words, that they are marked by an 'internal diaspora', an 'other-from-within' (1996, 245). In another sense, childhood as a site of experimentation, is explored in Achebe's *Arrow of God* (1964) through Ezeulu's attempt at using his child to interact with the missionaries. Childhood therefore occupies a space in the tradition and change equation symbolized in the metaphor of 'mask dancing' in *Arrow of God*. While mask dancing is obviously patriarchal and highly gendered, given its exclusivity to only titled men, yet it is significant to children. Ezeulu's perception that understanding life is akin to a mask dancing, to establish rapport and the necessary network, underscores the importance of childhood in the novel. The point is that Achebe's early works construct multiple cultural views that accommodate varying and diverse identities. The image of children is a significant metaphor for transition, change, cultural mobility and experimentations.

Representations of childhood in Nigerian fiction are also prevalent in the works of notable African feminist writers such as Buchi Emecheta,

Flora Nwapa and Zaynab Alkali among others. With a gender perspective, these writers negotiate the concept through the fate of the girl child. Several critics however refuse to associate these feminist child portraitures with motherhood (Ikonné 1992; Agbasiere 1992; Okereke 1992; Nnaemeka 1997; Uwakweh 1998; Alabi 1998). The point is that the exploration of childhood in works of Nigerian female writers is subsumed within the overall feminist agenda. It also provides an entry point to what Oakley (1994) calls 'malestream' literature.

Consequently, the feminine temperament that overshadows the portraiture of the child has resulted in a peripheral position for childhood in African critical discourse, and hence, motherhood occupies an important position in the thematic explorations. However, it can be reasonably argued that motherhood as a social construct has brought attention to the evolution of teenage age brackets, something more of 'girlhood' in contradistinction to childhood, which ordinarily may make the concept homogenous in societies. Feminist criticism of childhood in Nigerian fiction is therefore a subset of gendered notions. This is a phenomenon that has assumed a strategic location in imaginative literary expressions and scholarship in several contexts – including, of course, the diaspora.

The figure of the child as occupying a transitional phase between several cultural worlds is often foregrounded in African literary imagination. The representative images take the forms of innocence, essence of struggle, socio-historical engagement as well as the future of the polity. With Ben Okri in *The Famished Road* (1991) as a kind of path-breaker in character portraiture of a child hero, Azaro, whose powers clearly transcend the physical, the flourishing of children and youth protagonists, or to put it in another way, the ubiquity of the bildungsroman, is understandable. The characterization of children represents an array of worldviews at different stages of their lives, thus confirming that the fiction coming out of Nigeria in the twenty-first century is characterized by the use of children, youthful protagonists and the resultant provocation of new critical paradigms.

Interestingly, third-generation Nigerian writing features children who have 'come of age'. The child represents an icon of both formal and generational value. As characters and narrators, the child heroes project acutely the depth of the abyss they are in and portray a society in ceaseless strife and perpetual debacle. However, it is indubitable that there are obvious limitations and inhibiting factors with a view to fulfilling their engagement. The narrative advantage of the novel (McCarthy 1961) seen as a strategic form to convey the aspirations of the modern world, is evidently an added advantage for the third-generation Nigerian writers. In other words, the form of the novel creates an atmosphere for intense thematic and stylistic dissipations. Therefore, birthing child narration as a device within narrative fiction is a way of proving the resourcefulness of the genre.

In the Nigerian context, using child narration to capture the disaster of poverty, low quality of life, lack of access to adequate healthcare, and environmental degradation, paint a total and factual picture of post-independence decadence. The characterization of Kambili in Chimamanda Adichie's, *Purple Hibiscus* (2003) is an exploration into the psychological state of the child heroes. Robert Mollinger rightly reveals that 'there is a search for patterns of behavior, unconscious motivations and in general the typical way the person relates to himself and others' (1981, 12). This is where the device of child narration readily functions as a strategy for narrating the realities of post-independence Nigerian society, as exemplified in *Purple Hibiscus*. As a leading figure of her generation, Adichie, through this her first novel, consciously engages and domesticates post-independence disillusionment. This is clearly evident in the thematic concerns and the character portraitures of the novel. It is, therefore, a remarkable attempt at socio-historical engagement, first by being inward-looking and progressively pigeon-holing society with a view to positively engaging the social malaise confronting the self.

Anthony Oha rightly observes that 'Adichie presents a series of fictional surprises as she consciously oscillates between history and art. The need to expose the traumatic situation in Africa has often occupied the minds of modern day writers in Africa' (2007, 200). She achieves this in her deconstruction of the myth of the father figure in Eugene and the empowerment of hitherto invincible faces in the literary traditions before her. This is in contradiction to female characterization in the Achebe generation, where patriarchal subjection of women, to use the words of Charles Fonchingong 'is central to the plot construction and characterization of African male writers, the patriarchal subjection of women ... and a woman's honour and dignity often consist in her strict adherence to idealized norms of wifehood and motherhood' (2006, 138). This is what Adichie's character portraiture of Kambili represents in a larger sense in the fusion of child innocence and potential feminine will. Heather Hewett explains this by locating Kambili as an agency of voice against the backdrop of silence. In her words:

Only in escaping his grasp can she become the author of and witness to her own life; only in narrating her life story can she begin to heal the traumatic dismemberment between her voice and her consciousness; only in speaking out can she begin to exist as a whole person with a future as well as a past. (Hewett 2005, 88)

In other words, Kambili represents a subtle challenge to the *status quo*, as far as her role as narrator and protagonist in the universe of the novel is concerned.

The dislocation of family values, as well the obvious disenchantment in the worldview of the novel, not only bears true allegiance to the postcolonial realities, but it is also reinforced by the narrative mode. In this respect, the terror unleashed on the household by Eugene in *Purple Hibiscus*, in the name of principles and religious high-handedness, produces children that never enjoy the bliss of the home. For Jaja and Kambili, their home is no better than a detention camp, ruled by Eugene, the high-handed hypocritical father. Instances of domestic violence and wife battery are proofs in this regard. As such, deviance and protest become the hallmark of the children's disposition from childhood. In fact, Kambili is relegated to perpetual silence which is why she could hardly cope with the strength of will of Amaka, on their visit to Enugu. The child narrative strategy employed by Adichie affords an opportunity of a panoramic view of the disconnect in Eugene's family.

Kambili externalizes the painful realities of domestic tyranny and repression. As a young girl who yearns for exposure, she gives the reader an opportunity to appreciate her peculiar environment; she ultimately airs her condition from the point of view of an all-seeing omniscient observer. Notwithstanding that she is a girl, Kambili wriggles out of the stereotyping to be the voice of commitment, which can be located within the preoccupation of the contemporary African novelist for socio-historical engagement as a fall out of post-independence disillusionment.

Therefore, Adichie's *Purple Hibiscus* demonstrates the need for continued socio-historic commitment in the face of fresh challenges in third-world societies, which continue to ravage the lives of the people. As Ayo Kehinde (2011) explains, 'a study of any writer may tend to be defective if an attempt is not made to locate his/her major thematic concerns within the totality of the history of his society. This is more pertinent when a discussion of an African writer is embarked upon' (2005, 224). In this regard, the larger socio-political issues addressed by Adichie's *Purple Hibiscus* help ensure that other novelists are true to their calling as committed African writers. Actually, the domestic strain in the novel suggests that the home, being the smallest unit of the society, is under threat of extinction, just as the larger society contends with issues of post-independence decadence.

The decline of values and infrastructural decay replete in the enabling society requires succinct and pungent thematic explorations to pass on the messages. This aligns with Hama Tuma's observation on the loss of sovereignty by Africa and the tragedy of the continent being ruled by 'kleptocrats who have mortgaged its future to the World Bank and the IMF, ravaged by maladies ranging from malaria to AIDS, humiliated and plundered – Africa is in a dire state' (2002, 1). This simply implies that, in thematizing these realities, writers can create a connection in their works with the state of affairs. One clear way of doing this is through narrative techniques that convey the situation as emotively as possible. Child narration is clearly a brilliant way of using a child's testimonial to show the extent of the rot. In fact, just as in actual war or conflict situations, women and children are the vulnerable populations. This is where the literary dexterity of Adichie is foregrounded – Kambili in *Purple Hibiscus* is a construction of the use of both gender and demographic figures through whom the socio-economic woes of the society are visibly shown.

In essence, the home front provides a platform for launching into the dissonance of the outside world. Kambili as the omniscient child narrator in *Purple Hibiscus* captivates the mind with the accounts of her domestic circumstances. The situation suggests that, rather than growing up amidst parental pampering, the child heroes encounter suppression and dehumanization. The family thus becomes a negative setting where the children suffer untold psychological trauma. They are literally made to suffer in silence. In *Purple Hibiscus* Kambili intones: 'I wanted to tell the girl that it was all my hair, that there were no attachments, but the words would not come' (2003, 141). Jaja and Kambili are like outcasts and this clearly manifests itself when they visit Nsukka where the two siblings do not fit in with the others. Andrée Greene aptly describes this as a deliberate and conscious attempt by Adichie to create 'a mood of surveillance, repression, silence, and swallowed voices at every societal level' (2007, 1).

The point being made is that, by deploying the characters whose experiences are being thermatised as narrators, the novelist constructs the setting of the home as the agent of social dislocation. This also goes to show that the post-independence decadence is not an issue that manifests in the society as a whole, but one which is deeply rooted in the disintegration of the family. Adichie deploys her artistry effectively to engage the apparent realities of post-independence disillusionment and socio-historical fragmentation, which Kehinde refers to as the theme of 'postcolonial betrayal' that has become 'a common motif in contemporary African literature' (2011, 226). One may infer from the above that, in projecting the misery and frustrations of the self, especially in postcolonial settings like Nigeria, Adichie elicits sympathy from the reader through her choice of child narration. In other words, child narration in the novel becomes a device of engaging postcolonial angst, in a deeper way than the conventional use of narrative technique as a literary device.

It should be stated that the novel's treatment of satire and social lampooning bears witness to the hypocritical posturing of human beings. As Eugene, Kambili's father, instantiates, it is inconceivable how a man can expect to thrive as a dual personality. This is in a sense the way Adichie casts the character of Eugene. For a man whose conduct at home is tyrannical to be a self-confessed democrat, leaves much to be desired. If, indeed, he believes in the ideals of freedom and human rights, his home naturally ought to be a model of such values. As the one sole financier of *The Standard* and the fiery journalist, Ade Coker, it is inconceivable that Eugene would descend so low as to perpertrate domestic violence, as represented in wife battery and child suppression. In other words, Eugene's domestic oppression beclouds his pro-democracy posturing in the larger society.

More pertinently, Eugene's hypocrisy is clearly demonstrated through Adichie's child narration. One feels the pain of Kambili as she and Jaja struggle through existence under Eugene's high-handedness. The point is that Kambili's voice is piercing and revealing. She provides a platform for appreciating the agony of domestic violence. She assumes the voice of the voiceless, ably represented by her mother, and Papa-Nnukwu, the grandfather. It follows therefore that the child narrative technique is a vista of thematic exploration. One can observe how the crisis in *Purple Hibiscus* is deftly orchestrated through the child narrative mode adopted.

To put the argument in perspective, one is of the opinion that the various thematic preoccupations of *Purple Hibiscus* are firmly rooted in the child narrator's ability to capture the experiences effectively. For example, in describing the infrastructural decay at the University quarters where Aunty Ifeoma lives, Kambili's words evoke a string of ironic comparisons which subtly capture the low quality of life in the University community: 'we came to a tall bland building with peeling blue paint' (Adichie 2003, 112). The crux of the description lies in the words 'bland' and 'peeling', which indicate neglect. Also, in describing the interior of Aunty Ifeoma's house, Kambili reveals:

> as we entered the living room, I noticed the ceiling first, how low it was. I felt I could reach out and touch it; it was unlike home, where the high ceilings gave our rooms an airy stillness ... the seams of the cushions were frayed and slipping apart. (ibid., 113-14)

The description above clearly suggests poverty and abandonment, and it is a subtle commentary on the state of education and public institutions in the country. As shown below, Kambili depicts anti-press policies, freedom, a litany of press victimization and corruption in high places:

> I imagined Ade Coker being pulled out of his car, being squashed into another car, perhaps a black station wagon filled with soldiers, their guns hanging out of the windows. I imagine his hands quivering with fear, a wet patch spreading on his trousers. (ibid., 38)

One can see in the novel's first-person narrator, Kambili, the child heroine who is also the narrative voice, a deliberate self-asserting ethos. Her name, Kambili, which means 'let me be' therefore becomes the centripetal force through which she navigates the quest of autonomy and self-direction, not only for herself, but also for a family and a country as a whole. This is an optimistic statement for her challenging and devastating location in Nigeria's troubled society. The novel therefore reinforces the postcolonial literary tradition by attempting to dismantle the patriarchal order represented in the lingering cultural struggles with colonial values. It is also obvious that the characters of that tradition, represented by Eugene are often transformed or destroyed by the recognition of their colonized consciousness.

Therefore, the use of child narration can be said to assist in actualizing the desire of Adichie to explore the postcolonial challenge through her thematization of domestic violence in the family of Eugene Achike. Eugene as a fictional archetype thus represents, from his Catholic middle-class vantage point, the remnants of the old-school colonial education, and Western ideas that consistently devalue traditional Igbo culture and experience. The high-handed Eugene furthers patriarchy through the physical and psychological terrorism he unleashes on his family members. Notwithstanding this, he deploys his resources to promote the struggle in the larger community. In this way Adichie exposes humanistic hypocrisy and pretensions in *Purple Hibiscus* and clearly reveals the factors that thwart the desire for self-actualization by Kambili. Adichie therefore delineates the forces which influence her characters and the choices they are conditioned to make. Though the characters are representative of supposed success in the social hierarchy, they are unable to blossom.

The prosecution of feminism as an ideology and tool for affirmative action as presented in *Purple Hibiscus* is certainly thought-provoking. For one, it certainly may not be a feminist strategy to commit murder. As such, the fact that Beatrice, Eugene's wife, could resort to the dastardly act of murder of her own husband raises vital questions about Adichie's brand of feminist ideology. Even though this aligns with Adichie's personal projection of feminist crusades which underscores the need for challenging patriarchy and gaining true liberation, it is unlikely that more violence, which the murder of Eugene symbolizes, is a viable option, i.e. is doubtful whether murder is the solution to Eugene's domestic tyranny. This is because the poisoning of Eugene eventually shatters the home. It leaves, Eugene dead, Jaja behind bars and Beatrice a psychological wreck. However, the action merely shows that the self has the capacity to be decisive and must not be undermined. Violence eventually becomes, at both domestic and public levels, the only path to social change and liberation. This is what the action of Kambili's mother, who is secretly poisoning her husband, typifies. The foregoing observation notwithstanding, Ogaga Okuyade seems to accommodate Adichie's feminist temper in *Purple Hibiscus* when he writes that 'her feminist intention [is] bold and uncompromising, though, it is only an invocation of pre-existing stasis, and it is an emphatic statement of resistance to the dominant group' (2009, 287).

However, one hardly finds this to be a helpful resolution, but rather, the challenge is how not to inspire social and domestic disintegration through violence. One suspects that this resolution by Adichie is another deliberate attempt at foregrounding the limitation of the child narration. Beatrice's victory appears pyrrhic, and in fact, to agree with Daria Tunca, '[i]f Kambili has indisputably developed a form of resistance against Eugene, her quest for independence nevertheless remains an ambiguous one' (2009, 14). The child narration technique deployed in Adichie's *Purple Hibiscus* is a device used to engage with post-independence disenchantment in the universe of the novel. This lends credence to the view of Kwame Dawes that the child voice in Adichie's *Purple Hibiscus* serves as a means of airing trauma as 'she tells her story with something akin to the psychological disinterest of a deeply traumatized person' (2005, 3).

It is strongly contended that Chimamanda Adichie skilfully deploys child narration to conjure moods of repression, silence and suppressed voices in her novelistic milieu. With Ifeoma as the only visible respite, and her home in Nsukka a get-away, Kambili's voice is gradually discovered, while the child narration becomes piercing and affirmative. The character soon discovers her innate qualities and rights to liberty, identity and emotions. However, the temporary hope gained through Ifeoma, a progressive university professor, does not last as she is eventually forced to relocate to the United States as a result of larger questions of survival. Yet, she leaves Kambili with the ideals of feminism and a consciousness of the realities of post-independence Nigerian society, where intellectuals, artists, writers and other progressive figures are forced out in a bid to escape political persecution and economic hardship.

It could be seen therefore that the technique of child narration reveals Kambili's frustrations and that of the archetypal vulnerable child in this milieu. Frustration and depression become synonymous with such characters as Kambili in their depiction as victims of domestic negative realities as revealed in their dislocated and unfriendly family settings. As beings who seek positive self-assertion, such child characters are compelled to fashion out an escape. In fact, in *Purple Hibiscus*, Adichie draws attention to this fact in a graphic way by illustrating the actual circumstances of the enabling society, where Greene observes: 'Again, hope collides with the facts of contemporary African life, and intellectuals, artists, writers, and dissidents leave their countries to earn a living or avoid political persecution' (2007, 1). In this scenario, the options available for victims are not many, as the society frustrates attempts at positive self-assertion.

In summary, the dynamic capacity of Adichie as a contemporary Nigerian writer of the third generation is clearly manifested in the continued evolution of techniques and strategies that combine to engage the divergent subject matters of the enabling milieu, as evidenced in her use of child narration in *Purple Hibiscus*. It is, therefore, suggested that the use of child narration in the novel generates and sustains narrative empathy thereby deepening its thematic objectives. The metaphorical construct of vulnerability as a paradox of empowerment is thus fully accentuated in this exploration of the child perspective in the novel.

Works Cited

Achebe, Chinua. *Things Fall Apart*. London: Heinemann, 1958.
—. *Arrow of God*. London: Heinemann, 1964.
Adichie, Chimamanda. *Purple Hibiscus*. Lagos: Farafina, 2003.
Agbasiere, J. 'Social Integration of the Child in Buchi Emecheta's Novels'. In *Children and Literature in Africa*. Eds Ikonné, Chidi, Oko, Ebele and Onwudinjo, Peter. Ibadan: Heinemann, 1992.

Alabi, Adetayo.'*Gender Issues in Zaynab Alkali's Novels*'. In *Childhood in African Literature: A Review*. Ed. Jones, E. Trenton, NJ: Africa World Press, 1998.

Beti, Mongo. *The Poor Christ of Bomba*. London: Heinemann, 1971 [1956]. Mission to Kala. London: Heinemann, 1970 [1958].

Dawes, Kwame. 'Review of *Purple Hibiscus*, by ChimamandaNgoziAdichie' *World Literature Today* 79.1, 2005: 84.

Desai, S. K. 'The Theme of Childhood in Commonwealth Fiction'. *Commonwealth Literature: Problems of Response*. Ed. C. D Narasimhaiah. Madras, India: Macmillan, 1981: 38–48.

Fonchingong, Charles. 'Unbending Gender Narratives in African Literature'. *Journal of International Women's Studies* 8.1, November 2006: 135–47.

Greene, Andrée. 'Homeland: The New Generation of Nigerian Writers'. *Boston Review* March/April 2007. https://bostonreview.net/greene-homeland. Retrieved on 14 March 2009.

Hall, Stuart. 'When was "The Postcolonial"? Thinking at the Limit'. In The Post-Colonial Question; Common skies, divided horizons. Eds Chambers, I. and Curti, L. London, UK: Routledge, 1996.

Hewett, Heather. 'Coming of Age: Chimamanda Ngozi Adichie and the Voice of the Third Generation'. *English in Africa* 32.1, 2005: 73–97.

Ikonné, Chidi, Oko, Ebele & Onwudinjo, Peter (Eds). *Children and Literature in Africa*. Ibadan: Heinemann, 1992.

Kehinde, Ayobami. 'An Aesthetics of Realism: The Image of Postcolonial Africa in Meja Mwangi's *Going Down River Road*'. *EnterText* 4.2, 2011: 223–53.

Laye, Camara. *The African Child*. London: Collins, 1959.

McCarthy, Mary. 'Characters in Fiction'. In *On The Contrary*. New York: Farrar, 1961.

Mollinger, Robert. *Psychoanalysis and Literature: An Introduction*. Chicago, IL: Nelson-Hall, 1981.

Mudimbe, Valentin Y. *The Idea of Africa*. Bloomington, IN: Indiana University Press, 1994.

Nnaemeka, Obioma. (ed.) *The Politics of (M)othering: Womanhood, Identity and Resistance in African Literature*. London: Routledge, 1997.

Oakley, Ann. 'Women and Children First and Last: Parallels and Differences between Children's and Women's Studies'. In *Children's Childhoods Observed and Experienced*. Ed. Mayall, B. Lewes, UK: Falmer Press, 1994.

Oha, Anthony. 'Beyond the Odds of the Red Hibiscus: A Critical Reading of Chimamanda Adichie's *Purple Hibiscus*'. *Journal of Pan*

African Studies, 1.9, 2007: 199–211.

Ojaide, Tanure and Obi, Joseph. *Culture, Society and Politics in Modern African Literature: Texts and Contexts*. Durham, NC: Carolina Academic Press, 2002.

Okereke, Grace E. 'Children in the Nigerian Feminist Novel'. In *Children and Literature in Africa*. Eds Ikonné, C., Oko, E. and Onwudinjo, P. Ibadan: Heinemann, 2002 [1992].

Okolie, Maxwell. 'Childhood in African Literature: A Literary Perspective'. In *Childhood in African Literature*. Ed. Jones, E. D. Trenton, NJ: Africa World Press, 1988.

Okri, Ben. *The Famished Road*. London, UK: Jonathan Cape, 1991.

Okuyade, Ogaga. 'Changing Borders and Creating Voices: Silence as Character in Chimamanda Adichie's *Purple Hibiscus*'. *Journal of Pan African Studies* 2.9, 2009: 245–59.

Oyono, Ferdinand. *Houseboy*. London, UK: Heinemann, 1966.

Tuma, Hama. 'The Role and Ordeal of the African Writer'. Lecture at Columbia University, 2003.

Tunca, Daria. 'An Ambiguous "Freedom Song": Mind-Style in Chimamanda Ngozi Adichie's *Purple Hibiscus*'. *Postcolonial Text*, 5.1, 2009: 1–18.

Uwakweh, Pauline.'Carving a Niche: Visions of Gendered Childhood in Buchi Emecheta's *The Bride Price* and Tsitsi Dangarembga's *Nervous Conditions*'. In *Childhood in African Literature*. *African Literature Today* series, 21. Eds. Jones, E. D. and Jones M. Trenton, NJ: Africa World Press; London, UK: James Currey, 1998.

Wright, Michelle. *Becoming Black: Creating Identity in the African Diaspora*. Durham, NC: Duke University Press, 2004.

8

'Fragile Negotiations'
Olanna's Melancholia in *Half of a Yellow Sun*

PAULINE DODGSON-KATIYO

Commenting on the writing of *Half of a Yellow Sun* in her essay 'African "Authenticity" and the Biafran Experience' (2008), Chimamanda Ngozi Adichie admits that her character Okeoma is based on a romantic image of the poet-soldier Christopher Okigbo who died during the Biafran War (also known as the Nigerian Civil War; July 1967 – January 1970).[1] She had wanted to pay tribute to Okigbo as a man who lived life to the fullest and who 'exemplifies the monumental loss of human capital that Biafra represented' but she had 'used only an essence of the real Okigbo' (2008: 51). Her sense that she had romanticized Okigbo is indicatory given that she insists in the essay that she did not want her novel to romanticize the war or suggest that Biafra was a *'utopia-in-retrospect'* (ibid.: 50). The war had left Biafrans with the knowledge that they were a 'defeated people' and with a feeling of 'collective shame' (ibid.).

Adichie's view on the aftermath of Biafra resonates with that of the political anthropologist Ifi Amadiume. Writing in 'The Politics of Memory' (2000) on justice and the responsibility of the intellectual in conflict situations, Amadiume denounces the Nigerian head of state Yakubu Gowon's stance in his victory speech at the end of the war in which he claimed that unity was the only way forward if Nigeria were to prosper. This government will to unity, Amadiume argues, denied war victims the possibility of expressing their grief and testifying to their suffering:

---

[1] This romanticized representation is based on Wole Soyinka's description of a meeting with Okigbo (see Soyinka 1975: 156; Adichie 2008: 51). In her Author's Note to *Half of a Yellow Sun*, Adichie states that Okigbo's life and his work *Labyrinths* inspired the characterization of Okeoma.

Especially because the Biafrans were defeated, prohibiting an open discourse on the Biafran war was a bad policy: it denied ordinary civilian victims a chance to express their suffering, grief and anger. They were denied the right to tell their own truth and expose the wounds of the past, which remain hidden in Nigeria's body politic. The unvoiced suffering of trauma continues to surface at critical moments. (Amadiume 2000: 41)

Part of Amadiume's essay discusses the position taken on Biafra before and after the war by Wole Soyinka as a prominent intellectual. Although critical of him for opposing the secession of Biafra, Amadiume approves the opinion he expresses in *The Open Sore of a Continent* 'that the factors that led to Biafra neither were ephemeral nor can be held to be permanently exorcised' (Soyinka 1996: 32). Adichie too refers to Soyinka's view on the war. Citing his prediction in *The Man Died* that it will be a long time before 'passions die out' over the war, she suggests that one of the reasons for the continuing passions (and divisions) is that people do not know about the war, that lack of knowledge keeps the passions alive.[2] Therefore, she wanted to write about a war that Nigerians had chosen to forget in the hope that her novel would make it possible 'to collectively acknowledge what happened' ('African 'Authenticity' and the Biafran Experience' 2008: 53).

This emphasis on knowledge and revealing a hidden history may explain why Adichie has said that the character with whom she most identifies is the houseboy Ugwu, the first focalizer in the novel (Adichie 2006). The reader is shown Ugwu's attempts to acquire an education as part of the decolonizing mission of his employer, the radical university lecturer Odenigbo. We learn (although not until the novel's end) that Ugwu later becomes a new postcolonial historian. Descriptions of his history of colonialism and of Nigeria and Biafra are inserted into the fictional narrative, replacing the putative and never published book proposed by the colonially educated expatriate Richard. However, as Adichie grew up in 'the shadow of Biafra', the war for her 'is not mere history ... it is also memory' (Adichie 2008: 50). She recalls that the war haunted her family: her father was unable to bury his father who died during the war and only later saw his unmarked grave; her mother never speaks of the death of her father in a refugee camp but she recalls having to fight for food at the relief centre in order to feed her children.

Given her family's painful memories, Adichie feared that she would

[2] Biafra was the subject and setting of fiction and non-fiction after the war. Adichie's concern was that Nigerians of her generation did not know enough about the war (2008: 53).

be taking a risk in writing about the war, a risk that her novel would only perpetuate the Western association of Africa with war, a stereotypical and generalizing view that ignores the dynamism of the African past. Her dilemma was complicated further by her own worldview, which she admits is 'largely a dark one' and which has led her to 'sometimes wonder whether being African means that I must always indulge in fragile negotiations in order to fully explore my artistic vision' (ibid.: 47). The phrase 'fragile negotiations' is one I want to take up, particularly in relation to Olanna, the central female character in the novel. It is my contention that fragile negotiations are what characterize Adichie's writing of Olanna. Ugwu's history, just by virtue of being written, presents a strong narrative of survival. However, there is another necessary narrative of trauma, mourning and melancholia that circulates around Olanna and memory, which compensates for the romanticization of Okeoma/Okigbo by *showing* the 'monumental loss' to which Adichie refers. I intend to analyse Olanna's relationships to her lover Odenigbo and to her twin sister Kainene in terms of melancholia and to link this analysis to the traumatic events Olanna witnesses and to the ways in which these events compulsively recur in the novel.

In Ugwu's eyes, Olanna is nearly perfect. Admiring her appearance and her speech, and what he sees as her uniqueness, he believes she should be in a glass case. Glass, of course, is fragile and, throughout the novel, Olanna's strength is revealed but also her fragility when that strength fails her. Her vision of life, like Adichie's, is largely a dark one and her grief and the depression that is referred to as 'Dark Swoops' deprive her of the happiness she desires and that Ugwu thinks she deserves. Lacking confidence in herself, Olanna admires the self-confidence of Odenigbo and puts on his aftershave in an attempt to be like him, 'as if the scent could, at least for a while, stifle her questions and make her a little more like him, a little more certain, a little less questioning' (Adichie 2009: 27). At the university gatherings at Odenigbo's house, Olanna fears that she cannot keep up with the intellectual conversation, 'that there was a glaze of unoriginality to all her ideas', and that one of the guests, Miss Adebayo, 'could tell, from her face, that she was afraid of things, that she was unsure, that she was not one of those people with no patience for self-doubt' (ibid.: 51–2). Kainene tells her that not only is she too keen to please but she also feels sorry for people who don't need her sympathy. Before, during and after the war, Olanna shows signs of melancholia. The psychoanalyst Sigmund Freud in his essay 'Mourning and Melancholia' distinguishes between these two conditions, describing mourning as a 'normal' state that will end after a period of time and melancholia as pathological, an illness with no clearly defined end. However, as Sam Durrant points out in *Postcolonial Narrative and the Work of Mourning*, other distinctions Freud makes in his essay are unclear (2004: 9). Both mourning and melancholia are centrally concerned with loss of a loved person or a loved object (such as one's country) or an ideal (such as liberty). Nevertheless, Olanna's experiences suggest that she suffers from some of the symptoms of depression that Freud describes as melancholia.

According to Freud, the occasions that give rise to melancholia 'extend for the most part beyond the clear case of a loss by death, and include all those situations of being slighted, neglected or disappointed, which can import opposed feelings of love and hate into the relationship or reinforce an already existing ambivalence' (2001: 251). On two occasions before the war, Olanna believes she has lost Odenigbo. The first is when his mother calls her a witch and Olanna angrily leaves his house because he will not defend her; the second is when she learns that Odenigbo has slept with and impregnated Amala, a young woman whom his mother had brought from the village for that purpose. After the first incident, Olanna feels that 'Odenigbo's mother's visit had ripped a hole in her safe mesh of feathers, startled her, snatched something away from her. She felt one step away from where she should be' (Adichie 2009: 104). In her desire for security, she decides not to leave Odenigbo but to commit herself more fully to him by having his child. When she leaves him the second time, she feels she has become a 'stranger' (ibid.: 230) to herself and that she is still letting Odenigbo run her life. Unable to conceive, she learns of Amala's pregnancy and thinks she is useless because 'a child nestled now in a stranger's body instead of in hers' (ibid.: 232). On both occasions, Olanna is, ostensibly, able to recover; she returns to Odenigbo and, after Amala rejects her baby daughter, acts decisively and adopts the child.

However, during the war, Olanna continues to have ambivalent feelings towards Odenigbo as he changes from being the confident person she would like to emulate to someone who has lost his ability to take control of situations. She again suspects him of having an affair, this time with Alice, a woman with whom she had laughed about sexuality and with whom she felt 'a vulgar and delicious female bond' (ibid.: 336). Odenigbo's loss of control is particularly evident in his depression following the news of his mother's death and his behaviour after they receive the erroneous news that Ugwu has been killed. As Odenigbo becomes depressed, neglects his work and starts to drink heavily, Olanna feels an anger towards him which is exacerbated by her own sense of inadequacy. Freud, commenting on the poor self-image of the person suffering from melancholia, suggests that there is a stage when the clinician perceives that the patient's self-accusations 'fit someone else, someone whom the patient loves or has loved or should love' and that these 'self reproaches are reproaches against a love object which have been shifted away from it on to the patient's own ego' (2001: 248). Olanna feels guilty because she was not more accommodating towards Odenigbo's mother; she wants to help him to grieve but cannot connect with his mourning. Echoing a fear expressed by Odenigbo that she has become inward-looking, she wonders 'if this was her own failure rather than his, if perhaps she lacked a certain strength that would compel him to include her in his pain' (Adichie 2009: 322). When they wrongly believe that Ugwu has died, Olanna is unable to have a physical relationship with Odenigbo: 'his touch made her skin crawl and she turned away from him and went outside to sleep on a mat on the veranda, where Ugwu had sometimes slept' (ibid.: 382). In her rational mind, she knows that Odenigbo is not to blame for Ugwu's death but, nevertheless, thinks that 'his drinking, his excessive drinking, had somehow made him complicit' (ibid.). Olanna tells Kainene, 'I want this war to end so that he can come back. He has become somebody else' (ibid.: 388).

Kainene too is the object of Olanna's love. However, the relationship between the sisters, who had been close as children, changes after they return from study abroad. Olanna appears to need Kainene more than Kainene needs her: 'they had simply drifted apart, but it was Kainene who now anchored herself firmly in a distant place so that they could not drift back together' (ibid.: 37). When Olanna phones Kainene for support, Kainene asks if something has happened: 'Olanna felt a rush of melancholy; her twin sister thought something had to have happened for her to call' (ibid.: 102). The serious breach in their relationship comes after Kainene discovers that her sister has had sex with her lover, Richard, and suspects that it is a response to Odenigbo sleeping with Amala. Kainene upbraids Olanna for this betrayal of trust because she is 'the good one and the favourite and the beauty and the Africanist revolutionary who doesn't like white men' and 'the good one shouldn't fuck her sister's lover' (ibid.: 254). Given her own critical response to Odenigbo's infidelity, Olanna's seduction of Richard – 'she was clear-headed; she knew what she wanted to do and what she was doing' (ibid.: 234) – is extraordinary. Even more extraordinary for the reader is the way Adichie describes how, after the act, Olanna is filled 'with a sense of well-being, with something close to grace' (ibid.). This semi-religious imagery continues when, after she has told Odenigbo what she has done, Olanna wonders whether she should have told him 'that she regretted betraying Kainene and him but did not regret the act itself. She should have said that it was not a crude revenge, or a scorekeeping, but took on a redemptive significance for her. She should have said the selfishness had liberated her' (ibid.: 244). Olanna's liberation through selfishness suggests a sense of entitlement that seems out of character for someone who wants to please others. However, it is in keeping with the way Olanna feels about Kainene.

At one level, Olanna and Kainene can be considered to fit into the pattern of paired women, a convention in African literature identified by Florence Stratton and found in the work of a writer much admired by Adichie, Flora Nwapa. According to Stratton, 'the defining feature of the form ... is the familial or social juxtaposition of two female characters (sisters, cousins, co-wives, best friends) who, in their response to male domination, are the antithesis of each other, one passively submitting, the other actively resisting' (1994: 97). This is how the reader is, at first, encouraged to see the two women characters. Kainene's story (told to Richard) of how, when she was fourteen, she spat in her father's glass of water and 'Olanna ran and changed the water' (Adichie 2009: 114) illustrates their difference. However, their twinship complicates the pairing. Twin relationships in literature may, as in other literary representations of doubling, evolve around ambivalence. Moreover, to some extent Kainene is a foil for Olanna and for Richard since we see her largely through their eyes. Richard recognizes that Kainene, despite her assertiveness, resents her sister's attractiveness and supposed goodness. More importantly, Olanna wishes she were more like Kainene. She wants Kainene's self-assurance, her 'supreme confidence' (ibid.: 218) to be transferred to her so that she can be stronger. This desire of Olanna to be complete by becoming like Kainene, as if Kainene is a missing part of herself, explains her sense of entitlement but also her melancholia when Kainene insists that her act is unforgivable precisely because she is her sister.

The novel's non-linear structure presents the reader with the traumatic experience of Olanna during the massacre (in the late 1960s in Part II) before we learn the full story of the birth of her child, Baby, and of Kainene's rejection of Olanna (in the early 1960s in Part III). During this period, Olanna's depression is largely represented through the recurrence of the violence she has seen. Visiting her former lover, Mohammed, in Kano during the attacks on the Igbo in the North in 1966, she sees the dead bodies of two of her relatives, Aunty Ifeka and Uncle Mbaezi, and learns that her cousin Arize and her husband have also been killed. On the train journey back after Mohammed has helped her to escape, she sees the decapitated head of a child carried by her mother in a calabash. Olanna goes into a deep depression (her 'Dark Swoops'), finding it difficult to breathe, sleep or walk. She compulsively repeats the trauma of the deaths in her family and of seeing the mutilated child.

The memory of her relatives recurs just before and then after the secession of Biafra. Making love to Odenigbo, shortly before a pro-Biafra rally, she thinks of Arize's 'pregnant belly' and 'how easily it must have broken, skin stretched that taut' (Adichie 2009: 160). When Odenigbo raises his arm during a speech, she remembers how Aunty Ifeka's twisted, bloody arm had looked in death. Olanna thinks that 'perhaps Aunty Ifeka could see this rally now, and all the people here, or perhaps not, if death was a silent opaqueness' (ibid.: 163). Later, when they are living in Odenigbo's village, Olanna cannot 'visualize a war happening now ... It was often difficult to visualize anything concrete that was not dulled by memories of Arize and Aunty Ifeka and Uncle Mbaezi, that did not feel like life being lived on suspended time' (ibid.: 185). Olanna feels empowered at a meeting where people are united but then goes back into a deep depression when Odenigbo, after having claimed that Mohammed is complicit in the killings because of his ethnicity, suggests that Arize would have been raped and mutilated. She feels angry both because of what he has said and because he assumes that she will forgive him for saying it.

In *Unclaimed Experience*, Cathy Caruth, analysing trauma and narrative, asks: 'Is the trauma the encounter with death, or the ongoing experience of having survived it?' She argues that within trauma stories, there is 'a kind of double telling, the oscillation between a *crisis of death* and the correlative *crisis of life*: between the story of the unbearable nature of an event and the story of the unbearable nature of its survival' (1996: 7, original emphasis). This is illustrated when Olanna is summoned to attend a family gathering to explain what she knows of the deaths of her relatives. When she is asked how she knows they have died, she wants Aunty Ifeka's sons to 'question her for being alive, instead of dead like their sister and parents and brother-in-law' (Adichie 2009: 193). In telling of the deaths, Olanna has given the family the right to mourn, move on and count the dead as 'gone forever' but she, the teller, continues to experience the trauma. She knows that 'the heavy weight of four muted funerals weighed on her head, funerals based not on physical bodies but on her words' (ibid.).

The crisis of life becomes more unbearable when there is no witness to Kainene's supposed death and, therefore, not even words on which to base a funeral. After the sisters' reconciliation, Kainene goes on *afia* attack (buying provisions behind enemy lines) and never returns. Olanna is unable to accept that she has lost Kainene. At first, she thinks about this in the material terms of Kainene coming back and finding a deserted house. Later, she consults a *dibia* (traditional healer) because, as she tells the sceptical Odenigbo, she believes 'in anything that will bring my sister home', including reincarnation: 'When I come back in my next life,' Olanna insists, 'Kainene will be my sister' (ibid.: 433). However, in this life, the only way she can claim her sister is through memory, or through identification. I suggested above that Olanna needs Kainene in order to feel whole. Here, I further suggest that this is even more the case when Kainene is missing. In Freudian terms, Olanna's ego identifies with the lost Kainene, whose shadow has fallen upon it, and there is a 'cleavage between the critical activity of the ego and the ego as altered by identification' (Freud 2001: 249). When Olanna's father, echoing her name, calls her 'my gold', she wishes he wouldn't because she feels she is now 'tarnished' (Adichie 2009: 431). Richard's realization that 'he would never see Kainene again and that … he would see things only in shadow, only in half glimpses' (ibid.: 430) allows him to mourn because he knows what he has lost. Since Olanna does not have that same realization, her mourning cannot be complete and Kainene remains with her in another form of twinning as a ghost or spectre. As previously quoted, a quarter of a century after the end of the war, Soyinka referred to the factors that caused the secession not being 'permanently exorcised'. Soyinka's choice of the verb 'exorcised' rather than 'eradicated' is an interesting one. The deconstructionist philosopher Jacques Derrida argues that 'effective exorcism pretends to declare the death only in order to put to death … it certifies the death but here it is in order to inflict it' (1994: 59). Olanna's refusal to let go of Kainene shows the impossibility of exorcism in loss and trauma. Exorcizing ghosts means permanently losing the person you love and, in this case, also losing the country and ideal shared with them, Biafra. When Odenigbo tells Olanna that in burning Biafran money, she is 'burning memory', she responds that she will not base her memory on anything material that can be taken from her. Her memory, she says, is inside her (Adichie 2009: 432).

Adichie's fragile negotiations are around the ways in which events and their consequences and relationships come together. Before Kainene's disappearance, it is her experience of violence that brings about her reconciliation with Olanna. After she has seen the decapitation of her steward Ikejide in a mortar attack, an event she relives, Kainene remembers that Olanna had seen a mother carrying her child's head. Unable to forget the death of Ikejide, someone she later admits she 'never really noticed' (ibid.: 390), she realizes that she wants to see again the sister who also lives with violent and painful memories. Kainene expects an affirmative response when she says to Richard "'You know Olanna saw a mother carrying her child's head'" but in fact 'he did *not* know' (ibid.: 318) because she had not told him. Kainene herself did not hear the story directly from Olanna but from Odenigbo. Knowing and not knowing and how they either converge or remain apart are at the heart of the novel. There are hints throughout Part II that there have been several serious and, as yet, unhealed rifts in the relationships of Olanna, Odenigbo, Kainene and Richard but, in this part of the novel, we are not told enough of the personal stories to be able to flesh them out and put them together. This withholding and then revealing is itself a technique that relies on repetition, intimating that events not yet known have already happened. Adichie's telling of the Biafra story also involves recurrences, especially the traumatic repetitions of what Olanna witnesses. The repetitions of the story of the child's head illustrate not only the compulsive need to tell but also how knowing and not knowing intersect[3] in the telling.

The initial telling in the novel is in the first entry on Ugwu's writing of his book, the story acting as a prologue to the book itself. A silent woman on a train is 'caressing the covered calabash on her lap in a gentle rhythm' until she asks Olanna and others to look inside. Ugwu repeats the details Olanna has told him of the woman's bloodstained wrapper, the designs of the calabash and the child's head with its 'scruffy plaits falling across the dark-brown face'. After writing this, Ugwu refers to other occasions when women carried all or part of their dead children's bodies with them. We are told that 'he is careful not to draw parallels' (Adichie 2009: 82) but the fact that the comparisons are made will, as Aghogho Akpome points out, ensure that the reader will link these events (2013: 27). The next telling, at the end of chapter 11, is a description of what Olanna experienced on the train from her perspective. In this version, it is not the woman who caresses the calabash but Olanna who is 'gently caressing the carved lines that crisscrossed the calabash'. When she looks into the calabash what Olanna sees is 'the ashy-grey skin and the plaited hair and rolled-back eyes

---

[3] In this comment, I adopt a phrase of Cathy Caruth, who states that it is 'at the specific point at which knowing and not knowing intersect that the language of literature and the psychoanalytic theory of traumatic experience precisely meet' (1996: 3).

and open mouth' of a girl (Adichie 2009: 149). The 'scruffy plaits' of Ugwu's account are replaced by Olanna visualizing the mother oiling her child's hair and carefully dividing it into sections. In chapter 34, Ugwu's version of the calabash story and what Olanna experienced are brought together as she speaks and he writes down the story. In this version, Olanna describes the child's hair, its thickness that would have made it hard to plait and the look of the child's eyes and skin. She continues to tell Ugwu all she remembers of what happened on the train because the earnest way he is listening to her 'suddenly made her story important, made it serve *a larger purpose that even she was not sure of*' (ibid.: 410; emphasis added).

That larger purpose could be said to be realized when Ugwu uses the story as the prologue to his historical book. However, his telling – the first version we read – is out of context and inadequate, weakened not only by the parallels he draws which make it one of the many stories of atrocities in wartime but also because, in its careful attempt at objectivity, it cannot express fully what the witness Olanna experienced and continues to live with in her waking and sleeping life. According to Caruth:

> The repetitions of the traumatic event ... suggest *a larger relation to the event that extends beyond what can simply be seen or what can be known,* and is inextricably tied up with the belatedness and incomprehensibility that remain at the heart of this repetitive seeing. (1996: 92; emphasis added)

This characteristic of trauma – of the traumatic event being compulsively repeated but not fully known – can be contrasted to Olanna and Odenigbo's understanding of what Okeoma's death means to them and to Biafra. In a similar manner to Ugwu's retelling of Olanna's story, Dr Nwala, the friend who tells them of Okeoma's death, brings in extraneous material. He embeds Okeoma's death in a discourse about poems that Okeoma may have written but which, if so, are now lost:

> I saw him last month, and he told me he was writing some poems and Olanna was his muse, and if anything happened to him I should make sure the poems went to her. But I can't find them. The people who brought the message said they never saw him writing anything. So I said I would come and tell you he has gone but I did not find the poems. (Adichie 2009: 391)

In foregrounding the poems and not Okeoma's death, Dr Nwala would appear to be giving the wrong message but, for the reader, the poems are significant in their absence. The idea of the missing poems further enhances the sense of 'monumental loss'. The recent and future creativity of Okeoma (and by extension, Okigbo[4]) is lost during the war as work is missing or destroyed and potential work will never be written. For Olanna, what matters is that Okeoma has died and she realizes, before Odenigbo, what the garbled message means and interprets it. It is known in a way that Olanna's trauma is not known. After expressing her pain by screaming, she and Odenigbo make love, in a genuine expression of shared mourning.[5]

In my analysis of Olanna's grief and loss, I have concentrated on the ways in which this could be understood through early psychoanalytic work on melancholia. In conclusion, I want to consider whether the novel itself, in its use of repetition and trauma, goes beyond melancholia and becomes an act of mourning. Durrant's ideas on post-colonial narrative and mourning, largely derived from Freud and Derrida, are illuminating here. Durrant writes on novels by three authors – J. M. Coetzee, Wilson Harris and Toni Morrison – in relation to colonialism and memories of racial oppression. He argues that

> melancholic rituals [of characters in these novels] accrue a wider political significance and thus need to be reinterpreted as modes of collective mourning ... their immoderate grief needs to be recognized as a precisely proportionate response to history, a way of bearing witness to losses that exceed the proportions of the individual subject. (2004: 10–11)

This, I suggest, can also be applied to work that bears witness to loss and grieving in civil war. Adichie rightly points out that the novel is about love and human endeavour, not just about war (2008: 53) but it is also an act of mourning, a collective act which involves the reader through empathy and interpretation. Writing on trauma and literature, Laurie Vickroy argues that 'an audience needs assistance in translating unfamiliar experience in order to empathize with it'. She adds that 'readers are often oriented and receive information via a character's/ narrator's memory and consciousness, engaging readers to reconstruct the past, along with the often unwilling characters' (2002: 11). In *Half of a Yellow Sun*, Olanna's melancholia, rather than being different and separate from mourning, exists within mourning. She loses her role as Okeoma's muse when he dies. However, the repetitions and rewriting

---

[4] According to Donatus Ibe Nwoga, work written by Okigbo was lost when 'Nigerian soldiers destroyed Okigbo's residence ... near Enugu in 1967' (1984: 35).
[5] Zoe Norridge offers a powerful reading of the linking of physicality and pain in Olanna's response to Okeoma's death (2012: 32–3).

of the trauma she experiences and the representation of her melancholia provide the reader with a way of understanding and interpreting what has been lost. Rather than exorcizing, it enables a collective acknowledgement of a repressed past and an awareness of its significance in the present.

Works Cited

Adichie, Chimamanda Ngozi, Interview with Mariella Frostrup. *Open Book*. BBC Radio 4 (20 August 2006).

—. 'African "Authenticity" and the Biafran Experience.' *Transition*. 99.1 (2008): 42–53.

—. *Half of a Yellow Sun*. London: Fourth Estate, 2009 [2006].

Akpome, Aghogho. 'Narrating a New Nationalism: Rehistoricization and Political Apologia in Chimamanda Ngozi Adichie's *Half of a Yellow Sun.' English Academy Review* 30.1 (2013): 22–38.

Amadiume, Ifi. 'The Politics of Memory: Biafra and Intellectual Responsibility.' *The Politics of Memory: Truth, Healing and Social Justice*. Eds Ifi Amadiume and Abdullahi An-Na'im. London and New York: Zed Books, 2000.

Caruth, Cathy. *Unclaimed Experience: Trauma, Narrative, and History*. Baltimore, MD and London: Johns Hopkins University Press, 1996.

Derrida, Jacques. *Specters of Marx: The State of the Debt, the Work of Mourning & the New International*. New York and London: Routledge, 1994.

Durrant, Sam. *Postcolonial Narrative and the Work of Mourning: J. M. Coetzee, Wilson Harris, and Toni Morrison*. Albany, NY: State University of New York Press, 2004.

Freud, Sigmund. 'Mourning and Melancholia.' *The Standard Edition of the Complete Psychological Works of Sigmund Freud*, Volume XIV: *On the History of the Psycho-Analytic Movement, Papers on Metapsychology and Other Works*. London: Vintage, 2001 [1917].

Norridge, Zoe. 'Sex as Synecdoche: Intimate Languages of Violence in Chimamanda Ngozi Adichie's *Half of a Yellow Sun* and Aminatta Forna's *The Memory of Love'. Research in African Literatures* 43.2 (2012): 18–39.

Nwoga, Donatus Ibe. 'Christopher Okigbo: The Man and the Poet'. *Critical Perspectives on Christopher Okigbo*. Ed. Donatus Ibe Nwoga. Washington, DC: Three Continents Press, 1984.

Okigbo, Christopher. *Labyrinths with Path of Thunder*. London: Heinemann, 1971.

Soyinka, Wole. *The Man Died: Prison Notes of Wole Soyinka*. Harmondsworth: Penguin, 1975 [1972].

—. *The Open Sore of a Continent: A Personal Narrative of the Nigerian Crisis.* Oxford and New York: Oxford University Press, 1996.

Stratton, Florence. *Contemporary African Literature and the Politics of Gender.* New York and London: Routledge, 1994.

Vickroy, Laurie. *Trauma and Survival in Contemporary Fiction.* Charlottesville, VA and London: University of Virginia Press, 2002.

9

The Biafran War & the Evolution of Domestic Space in *Half of a Yellow Sun*

JANICE SPLETH

In *Half of a Yellow Sun*, Chimamanda Ngozi Adichie contributes yet another narrative to the genre of the Nigerian war novel. The action of her work spans the turbulent decade of the sixties, and the story is narrated from several different points of view representing various stakeholders in the conflict. As a war novel, however, this narrative challenges the conventions, providing ample information about the political causes and military progress of the war, but showing as well how these developments touched the private lives of individuals, emphasizing the role played by non-combatants. According to the United States Agency for International Development (2000), 95 percent of all casualties in the intrastate conflicts that have destabilized Africa since independence have been civilians,[1] and in *Half of a Yellow Sun*, Chimamanda Ngozi Adichie chooses to confront civil strife in Nigeria largely through the eyes of Biafra's civilian population. The author thus refuses the familiar heroic war narrative as it has been told from the exploits of Sundiata and Chaka to the cinematic adventure of *Days of Glory* (1944), replacing the traditional battlefield as her centre of interest with the domestic space of family life, which, if rarely the site of key military engagements, proves highly effective in illustrating the changing fortunes of a people at war.

In addition to the very real nature of civil war and its consequences for civilian populations, Adichie's decision to privilege domestic space might, in some archetypal way, be considered more generally a characteristic of writing by women, inasmuch as they have a tendency to privilege interior space. An early but often cited experiment by the psychologist Erik Erickson presented both boys and girls with toys

[1] Craig McLuckie's checklist (1987) is a good starting point for further reading of literature inspired by the war.

and a plot in order to examine gender differences. Girls focused on designing the interior of a house, situating people and animals within a closed area, 'in a static position that was peaceful' as opposed to boys' tendencies to transcend boundaries and to use the same toys aggressively and competitively. Erickson attributed this inclination to the differences in women's bodies, 'the provision of home and nurture for the 'other' ... being a basic aspect of woman's physical being' (Sweeny 2006, 135). In Igbo households in Nigeria, domestic space is the domain of the wife and, even among the elite, when women work outside the home, the organization of domestic work remains 'unquestionably gendered' and 'their husband's share of domestic work is minimal' (Okeke-Ihejirika 2004, 145). The focus on domestic space in the novel, whether a reflection of the writer's gender, the culture of the Igbo people, or the particular circumstances of the war, must necessarily produce a gendered view of the Biafran conflict.

Among the principal protagonists within the novel's rather sizeable cast of characters is Olanna, a university-educated Igbo woman whose household constitutes one of the focal points for the narration and whose domestic space becomes an essential theatre for the unfolding of events. With her partner and ultimately husband, Odenigbo, a professor of mathematics at the University of Nigeria in Nsukka at the time of Biafran secession, their daughter Baby, and the young houseboy Ugwu, Olanna experiences the displacement and deprivation that characterize many of Africa's civil wars and provide a crucial perspective from which to watch the changes taking place in her community. The purpose of this analysis will be to explore the evolution of Olanna's domestic space within the structure of the narrative both as a microcosm of the war's impact on the people and state of Biafra and as a stage for dramatizing post-independence social change, the nation metaphorically or metonymically represented by the home.

In very many ways, the displacement of Olanna's family reflects the various military successes of Nigeria in its campaign to reclaim its seceding Eastern territories. The couple celebrates the birth of Biafra on 30 May 1967, in Nsukka, a city that nurtured the secessionist movement and quickly became a key target for government troops hoping to demoralize the new republic by striking at its intellectual heart. By mid-July, the city had fallen. Olanna found herself taking refuge first in Odenigbo's hometown of Abba, and when that is threatened, in the resituated administrative and military capital of Umuahia where Odenigbo will be employed in war work until the town is evacuated in April 1969. Fleeing the advancing Nigerian army, the household relocates finally to Orlu, 'one of the largest remaining towns left on

Biafran-held territory' at the end of the war. The refugees move in with Olanna's sister, who had been obliged to flee Port Harcourt during the bombardment and has taken on the responsibility of provisioning a refugee shelter in Orlu. As these various urban centres fall to the Nigerian military, the contours of Biafra shrink and the remaining civilian population is squeezed into an ever smaller geographical space. Zdenek Cervenka observed: 'On May 30, 1969, the second anniversary of the declaration independence, Biafra's territory was only one-tenth of its original size, an area of barely 2,000 miles' (1972, 69). With the borders of the republic constantly in flux, the frequent dislocation of Olanna's household effectively mirrors that of the throngs of her compatriots who flood the roads before the advancing battalions. She and her family are forced to leave their home on multiple occasions, often with little or no preparation for the flight, and each time, she must completely set up housekeeping again. In each case, the circumstances of the family are reduced in much the same way that Biafra itself is eventually reduced to a mere enclave. John de St. Jorre estimates the population wedged into Biafra's remaining territory at the end to have been 'between three and four million' (1972, 404–5).

The passages describing the various homes that Olanna makes for the family constitute an important part of the chapters devoted to her perspective on the progress of events. As the daughter of a wealthy and politically influential chief, Olanna had been raised in a lavish setting and was accustomed to the privileges of the Nigerian elite. Her decision to set up housekeeping with her 'revolutionary' lover in the Eastern Region of the country was seen by her family as a lowering of her social status. While certainly not as grand as her parents' palatial ten-room mansion in Lagos with its army of servants, the university housing that she shares with Odenigbo on Odim Street in Nsukka prior to the outbreak of hostilities is nevertheless quite comfortable and spacious with its well-manicured lawn, flowering shrubs, and gardens. Thinking of the productive way that every plot of land was utilized back in his village, Ugwu is aghast at 'so much wasted space' (Adichie 2007, 19). In the house itself, there are three bedrooms, a study for Odenigbo's ample library, living and dining rooms, a bathroom with a bathtub, and a well-appointed kitchen. In the yard are quarters for the houseboy. Food is always plentiful in Nsukka before the war and is often at the heart of interactions between characters. Ugwu's discovery that meat is on the menu every day is highlighted in the very first paragraph of the novel's opening section. The ascension of Olanna as the new mistress of the household is dramatized by her volunteering to show Ugwu 'how to cook rice properly' (ibid., 23) after his efforts at fried rice result in a particularly tasteless meal, and the opening battle between Olanna and her future mother-in-law is waged in the kitchen where the latter has brought ingredients from the farm to make a 'proper soup' for her son. Olanna and Ugwu go regularly to the market for provisions, and hospitality is generous, with visitors being represented as much by their preferred beverages and eating habits as by their personalities and opinions. These passages provide useful information for the construction of the narrative in terms of setting and character development, but they are also valuable by virtue of the contrast that Adichie is establishing with the changing circumstances of the household and the decreasing availability of food as more of the country falls to the Federal Army and starvation and famine become veritable strategies of war.

Olanna and Odenigbo's home serves as a meeting place for political discussions among university intellectuals as events throughout Nigeria lead inevitably to a call for secession in the East, and the fall of Nsukka comes only shortly after Nigeria's announcement of a 'police action to bring back the rebels of Biafra' (ibid., 177). With an attack on the university town imminent, the family has only enough time to grab a few things and lock up before getting in the car to join other evacuees on the road: 'women with boxes on their heads and babies tied to their backs, barefoot children carrying bundles of clothes or yams or boxes, men dragging bicycles' (ibid., 179). For a time, Odenigbo's family home in Abba serves as a refuge, albeit a far humbler abode and far less modern. Olanna regrets 'the things left behind': 'her books, her piano, her clothes, her china, her wigs, her Singer sewing machine, the television', but learns not to talk about them, focusing instead on 'the win-the-war effort' (ibid., 185). Cooking is far simpler without the stove, toaster, pressure cooker and spices that she had not been able to bring with her. These and other tangible signs of her Western lifestyle, her education, and her family's wealth fall by the wayside in the face of changes wrought by the war. When the arrival of more refugees heralds the encroaching Nigerian forces, she instructs Ugwu to pack. He muses that 'they did not have much anyway, it was not like Nsukka where he had been paralyzed with so many choices that he had taken very little' (ibid., 194). Meredeth Turshen draws attention to displacement and dislocation as essential components of women's experience in intrastate wars: 'The number of people uprooted in Africa's civil wars is staggering: half the population of Liberia, half of Rwanda, five million Mozambicans' (1998, 15). During the Biafran conflict, 'more than 500,000 civilians became refugees or internally displaced persons' (Rubenzer 2007, 568). Olanna's experience is in many ways representative of those civilians as she once more dismantles her household only to be obliged to set up housekeeping again in unfamiliar surroundings and increasingly reduced circumstances.

In Umuahia, a colleague of Odenigbo's finds accommodation for him: a two-bedroom house with a thatch roof, unpainted walls, and a pit latrine in the outhouse. There is a kitchen, however, and living and dining rooms. The electricity is available until eight o'clock in the evening. When Ugwu observes that 'this is not a good house, mah' (Adichie 2007, 197), Olanna points out that many others are sharing houses. Umuahia will be one of the targets of the Federal Air Force, often accused by the press of indiscriminate bombing of civilians. While Nigeria eventually sought to address the situation, fatalities in 1968 were considerable. Cervenka quotes the Ghanaian *Evening Star* in its assertion that it was 'a crying shame of humanity to pursue the almost inhuman bombing of innocent children and women, such as characterized the recent stage of the war' (1972, 62). Adichie graphically illustrates the disruption of domestic bliss caused by the bombings. Having finally overcome her reservations about marriage, Olanna agrees at last to officially marry Odenigbo. Her wedding reception, postponed by the onset of war and eventually held in her new home in Umuahia, is interrupted by an air raid. There will be no photos of the bride because the photographer broke his camera in the confusion. The resulting insecurity will lead to a disturbing addition to what might normally be considered the family's domestic space, the construction of a bunker by Odenigbo and the men in the neighbourhood. Under the onslaught, Olanna threatens to spend all her time there, protecting Baby from the constant bombardment.

While her husband serves his new country by working at the Manpower Directorate and often goes into the countryside to rally the people, Olanna, like other housewives and mothers in the community, copes with circumstances that worsen with each day of the blockade and the increasing scarcities it brings. In ordinary times, the heavily populated parts of Eastern Nigeria had had to import food to provide adequate protein for the population. From the beginning of the war, therefore, the physical and economic isolation of the republic had become an important and effective part of the Nigerian strategy to force capitulation. The success of the blockade led not merely to shortages but to malnutrition and starvation, such that 'in December 1968, it was reliably estimated by the International Committee of the Red Cross that some 14,000 people were dying every day in Biafra' (Cervenka 1972, 48). This crisis attracted the attention of the outside world and brought humanitarian organizations into the conflict.

According to de St. Jorre, 'the resulting relief operation began to grow until by the summer of 1969 it had surpassed all other similar crises since the Second World War' (1972, 238). During the early part of the conflict, the family, considerably better off than many of its neighbours, is far from starvation, but the household changes perceptibly nevertheless as Olanna and Ugwu cope with the lack of available food and medicine. While hospitality had been virtually a daily affair in Nsukka, where Odenigbo's university friends gathered in his home to talk politics, Ugwu 'no longer served pepper soup or drinks' to visitors (Adichie 2007, 197). At breakfast, Odenigbo and Olanna share a single tea bag. When Baby falls ill, the doctor cannot provide the necessary antibiotic and sends Olanna to the black market, where women trade in enemy territory and necessities can be available – for a price. Olanna stands in line to obtain precious dried eggs from relief agencies with which to tempt Baby's waning appetite. Later, these agencies – the World Council of Churches, the Red Cross, Caritas – will become an important source of protein even for someone of Olanna's standing, complementing the normal marketing, although 'Ugwu hated relief food. The rice was puffy, nothing like the slender grains in Nsukka, and the cornmeal never emerged smooth after being stirred in hot water' (ibid., 283). By the time Biafra surrenders, roasted bush rat will be considered a delicacy.

Cynthia Cockburn has observed that the tendency for war to disrupt everyday life is peculiarly significant for women 'who in most societies have a traditional responsibility for the daily reproduction of life and community in ways that are both class and gender specific' (2004, 35). The male and female perspectives on the war reflect the different areas for which each member of the couple is responsible, as we see in Adichie's novel. Odenigbo focuses on the wider issues of the nation, while Olanna is preoccupied by the domestic realities of daily survival, making a home, feeding her family, and raising their child:

> His eyes saw the future. And so she did not tell him that she grieved for the past, different things on different days, her tablecloths with the silver embroidery, her car, Baby's strawberry cream biscuits. She did not tell him that sometimes when she watched Baby running around with the neighbourhood children, so helpless and happy, she wanted to gather Baby in her arms and apologize. (Adichie 2007, 262)

Olanna thus laments the loss of those objects that had allowed her take pride in her household, given her a sense of identity, and distinguished her in terms of class and privilege. She longs for them not only for herself, but also for her daughter, clearly feeling that she has failed in some essential way to provide as a mother. Throughout much of the war, however, she lives well compared to others in a town that is flooded with destitute refugees.

When the profiteering landlord decides to rent their house to a wealthier tenant, the family is again forced to move. Their new home is merely a single room in a long strip of a building with nine rooms side by side, each giving on to a narrow veranda. At one end, there is a kitchen; at the other, a communal bathroom. Privacy virtually disappears, as four people must adjust to sharing a small space together with only a thin curtain separating the adults' sleeping quarters from those of Baby and Ugwu. The neighbours include both natives of Umuahia and refugees, most of whom are relatively uneducated. One unit houses a family of sixteen people. Ugwu is conscripted, and Odenigbo, unable to cope with the prospect of failure and defeat, becomes increasingly depressed after the death of his mother at the hands of Nigerian soldiers. She had quite simply refused to leave her home, despite her son's urging. Her death illustrates the way that civil wars are so rarely limited to the actual battlefields more characteristic of the classic male war narrative, and it serves as just one more example in the novel of the intrusion of the war's violence into domestic space.

Without the accustomed support of her husband and houseboy, Olanna is thus left alone with the daily more arduous task of scavenging food for the family, standing in line at the relief centres, and even begging influential friends for help. It is at this point in the story that Olanna finds herself closest to the ordinary people. The evenings in the living room with a few Western-educated colleagues are no longer possible, and Olanna's social life moves to the veranda where she begins to know her less affluent neighbours, teaching their children English, sharing her precious care-packages from friends outside Biafra, learning survival strategies from those who have always had fewer opportunities and more challenges, and watching Baby as she plays with children who would never have been part of Olanna's social circle in the past. At the same time that the progress of the war and the toll it takes on the nation are given human dimensions by their depiction within Olanna's family, Adichie also provides a specific illustration of Biafra's ambition to create a more-democratic, egalitarian society as put forward in 'The Principles of the Biafran Revolution' (Ojukwu 1969). In her summary of the mythic vision that Biafra represented, Ann Marie Adams tells us: 'Biafra, as a theorized ideal, represents a country where all peoples, regardless of their tribal affiliations or ethnic heritage, can benefit from the wealth of their nation without being subject to the corruption of a national bourgeoisie' (2001, 292). Adichie shows that this dream did not succeed entirely, but that there may indeed have been progress. Instead of propagating the social structure inherited from the colonial period, a hierarchy that had placed Olanna and Odenigbo in a privileged position by virtue of their education and, in her case, her father's role as chief, the Biafran secession and its consequences had, at least for a time, reduced the social distance separating the couple from the average Biafran, uniting women especially in a sisterhood of common challenges and common needs.

After the fall of Umuahia, the family flees to Orlu where Olanna's twin Kainene takes her in. While the house itself is comfortable, day-to-day existence is now a struggle – even with the two women working together, and much of the action involves finding and preparing food or dealing with the deteriorating physical and mental condition of the family. Ugwu, wounded in battle, needs to be cared for. With overcrowded hospitals and inadequate medical services, Odenigbo and Olanna arrange for him to recuperate in Orlu. Baby's hair is turning red and falling out. Kainene, who is striving valiantly to supply a refugee centre rife with kwashiorkor, disappears when she crosses enemy lines to trade for provisions. These developments illustrate the critical scarcity of food at the end of the war. Whereas news of severe malnutrition in Biafra had earlier brought a response from the international community and relief organizations, by June 1969, the International Committee of the Red Cross had been obliged by the Nigerian government to suspend its flights. According to Cervenka, 'the drastic reduction in relief supplies was undoubtedly one of the factors in Biafra's collapse' (1972, 144). One of the novel's characters returning empty-handed from a visit to the relief centre tells Olanna: 'They said they have nothing and that our emphasis now is on self-sufficiency and farming' (Adichie 2007, 405). Olanna questions the feasibility of such a project in the now land-locked enclave that is only a fraction of its original size, and crowded with refugees.

When the war ends in January 1970, the family returns to Nsukka, where they find the house vandalized, its furnishings stolen, and the books burned, but it is still standing. Odenigbo and Olanna have suffered losses, but they have survived, and while Olanna, like thousands of refugees separated from loved ones during the hostilities, continues to search for her sister and regrets the loss of her bank account to the Nigerian government, there are signs that the household, intended perhaps to represent the nation, will return to some kind of normalcy. We are told that 'the weeks passed and the water started running again and the butterflies were back in the front yard and Baby's hair grew jet black. Boxes of books came for Odenigbo from overseas' (ibid., 432). Bronwen Walter asserts that 'the trope of family is widespread in the figuring of national narratives – homeland, motherland, daughters and sons of the nation' (1995, 37) and, in this instance at least, the house on Odin Street appears to stand for the republic itself, defeated and humiliated but capable of beginning again.

This analysis of the evolution of Olanna's domestic space in *Half of a Yellow Sun* shows the extent to which the Biafran war had implications for women's lives. On one hand, 'home' in the novel might well be viewed as 'nation,' serving figuratively to illustrate the displacement of peoples, the shrinking of the republic in the face of its loss of territory, the consequences of blockades and aerial bombardment, and the egalitarian dream that animated soldiers and civilians alike. On the other hand, this reading of Adichie's narrative dramatizes the real human dimension of the role that civilians and especially women played in the struggle, finding the courage to survive in the face of constant displacement, insecurity, and deprivation, and learning to depend on each other in a solidarity born of experience rather than ideology. As Adams phrased it so effectively in her study of Emecheta's texts, 'it may not be a woman's world ... but Biafra was a woman's war' (2001, 295). Adichie makes it hard to imagine a serious interpretation of this moment in Nigerian history that does not take into account the war's intrusion into domestic space and the catastrophic disruption of everyday existence.

Works Cited

Adams, Ann Marie. 'It's a Woman's War: Engendering Conflict in Buchi Emecheta's *Destination Biafra*'. *Callaloo* 24.1 (2001): 287–300.

Adichie, Chimamanda Ngozi. *Half of a Yellow Sun*. New York: Knopf, 2007.

Cervenka, Zdenek. *A History of the Nigerian War 1967–1970*. Ibadan: Onibonoje Press, 1972.

Cockburn, Cynthia. 'The Continuum of Violence: A Gender Perspective on War and Peace'. *Sites of Violence: Gender and Conflict Zones*. Eds Wenona Giles and Jennifer Hyndman. Berkeley, CA: University of California P, 2004: 24–44.

De St. Jorre, John. *The Nigerian Civil War*. London: Hodder & Stoughton, 1972.

McLuckie, Craig W. 'Preliminary Checklist of Primary and Secondary Sources on Nigerian Civil War / Biafran War Literature'. *Research in*

African Literatures 18.4 (1987): 510–27.

Ojukwu, Emeka. *The Ahiara Declaration: The Principles of the Biafran Revolution*. Geneva: Markpress, 1969.

Okeke-Ihejirika, Philomena E. *Negotiating Power and Privilege: Igbo Career Women in Contemporary Nigeria*. Ohio University Research in International Studies Africa Ser. 82. Athens, OH: Ohio University Press, 2004.

Sweeny, Kathleen Curran. 'The Perfection of Women as Maternal and the Anthropology of Karol Wojtyla.' *Logos: A Journal of Catholic Thought and Culture* 9.2 (2006): 129–53.

Rubenzer, Trevor. 'Nigeria (1967–70)'. *Civil Wars of the World: Major Conflicts since World War II*. Ed. Karl DeRouen, Jr., and Uk Heo. Vol. 2. Santa Barbara, CA: ABC-CLIO, 2007: 567–84.

Turshen, Meredeth. 'Women's War Stories'. *What Women Do in Wartime: Gender and Conflict in Africa*. Eds Meredeth Turshen and Clotilde Twagiramariya. London: Zed, 1998: 1–26.

United States Agency for International Development. Office of Women in Development. 'Intrastate Conflict and Gender'. *Gender Matters Information Bulletin* 9 (2000): 1–4.

Walter, Bronwen. 'Irishness, Gender, and Place'. *Environment and Planning D: Society and Space* 13.1 (1995): 35–50.

10

Corruption in Post-Independence Politics
Half of a Yellow Sun
as a Reflection of *A Man of the People*

CHIKWENDU PASCHALKIZITO ANYANWU

The publication of *Half of a Yellow Sun* (2007) ostensibly erased doubts in the minds of many critics that Chimamanda Ngozi Adichie has come as Chinua Achebe's literary progeny. Regarding this publication Joyce Carol Oates writes: 'a worthy successor to such twentieth century classics as Chinua Achebe's *Things Fall Apart*' (2007). However, a good number of readers were already certain about Achebe's profound influence on Adichie's writing with her first novel, *Purple Hibiscus*. Ike Anya titled his interview with Adichie 'In the Footsteps of Achebe: Enter Chimamanda Ngozi Adichie...' (2003). Anya's title certainly resonates with any reader who opens Adichie's first novel to see the opening line – 'Things started to fall apart' – evoking the title of Achebe's first novel, *Things Fall Apart*. To this, Heather Hewett responds:

> How better to alert the reader that familiar terrain – both the events and the Nigeria of Achebe's novel – will be rewritten and remapped? Adichie's rewriting pays homage to one of the forefathers of Nigerian literature (indeed, of Anglophone African literature) while it also challenges him. (Hewett 2005, 79)

Arguably, Adichie works on Achebe's ideologies and themes and it is not surprising that Achebe ascribed to her attributes associated with (Achebe) himself.

> We do not usually associate wisdom with beginners, but here is a new writer endowed with the gift of ancient storytellers. Chimamanda Ngozi Adichie knows what is at stake, and what to do about it ... She is fearless, or she would not have taken on the intimidating horror of Nigeria's civil war. Adichie came almost fully made. (Achebe 2007, blurb)

'With the gift of ancient storytellers' – Achebe does not differ from Oates in saying that *Half of a Yellow Sun* is a worthy successor to *Things Fall Apart* because the author of *Things Fall Apart* certainly possesses the gift of ancient storytellers. In writing *Things Fall Apart* (and his other novels) Achebe shows that he knows what is at stake and what to do about them. This is the sense Ernest Emenyonu evokes when in the late 1970s he held that Achebe was the only writer so far to deal with all the themes arising from Africa's contact with Europe 'in a progressive order' (1978, 103). Simon Gikandi also testifies to this when he writes that Achebe was the one 'able to capture the anxieties of many African readers in the 1950s' (2000, x). He was fearless and came fully made with his first novel successfully challenging the dominant (imperial) canon, and paved the way for successive African writers. With these similarities, and with Adichie's faithful admiration of Achebe as one of the greatest writers the world has produced (Anya 2003), reading Achebe in Adichie becomes predictable. In *Purple Hibiscus*, for instance, Adichie experiments with Achebe's dualism, the ideology of *ife kwulu, ife kwudebe ya*, or what Cynthia Wallace refers to as 'critique and embrace' (2013) in her treatment of Christianity and Igbo traditional religion. This paper further reveals how both authors are connected, while carefully examining their treatment of corruption in post-independence politics, even though Adichie, with the panoptic lens availed her by historical location, goes beyond Achebe's prophetic military coup to narrate the consequent civil war. Before drawing up the parallels, let us look at the political background of the 1960s when the two novels were set.

Nigeria in the 1960s was fraught with political unrest and anxieties, evaporating the pre-independence excitements and the hope of freedom from the excruciating colonial regime. Political independence from the colonial regime, as Achebe describes it, was a complete hoax (1979, 82). Consequently, Achebe upholds that the work of the writer was not done yet because 'he found himself with a new terrifying problem on his hands' – the emptiness of political independence and the will of the colonial master being propelled by black stooges (ibid.). With his trilogy in direct confrontation with colonial regime, the post-independence politics posed a different kind of problem because the colonial masters were in remote control of the so-called indigenous government. Frantz Fanon explains why:

> The national middle class which takes over power at the end of the colonial regime is an under-developed middle class. It has practically no economic power, and in any case it is in no way commensurate with the bourgeoisie

of the mother country which it hopes to replace. In its wilful narcissism, the national middle class is easily convinced that it can advantageously replace the middle class of the mother country. But that same independence which literally drives it into a corner will give rise within its ranks to catastrophic reactions, and will oblige it to send out frenzied appeals for help to the former mother country. (1963, 120)

Chinweizu refers to this national middle class as petit-bourgeois Africans or African moderates, groomed 'for their new duties as local foremen and gendarmerie for the European bourgeoisie' (1987, 160).

In Nigeria, Achebe writes that Britain made certain they handed over power to the North that contributed nothing to the independence struggle (1975, 82). Adichie re-echoes this very succinctly: 'The British preferred the North' (2007, 115). Alexander Madiebo observes that, out of nineteen major military installations, seventeen were located in the North, with one each in the East and the West. It was only in 1965 that two installations were moved from the North to the West, 'after the political coming into being of the Sardauna-Akintola alliance' (1980, 10). In government, Eghosa E. Osaghae writes that the North was granted 50 percent (later increased to 52 percent) of the seats in the House of Representatives, meaning 'that the region could single-handedly obtain the dominant position under the majoritarian system the country inherited at independence' (1998, 6). According to a colonial administrator at the time, Harold Smith: 'The chosen people were totally unprepared for independence' (1991); but that was to ensure the British retained remote control of the colony. In this lies the emptiness of the independence to which the people looked forward.

In 'Pitfalls of National Consciousness' Fanon explains that the period preceding independence is always one of hope as natives see their struggles as the panacea that would terminate colonial abuses like 'forced labour, corporal punishment, inequality of salaries, limitation of political rights, etc.' (1963, 133). However, as soon as the independence is granted, the people realize that those who had been champions of freedom and embodiments of public aspirations are no more than egoists wishing to 'become the president of profiteers' (ibid., 133) and the rules change to: 'All animals are equal but some animals are more equal than others' (Orwell, 2003, 97).

Post-independence Africa became a period of disillusionment, which, Ngugi observes, also engulfed the African writer (1986, 10). It led to a breakdown in the relationship between the creative artist, who used his art to advance the call for self-government, and the political nationalist who the artist now perceives as having betrayed the cause.

This betrayal, in Obiechina's words, 'infused in the writers a certain radicalism as well as a sharpening of their social instincts' (1990, 123), which probably helped them to overcome disillusionment. Achebe's response was *A Man of the People* (1988); Wole Soyinka and Ayi Kwei Armah responded with *The Interpreters* (1965) and *The Beautyful Ones Are Not Yet Born* (1968), respectively. These novels more than anything else expose the corrupt politicians in the post-independence era, accusing them of

> expropriating from the masses the fruits of independence, and more specifically, of being venal, corrupt, irresponsible, hypocritical, and without vision and common sense. The failure of independence is regarded as evidence of the failure of the elite to justify themselves to the masses and validate their claim to leadership. (Obiechina 1990, 123)

'Within six years of independence', Achebe writes, 'Nigeria was a cesspool of corruption and misrule. Public servants helped themselves freely to the nation's wealth' (1975, 82). Consequently, young military officers, led by Chukwuma Kaduna Nzeogwu, struck on 15 January 1966 to bring an end to corruption (cf. Ademoyega, 1981, 63). The coup, however, was branded an Igbo coup, and a counter coup led by Murtala Mohammed was effected on 28 July of the same year, claiming the life of the Head of State, General Aguiyi Ironsi and leading to the massacre of soldiers from the Eastern Region, the pogrom on their civilians, the birth of Biafra and the war to bring Biafra back to Nigeria.

Writing *A Man of the People* within this period, Achebe could only forecast the future but only wished that the new independent nation came out of it better and wiser; but it came off worse. This is probably why Adichie, a post-war child, considers it important to get the whole picture and, in doing so, revises the theme of corruption as presented by Africa's foremost novelist before advancing into the events that brought the decade to a miserable conclusion.

A *Man of the People* introduces us to a government totally dominated by corrupt politicians, with Chief Micah A. Nanga as a prototype. He dishonestly becomes a minister by leading the pack of back-bench hounds that 'yapped and snarled shamelessly' for the empty ministerial seats created by the exit of the more honest and intellectual ministers (1988, 5–7). The intellectual ministers are forced and hounded out of Parliament by the ruling party that wants to retain power by all means.

The absence of intellectuals at the helm of affairs in the country is thus captured in *Half of a Yellow Sun*: 'The new Nigerian upper class is a collection of illiterates who read nothing' (2007, 64). Chief Ozobia, the father of Kainene and Olanna, fits into this picture when Susan, the British expatriate talks about him to Richard:

> Chief Ozobia owns half of Lagos but there is something terribly *nouveau riche* about him. He doesn't have much of a formal education, you see, and neither has his wife. I suppose that's what makes him obvious. (2007, 59)

Chief Ozobia represents the new Nigerian elite and is ostentatious like Nanga, 'that corrupt, empty-headed, illiterate capitalist' (1988, 74), throwing and attending parties and dinners. When Ozobia invites Chief Okonji, the finance minister, to a dinner, it is with the intention of being awarded a building contract, and he would stop at nothing, even using Olanna, the beautiful one, as bait. In the manner of a corrupt minister, Okonji offers Olanna a place in the ministry at a party at the Ikoyi Club, and seeks her consent at her parents' dinner table. This calls to mind Chief Nanga's invitation to Odili to find him scholarship through the back door. While Odili accepts Nanga's invitation, Olanna declines Okonji's offer, preferring a lecturing job at the University of Nigeria, Nsukka. Adichie's physical description of Okonji as one who appears to salivate when he smiles, suggests an unpolished fellow, who must have been used to replace the first-rate economist in *A Man of the People*. In his narrative, Achebe writes about the sacking of the excellent Minister of Finance, with newspapers supporting the Prime Minister, agreeing one does not need to be an economist to be a finance minister (1988, 4). It is my opinion that Adichie fully understands her duty of complementing her forebear, taking advantage of her historical location that offers her a panoptic view of the events of the 1960s. Adichie, sometimes, fills the gaps with what is known in history and other times with her imagination. In *Half of a Yellow Sun*, she depicts the kind of man that replaces the finance minister sacked in *A Man of the People*; she names the minister and uses the real name of the Prime Minister at the time, Balewa, just as she does with the names of the principal actors during the revolution, such as Nzeogwu, Gowon, Ojukwu and Zik. Achebe's fictitious Bori is replaced with the real name, Lagos. Minister Okonji tells the Ozobias of his meeting with Balewa, to signify his closeness to the Prime Minister and, of course, boost his ego – and perhaps to woo Olanna. The connection Adichie constructs here – Ozobia–Okonji–Balewa – is her illustration of Achebe's comment on post-independence society: 'A common saying in the country after independence was that it didn't matter *what* you knew but *who* you knew' (1988, 17). Odili is educated but knows nobody and so languishes in a village school, while Ozobia, an illiterate, owns half of Lagos and large businesses in the East, not because of 'what' he knows but because of 'who' he knows.

The finance minister is so involved in the corrupt practices of the government that when the soldiers struck, Okonji is one of those killed. The news of Okonji's death excites Odenigbo and his guests who had gathered to celebrate the coup; and they chuckle, showing that Okonji is one of the corrupt figures the public despises. 'This is the end of corruption!' one of the guests exclaims (Adichie 2007, 123). Olanna speaks with a subdued voice, hearing of Okonji's death and is afraid that her parents might be killed, too, because she knows they are part of the corrupt system, having heard the leader of the revolution, Major Nzeogwu, announce that

> the aim of the Revolutionary Council is to establish a nation free from corruption and internal strife. Our enemies are the political profiteers, the swindlers, the men in high and low places that seek bribes and demand ten percent. (Adichie 2007, 123)

Odenigbo reassures the anxious Olanna: 'Your parents are fine, *nkem*. Civilians are safe.' Here, Odenigbo excludes politicians from civilians. Adichie defines a politician as a *politician*. There is a tone of monstrosity in what the houseboy, Ugwu, thinks about politicians, and he therefore finds it difficult to console Olanna over Okonji's demise:

> He wished he could truly feel sorry for her friend the politician who has been killed, but politicians were not like normal people, they were *politicians*. He read about them in the *Renaissance* and *Daily Times* – they paid thugs to beat opponents, they bought land and houses with government money, they imported fleets of long American cars, they paid women to stuff their blouses with false votes and pretend to be pregnant. Whenever he drained a pot of boiled beans, he thought of the slimy sink as *politician*. (Adichie 2007, 126)

With this passage, Adichie suggests that she consciously skipped the election that took place within that period, which led to the revolution. She seems to say she is contented with commenting on the story Achebe had already provided about politicians and the election. In *A Man of the People*, politicians like Nanga and Odili employ thugs; Nanga uses government money to build a four-storeyed house, has a Cadillac (an American car) and a fleet of buses. More striking is Adichie's mention of women who 'stuff their blouses with false votes'. This parodies Achebe in the passage that reports the violence that claims the life of Max (leader of Odili's party, CPC) while investigating the report that Chief Koko's wife was using women to 'breast-feed the ballot box, i.e. smuggling wads of ballot paper concealed in their brassieres into the polling booths' to favour her husband (Achebe 1988, 142). Comparing the two passages reveals Adichie's comic instincts at work, for she seems to say to her master that women are first delivered before they breast-feed. Heather Hewett is, therefore, correct in stating that Adichie does not only rewrite Achebe, she also challenges him (2005).

In keeping with her faithful discipleship, Adichie adapts Achebe's metaphor of the small thief to satirize society's attitude to corruption. The small thief is in great danger while the big thief is glorified. In *A Man of the People*, some critics of the novel consider as the central metaphor, the story of Josiah, the shopkeeper, who steals the blind man's walking stick to make a charm that would attract more customers. Achebe uses it to contradict and criticize the new 'nation' founded by the colonial regime as lacking the basic moral principles that can keep corruption in check. While Josiah is ostracized for his corrupt practice, the people beat drums and dance for Nanga who is stealing from them on a much higher scale and, when Josiah aligns himself to Nanga, no one raises an eyebrow. Bernth Lindfors observes that, 'Unlike the village where the unscrupulous Josiah is quickly and effectively outlawed, the country as a whole has no kind of political morality by which to judge and condemn a Nanga' (1978, 260). There is a mirroring of this irony in *Half of a Yellow Sun* when Mrs Ozobia is on the verge of sacking one of their house helps for stealing a few cups of rice, but for Olanna's intervention. Olanna asks the servant who has been kneeling and pleading, to stand up and then challenges her mother: 'Mum, if you're going to sack him, then sack him and have him go right away'. Mrs Ozobia could not face the challenge and, therefore, tells the servant that she is giving him another chance. Reflecting on this incident, Olanna says to Odenigbo:

> My father and his politician friends steal money with their contracts, but nobody makes them kneel to beg for forgiveness. And they build houses with their stolen money and rent them out to people like this man and charge inflated rents that make it impossible to buy food. (2007, 221)

This trend is very common in contemporary Nigeria. Often, there are stories, videos – especially through social media – about mobs setting petty thieves on fire while politicians and their associates who steal billions of money are adored and glorified. Thieves are heavily punished in the village, but the same people hail national thieves, and Achebe reasons that it is because the village has a mind and could say no to sacrilege there, but 'in the affairs of the nation there was no owner, the laws of the village became powerless'. Gikandi relates that Achebe, in writing this novel, observed that

> the world ushered in by political independence had been one of estrange-ment and confusion for African peoples. Independence, noted Achebe, had begotten a pulverized reality in which the gap between nationalist rhetoric and political practice was becoming obvious, and it was difficult for people to get a grip of the 'new cloud' that had appeared on the African sky. (Gikandi 1991, 113)

It becomes all too confusing for the people can only say 'let them eat', since they did not commit suicide when the white man was eating alone (Achebe 1988, 144). Pre-independence propaganda convinced the common people that the colonial regime was oppressive and denied them of the fruits of their labour. However, the African poli-ticians, who appeared as benevolent patriots bringing the colonial maltreatment to an end, did little or nothing to change the status quo and improve the condition of the ordinary people. Under the indige-nous politicians, leadership was translated into eating and nationhood defined as cake-sharing with 'self-interest masquerading as Africani-zation' (Lindfors 1978, 258). The African politicians enriched them-selves through corrupt means at the expense of the masses, and the people were unable to control them because the new form of govern-ment introduced by the West was very strange to them.

In *A Man of the People*, through the story of Josiah and the blind man's walking stick, Achebe shows that enriching oneself through corrupt means and being out of control is detestable in the traditional Igbo society. It is true that materialism has been one of the charac-teristics of the Igbo before the advent of Europeans, but the spiritual dimension of Igbo life was strong enough to keep materialism under control (Achebe 1978, 11), such that no one could hold his place in the community if his source of wealth became questionable. This is the major lesson of the first Igbo novel, *Omenụkọ* (Pita Nwana 1933, see Chapter 1), where the hero had to escape into exile after selling his apprentices. This traditional condemnation is heard in the voice of Odenigbo's mother concerning Olanna's father, when she visits to take control of her son's destiny, albeit, through diabolic means.

> I heard her father came from a family of lazy beggars in Umunnachi until he got a job as a tax collector and stole from hard-working people. Now he has opened many businesses and is walking around in Lagos and answering a Big Man. (Adichie, 2007, 97)

In *A Man of the People*, Achebe uses the masquerade metaphor to explain how the moral principles of traditional religion keep the social elements in check against excesses.

> While the Mask danced here and there brandishing an outsized matchet the restraining rope round his waist came undone. One might have expected this sudden access to freedom to be followed by a wild rampage and loss of life and property. But the Mask tamely put his matchet down, helped his disciples retie the rope, picked up his weapon again and resumed his dance. (ibid., 97)

Symbolically, Achebe condemns the political 'masquerades' (*nnukwu mmanwu* as they are called in Igbo) that are uncontrollably corrupted. A corrupt masquerade, in essence, is ironic because masquerades in precolonial Igbo society were political agents, performing religious and social duties. Their spiritual (religious) dimension, symbolized by the rope tied around their waists (Killam 1977, 87–8), controlled their social dimension – and therefore they knew how to behave even with their 'outsized matchets'. Even as colonization and Christianity did much harm to the restraining rope of religion that it 'came undone', Achebe observes that the traditional masquerades were still guided by the moral principles of traditional religion.

This masquerade phenomenon in Achebe, I suppose, fascinated Adichie such that she takes to a hermeneutical re-presentation of the metaphor to the readers of both novels, with a view to calling their attention to its symbolic value. Achebe only tells the story and leaves it to his readers to discover its raison d'être within the narrative, but Adichie takes one more step to prompt the reader:

> Mr Richard took photographs, wrote in his notebook and asked questions, one after another – what was that called and what did they say and who were those men holding back the *mmuo* with a rope and what did that mean [...] (Adichie 2007, 211)

It is arguable whether the *ori-okpa* festival, to which Ugwu took Richard, is integral to the story of *Half of a Yellow Sun* and if it moves the story forward. Adichie, in my view, includes the festival in order to make Achebe more accessible, aware of the cultic nature of Achebe's 'simple' language.

Furthermore, Achebe uses marriage relationships as a subplot in the discourse, and so does Adichie. In *A Man of the People*, the marriage between Nanga and Edna collapses just as does the marriage between

Odenigbo and Amala in *Half of a Yellow Sun*. These are forced unions and one can hear both authors questioning Nigeria's legitimacy as a nation, having been forced together by the colonial regime. In this way, colonialism is indicted as the root cause of corruption and injustice in post-independent Nigeria.

In forcing their children into inadequate relationships, Edna's father (Achebe 1988) and Odenigbo's mother (Adichie 2007) act like the colonialists who coerce nations bereft of cultural homogeneity into one government (Appiah 1992, 161–2), thereby creating a nameless country without a 'mind' (Achebe 1988), which Adichie translates into a nameless 'Baby'. She describes Nigeria at independence as 'a collection of fragments held in a fragile clasp' (Adichie 2007, 155). What Odenigbo's mother does, using 'charm' to force Amala on her son, produces a chain reaction that destroys a web of relationships, as Odenigbo's act leads Olanna to sleep with Richard, her twin sister's boyfriend. Through these subplots we discover the authors' thesis that, (i) colonial regime is at the root of corruption in post-independent Nigeria: Achebe identifies Britain and America in this regard (1988, 126) and Adichie is convinced that Balewa, the Prime Minister, is Britain's stooge (2007, 110); (ii) corruption leads to destruction – not only of life and property but also of mutual trust. Thus, Edna abandons Nanga for Odili (Achebe 1988, 144–6) and Olanna realizes that distrust would always lie between her and Odenigbo (Adichie 2007, 244). In like manner, Major Madu declares to Kainene after the massacres of Igbo soldiers: 'Igbo soldiers and Northern soldiers can never live in the same barracks after this. It is impossible, impossible' (ibid., 140). This is the effect of corruption: it destroys existing relationships but the creative artist remains optimistic and seeks a way for regeneration.

To reverse the situation, the two writers had to discard the 'enforced but welcome journey' of the 'African petite bourgeoisie' that wanted independence at all costs (Chinweizu 1987: 160) by proposing unions without compulsion. In Achebe, the parties involved go through the required rituals as in the final union between Odili and Edna to realize a new 'nation', true to its etymology of a people born into relationships (Renan 1990, 9–10). Adichie, however, is contented with enough expressions of good intentions to follow the right processes in entering into a union as in the case of Odenigbo and Olanna. They wed in church when the war situation makes it difficult for them to carry out the traditional rites. It is good enough that they have the right intention, that they are truly reconciled. In comparison with Achebe, Adichie employs romance and marriage as subplot, but in the use of explicit sex, she again shows that she is not only interested in rewriting Achebe, but also in challenging him as she discards his modesty and cultural sensitivity.

The structure of *Half of a Yellow Sun*, which tasks the memory, is one great testimony of Adichie's revisionary mission of Achebe's work. By taking her reader back and forth, in time and space, Adichie again offers a graphic illustration of her literary forefather's invitation to go back and find out where the rain began to beat us. *A Man of the People* is a narrative in reminiscence. In reminiscence, we discover colonialism at the root of it all, enforcing unmatchable relationships that gave rise to unjust and corrupt governments; and as far as injustice and corruption are continuously adding more destructive horns to their monstrous heads as in Nigeria, a piquant revision of earlier writings on this theme will always be a welcome project.

Adichie's rewriting of *A Man of the People* is a good example of interpretation of a work of art with another work of art. For instance, one of the remarkable things about *A Man of the People* is that its publication coincided with the predicted military coup, and art and life, fiction and reality, became one. Adichie expresses this coincidence by her mix of real and fictitious names in *Half of a Yellow Sun*. The major difference between the two novels is the war narrative which Adichie embarked on, but which Achebe could not write about in *A Man of the People* because it happened later. Adichie believes that the war has remained up to this day, a determining factor in Nigerian politics and policies (Adichie 2006) – are considered brazenly unjust and corrupt. Placed against the post-war conditions of the defeated Biafra, the policies make no sense of the post-war slogans of 'No Victor, No Vanquished!' and of the 'three Rs' of reconciliation, rehabilitation and reconstruction. As a result, Achebe writes:

> I believe that in our situation the greater danger lies not in remembering but in forgetting, in pretending that slogans are the same as truth; and that Nigeria, always prone to self-deception, stands in great need of reminders. (Achebe 1975)

Adichie emerges as one of those great reminders in a Nigeria where collective amnesia has become a major malaise, with History pushed aside as a subject in secondary schools; and, like a faithful disciple in adherence to the master's voice, or, rather a literary offspring who grew up in the same house her forebear lived in at the University of Nigeria, Nsukka, Adichie dubs *Half of a Yellow Sun*, 'my refusal to forget' (BBC 2007). Day after day, injustice and corruption in Nigeria, refuse to give concerned minds any reason to forget. It is corruption and injustice that have tilled and fertilized the soil for the continuous springing up of groups, militant and non-militant, agitating for secession in Nigeria. Based on this uncertainty and Nigeria's apparent unwillingness to make amends, Adichie strikes a strong note by ending her story with the disappearance of Kainene, whose name means 'Let us wait and see!'

Works Cited

Achebe, C., *A Man of the People*. African Writers series. London: Heinemann, 1998 [1971].

—. *Morning Yet on Creation Day*. Lon/Ibadan: Heinemann Educational Books, 1975a: xiii.

—. 'The Role of the Writer in a New Nation' in G. D. Killiam (ed), African Writers on African Writing, London, Heineman, 1978: 11.

—. 'blurb'. In Adichie, C., *Half of a Yellow Sun*. New York: Harper Perennial, 2007.

Ademoyega, A. *Why We Struck: The Story of the First Nigerian Coup*. Ibadan: Evans Brothers, 1981: 63.

Adichie, C. N. 'Audio Interview with Mariella Frostrup', BBC Radio 4, 20 August, 2006.

—. *Half of a Yellow Sun*. New York: Harper Perennial, 2007.

Anya, I, 'In the Footsteps of Achebe: Enter Chimamanda Ngozi Adichie, Nigeria's Newest Literary Voice' (Interview), www.nigeriansinamerica.com/in-the-footsteps-of-achebe-enter-chimamanda-ngozi-adichie-nigerias-newest-literary-voice-2, 10 October 2003.

Appiah, K. A. *In My Father's House: Africa in the Philosophy of Culture*. Oxford: Oxford University Press, 1992: 161–2.

BBC NEWS, 'Award Surprises Nigerian Author', http://news.bbc.co.uk/2/hi/africa/6729435.stm 7 June 2007.

Chinweizu, *The West and the Rest of Us*. (New edn). Lagos: Pero Press, 1987: 160.

Emenyonu, E. *The Rise of the Igbo Novel*. Ibadan: Oxford University Press, 1978: 103.

Fanon, F. *The Wretched of the Earth* (trans. Constance Farrington). Harmondsworth: Penguin Books, 1963: 120.

Gikandi, S, *Reading Chinua Achebe, Language and Ideology in Fiction*. London and Portsmouth, NH: James Currey and Heinemann, 1991: 113.

Gikandi, Simon. 'Achebe and the Invention of African Literature'. In Achebe, C. *Things Fall Apart* (reprint) Oxford: Heinemann, 2000: x.

Hewett, H. 'Coming of Age: Chimamanda Ngozi Adichie and the Voice of the Third Generation'. In *English in Africa*, 32.1 (May 2005): 79.

Killam, G. D. *The Writings of Chinua Achebe*. London: Heinemann Educational, 1977: 87–8.

Lindfors, B. 'Achebe's African Parable'. In Innes, C. L. and Lindfors, B. (eds), *Critical Perspectives on Chinua Achebe*. Washington DC: Three Continents Press, 1978: 258.

Madiebo, A. A. *The Nigerian Revolution and the Biafran War*. Enugu: Fourth Dimension Publishers, 1980: 10.

Ngugi, *Writing Against Neocolonialism*. London: Vita Books, 1986: 10.

Oates, J. C., 'blurb', in Adichie, C, *Half of a Yellow Sun*, New York: Harper Perennial, 2007.

Obiechina, E. N. *Language and Theme: Essays on African Literature*. Washington DC: Howard University Press, 1990: 123.

Orwell, G. *Animal Farm*. London: Penguin, 2003 [1945]: 97.

Osaghae, E. E. *Crippled Giant: Nigeria Since Independence*. London: Hurst & Co, 1998: 6.

Renan, E. 'What is a Nation?' in Bhabha H. K. (Ed.). *Nation and Narration*., London: Routledge, 1990: 9-10 quoted from Raymond William, *The Year 2000*. (New York: Pantheon, 1983.

Smith, H. 'Rigging of Nigeria's Independence Elections by the British Government'. www.biafraland.com/harold_smith/harold_smith_frm.htm. 28 November 1991.

Wallace, C. R., 'Chimamanda Ngozi Adichie's *Purple Hibiscus* and the Paradoxes of Postcolonial Redemption'. *Christianity and Literature* 61.3 (Spring 2012).

11 .

Contrasting Gender Roles in Male-Crafted Fiction with *Half of a Yellow Sun*

CAROL IJEOMA NJOKU

During wars, women are ubiquitous and highly visible; when wars are over and songs are sung, women disappear.
Linda Grant De Pauw – *Battle Cries and Lullabies*, 1966

Sedimented lore – stories of male war fighters and women home keepers and designated weepers and weepers over wars' inevitable tragedies – have spilled over from one epoch to the next.
Jean Bethke Elshtain – *Women and War with a new Epilogue*, 1995

The first act of the feminist critic must be to become a resisting rather than an assenting reader and, and by this refusal to assent, to begin the process of exorcising the male mind that has been implanted in us.
Judith Fetterly – *The Resisting Reader*, 1998

Jean Bethke Elshtain's book *Women and War with a new Epilogue* remains one of the subversive attempts that resonate with the orthodox construction of masculinity and femininity in the American war narratives. The binary construction of masculinity and femininity, as Elshtain argues, flows from a tradition 'that assumes affinity between women and peace, between men and wars, a tradition that consists of culturally constructed and transmitted myths and memories … the personas of just Warriors and Beautiful Souls' (1995, 4). Hegemonic masculinity is built upon this traditional paradigm that 'embodies legitimacy of a patriarch – domination of men and subordination of women' (Connell 2005, 77). The problematic of such persuasive gender dichotomies imposed upon war narratives dominant (orthodox) images of male warrior / female victim, male combatants / female non-combatant, male life takers / female life givers and comfort givers, male aggres-

153

sors / female peace makers. These male-constructed binaries project war and military exploits as exclusive male preserve, and disavow the identity of bellicose females. Nigerian war narratives, particularly the male-authored narratives, borrowed heavily from this tradition. Elshtain critically revisited the scene of World War II and the American Civil history to liberate female heroines swallowed in the wilderness of masculine mythological history. Despite the fundamental difference in time and space, the Nigerian female authors provoked by simultaneity of female activism have raised their voices in counter-narratives – Flora Nwapa's *Never Again* (1975), *Wives at War and Other Stories* (1992); Buchi Emecheta's *Destination Biafra* (1982); and Rose Adaure Njoku's *Withstand the Storm: War Memoirs of a Housewife* (1986) – to retell the war stories from women's perspectives. The subversive attempts by 'these Igbo women writers contributed a great deal in addressing the silences but 'de-authorized female heroism and failed to pay attention to class inequalities/struggles and their impact on speech (de)legitimation' (Nnaemeka 1997, 261). Since the question of narrative – authenticity – is a demand for narrative, the unfinishedness of narrative (Derrida 2004, 85), this paper explores Chimamanda Ngozi Adichie's *Half of a Yellow Sun* as intervention into Nigerian war narratives – a rediscovery of the Nigeria-Biafra female heroine.

War and gender reality are complex issues that cannot be thoroughly captured in a mythic narrative. The reality of war is far more complex than portrayed in the traditional narratives. Gender fragmentation in war is even more complex than what the masculinized myth can espouse. As Carol Cohen profoundly acknowledged in *Women and War*, women's role in and experience of war are far more integral and complex considering their diverse individual identities, options and experiences shaped by such other factors as type of war, age, economic class, interest, race, clan, belief, ethnicity, religion, culture, sexuality, physical ability, geographical location, state citizenship and national identity (2013, 2). To romanticize war with traditional assumptions of masculinity and femininity implies that the real images of women in war can never be known; such has been the case with Biafra women in the Nigerian war novels.

Paradoxically, the myth of militarized masculinity makes women invisible at wartime. In the Nigeria-Biafra situation, the myth is bolstered by the Igbo maxim of *nwoke luchaa ogu nwanyi enwere akuko* meaning 'the men fight war, the women (as purveyors of war narrative) narrate the stories of men's exploits in warfare'. This orthodox myth imposed upon women the task of narrative in order to valorize male heroism, and foregrounds an implied metaphor that associate

women with gossip or praise singing. Storytelling, is therefore, meta-
phorized as an indoor activity for idle and protected women and children. The storyteller narrates her tales not as an eyewitness but as
a second class narrator because she/they are excluded from being
participant observers. The same traditional assumption of femininity
and masculinity punctuates the Nigeria-Biafra war narratives, as will
be seen in *The Combat* (Omotoso 2008), *The Last Duty* (Okpewho
1981) and *Girls at War* (Achebe 1988). These narratives feature the
traditional paradigm of 'arms and the man', which undermines
women's significant roles as combatants, leaders, decision makers
and active participants in war and national struggles. Derrida's epistemology of narrative insist upon representational truth and exactness,
conceptualized as '*the question of narrative ... with the demand for narrative
... Tell us exactly what happened*' (2004, 72, emphasis added). Our
task in this study is to deconstruct the author's navigation of truth in
the construction of female identities in the Nigerian war narratives
and the subversive reconstruction of 'patriarchal truth' particularly
in Adichie's *Half of a Yellow Sun* (2007).

Kole Omotoso's *The Combat* is an allegoric male narrative of the
Nigeria-Biafra war that recreates a paradoxical myth of a combat
between two male protagonists Ojo Dada and Chuku Debe. The duo
allegorically represent the two warring parties of the Nigeria-Biafra
war – General Odumegwu Ojukwu and General Yakubu Gowon (also
described in the novel as His Excellency and His Other Excellency
– HE and HOE) (2008, 17). The intended combat between these
male protagonists is a prevailing theme in the novel that initiates a
metaphor of 'valorized male warriors'. The combat ensues from their
inability to resolve a conflict relating to an alleged bloodshed – the
blood of Isaac (ibid., 19), which allegorically symbolizes the gruesome
bloodshed during the anti-Igbo pogrom of 1966. The alleged murder
of Isaac, a mythical child, vagabond, and son of a sexually-exploited
female hawker, Moni (*Moniker*) becomes the pivot in which the plot
of 'combat' continues to unfold. The story is intertwined in a satir-
ical allegory in which Moni is made both a victim and object of caricature. She is a victim of Ojo Dada and Chuku Debe's collaborative
sexual exploitations that later result in her early pregnancy, a protracted
court case to contest the child's paternity, the court's verdict against
her wish, her later ordeals, and those of her neglected child resulting
in his murder while a street boy. Moni is a street hawker in the novel.
She later becomes a society lady – De Madam – through dubious
money theft. But her character remains stunted and insignificant in the
fictional universe. The novel continuously ridicules her because of her

gender and persistently characterizes her as perverse, mindless, naïve, voiceless and insensitive.

The name, Moni, is an abridged word for *Moniker* which refers to money. Her body is portrayed as a potential resource for trade, and 'the male combatants' traded on her at will. Her image in this regard replicates the character of Aku in Isidore Okpewho's *The Last Duty* whose body becomes the most accessible battlefront for a debased male. To enhance the use of female caricature against the female protagonist, Omotoso's novel portrays *Moniker* as a vendor of her own body who unscrupulously sells her body either in cash or credit for monetary reward.

Moni came to realize that she has natural resources that seemed to be crying out for exploitation. But her limited horizon was only interested in the few shillings some of the men who picked her up readily gave her. Later she got into the hands of those men she came to label as 'do-now and-pay-later... But by this time she had begun to enjoy herself and was prepared merely to reckon, in her fingers, the amount of shillings these men owed her' (Omotoso 2004, 61).

An irony is intended by citing the above quotation. It is not cited as a realistic portrayal of images of the Biafran war but to reveal the serious epistemic violence that undermines women's genuine struggles for survival. Omotoso is not alone in such violent misrepresentation of women as notorious prostitutes and unconscionable wealth-seekers. Okpewho's *The Last Duty* reproduces the image of another helpless and vulnerable woman, Aku, who resorts to sexual trade as her viable means for surviving the hardships of war in the course of her husband's protracted incarceration:

> My skin is firm; my breasts are still handful ... I cannot now in all honesty say it would never come to the mind of any man to want me ... if I am at their mercy, and I know I am, then I should be prepared to accept their moods. (1981, 62–3)

The recurrent phenomenon of objectifying female characters as either chattels for men's gratification, battle ground for the display of men's sexual dominance, or other pictures of gender-based abuses are common features in the Biafran war narratives that foreground the myth of masculine hegemony. The mythic images characterize women with contemptible stereotypes that mirror them as weak, gullible and irresponsible.

In Achebe's *Girls at War* (1988), another male-crafted narrative, the myth is exaggerated in the metaphor of a debased war, infecting its female personages with a sickness that drags them through serious transformational dilemma. The female protagonist, Gladys, begins her exploit as a militia girl but later joins the band of female prostitutes who are 'ready to tumble into bed at the sight of stockfish and American dollar' (ibid., 116). The notoriety shown in her encounter with Reginald Nwankwo forms the basis for assessing her moral dilemma and inability to sustain patriotic spirit at wartime:

> She gave him a shock by the readiness with which she followed him to bed and by her language.

> 'You want to shell?' she asked. And without waiting for an answer she said, Go ahead but don't pour in troops!'

> What a terrible transformation in the short period of less than two years! (ibid., 119)

> '... You girls are fighting a war, aren't you?' (ibid., 114).

The predominant images of female degradation depicted in the three Biafran war narratives suggest a calculated attempt to create gender bias or what Akachi Adimora Ezeigbo describes as the myth of 'female annihilation and male self-realization'. There is no doubt that the Nigeria-Biafra war imposed unprecedented hardships on women left to shoulder the responsibilities of home-making, bread-winning, humanitarian services and community development. However, these women embarked on several improvised strategies that included 'attack trading', farming, social mobilization and win-the-war synergies as means of survival. Those who went into prostitution did so to feed themselves and their families. Egodi Uchendu testifies to 'those [Aniocha Biafra women] who yield to the pressure of the time like pawns in men's hands and those that are very resilient though may suffer greater economic challenges but maintain their integrity through struggle and hardship' (2007, 129–30). The last category of women has been hidden in the Biafran war narratives because of their authors' intention to masculinize the war by reproducing grotesque images of Biafran women.

Omotoso's use of the metaphor of men's combat similarly reflects the patriarchal maxim of *nwoke luchaa ogu* – a perspective of militarized masculinity. The affairs of combat, preparation and negotiations are exclusively institutionalized by the male characters like Ojo Dada and Chuku Debe 'HE and HOE' and their allies. Moni and other female characters are totally excluded from this masculine venture. They are characterized with insignificant features and drawn into contemptible positions that trivialized their passionate pursuit for wealth and pleasure. The weave of female myth in Omotoso's *The Combat* is bolstered by the same politics of gender suppression which undermines female relevance in order to give vitality to masculine hegemony. For example, in order to ridicule Moni's ignorance about 'the combat', she goes to celebrate the 10th birthday of her decaying son – Isaac, at the time when the whole attention of the men are centred on negotiation for peace or combat (2008, 23). When her celebration fails, she goes to watch the combat as a spectator (ibid., 26), not a combatant. Omotoso makes a caricature of Moni's ignorance about the combat and the prevailing national issues. Her personality is ridiculed, sidelined and romanticized to such an extent that she has no room for emancipation. She remains a conquered victim in the world of men. The author justifies his patriarchal position relying on the following assertion:

'Such things as Women's Lib,' Chuku Debe began to answer, 'take place only in the decadent West. There is no room for Women's Lib in Nigeria. Women knew their places. We all know our places here.' (ibid., 60)

The passage mirrors a patriarchal space in which the dynamics of masculinity and femininity are strictly polarized. The statement 'we all know our places here' indicates a fixed social structure that cannot be ventilated with the wind of change or civilization because it is skewed into the patriarchal thought, perception and belief system. But a counter-narrative of the same war by Nwapa, Ezeigbo and Adichie seem to vitiate the claim. These female narrators identify the challenges imposed by the war and the genuine efforts of the female characters to confront these challenges in other to win and survive the war. Through their narratives, the roles of women as both warriors and narrators become appreciated. Even the changes brought by the war in terms of female radicalization and expanded gender expectations are recognized by these narratives.

The inability of Omotoso's *The Combat,* Okpewho's *The Last Duty* and Achebe's *Girls at War* to sustain the quality of fictional credibility makes their narratives fatal. They failed in the imperative task of teaching and enlightening their readers through objective truth that fulfils Derrida's 'question of narrative' (2004, 72). Because truth is manipulated into a weapon of female suppression and patriarchal hegemony. When war narratives are reproduced through an undistorted gender lens, they form a reasonable historical substitute that can feed future generations with unbiased historical knowledge of a heroic past (Harry Eckstein and Ted R. Gurr, 56). Such a task is imminent in the case of narrativizing the Nigeria-Biafra history to achieve a standard level of objectivity in gender representation.

Subversion or counter-narrative in literature is anchored on the framework of postcolonial deconstruction, in which 'the subaltern' is empowered to challenge their distorted image and redefine themselves by re-presenting their true stories (Landry & Maclean 1996, 62). Notable among these include the several attempts made by feminist writers and critics to challenge female stereotype in war and non-war narratives. Awa Thiam, a Senegalese feminist in 1978 emerged with an attempt to speak out and revolutionize narrative in her *La Parole Aux Negresses*, translated into English as *Black Sisters, Speak Out* with the powerful and empowering statement that: '[African] [w]omen must assume their own voices – speak out for themselves,' while cautiously adding: 'It will not be easy' (1986, 12). While the last statement does not embody disillusionment on the struggle for female emancipation, it reiterates the difficulties on the path to regaining the subaltern's voice and power, a project that is championed in Gayatri C. Spivak's famous essay 'Can the Subaltern Speak?' Her answer to the hypothetical question is 'no'. Spivak's ideation on subalternization reflects serious violence caused by the misrepresentation of the subalterns in the narratives, constructed by the 'well-intentioned intellectuals' – supposedly their hegemonic lords. Her concept of subalternization is applied in the analysis of the patriarchal myth of female misrepresentation, the violent effects of these gendered myths and the interventions of female writers through their counter-narratives that focus towards resisting gender stereotypes and regaining female voice and power. To speak out, according to Spivak, is to become liberated from subject-hood, to tell one's own story and to construct one's own image and identity distinct from the distorted images of 'well-intentioned intellectuals' (2012, 12). The aim is not to deter the subaltern from being acquiescent; but according to Judith Fetterley in her *The Resisting Reader*, one must necessarily 'resist the author's intentions and design to create gender biases by a 'revisionary counter-reading' and critical deconstruction of distorted narratives (1978, xxii). Deconstructive reading and counter-narrative make it possible for female writers to re-visit a fictional space to reconstruct their images and achieve 'self re-presentation'. Adrienne Rich defines it as 'the act of looking back, of seeing with fresh eyes, of entering an old text from a new critical direction' (1986, 18).

Akachi Ezeigbo's critique of the evil of patriarchy and the appraisal of female radicalization in Cyprian Ekwensi's *Survive the Peace* indicates her viable attempt to valorize female activism and resist patriarchal narratives. She lauds the courageous efforts of Juliet Odugo as an

adventurous 'attack woman', and her resoluteness in resisting patriarchal confinement and female annihilation. Juliet remains a symbol
of female radicalization rather than notoriety. In deconstruction of
Juliet Odugo, Ezeigbo re-presents her as a redemptive instrument in
the struggles for survival and nation building other than an estranged
character. She appraises her courage in rejecting sexist and gender
oppression to a desired social liberty (1999, 143). Ezeigbo's deconstruction goes beyond textual space to reconnect the realities of female
values and experiences in a war and non-war situation.

In the same manner, Flora Nwapa's *Wives at War* (1992) recreates
the stories of the Nigeria-Biafra war through female perspectives. The
narrative metaphorizes the concept of war to reflect women's attack
against patriarchy. This projects *Wives at War* as a direct response to
the narrative bias in *Girls at War* (Achebe 1998). The story captures
different kinds of gender-based 'war' within the Nigeria-Biafra war
ranging from war against female annihilation to agitations against
non-female recognitions, war on resources and power control and
war for female emancipation. The cover page of the story gives signal
to these several themes of war. It embodies the images of provoked
female combatants whose agitations are demonstrated through their
stretched hands and inflected muscles waiting to strike their men. This
picture is supported with the inscription on their placards – *MONKEY
DE WORK BABOON DE CHOP*. The phenomenon of female war
is used as a recurrent theme in the entire story to depict the author's
intention to attack and subvert the myth of patriarchal dominance and
female passivity.

> 'You wait until the end of this war. There is going to be another war, the
> war of the women. You have fooled us enough. You have used us enough.
> You have exploited us enough. When this war has ended we will show you
> that we are a force to be reckoned with. You wait and see. What do you
> think we are? Instruments to be used and discarded?'

> 'Your offence is that you by-passed us. Without the women, the Nigerian
> vandals would have overrun Biafra; without women, our gallant Biafran
> soldiers would have died in hunger in the war fronts. Without women,
> the Biafran Red Cross would have collapsed. It was my organisation that
> organized the kitchen and transport for Biafran forces. You men went to
> office every day busy doing nothing.' (Nwapa 1992, 12–13)

The passage reflects Nwapa's intervention to challenge the female
narrative myth, a remarkable wave that signifies the rise of female
voice in fictional narratives. As a pioneer female voice in the Nige-

rian fiction and particularly in war narratives, she uses *Wives at War* to counter the vicious epistemic violence of female misrepresentation in the war – 'Your offence is that you by-passed us' (ibid., 13). She goes on to outline the unacknowledged efforts of the Biafran women which included: feeding and nursing of soldiers in the war fronts, reinforcement of the Biafran Red Cross, controlling the kitchen and transport departments. These were obviously important logistics of war that helped to determine its success and outcome. Nwapa indirectly projects the indispensable nature of the Biafran women in the war. The aim of her counter-narrative is to challenge the dominant patriarchal bias in the earlier narratives of the Biafran war. She achieves this objective by empowering her female characters with unflinching audacity to combat male suppression and misrepresentation: 'You have fooled us enough. You have used us enough. You have exploited us enough.' (ibid., 12). Her female characters eulogize their achievements in the war and boldly confront their men's hypocrisy and self-imposed redundancy. 'Without women, the Biafran Red Cross would have collapsed. It was my organisation that organized the kitchen and transport for Biafran forces. You men went to office every day busy doing nothing.' (ibid., 12–13).

The counter-narrative attack uncovers several aspects of female synergies in their collective efforts to win the war. The different female organizations mentioned in the story such as the National Women's Club, the Busy Bee Women's Club, and the Women's Active Service Club (ibid., 12) eloquently testify to their resilient contributions. The women's attempts to revolutionize war through their intended fight against patriarchal subjugation also replicate their symbolic confrontation with the obnoxious policies that preclude and limit their effective participation in the war, as depicted in the statement below.

We are independent. We are not affiliated to any redundant and planless group. We are the creation of Biafra and our aim is to win the war for Biafra. Right from the word, we organized women for real fight. We asked for guns to fight the enemy. We asked to be taught how to shoot. Did not women and girls fight in Vietnam? We asked to be taught how to take cover and how to evacuate women and children. But those who did not understand mounted strong propaganda against us. They said we were upsetting the women. But we were realistic. We knew Nigeria would fight us, so we must be prepared. (ibid., 14)

Wives at War is sustainable as a counter-narrative against the myth of hegemonic masculinity in the Nigeria-Biafra war narratives. It captures an upsurge of female activism that challenges the veracity of the conventional images that characterize the early narratives of the same war. By recounting the unacknowledged contributions of the Biafran women in the war, *Wives at War* becomes an effective instrument for subverting the images of the Biafran women in the war.

Chimamanda Ngozi Adichie's *Half of a Yellow Sun* emerges four decades after the Nigeria-Biafra war and nearly three decades after *Wives at War*. Despite their periodic differences, the novel identifies with the female struggles towards vocalization, re-presentation and emancipation of Biafran women. It recreates the story of the war in its different significant stages and tactfully portrays the important resilient roles of the Biafran heroines in their struggles to survive, win the war, and to rebuild a war-ravaged society. The novel remarkably distinguishes itself from other narratives by its ability to reproduce the Biafra war stories through different social, cultural, and diplomatic perspectives. The plot of the story connects the cause and effects of the war, its consequences on the Biafran families, the political scenario before the war, the corruption of leaders that led to the coup d' état and counter coup, the anti-Igbo pogrom, secession and war. These events are mirrored through the conversations among university intellectuals in their evening gatherings at Odenigbo's house at Odim Street of the University of Nigeria, Nsukka. Their regular meetings become a centre for national discourse. The novel resonates the early events that culminate into war and the interventions of the University women in rescuing the thousands of refugees that flee from the pogrom and their workshop that orientates the University community: 'In case of War'.

The major plot of the story revolves round the experiences of the Ozobia family particularly their twin daughters, Kainene and Olanna, before and during the war. The protagonist, Kainene, is represented as a male daughter in her family.

> 'Kainene is not just like a son, she is like two', her father said. He glanced at Kainene and Kainene looked away, as if the pride on his face did not matter (Adichie, 2007, 32)

Such masculine traits as depicted in the above statement characterize her throughout the novel as a business administrator, head of her own home, manager of her own contracts with the government and oil companies, controller of her relationship with her lover, Richard, an expatriate researcher. Kainene's leadership qualities become so glaring during wartime, when she takes the initiative to build and manage refugee camps to save the victims of the war. The novel describes her with imposing masculine tallness and vigour in embracing challenging tasks, speaking her mind and sometimes smoking like men. These images are juxtaposed to portray her as a woman-man or as a super-woman, an image that defeats male dominance. By institutionalizing Kainene as a 'male daughter' and heir, the novel destroys the traditional structures of male preference and family inheritance by male progenitor.

Kainene's success in the business world and her economic independence destabilize the patriarchal structures of gender inequalities and economic imbalance as found in Omotoso's *The Combat* and Okpewho's *The Last Duty*. *Half of a Yellow Sun* introduces a reversal of social roles where the male characters like Odenigbo, Richard and Ugwu have to depend upon Kainene for survival, especially at the critical period of the war. In order to truncate the age-long structures of masculine hegemony, Adichie equips her female character with the weapons of Western education and financial security. Kainene and Olanna are independent ladies of substance and social relevance, not like Omotoso's De Madam, who is bereft of intellectual freedom and voice. Kainene, for example, is a holder of a Master's Degree in Business Administration, while her twin sister, Olanna holds a Master's Degree in Sociology, and works as a lecturer at the University of Nigeria, Nsukka. Both characters are strongly empowered with all it takes to participate as active members of society, leaders and decision makers.

The novel diametrically recreates the binary relationship between the old and the new by remarkably projecting the dichotomy in Olanna and Kainene's social and economic independence and their mother (Lady Ozobia)'s marital subjugation. Lady Ozobia suffers the marginalization like Okpewho and Omotoso's women because she lacks the educational and economic empowerment of her daughters. She cannot acquire 'a room of her own' (Virginia Woolf, 47, alluding to Judith Shakespeare), the room of Western education and financial security, which is the secret of female emancipation. But the contemporary Igbo women in Adichie's novel enjoy their social freedom, equal gender relationship, freedom of choice and expression and active participation in the affairs of their society. The novel portrays this using Olanna's relationship with Odenigbo, her maturity in confronting her mother in-law's prejudice and later attempts to supplant her in her marital home because of childlessness. She transcends over these margins by her rational initiative to adopt Odenigbo's illegitimate daughter whom her mother in-law rejected because of her sex. These features characterize Olanna as a new Igbo woman who has not only surmounted male-female hegemony but has conquered female antagonism imposed by the patriarchal structure. Her maternal relevance in fostering Baby in addition to her spousal commitments to Odenigbo does not in any way limit her patriotic service for Biafra. Olanna continues in her diligent services as teacher during the war by rendering humanitarian services to Biafran children. She taught them about the Biafran flag:

> They sat on wooden planks and the weak morning sun streamed into the roofless classes. She unfurled Odenigbo's cloth flag and told them what the symbols meant. Red was the blood of the siblings massacred in the North, black was for mourning them, green was for the prosperity Biafra would have and, finally, half of the yellow sun stood for the glorious future. (Adichie, 2007, 281)

The novel stretches Olanna's space of motherhood to national service (mother of a nation). Despite her position, she identifies freely with the local women and integrates herself in their win-the-war synergies. It is through these synergies that she encounters Mrs Muokelu, whom she admires as a replica of Kainene in her masculine vigour. Mrs Muokelu is a leader of female mobilization to win the war. She carries Olanna through several orientations to survive the war and resuscitate her adopted daughter from kwashiorkor. Mrs Muokelu later joins the female attack traders as the Republic thins down due to massive death tolls and extreme hardship. Olanna also moves with her family members – Odenigbo, Baby and Ugwu, to settle in her twin sister's refugee camp at Orlu.

Kainene's refugee camp is a centre of revival and family reunion at such a time when there is no vestige of hope for many Biafrans. She reunites herself with her sister Olanna, her lover Richard, and her twin sister's family members. Other Biafran families are accorded refuge in this camp. She employs her personal resources and available humanitarian relief resources in running the centre. She explores improvised strategies such as farming as means of survival. In the dearth of food and economic supplies, she resorts to the perilous attack trading as the only available alternative for survival. Attack trading *(afia attack)* in the novel is employed as a metaphor of female militarization serving as part of their strategies to win the war. Trading or planting crops within the enemy's border is another display of female radicalization in their collaborative synergies to win the war. While the Biafran soldiers fight within the Biafran war fronts, the attack traders break into the threshold of the enemies' borders and face the danger of being abducted or killed by their enemies (Ezeigbo 1999, 142).

The dynamics of attack trading is explored first in Cyprian Ekwensi's *Survive the Peace* (1976) as an escape to female liberation. The attack women come back financially empowered and socially reinforced with greater connections that enhance their space of social relevance. Juliet Odugo, for instance, does not come back to the level of marital servitude but takes a national responsibility that positions her to a height of influence, power and independence. As she remarks in her dialogue with James Odugo, her former husband: 'War changes everything' (Ekwensi 1976, 80). However, Adichie's 'attack women' exist in a continuum that breaks the boundaries of narrative closure. Kainene's attack adventure puts her in a space that knows no boundary, where her resourceful existence remains continuous and endless. The novel has no ending with regard to female imperative life in the war. Olanna searches for Kainene with passionate expectation but she does not return to her previous abode because the attack trade becomes a voyage to a limitless horizon of female endeavour.

Kainene remains the heroine in Adichie's *Half of a Yellow Sun* not only because of her ability to break a marginal ground but as a result of her enormous exploits to win the war and redeem the war-ravaged Biafran society. She makes personal donations to Biafra, takes up a contract to support the war, participates in administering sensitive humanitarian logistics during the war, makes the personal sacrifice of her initiatives and talents and explores challenging avenues for rescuing the Biafran population under her patronage. Her attack exploits metaphorically end the storyline, but her enormous roles stretch beyond narrative possibility, making her an enigmatic heroine.

In conclusion, the challenging counter-narratives of Nwapa, Ezeigbo and Adichie truly objectify them as sisters destined for a common mission of emancipation – 'lifting womanhood from the bog of tradition, superstition and custom' (Opara 1999, 17) and charting their redemptive course that strengthens the potentialities of women for actualized existence. Their liberation movements connect them to their female contemporaries like the feminist, womanist, femalist, gynist and Africana feminists. They foreground millions of women abused and battered domestically at home, in their workplaces, battlefields and refugee camps without remedy or redress. Their narratives re-present the unacknowledged patriotic sacrifices of women as sisters, mothers, wives, humanitarian workers and participants in war and nation building, which often are predominantly problematized in male-authored narratives. Adichie and her forebears in the Nigerian war narratives have made significant efforts to challenge the recurrent myths of hegemonic masculinity by reappraising female heroism in the war. These writers employ counter-narrative as their linguistic conduit to transcending patriarchy and charting the path to freedom and self-awareness. *Half of a Yellow Sun* in particular recreates the Biafran war history to celebrate the tapestry of Igbo woman's valour and resilience at wartime; and to counter the orthodox bias of 'passive female purveyor' – entrenched in the myth of *nwoke lucchaa ogu nwanyi enwere akuko*. Its images of educated, vocal, valiant and committed female players in the struggle to win the war and rebuild the ravaged Biafran Republic undoubtedly indict the patriarchal structures that undermine female heroism. The novel fulfils the legacy of creative enlightenment, mental liberation and emancipation. It is obvious that a plausible sense of history can not only be redemptive but sustains the hope and courage for confronting the future. Adichie's strategy of retelling the Biafra war stories through womanist perspectives uncovers the untold truth about Biafran female heroines, signals hope for future struggles and reemphasizes the woman's significance in the human struggles for victory and survival.

Works Cited

Achebe, Chinua. *Girls at War and Other Stories*. London: Heinemann, 1988. Print.

—. 'The Novelist as Teacher.' *African Literature: An Anthology of Criticism and Theory*. Ed. Olaniyan, T. and Quayson, A. Hoboken, NJ, Chichester, UK and Brisbane, Australia: Blackwell, 2007, 103–7.

Adichie, Chimamanda. N. *Half of the Yellow Sun*. London: Harper Perennial, 2007.

Amadiume, Ifi. *Male Daughters, Female Husbands: Gender and Sex in an African Society*. London and New Jersey: Zed Books, 1987.

Cohen, Carol. *Women and Wars*. Cambridge: Polity Press, 2013.

Connell, R. W. *Masculinities*. Los Angeles, CA: University of California Press, 2005.

Derrida, Jacques. 'Living On'. *Deconstruction and Criticism*. Eds. H. Bloom, P. De Man, J. Derrida, G. H. Hartman and J. H. Miller. New York: Continuum, 2004.

Eckstein, H. and Gurr, T. R. *Patterns of Authority: A Structural Basis for Political Inquiry*. New York, London, Sydney, and Toronto: John Wiley & Sons, 1975.

Ekwensi, Cyprian. *Survive the Peace*. London: Heinemann, 1976.

Elshtain, Jean Bethke. *Women and War with a New Epilogue*. Chicago, IL: The University of Chicago Press, 1995.

Emecheta, Buchi. *Destination Biafra*. London: Heinemann, 1982.

Ezeigbo, Akachi A. 'Cyprian Ekwensi's *Survive the Peace* as a Critique of War and Patriarchy'. *Beyond the Marginal Land*. Ed. C. Opara. Port Harcourt: Belpot, 1999: 135–51.

Fetterley, Judith. *The Resisting Reader: A Feminist Approach to American Fiction*. Bloomington, IN: Indiana University Press, 1978.

Landry, Donna and MacLean, Gerald. *The Spivak Reader*. New York: Routledge, 1996.

Njoku, R. A. *Withstand the Storm: War Memoirs of a Housewife*. Ibadan: Heinemann, 1986.

Nnaemeka, Obioma. 'Fighting on all Fronts: Gendered Spaces, Ethnic Boundaries and the Nigerian Civil War Author(s)'. *Dialectical Anthropology*. 22 (1997): 235–63.

Nwapa, Flora. *Wives at War and Other Stories*. NJ: Africa World Press, 1992.

—. *Never Again*. Enugu: Nwamife Publishers, 1975.

Okpewho, Isidore. *The Last Duty*. Harlow: Pearson Education Limited, 1981.

Omotoso, Kole. *The Combat*. Parklands: Penguin Books, 2008.

Opara, C. (Ed.). *Beyond the Marginal Land: Gender Perspective in African Writing* Port Harcourt: Belpot, 1999.

Rich, Adrienne. *Of Woman Born: Motherhood as Experience and Institution*. New York: Norton, 1986.

Spivak, G. C. 'Can the Subaltern Speak?: Gayatri Spivak and Post-Colonialism.' Retrieved 5 July 2012, https://mashrabiyya. wordpress.com/2012/07/05/can-the-subaltern-speak-gayatri-spivak-and-post-colonialism; http://culturalstudiesnow.blogspot. com.ng/2011/11/gayatri-spivak-can-subaltern-speak.html.

Thiam, Awa. *La Parole aux négresses. [Black Sisters, Speak Out: Feminism and Oppression in Black Africa]*. Trans. Dorothy S. Blair. London: Pluto Press, 1986.

Uchendu, Egodi. *Women and Conflict on the Nigerian Civil War*. New Jersey: Africa World Press, 2007.

Woolf, Virginia. *A Room of One's Own*. London: Penguin, 1945.

12

'A Kind of Paradise'
Chimamanda Ngozi Adichie's Claim to Agency, Responsibility & Writing

SILVANA CAROTENUTO

The language you taught me rolls
From your mouth into mine
The way kids will pass smoke
between them ... I feed you
My very own soft truth. We believe.
(Tracy K. Smith, 'Self-Portrait As the Letter Y',
in *The Body's Question* 2003, 60)

The creative singularity of the work of Chimamanda Ngozi Adichie seems resistant to theoretical interpretation, being always already informed by the translation of complex thoughts in a language and a form of writing whose goal is to communicate to her public, a vast audience, a global readership. Some might suspect a commercial interest in this choice of language; I would rather experiment with an interpretative approach which does not want to disrespect the clarity and the simplicity of Adichie's poetics, but which intends to give insights into the critical chance of sharing creative and theoretical languages.

The specific resistance I want to deal with, concerns the 'postcolonial question', nowadays often reflected in academic debates that appear obscure, self-referential, difficult to comprehend. In my experimentation, I would like to prove that the voices of some postcolonial authors share the same intellectual vocation as Adichie. Edward Said, Gayatry C. Spivak, Achille Mbembe, Fred Moten and Stefano Harney, Hélène Cixous and Denise Ferreiro da Silva are intellectuals, philosophers and writers organic to – Palestine, the Indian subcontinent, the African continent, the 'undercommons', *l'écriture féminine*, the excess of female desire, the globality of the diasporic world hybridized by migration, exile and displacement. Said offers us the first figuration of intellectual

169

organicity[1]; Spivak invites us to make it reach out for the un/limits of the planet; Mbembe knows the 'African question' and vindicates its singularity for the destinies of humanity; Moten and Harney emphasize the insubordination of the radical intellectual;[2] Cixous writes of women's laughter in the face of patriarchy; da Silva un/represents the radical desire of the black female body.

For her part, Adichie is a 'storyteller' organic to her art and her seducing and enjoyable language, bringing her 'amateurish' voice to the highest plane of poetic utterance (Said would find her public utterance as gifted as nothing else, in the resistance to the 'professionalism' he so critically suspected). Adichie's discourses, virally circulating on the internet, are globally followed; her novels – so dense as to gain already the quality of classics – are extremely popular; her feminism is even evoked by the female Deans of Italian universities when urging for the academic implementation of a politics of gender. We speak of Adichie; we discuss the issues she brings to our attention; we read and enjoy her writing. She finds the right and just language to utter and narrate stories of difficult realities, scenes of migratory experiences, and new utopias of future salvation.

My experimentation traces some of these sensitive 'questions' (the interrogative form is congenial to Adichie's poetics) by following their relevance woven around the claim of 'agency' for the ones deprived of creative existence by the modern – colonial/postcolonial – single story of the West, and, if contemporaneity remains patriarchal in its global socializations, around the urgency of an intense discussion on the question of gender. Alterity and female difference are consistent issues in the poetics of Adichie; it follows the extraordinary question of 'responsibility' – to oneself, the other, the past, the present and the future of the planet. Memory and utopia are the themes Adichie offers her audience with grace and simplicity. Art reigns over all; writing is what Adichie would perform even without a public, her necessity, the unconditionality of her desire. On this level, her public vindication for the 'multitude' of stories telling of women exposed to the dangers – erasure, disengagement, contraction – of history and society, power

---

[1] For E. Said's influence on postcolonial studies, Mbembe (2008) remarks: 'The cultural analysis of the discursive infrastructure and of the colonial imagination would gradually become the very subject of postcolonial theory.' The analysis of both the 'discursive infrastructure' and 'colonial imagination' is central to Adichie's creative work.

[2] '[T]he subversive intellectual enjoys the ride and wants it to be faster and wilder; she does not want a room of his or her own, she wants to be in the world, in the world with others and making the world anew' (Halberstam 2013: 10).

and culture, provides the metanarrative traits supporting her passionate investment in the construction of her singular 'writing'.

Inside/outside Adichie's public voice and intimate writing, there is a flavour or a sensibility which could be called 'religious'; in my experiment, Adichie's singular drive, and the thinking of the organic intellectuals I quote, are as sacred as worldly and earthly. The claiming of the stories negated by history gains a 'kind of paradise'; the declaration of feminism creates a culture of respect for the 'humanity' of women; the material/affective gesture of writing is a sacred 'shivering'. The planet opens its cosmos to the encounter with the Other, in full joy, sisterhood and love.[3] Adichie's 'belief' in the future is always already in full act...

The Organic Intellectual

> i collect
> wings what are
> you bird
> or animal?
> something that
> lights on trees
> breasts pawnshops
> i have seen
> another
> path to this
> rendezvous
> (Sonia Sanchez, 'Sonku' in *Like the Singing Coming
> off the Drums. Love Poems*, 1998, 15)

The time of the encounter with the Other is always a time of violation of innocence by – internal/external, past and present – experience. In 'The Danger of a Single Story' (2009b), Adichie narrates being saved from the universality of history by her encounter with the African literature of Chinua Achebe and Camara Laye.[4] In her early attempts to write, she used to imitate the 'models' provided by the Western

---

[3] 'I propose the planet to overwrite the globe ... the planet is in the species of alterity, belonging to another system and yet we inhabit it, on loan.' (Spivak 2003: 71).
[4] For the inspirational influence Achebe had on Adichie's work, see Whitaker (2011) and Franklin (2009). Adichie does not use the word 'universality' but she would agree with the postcolonial 'demonstration': 'Postcolonial thought demonstrates that colonialism itself was a global experience which contributed to the universalization of representations, techniques and institutions ... It shows that this process of universalization, far from being a one-way street, was basically a paradox, fraught with all sorts of ambiguities' (Mbembe, 2008).

'single story' of the other, up to the moment she enjoyed the chance of inscribing her alterity on the page, the alterity of the ones never included in the Western single story, that the univocacity of its vision is only rendered in abusive and discriminatory traits. The experience is persistent and consistent; when Adichie is 19 years old, at university in the United States, the meeting with a flatmate proves the shock of seeing herself inscribed, according to simplified and incompressible schemes, into a hypothetical and definite African identify. In 'We Should All Be Feminists' (Adichie 2014), in a similar way, she encounters the word 'feminism' when, during a discussion among adolescents, a friend accuses her of being a 'feminist'. It is a word she did not know at the time, and that, from that first encounter, will never stop substantiating her personal life and her evolution as a public figure. How could it be otherwise, if what still necessitates of feminism, in a more remote infancy, forbade her to assume, as she deserved, the role of class leader because she was a girl?

The expression of the danger of the single story, the public discussion on the condition of women: this is Adichie's intellectual mission. She identifies the causes and the mechanisms of the implementation of narrative empire and imperial patriarchy. Adichie speaks of 'power' and 'society': power turns a provisional story into the definite one, to the detriment of the complexity of the other; society – the socializing process – defines the criteria of acceptability, respect and opportunity that rule the lives of women everywhere in the world. Power plays the definition of the ways, subjectivities and times of narration, in the refusal of the plurality of existing and relevant stories; society defines the contests, premises and forms of policing the desires of men and women.

What is indeed fatal is that power and society share a danger, one that impedes knowledge and understanding, and a mechanism, one that affects the historical, social and personal un/conscious: the instilment of pity and the patronizing attitude to the other; the interiorization of gender's social norm/ality. In the world of the other, the danger allows the – always possible – fall into 'the trap of the radicalization and race glorification' (Mbembe 2008), for instance, African literature's single story of 'authenticity'. In the world of feminism, the interiorization of the norm can always already induce 'the greatest crime' of female misogyny: women hating women, mobilizing their puissance against themselves, executing virile needs (Cixous 1976). In the world of Adichie, they prove her own involvement in what she so radically criticizes. She has often read the other through the lens of stereotypes, interacting with the boy working in the house under the spell of the single story of poverty provided by her mother, or involuntarily assuming the media coverage of the Mexican clandestine as 'abject'. She has given herself up to social expectations, for example in the appropriateness of the dress code chosen for a lecture with students. She has often felt her un/conscious vulnerability to the presuppositions of femininity.

The organic intellectual might be using the confessional mode to prove the 'sense of drama and revolt' (Said 1997, 17) that Said expected from any engaged voice to incite attention in his/her public. Indeed, once the communicative and participating contact is gained, Adichie's vocation attracts her public into a space that is ethical more than instrumental. If she is herself touched and affected by power and society, it follows that 'we all' partake in subjugated exposure to the universality of history and to the interiorization of the norm.[5] 'We all' should feel 'responsible' for the destinies of the other in the historical world, and for the injustice experienced by female alterity in society: the act of

> responsibility towards oneself and towards an inheritance ... It is a thought of responsibility, responsibility in terms of the obligation to answer for oneself, to be the guarantor of one's actions. The ethics underlying this thought of responsibility is the future of the self in the memory of what one has been in another's hands, the sufferings one has endured in captivity, when the law and the subject were divided. (Mbembe 2008)

In 'The Danger of a Single Story', Adichie speaks of our responsibility in impressing another origin to historical negation:

> Start the story with the arrows of the Native Americans, and not with the arrival of the British, and you have an entirely different story. Start the story with the failure of the African state, and not with the colonial creation of the African state, and you have an entirely different story. (Adichie 2009b)

The imperative is ethical, indecisive, gaining substance in the interrogative form that follows:

> What if my roommate knew about my friend Funmi Iyanda, a fearless woman who hosts a TV show in Lagos, and is determined to tell the stories that we prefer to forget? What if my roommate knew about the heart procedure that was performed in the Lagos hospital last week? What if my roommate knew about contemporary Nigerian music? ... What if my roommate knew about the female lawyer who recently went to court

[5] Mbembe (2008) calls it a 'politics of fellow-creatures'; 'a stress on humanity-in-the-making'.

in Nigeria to challenge a ridiculous law that required women to get their husband's consent before renewing their passports? What if my roommate knew about Nollywood, full of innovative people making films despite great technical odds? ... What if my roommate knew about my wonderful ambitious hair braider, who has just started her own business selling hair extensions? Or about the millions of other Nigerians who start their businesses and sometimes fail, but continue to nurse ambition? (ibid.)[6]

What would have happened, might happen, and will happen if ...? Adichie's interrogations echo Said's mandates to the organic intellectual who, in posing questions and operating dissections, recalls to memory 'everything we tend to neglect in the urgency of uniting to the judging chorus, to the collective action' (Said 1996, 46). At the same time, if Adichie is thinking of Nigeria, it is Africa to substantiate her call to the 'multiplicity' of necessary stories:

Look at any single thing on the continent, it always comes under the sign of the multiple ... One of the tragedies of colonialism has been to erase that element of multiplicity which was a resource for social development in pre-colonial Africa and which was replaced by the paradigm of 'the one', the kind of monotheistic paradigm. So how do we recapture the idea of multiplicity as precisely a resource for the making of the continent, its remaking, but also for the making of the world? (Mbembe 2008)

Africa informs its own destiny and the destinies of the world; in Adichie's 'recapture', African multiplicity opens the humanity of 'we all' to a zone of future coexistence and comprehension, a 'kind of paradise':

Stories matter. Many stories matter. Stories have been used to dispose and to malign. But stories can also be used to empower, and to humanize. Stories can break the dignity of a people. But stories can also repair that broken dignity. When we reject the single story, when we realize that there is never a single story about any place, we regain a kind of paradise. (Adichie 2009b)

This line of thought works also for the destinies of our global world, built on the discrimination of the difference of women. 'We all' should acknowledge the condition of women; if it is true, as it is, that 'there is no escape from the need of justice' (Mbembe 2013), and that 'Anger has a long history of bringing about positive change' (Adichie 2014, 21), 'we all' should feel rage at the injustice of gender dynamics. 'We

[6] See Azuonye (2010).

174

all' should interrogate the premises of education and, starting from our subjectivity, unlearn and dismantle any un/conscious interiorization: 'I have chosen to no longer be apologetic for my femininity. And I want to be respected in all my femaleness. Because I deserve to be' (ibid., 39). Once again, Adichie's interrogation – 'What if, in raising children, we focus on ability instead of gender?' (ibid., 36); 'What if she saw it as something normal and natural, that he should help care for his child?' (ibid., 37) – marks the opening of imagination and self-creation to the non-said, the unimaginable-unimagined future of an answer, substantiating the 'dream about and the plan for' (ibid., 25) a culture of respect: 'Culture does not make people. People make culture: if it is true that the full humanity of women is not our culture, then we can and must make it our culture' (ibid., 46). Our responsibility is to allow the dream to inform the plan; if in the eventuality the dream stays a dream, it will have imparted a lesson of postcolonial thinking:

> Postcolonial thought is also a dream: the dream of a new form of humanism, a critical humanism founded above all on the divisions that, this side of the absolutes, differentiate us. It's the dream of a polis that is universal because ethnically diverse. (Mbembe 2013)

The Organic Writer

> I go ahead intuitively, and without looking for an idea: I'm organic …
> I immerse myself in the near pain of an intense happiness –
> and to adorn me leaves and branches are born out of my hair
> (Clarice Lispector, *The Stream of Life*, 1989, 16)

I would like to anticipate a note of clarification to my analysis of Adichie's collection of stories, *The Thing Around Your Neck* (Adichie, 2009a). What follows does not intend to be exhaustive of the complexity and the beauty of the collected stories; still, my reading is deconstructive, not in ideological terms, but as an intimate appreciation of the art of writing. At a certain point in their progress, the stories created by Adichie present a metanarrative reflection, a thread structured by clear and direct comments on writing. I decide to follow this thread, without wanting to dismiss the multitude of other elements that weave Adichie's passion as a storyteller.[7] In this sense, I decide –

---

[7] Griswold explains that 'Nigerian novelists see themselves as storytellers. They tell stories of a particular kind and with a particular intent, however, for these writers understand themselves to be bearing witness to Nigerian social experience' (2000: 3).

it is my responsibility – to read the stories according to their internal rhythm of writing, in the order in which Adichie wrote the stories, which is different from the one gathered in the published collection: 'the stories in this collection are stories I've been working on really for the past nine years. So, I've had time to let things, you know, percolate' (Adichie in Raz, 2009). Assuming the 'percolation' of Adichie's writing through the agency and the responsibility of 'we all', my choice seems appropriate to show – quickly, too quickly, I apologize – the organicity (roots, praxis, matter, promise, exposure and gesture) of the approach of Adichie as a writer to (the) writing (of the other, of power and society, culture and art). I assume responsibility for the partiality of my choice, hoping it might provide insight into how Adichie takes care in her own writing of the simple truth she utters on the public scene: 'how impressionable and vulnerable we are in the face of a story' (Adichie, 2009b).

The Thing Around Your Neck consists of twelve stories written in the timespan from 2002 to publication in 2009. This text regains its 'kind of paradise' with the multitude of stories it collects, its culture of respect for women knitting together immigration and gender:

> I think gender affects the way we experience immigration. And just observing immigrant communities in the U.S., I think that – and I think immigration in itself is a difficult thing, that it sort of involves layers of losses and gains. And I find that women, it seems to me, deal with immigration differently, and I'm interested in that. (ibid.)

Adichie is an organic writer. She goes to the 'roots' of writing, where her vocation finds a specific dialectic: writing must keep memory of what substantiates it, witnessing its legacy for the coming of the future. Past and future / witness and advent: in 2002, 'The American Embassy' deals with this basic radicalism.[8] One morning, indifferent to her surroundings, a woman queues outside the American Embassy, waiting to receive the answer to her visa application. Her child has been killed by the soldiers who were looking for her husband, a radical and engaged journalist who uses writing to criticize the Nigerian establishment, as the woman dramatically understands, out of 'utter selfishness'. The story is focused on impressing on the

---

[8] Mbembe (2008), sharing the critique with Adichie, would interpret the scene according to a precise lack of responsibility: 'The global politics of the United States today is a politics that seeks to free itself from all constraints. In the name of security, it seeks exemption from all responsibility. This politics of boundless irresponsibility must be subjected to a firm, intelligent and sustained critique.'

page the atrocities lived by the woman, together with the ability of writing to witness the horror. At the same time, writing seems unable, if not in silence and by dismissal, to claim the future from the 'faces' of the ones in charge. The instant when the woman is exposed to the verdict of the personnel who might entrust her the visa, closure is inscribed on the page: 'Her future rested on that face. The face of a person who did not understand her ... She turned slowly and headed for the exit' (ibid., 141).

Incomprehension and refusal: the woman will, perhaps, one day, 'recapture that category of the future and see to what extent it could be remobilized in the attempt at critiquing the present, and reopening up a space not only for imagination, but also for the politics of possibility' (Mbembe 2013). To recapture its possibility, indeed, writing needs 'time' and 'agency': 'New Husband' (in the published collection, 'Arrangers of Marriage', Adichie 2009a, also 2003) and 'Imitation' narrate the instances of two women whose innocence is exposed to the experience ('fort/da') of discovering what they did not know, what they need to understand, before they can vindicate their difference for the advent of the future.

In 'New Husband', a woman arrives in the United States to discover the deceit of the man she has married by arrangement, the fallacy of his mainstream life, performance, and conformed language, even his failure in providing her with the Green Card their marriage should guarantee. If 'agency' is assumed as a given, writing necessitates 'time' to operate its creativity: when the woman decides to leave her husband, the only female friend she has, invites her to a different wisdom: '"You can wait until you get your papers and then leave," ... She was right, I could not leave yet.' (Adichie 2009b, 186). Time is as necessary to writing as it is agency, decision, 'will' (Carotenuto 1998): in 'Imitation', a rich husband keeps his wife in America, while he lives in their Nigerian house with his new girlfriend. Through a game of copies and originals, some Benin masks are the commercial treasures that constitute the husband's collection; for the woman, their sculptured eyes speak an idiom that strongly affects her sensibility. At the arrival of the first original in the house, her decision is immediate, uttered in the voice of agency: '"We are moving back at the end of the school year" ... She stresses the "we" ... She gently turns him around and continues to soap his back. There is nothing left to talk about. Nkem knows: it is done' (Adichie 2009b, 41–2).

Something round, made of me and her and him.
Something akin to one large ballooning finger, here,

at the full lips of my belly's button where I could feel
the warmth of food; milky brown thick sugar passing

from her body's oven into my own whole-wheat capsule.
(Nikky Finney, 'The World Is Round: The Breast of the Garment
Measured', in *The World Is Round. Poems*, 2013, 3)

Indeed, something is done to writing; the axe of Adichie's writing
turns round itself to test the matter/matrix of its evolution, difference and safety. After the reflection on testimony and future, on time
and agency, in 2004, in *The Thing Around Your Neck*, a young Nigerian
woman is narrated in her exile in the States, due to the 'lucky chance'
of a visa won from the American lottery. She is a complex woman,
but the empire of the single story exposes her to constant simplifica-
tion and stereotyping. During a visit to the family who has long been
living in America, the girl is even exposed to her uncle's sexual abuse.
Power and patriarchy: she finds her ways of surviving, but a sense
of invisibility suffocates her, her body oppressed by a feeling that
impedes breathing: 'At night, something would wrap itself around
your neck, something that very nearly choked you before you fell
asleep' (Adichie, 2009b, 119). 'The thing around your neck' – the
sentence impresses its versatility on Adichie's writing. Against the
emptiness, the void and the 'nothing' that are the common traits of
the migrant's life, writing vindicates 'something': the 'thing'. The
meaning of the 'thing' is left unknotted, staying around the neck as
the secret of the story. Does 'the thing' belong to the unconscious?
Does it embody non-representability, alterity to the already-said,
indefinite matter? Denise Ferreira da Silva evokes 'the Thing' as
the black body's 'undecidable female desire and excess', which, in its
difference from the 'object of no value' that Hegel used to read in
blackness, produces its unforeseeable difference, 'other desires, other
figuration of existence, or any other and all possible modes of being
human in the world' (da Silva 2013, 53):

> Without Patriarchy and without History … the desire promised by the
> sexual female body remains an untraced guide for a radical praxis, which is
> also a racial critique and a feminist intervention, able to counter the effects
> of subjugation produced by appropriations of the global subaltern in the
> name of freedom. (ibid: 56)

What writing knows is that the thing circles around the body, affecting
'your' neck. 'Her' neck, 'my' neck, 'our' neck – in auto/biography and
commonality, Adichie's grammar writes its 'compositional' effect.

Everything is compositional … a process of becoming as a relation; a relation in which the 'I', meaning the subject, is understood as being made and remade through the ethical interaction with what or who is not him. In fact, the idea that other is another me, the other is the other only to the extent that he or she is another me. That the other is not outside of myself, I am my own other to a certain extent. (Mbembe 2013)

In a similar way, the agency and the responsibility required by writing to relieve the pain the thing is, are absolute, direct and decisive.[9] Writing calls for writing. If the story still appeals to romance, narrating the girl's encounter with a boy who seems attentive, understanding, generous and loving, the page cannot but inscribe that 'a lot was wrong' (Adichie, 2009b, 126). What offers the escape from the 'impossible impasse' is, literally, writing. The girl has been sending money home without a note or a message; money, and nothing else. Caught in her invisibility, she cannot write; she would love to write, but she is unable to write: 'There was nothing to write about … you wanted to write … You wanted to write about … You wanted to write about … You wanted to write about … You wanted to write about … You wanted to write … you wrote nobody' (ibid., 118–19). One day, she sends a note to Nigeria; soon after, the letter of her mother tells her of her father's death. The decision proves no hesitation; at the airport, the 'thing around your neck' finally loosens its suffocating grip, and 'you hugged him tight for a long, long moment, and then you let go' (ibid., 127).

> … a thing of intense intrigue,
> the brush's bristles oozing pallid
>
> matter, constructed flesh, tragic
> between what can and can't be seen.
> (Randall Horton, 'Girl Model J', 2013, 13)

'Let go': from now on, writing will offer hospitality to the other, creating its paradise of stories and fighting for the respect culture of female humanity through Adichie's reflection on the constitutive principles, the productive exposures, the creative traits and the sacrality of its gesture.

In 'A Private Experience', two women, a Catholic student and a subaltern Muslim, experience the violence of riots in the capital; the

---

[9] In *Americanah*, the discourse on responsibility is linked to blog writing, which plays an innovatively self-conscious case in the novel: 'Remember people are not reading you as entertainment, they're reading you as cultural commentary. That's a real responsibility' (2013: 386). See Guarracino (2014), for the centrality of Adichie's interest in new forms of writing.

woman leads the girl into an abandoned supermarket, saving her life. The focus is concentrated, private, producing the 'bond' of the unforgettable 'souvenir' – 'a stone stained the copper of dried blood' (Adichie, 2009b, 56) – that will remain in the girl's remembrance forever. In 'Ghosts', an old Nigerian professor meets a colleague he believes to have died during the Biafra war. The encounter is the motif of a series of scenes where 'souvenir' encounters 'survival': the professor is a survivor, in the same way as the man he meets. He could be a ghost; the man of letters would not be surprised: his own survival is allowed by the return – the visits – of his dead wife. She comes back to massage him, every morning announced by the sound of 'doors opening and closing' (ibid., 73). This sensation, this feeling, is indeed an affirmation of life, the double genitive 'of' writing celebrating 'what lies at the heart of a new culture that promises never to forget the vanquished' (Mbembe 2013).

What kind of writing might assume the responsibility for the past and for the future at the same time? In 'Jumping Monkey Hill', a seminar in creative writing is run by an English scholar, who gathers writers from Africa and judges the works they create on the premises. In one of the rare occasions in which Adichie uses a meta-fictional device; writing literally inscribes difference on the page: the tale of the seminar's anxious atmosphere mirrors, by splitting, into the tale written at night by one female participant to the workshop. This story is the embodiment of the required task, the proof of a possible talent, the girl's laughter in the face of canonical standard and judgemental formality:

> 'The whole thing is implausible'...
> He was watching her, and it was the victory in his eyes that made her stand up and start to laugh ... She laughed and laughed ...
> There were other things Ujunwa wanted to say, but she did not say them. There were tears crowding up in her eyes but she did not let them out. (Adichie, 2009b, 114)

The process of 'self-writing' has started, and will continue, under the spell of the tears and the joy of creation, in the assumption of responsibility to what can be called 'the unmasking of falsification':

> ... the stock of falsehoods and the weight of fantasizing functions without which colonialism as a historical power-system could not have worked ... duplicity, double-talk and a travesty of reality. ... this economy of duplicity and falsehood ... the transference of this self-hatred to the Other. (Mbembe, 2008)

'Tomorrow is Too Far' constructs various scenes or different versions of what binds a girl to her brother's death. Writing goes back and forward in time and space (Sharobeen 2015), narrating the stories of the girl's grandmother, mother and friend, in dealing with the accounts the girl gives of what happened the afternoon the child fell from the tree. Narrated, re-narrated and narrated again, the re/construction of the girl's lies desperately tries to negate her responsibility in the traumatic event – a ghost that will stay in the fibre of experience, tormenting the texture of writing.

In order to assume responsibility, writing needs no lie or 'model', as it is painfully understood by the Nigerian girl 'with diploma', who, in 'On Monday of Last Week', keeps faith in the human relationship she might create with the Afro-American mother of the child she babysits. She falls in love with the woman the instant she asks her to sit as the 'model' of the paintings she creates in the basement. Is this an offer of communality, singularly addressed to her, the precious sign of sisterhood and female love? In disillusionment, the woman makes the same request to whoever arrives in the house.

Rather than to models, the drive of writing goes to invention and strength: 'Cells One' narrates the experience of a spoilt university boy who, taken to prison and there exposed to violence and abuse, gains a new ethical awareness in his life. 'The Headstrong Historian' expands this difference by adding courage; it is the story of a girl whose education has been strenuously supported by her grandmother, the matriarch of pottery, who believes in female lineage and bondage. At the end of the process of narration, the girl finds the courage to finish her history text, dedicated to *Pacifying with Bullets: A Reclaimed History of Southern Nigeria*. The book is criticized by her academic colleagues, who suggest changes in topic and style. In truth, critique cannot change the graceful (if Grace is her name) determination to offer her writing to the honour of her beloved ancestor:

> On that day as she sat at the grandmother's bedside in the fading evening light, Grace was not contemplating her future. She simply held her grandmother's hand, the palm thickened from years of making pottery. (Adichie, 2009b, 218)

She is not contemplating the future: on the ladder of writing, there is one last step to climb (Cixous 1993). Adichie's last story, 'The Shivering', depicts the relationship between two Nigerian people, an expatriated guy who believes in religion, and an atheist girl. They meet in an instance of fragility for the girl; he would support her with prayers, but the girl refuses. Indeed, since their first encounter, a bond of friendship has been establishing between them; at the end of the story, the – 'shivering' – gesture of writing draws the picture of the friends enjoying the blessing of the gaze of a 'Madonna with baby': 'At first they stifled their laughter and then they let it out, joyously leaning against each other, while next to them, the woman holding the baby watched' (Adichie, 2009a, 166).[10]

The joyful proximity and the visionary company of/with others: in the end, the postcolonial gesture of writing opens and relaunches the future in a singular fashion, responsible to itself, for the other, and before the Other. It is the African celebration of 'the poetic productivity of the sacred': 'After all, what would Africa be without the sacred? Here the sacred represents the imaginative resource par excellence. The sacred is to be understood not only in relation to the divine, but also as the "power of therapy"' (Mbembe 2013). Adichie's therapeutic writing might be 'religious'. In the conclusion of my experiment, I rather believe that the 'kind of paradise', the respect for 'humankind' and the 'sacrality' of Adichie's writing follow the traces of a vocation which, inscribed on the earth and throughout the planet, here and now (Carotenuto, 2000), organically calls for the multiplicity, the equality and the poetry of the future of humanity.

[10] See McCandless (2010). On the other side of violence, see the upsetting image of the amputee mother breastfeeding her amputee baby in 'Concerning violence' (2014) by Göran Hugo Olsson: http://dogwoof.com/concerningviolence. In her 'Preface' to the film, Spivak (2014) remarks: 'The most moving shot of this film is the black Venus, reminding us of the Venus of Milo with her arm gone, who is also a black Madonna, suckling a child with bare breasts. This icon must remind us all that the endorsement of rape continues not only in war but also, irrespective of whether a nation is developing or developed – in women fighting in legitimized armies. Colonizer and colonized are united in the violence of gendering, which often celebrates motherhood with genuine pathos.'

Works Cited

Adichie, Chimamanda Ngozi, 'New Husband', *Iowa Review* 33.1, 2003: 53-66

—. *The Thing Around Your Neck* (London: Fourth Estate, 2009a).

—. 'The Danger of a Single Story', TEDGlobal 2009b www.ted. com/talks/chimamanda_adichie_the_danger_of_a_single_story (filmed July 2009), www.ted.com/talks/chimamanda_adichie_the_ danger_of_a_single_story/transcript (October 2009).

—. 'We Should All be Feminists', TEDxEuston 2013 http://tedxtalks.

ted.com/video/We-should-all-be-feminists-Chim (12 April 2013).

—. *Americanah* (New York: Alfred A. Knopf, 2013).

—. *We Should All be Feminists* (London: Fourth Estate, 2014).

Azuonye N., 'What is Illuminating about Adichie's 'The Danger of a Single Story'?' *AfricaResource*, 7 June 2010, www.africaresource.com/essays-a-reviews/literary/753-what-is-illuminating-about-adichies-the-danger-of-a-single-story.

Carotenuto S., 'A Will-To-Power in the Crossing of Space and Time: *An Atlas of the Difficult World* by Adrienne Rich', *Anglistica*, 2.2, 1998.

—. '*Here and Now*: the Leprosy of Nationhood in Sonia Sanchez's Poetics', *Anglistica*, 4.2, 2000.

Cixous H., 'The Laugh of Medusa', *Signs*, 1.4, 1976.

—. *Three Steps on the Ladder of Writing* (New York: Columbia University Press, 1993).

Ferreira da Silva D., 'To Be Announced. Radical Praxis or Knowing (at) the Limits of Justice', *Social Text* 114, 31.1, 2013.

Finney, N., 'The World Is Round: The Breast of the Garment Measured', *The World Is Round. Poems* (Evanston, IL: TriQuarterly Books/ Northwestern University Press, 2013).

Franklin R., 'Things come Together', *New Republic* 6 October 2009, www.newrepublic.com/article/books-and-arts/things-come-together.

Griswold W., *Bearing Witness: Readers, Writers, and the Novel in Nigeria* (New Jersey: Princeton University Press, 2000).

Guarracino S., 'Writing "So Raw and True": Blogging in Chimamanda Ngozi Adichie's *Americanah*', *Between*, IV.8, 2014.

Halberstam J., 'The Wild Beyond: With and for the Undercommons', in S. Harney and F. Moten (2013).

Harney S. and F. Moten, *The Undercommons. Fugitive Planning & Black Study* (New York: Minor Compositions, 2013).

Horton, R., 'Girl Model J', *Pitch Dark Anarchy: Poems* (Evanston, IL: TriQuarterly Books /Northwestern University Press, 2013).

Lispector, C., *The Stream of Life* (Minneapolis, University of Minnesota Press, 1989).

Mbembe A., 'What is postcolonial thinking? An interview with Achille Mbembe', by Olivier Mongin, Nathalie Lempereur and Jean-Louis Schlegel, *Eurozine*, 1 September 2008 (first published in *Esprit*, 12, 2006) www.eurozine.com/articles/2008-01-09-mbembe-en.html.

—. 'Africa and the Future: An Interview with Achille Mbembe', *AfricaCountry*, 20 November 2013 http://africasacountry.com/2013/11/africa-and-the-future-an-interview-with-achille-mbembe (edited version of the interview first published in *Swissfuture*, March 2013).

McCandless H., '*The Thing Around Your Neck* by Chimamanda Ngozi Adichie' (review), *IdentityTheory*, 2 February 2010, www.identitytheory.com/the-neck-chimamanda-ngozi-adichie.

Okwuje J., 'The American Embassy' by Chimamanda Ngozi Adichie (a review), https://okwujeisrael.wordpress.com/2012/09/26/the-american-embassy-by-chimamanda-ngozi-adichie-a-review.

Raz G., 'Irritation and Space: A Nigerian Writer in America', *NPR* Interview with Chimamanda Ngozi Adichie, 21 June 2009, pennstatereads.psu.edu/transcript1.docx.

Said W. E., *Representations of the Intellectual: the 1993 Reith Lectures* (London: Vintage Books, 1996).

Sanchez, S., 'Sonku', *Like the Singing Coming off the Drums. Love Poems* (Boston, Beacon Press, 1998).

Smith, K. T., 'Self-Portrait As the Letter Y', in *The Body's Question* (Saint Paul, MN: Graywolf Press, 2003).

Spivak G. C., *Death of a Discipline* (New York, Columbia, U.P., 2003).

—. 'Preface', *Film Quarterly*, 68.1, 2014.

Sharobeen M. H., 'Space as the Representation of Cultural Conflict and Gender Relations in Chimamanda Ngozi Adichie's *The Thing Around Your Neck*', *Rocky Mountain Review of Language and Literature*, 69.1, 2015.

Whitaker A., 'The Novelist as Teacher', *Cross/cultures: Readings in the Post/ Colonial Literatures*, 137, 2011.

13

Dislocation, Cultural Memory
& Transcultural Identity in Select Stories
from *The Thing Around Your Neck*

MAITRAYEE MISRA & MANISH SHRIVASTAVA[1]

From the very beginning of human civilization, from the day man had built the first shelter and a society to live in, the concept of 'location' became relevant to his existence on this planet. Religio-philosophical ideas like the 'great chain of being' or the 'ladder concept' in medieval and renaissance Europe also insisted on the very similar concept of location of the human being in the hierarchy of existence. The issue of location is relevant for everything which is derivative of spatiality, and also to some extent, of temporality. A kingdom, a country, the modern day nation – everything is subject to a boundary, and therefore, a location. In this context, it may not be a digression to remember the lines of King Lear spoken to Goneril during the division of his kingdom, just to insist on the relationship between location and the boundary that determines the spatiality of location: 'Of all these bounds, even from this line to this / With shadowy forests'(I.i, lines 70–71). One easily remembers that at that time Lear was still the King, demonstrating his division, holding a map of his kingdom. We use this reference just to point out that the concept of location is interlinked not only with kingdom, country, sovereignty or a map on a spatial level, but also with the issue of identity on a purely cognitive level. The politics of location and 'dislocation' has many more things to do with the boundary of a country, a cultural space and most obviously, with identity in this twenty-first century probably as never before.

In this paper our primary objective is to focus on the interplay of the politics of location and culture and the resultant formation of a transcultural identity with particular references to some dislocated

[1] The authors acknowledge the invaluable assistance of Dr Asis De at various stages of the preparation of this essay.

individuals in three short stories of Chimamanda Ngozi Adichie in her collection entitled *The Thing Around Your Neck* (2009). Herself a 'dislocated' writer, Adichie ever remains sensitive to issues like dislocation, cultural assimilation and the shaping of a 'new' type of identity that is often close to transcultural. Whether Adichie likes it or not, her writings are usually branded by Western academia mostly as postcolonial African/ Nigerian literature. The politics of location plays a crucial role here, as it relates Adichie's country of origin to her writings. Even if her novel *Americanah* (2013) was published first in the United States by the publisher Alfred A. Knopf, it would conventionally not be seen as 'American' literature, but instead as an Anglophone novel published in America and written by a 'dislocated' Nigerian writer. The issues of dislocation of the writer, and also the use of English as the language of the literature she produces, relate each of her works within the context of postcolonialism.

Historically, colonization was the European form of imperial expansion that has left an indelible impact on the socio-economic and politico-cultural realms of existence in the erstwhile colonies both in Africa and Asia. Even the present political boundaries of many African and Asian nations, which were formerly European colonies, are the makings of the concerned colonial powers – 'borders may seem to operate in a converse manner ... as sites that enforce the colonial control over colonized people's lives' (Thieme 2003, 33). Undoubtedly, European colonization affected the economy of the colonies badly but at the same time (probably for their own gain) made the concerned European language the language of administration and power. Nigeria, being a British crown colony, adopted English as the language of administration and power from the colonial period and, quite amazingly, the tradition continues even after 1960. Alongside the mindless exploitation of British colonization, some readers have considered the introduction of a Western educational system as a mode of cultural exchange between the colonizers and the colonized Africans. However, it is more rational to see the introduction of Western knowledge systems and the English language to the colonized Africans, as a means of exercising more political and cultural control over them. 'Dislocated' British colonizers also felt the need for an apparent and partial cultural assimilation with the African people 'located' very much within their own cultural space. But simultaneously, the cultural identity of the Nigerians started changing as they came in contact with the European cultural space even though most of them did not cross the political boundary of the British-ruled Nigeria.

After the decolonization in 1960, Nigeria unfortunately witnessed violence as never before – in the form of a civil war that involved the major ethnic groups of the Igbo, Hausa-Fulani and the Yoruba. Due to the long-term aftermath of socio-political instability, many Nigerian upper and upper-middle-class families found it better to send their wards to a number of European countries and to the U.S. for education, jobs and a better life. It was a reverse flow of history that the English-educated young Nigerians chose to be 'dislocated' into a different English-speaking world than their own. It was fashionable for the Nigerian elites – the politicians, the bureaucrats and the businessmen, to buy houses and apartments in the United Kingdom and the U.S., fearing the volatile political situation in their country, and as for the scholars, the U.S. and Europe became favourite places for migration. Adichie herself won a scholarship at the age of 19 years, and left Nigeria for the U.S. to study communications at Drexel University in Philadelphia. Her own 'dislocation' and the memory of her own Nigerian cultural space have certainly contributed to her writings and her concern with the issue of identity, as she acknowledges in an interview with Carl Wilkinson (2005):

> Before I went to live in the U.S. at the age of nineteen, I was not concerned with the topic of identity. Leaving Nigeria made me much more aware of being Nigerian and what that meant. It also made me aware of race as a concept because I didn't think of myself as black until I left Nigeria … In many ways travel becomes the process of finding … I'm not sure I would have this strong sense of being Nigerian if I had not left Nigeria.

This paper concentrates on three stories of Adichie as case studies from her story collection entitled *The Thing Around Your Neck* (2009) and attempts to focus on the issues of dislocation, cultural memory, mimicry, identity crisis, hybridity and the formation of a transcultural identity for better cultural assimilation. The stories selected for discussion are 'Imitation', 'The Arrangers of Marriage' and 'The Thing Around Your Neck'. As Adichie divides her time mainly between the U.S. and Nigeria, it is natural for her to depict the first-hand experience of the dislocated individuals striving hard for cultural assimilation in the host country in a credible manner. In fact, most of the fictional characters in her short stories are diasporic: either coming from Nigeria to America, or getting back to Nigeria from America. What is more interesting about her stories is that most of the well-depicted dislocated fictional characters are women, as she explains to Guy Raz in an interview (2009): 'gender affects the way we experience immigration … I think immigration in itself is a difficult thing … And I find that women … deal with immigration differently, and I'm interested in it.' This makes it clear how Nigerian women have benefited from the Western education introduced by the British colonizers during the colonial period. It seems that Adichie takes a particular care in telling some personal and painful stories of dislocated Nigerian women who have relocated to America through marriage, and may be seeking better education and jobs – or have some obscure dreams to fulfil.

Each dislocated woman in Adichie's fictional world has her own story, where she takes up the challenge to balance her life through several acts of interpreting her present situation in 'dislocation', of memorizing the past, learning new lessons to adapt in the host country and thereby facing the challenge of the unpredictable future in her own unique way. The initial culture shock after dislocation opens up the process of disillusionment, which gradually affects both their energy and psyche, and they start suffering from loneliness, despair, disappointment, psychological trauma and identity crisis. Sometimes this even makes them regret leaving their homeland, and consequently the characters start missing the softness, the delicacies, and the warmth of the cultural space of their place of origin. Eventually these fictional women in Adichie's short stories start walking down 'memory lane' to excavate the ruins of the past along with living in the present and learning the lessons of assimilation in an alien cultural space. Here lies Adichie's mastery in weaving the collage of two cultures and the urgent human struggle to reconcile them. The issue of the weaker sex adds to the struggle a unique dimension of desperation alongside the common issue of colour. But the fictional women believe not in giving up, but rather in adjusting to the situation and shaping an identity which is more transcultural in nature: 'It is true indeed that the world is shrinking. But to live meaningfully in a globalised world does not mean giving up what we are, it means adding to what we are' (Adichie 2014, 8).

'Imitation', the second story in *The Thing Around Your Neck*, depicts the plight of Nkem, who is married to a rich Nigerian named Obiora and then arrives at the 'lovely suburb near Philadelphia' in America with him. She leaves her country behind for America when 'She was pregnant' (2009, 24). Nkem belongs to those sets of women who value the marital bond above everything under the sun and follow their husbands without any question or doubt. For this reason, she strives to fit in the new cultural space, keeping in mind her husband's demands from family life. At the same time, she feels proud of becoming the wife of a man who belongs to the 'Rich Nigerian Men Who Sent Their Wives to America to Have Their Babies league' (ibid., 26) and is one of the 'Rich Nigerian Men Who Owned houses in America League' (ibid.).

Even when Obiora finds an elementary school for Adanna, their first child, she feels mesmerized by the magic of the dream country. Apparently she seems to be happy, as her dislocation is purposeful and meant only for the realization of her dream space. She even feels grateful to Obiora in his attempts to reduce her initial culture shock by creating a microcosmic Nigerian space inside their house in the Philadelphian suburb by decorating the domestic space with African artefacts and by keeping a Nigerian maid to assist Nkem in her housekeeping. But, quite ironically, the dream space is shattered as Obiora goes back to Nigeria and starts visiting Nkem and the children 'only in the summer. For two months' (ibid., 27).

Nkem takes this loneliness for granted, keeping in mind only the education and future of her children, but cannot resist herself from being traumatized when, through her friend Ijemamaka, she comes to know about Obiora's girlfriend. This incident leaves her utterly spent, lonely, and more confined than ever, and she feels the fragility of their marital bond to such an extent that 'the flatness on one side of the bed' (ibid., 29) does not escape her sight. She truly realizes that her dislocation has taken a toll on her own life. Despite acts of mimicry of the kind that regularly occur in the American cultural space, she feels herself drawn back to her past and seeks happiness only in the memories of her homeland. Her new discovery of a meaningless married life makes her think that 'she does miss home' (ibid., 37), her own cultural space in Nigeria, a place where she does not need to compromise fibrous potatoes for yams, and basmati for the 'jollof' rice; a place where the 'Lagos sun glares down even when it rains' (ibid.). The issue of marital infidelity on the part of Obiora becomes more complex as Nkem reflects over her teenage years, the days of her misfortune, when 'she dated married men' (ibid., 31) and in return those men used to buy new sofas for her household, paid her father's hospital expenses or fixed their roof. As she recollects more and more, the reader becomes anxious about the materialistic nature of life – as in America, so in Nigeria – a life where the border between morality and corruption is always blurred, where life is measured in terms of materialistic gains and loss. In her helpless surrender to the material market of life, everything was so strategic. This was what she could do as an *ada*, the first daughter of her parents.

In spite of all these memories Nkem finds that 'America has grown on her, snaked its roots under her skin' (ibid., 37), and she has also learnt to cope with the culture of America like her husband Obiora. To an extent she enjoys her partial assimilation in the new American cultural space and she finds it rather safer than her past life in Nigeria: she feels herself safe in America when driving back home late night;

she finds that there are no fears of robbers here. Even the 'restaurants served one person enough food for three' (ibid.). Moreover, America has taught her 'egalitarianism' (ibid., 29) for which she is able to share her household problems with Amaechi, the house maid. She has learnt to make cookies, goes to Pilates class. Do all these acts of mimicking make her fully American? Although confident enough, is Nkem able to assimilate fully in the new cultural space? Rather she is in an identity crisis, as memories cannot be effaced from the mindscape. As a result she cuts her hair and texturizes it, because she has come to know that Obiora's girlfriend in Lagos has 'hair (that is) short and curly' (ibid., 22). Being a diasporic Nigerian woman, Nkem wants to identify herself with that Nigerian girl instead of with American women. Towards the end of the story she utters the very words 'she had not planned to say' (ibid., 41), which 'seems right' and 'what she has always wanted to say' (ibid.). She expresses to Obiora that she wants to move back to Lagos with her children despite all the amenities America provides her. Nkem defeats her identity crisis by valuing her cultural space of origin more than any other place on earth.

The second story in this discussion is 'The Arrangers of Marriage', which tells the tale of Chinaza Okafor, an orphan fostered by her Uncle Ike and Aunty Ada in Nigeria. They think that they 'have won a lottery' as they become successful to arrange the marriage of their girl with 'an *ezigbo di!* A doctor in America' (2009, 170). To 'avoid being called ungrateful' (ibid.) Chinaza yields to their wishes and, keeping aside her dreams to take the Joint Admissions and Matriculation Board entrance exam to secure a place in the university, she accepts the 'lottery' prize by marrying that Nigerian doctor already settled in America and starts off for America with some 'ground *egusi* and dried *onugbu* leaves and *uziza* seeds' (ibid., 168) in her bag. She feels severely distressed from the very beginning of her diasporic life in America as her preconceived fancies for a 'house like those of the white newlyweds' (ibid., 167) shown in the typical American films, are replaced rather by a 'furniture-challenged' (ibid., 168) flat which 'lacked a sense of space' (ibid., 167). Chinaza has to pass through various cultural shocks, Ofodile being her guide in the new cultural space, continuously correcting her language problems. She learns what the Americans do and what they do not, and she becomes gradually habituated in adopting some typically American word usage: for example, 'busy' for 'engaged', 'Hi' for 'You're welcome', 'cookies' for 'biscuit', or 'elevator' for 'lift'. Ofodile actively nags to remind her that 'this is not like Nigeria' (ibid., 173) and also explains to her: 'If you want to get anywhere you have to be as mainstream as possible. If not, you will be left by the roadside' (ibid., 172). This comment by Ofodile emphasizes the necessity of cultural assimilation in the host country and obliquely highlights the importance of mimicry as a strategic tool for cultural assimilation. She is highly shocked to discover that her husband Ofodile has sworn an affidavit to change his name, and is now known as Mr Dave Bell in America. This could be interpreted as Ofodile's strategic attempt to get assimilated in the cultural space of America and a well-thought-out plan to secure the Green Card there. Chinaza also painfully notices that her husband has become such a cultural hybrid that he does not even allow any cultural trace of the language of his homeland as he reminds her to 'speak English at home too' (ibid., 178). She loses herself the very moment that Ofodile confesses to her his first marriage with an American girl to secure the residential permit in America – the Green Card.

Adichie cleverly portrays how the Nigerians' belief 'that any fate, any prospects awaiting any Nigerian in America are as a matter of course better than when having to stay at home' (Mami 2014, 7) are smashed when the diasporic Nigerian individual really starts facing the cultural space of the host country. This is the case with Chinaza. But memory plays an important role in weaving the present with the past and she is seen to recollect the situations of her homely cultural space, where she did not have to drink 'bland tea' (Adichie 2009, 171) or eat pizza which she thought was never cooked properly. At home she could bargain while shopping, and is able to examine the food-stuffs by touching them, which is hardly possible in America. She finds the concept of a 'food court' (ibid., 176) – quite popular in America – 'something lacking in dignity' (ibid.) Ofodile's serious and strategic attempts to be perfectly assimilated in the American cultural space puzzles her. She suffers from an acute identity crisis and feels rest-less. That her identity is at stake becomes clear when Ofodile fills an application form with the name 'Agatha Bell' (ibid., 173) in the space allotted for her. Whatever the situation, Chinaza discovers a comfort zone for herself only in the kitchen where she feels a little respite as she cooks Nigerian food and speaks Igbo to herself during cooking. When Ofodile buys her a Good Housekeeping All-American Cookbook and forbids her to speak Igbo, she again finds a way out in teaching Nia, an African American to say certain phrases in Igbo. But as the knowl-edge of Ofodile's earlier marriage constantly irritates and bewilders her, she leaves his place and finds herself in a no man's land. When Nia suggests that she talk to her uncle and aunt in Nigeria, Chinaza refuses and explains that there is 'nobody to talk to at home' (ibid., 184) as she no longer wants to show her gratitude to the arrangers of her marriage. The two-fold disappointments – 'the insecurity, the callous and sadistic machinations of the arrangers of marriage and the entire deceptive appearance and allusion of America' (Asoo 2012, 17–18) make her very much unwilling to return to her husband because he is no longer the man that she used to know. So when Nia asks Chinaza, if she did not call her husband by name for cultural reasons, she painfully replies: 'I wanted to say that it was because I didn't know his name, because I didn't know him' (Adichie 2009, 185). This in-between state of her identity makes her realize that she 'could not leave yet' – she needs to 'get a job and find a place and support ... and start afresh' (ibid., 186) to possess an identity for herself and something that would belong only to her.

Apart from Nkem's and Chinaza's identity crisis, the nature of Akunna's as depicted in 'The Thing Around Your Neck' is a little different. Here Adichie begins the story again with a lot of dreamy assumptions about America – 'You thought everybody in America had a car and a gun; your uncles and aunts and cousins thought so, too' (Adichie 2009, 115). Akunna, who is the lucky one among the other family members to win the 'American visa lottery' (ibid.), belongs to a poverty stricken family in Nigeria. To describe her dismal condition in the domestic cultural space in Nigeria, Adichie brings forth some of Akunna's childhood memories, like the incident of her father's hitting a big car and begging the big man's pardon making him 'just like the pigs' (ibid., 122); or her mother's inability to bribe the teachers of the local secondary school by giving a 'brown envelope' (ibid., 116) so that they provide an 'A' grade to Akunna's brother. In this context, the American visa becomes a 'phantasmal relief from the daily humiliation' (Mami 2014, 8) in the domestic cultural space. Before setting a foot in America, Akunna, alongside her own dreams, also carries the burden of the expectations of her cousins and relatives for foreign gifts like 'handbags and shoes and perfumes and clothes' (Adichie 2009, 115).

Akunna receives the first lesson about America from one Nigerian uncle, who allowed her to stay at his place with his family in Maine in the U.S., and also enrolled her in a community college nearby: 'America was give-and-take. You gave up a lot and you gained a lot, too' (ibid., 116). In that college she faces some awkward situations as the American girls asked her about her hair style, her English and her home, and all these queries make her feel inferior; she perceives these questions as points of difference and recoils from them more and more. She only feels homely now at her uncle's place where she shares *garri* (a typical Nigerian food) for lunch and is able to speak in her mother tongue. But this security of the homely cultural space in America comes to an end when her uncle attempts to molest her, and she is harshly reminded of the first lesson she got from this person. Adichie cleverly pushes her protagonist into a tough situation where Akunna has to take decisions for herself, where the comfort zone of reliance on familiar persons is crushed.

Akunna now starts working in a Connecticut restaurant as a waitress and tries to fulfil her urge to study by visiting a public library. Her struggles and pain in a foreign land remind her of the domestic cultural space in Nigeria, with all its poverty and hopelessness. She recollects the pangs of poverty there, thinking of her aunts 'who hawked dried fish and plantains', and uncles who showed their excellence in maintaining 'families and lives into single rooms' (Adichie 2009, 117). She thus torments herself peculiarly with all these personal cultural memories, but still she does not write to her family. Indeed she realizes that her distress and suffering in this new country is not so big an issue and there is 'nothing to write about' (ibid., 118) though, quite amazingly, she wants to speak more and more about America. At night when she thinks of her inability to buy gifts and presents for her relatives in Nigeria, it seems that 'the thing' around her neck starts to tighten. Several times in the narrative Adichie uses the expression 'you wanted to write' probably to express the difficulty of speaking. In this traumatic situation, she finds an American boyfriend who has already visited 'Ghana and Uganda and Tanzania, loved the poetry of Okot p'Bitek and the novels of Amos Tutuola' (ibid., 120). Her crisis starts reducing when she finds that also her boyfriend's 'parents were different' (ibid., 125) and they are even interested in Nigerian food and literature of 'Nawal el Saadawi'. She is astonished when they do not judge her as 'an exotic trophy, an ivory tusk' (ibid., 126) and naturally she feels relieved that 'the thing that wrapped itself around' her neck 'starts to loosen, to let go' (ibid., 125).

In this story 'The Thing Around Your Neck', there are multiple references to Akunna's act of memorizing the domestic cultural space of Nigeria, and in her desperate attempts to establish an identity for herself by working as a waitress, in her initial homelessness and joblessness, one would certainly notice the diasporic Nigerian woman's identity crisis. But what about the issue of mimicry, with which Adichie deals so powerfully in the earlier stories? It is not always true that every dislocated individual needs to mimic for acculturation or assimilation. If critically considered, it becomes clear that the women in the previously cited stories (Nkem and Chinaza) are married women and, in most cases, their mimicry is inspired by their compulsion to compromise. In the case of Akunna, her first privilege is that she is a single woman who may enjoy her freedom without any compromise. Second, she has found, quite luckily, an American boyfriend (unlike the Nigerian husbands of Nkem and Chinaza), who facilitates her acculturation in the American cultural space with more care and love. Her boyfriend does not allow any situation to arise that may make her conscious about her 'difference'.

Now Akunna has something to write about and she writes her first letter to her home in Nigeria. But in return she receives a letter from her mother that carries the news of the death of her father five months earlier. She feels paralysed again, and this time the shock comes from her home. Her desire to achieve a new identity that she has nurtured throughout these five months after her dislocation in America simply breaks into pieces. The news of her father's death reminds her of the crisis in her country and she finds no escape from the stiff realities around her. She decides to return to Nigeria, not as someone defeated by circumstances, but as someone who has made herself strong enough in facing new challenges. Adichie never mentions whether there is any possibility that Akunna would return but, towards the end of the story, the arrival of her boyfriend at the airport and the reference to her Green Card could be taken as the 'thing' that hangs around her neck like a reminder to get back to America within one year: 'He asked if you would come back and you reminded him that you had a green card and you would lose it if you did not come back in one year' (2009, 127). This Green Card is obviously a token of her transcultural identity that she has successfully achieved, to her credit.

Adichie in these three short stories skilfully portrays the lives of three dislocated Nigerian women – Nkem, Chinaza and Akunna – who struggle hard to find a place in the new cultural space in America in their own unique ways. Out of these three, two are dislocated by marriage; Akunna, who comes to establish herself and to support her family, is the exception. But surprisingly, the tiny and highly fragile dream space of each woman is wounded by the lashes of the American reality. In each story, all their preconceived notions about America, the country of their destination, prove to be terrible in course of time. That the 'American dream is therefore an illusion, and a dream deferred' (Wirngo Siver 2012, 25), becomes very difficult for them to accept. They might have adjusted calmly to their new cultural spaces, but when they receive the shocks from their husbands and uncle, coping with their situations becomes more critical. They were so traumatized that they seemed to lose their voice and also their individual identities. Adichie nicely depicts this matter in 'Imitation' where Nkem, in spite of knowing Obiora's infidelity, never questions him directly, and cuts her hair as a modest gesture of protest. Through Ofodile's nagging nature in 'The Arrangers of Marriage', the language of the host country itself squeezes the voice of Chinaza's private space in the kitchen. Akunna in 'The Thing Around Your Neck', sometimes 'felt invisible' (Adichie 2009, 119) and is in limbo, unable to write letters to her home, although she has so much to say.

Individuals at the time of their dislocation from the home country carry with them to the host country their 'belief, tradition, customs, behaviours and values' (McLeod 2000, 211). All these possessions and belongings are sheltered in their memory, which is again essentially cultural. This memory 'is firmly situated in the present' (Hirsch and Smith 2002, 2) and becomes a back-up system for the dislocated individuals to return to their homes. After facing the shocks one after another in the new cultural space, each of Adichie's women characters shelters herself in memories that help to recollect home either as a 'haven filled with nostalgia, longing and desire ... or as a site and space of vulnerability, danger and violent trauma' (Agnew 2008, 10). The cultural memories of their homeland become a panacea to the strife of their present situations. But these memories are sometimes so shocking that when they look back to their Nigerian past they only find corruption, poverty, joblessness and lack of education. Still they try to access and relate their memories to the life left behind; as Bhabha suggests, dislocated beings should 'reinscribe the past, reactivate it, relocate it, *resignify it*' in order to interpret it as 'an ethics of "survival" that allows [them] to *work through the present*' (original emphasis, 2010, 59).

These dislocated women often 'acknowledge an earlier existence elsewhere and have a critical relationship with the cultural politics of their present home' (Hua 2008, 195). In each of these three stories, the protagonists' attempts to connect their past with their present have nicely depicted the disparities between the two cultures. For the dislocated beings, negotiation is an important factor because it can only help them to accommodate themselves in the newer cultural space. In order to negotiate with the new place, they witness a clash of two cultures as they are unable to erase the cultural memory of their home country. In these selected stories also, we explore how 'Nigeria's corruption and its emphasis on family relations are contrasted with American ease and forced closeness' (Nayar 2009). Adichie's protagonists try their best to negotiate between the cultures of their home country and the host country: Nkem loves 'the abundance of unreasonable hope' (Adichie 2009, 26) in the Americans; Chinaza unites all her mental strength and hopes to make a place of her own; and Akunna, in spite of setting foot in her home, doesn't forget her Green Card, the only pass to return. At the point where two different cultures meet, a third space is generated and it creates in them a conscious urge to develop a new identity for better social adaptability. This consciousness also 'fosters an inclusive, rather than exclusive, understanding of culture as characterised by differences' (Nordin et al. 2013, x). The dislocated fictional characters of Adichie's short stories realize that it is beyond their ability to erase the differences between the cultures of their country of origin and their country of residence, but they can at least mould themselves to such a level of flexibility that it becomes easier for them to acculturate in any sort of cultural space.

At the end of all these stories Adichie's 'dislocated' women – Nkem and Chinaza – feel that they need to shape a new type of identity that would be tolerant of any kind of cultural practice in any new cultural space. The inclusivity of newer cultural practices promotes transcultural awareness and a consciousness of cultural diversity in them. Though Akunna decides to return to Nigeria after getting the news of her father's death in the letter from her mother, she keeps open every possibility to return to the U.S. again within one year, the maximum period her Green Card would allow her. Her return to Nigeria could be seen as the victory of cultural memory over the struggle and busy schedule of dislocation. All the women in Adichie's three stories establish that, unless they shape an identity flexible to the challenges of their diasporic realities, the 'new' world is not going to be a happy space for them. Just as not all memories related to their cultural past are happy, so it is in their dislocated present. But, the newly achieved transcultural identity empowers them to enrich their lives by adding things that are full of hope and promise for the days to come in any location on the planet.

Works Cited

Adichie, Chimamanda Ngozi, 'I Left Home to Find Home'. Interview, by Carl Wilkinson, *The Observer*, 6 March 2005, www.theguardian. com/travel/2005/mar/06/observerescapesection3.
—. 'Irritation and Space: A Nigerian Writer in America', Interview by Guy Raz, *NPR*, 21 June 2009, www.npr.org/templates/story/story. php?storyId=105588688.
—. *The Thing Around Your Neck* (London: Harper Perennial, 2009).
—. 'What Forms the Core of Igbo Society', *The Trent*, 25 June 2014, www.thetrentonline.com/chimamanda-adichie-forms-core-igbo-society-must-read.Agnew, Vijay, Introduction. *Diaspora, Memory, and Identity: A Search for Home*, Ed. Vijay Agnew (Toronto: University of Toronto Press, 2008 [2005]): 3–17.

Asoo, Ferdinand Iorbee, 'The Short Stories of Chimamanda Ngozi Adichie', *AFRREV IJAH: An International Journal of Arts and Humanities* 1.4, 2012: 13–27.

Bhabha, Homi K. 'Culture's In-Between'. *Questions of Cultural Identity*, Eds Stuart Hall and Paul du Gay (London: Sage, 2010): 59.

Hirsch, Marianne and Valerie Smith, 'Feminism and Cultural Memory: An Introduction'. *Signs: Journal of Women in Culture and Society*, 28.1, 2002: 2.

Hua, Anh, 'Diaspora and Cultural Memory'. *Diaspora, Memory, and Identity: A Search for Home*, Ed. Vijay Agnew (Toronto: University of Toronto Press, 2008 [2005]): 195.

Mami, Fouad. 'Circumnavigating Cultural Reification: A Study of Chimamanda Ngozi Adichie's *The Thing Around Your Neck*', *Romanian Journal of English Studies* 1.1, 2014: 215–25.

McLeod, John, *Beginning Postcolonialism* (Manchester and New York: Manchester University Press, 2000): 211.

Nayar, Pramod K. 'Passion minus the Melodrama', Review of *The Thing Around Your Neck*, by Chimamanda Ngozi Adichie. *Daily News & Analysis* (India), 9 August 2009, www.dnaindia.com/lifestyle/report-passion-minus-the-melodrama-1280776.

Nordin, Irene Gilsenan, Julie Hansen and Carmen Zamorano Llena, Introduction. *Transcultural Identities in Contemporary Literature* (Amsterdam/NewYork: Brill/Rodopi, 2013): x.

Thieme, John. *Post-Colonial Studies: The Essential Glossary* (London: Arnold, 2003): 32–3.

Wirngo Siver, Comfort. 'Self-Migration and Cultural Inbetweenness: A Study of Chimamanda Ngozi Adichie's *The Thing Around Your Neck*'. MA thesis, University of Yaounde I, Cameroon (2012).

14

'Reverse Appropriations' & Transplantation in *Americanah*

GICHINGIRI NDIGIRIGI

This paper probes the transnational mobility embodied in the character of Ifemelu in Adichie's 2014 novel, *Americanah*, informed principally by James Clifford's essay titled 'Traveling Cultures' (1992), and Mary Louise Pratt's arguments in the chapter 'In the Neocolony: Modernity, Mobility, Globality', in her 2008 book *Imperial Eyes*. These two significant studies of global mobility and the ensuing contact zones and transculturation are useful lenses for reading the entangled futures of Africa(n) diasporas in Europe and North America. I am particularly intrigued by Adichie's decision to reverse the traditional migrant narrative where the aspiring male travels to the metropole, leaving his hopeful girlfriend in Africa or the Caribbean, waiting to be brought over when the man has settled. *Americanah* features an aspiring female character who charts her way into a successful life and career in the United States before deciding to give it all up and relocate to Nigeria, unlike her Aunt Uju who continues to pursue the elusive American dream.

Travelling to and dwelling in metropolitan spaces gives Ifemelu the opportunity to eventually get to know Americans well enough to write about their 'tribalisms' in a popular blog. Though it turns out that her 13-year stay in America is equivalent to Clifford's notion of 'dwelling in travel/in-betweenness' (1992, 109), Ifemelu inverts the dominant narrative of 'culture collecting' and the traditional assumptions that the 'informant' is a localized 'native' while the ethnographer is the cosmopolitan/intercultural hybrid traveller, whose privileged position Clifford problematizes. *Americanah* invites us to ponder Clifford's question: 'What happens when the traditional ethnographic informant becomes a traveler to the metropole [as Ifemelu does to New York, Philadelphia, Baltimore and London]?' If 'reverse appropriations' (Clifford 1992, 98) occur when the ethnographer in the middle of the village becomes the object of study, how do Ifemelu's reverse appropriations redefine the 'localized' when she 'pitches tent' in the metropole? I argue that as the 'writer', she engages in what Arjun Appadurai, writing in a different context, calls 'representational essentializing'. Ifemelu engages in the "'metonymic freezing" in which one part [of American society] comes to epitomize them as a whole', to modify Clifford/Appadurai (ibid., 100), even as she unpacks the differentiated African and black subject(s). As writer/inscriber, she inverts the localizing moves of travel writing that position non-Western people as 'natives', but she, too, cannot avoid being seen and equally frozen. Paradoxically, when Ifemelu returns to Nigeria, we are told that she 'discovers' Lagos again (Adichie 2014, 586). But her American-inflected gaze is read by her in-dwelling Nigerian friends and co-workers as that of an alien traveller.

Upon her return to Nigeria, Ifemelu's former boyfriend Obinze remarks that Ifemelu changed in America. She became 'more self-aware, she's gone and conquered' (Adichie 2014, 534). In the second section of the paper, which dwells on transplantation – both in the US and upon her return to Nigeria, I read Ifemelu through Pratt's arguments in 'In the Neocolony'. She helps to illuminate Ifemelu's self-realizing individualism and 'metropolitan modernity' (2008, 224). Amplifying Pratt's key arguments that the decolonization of 'modernists of the neocolony … requires that one pass not around but through the subject-producing discourses of the metropole' (ibid., 232), I discuss Ifemelu's emergence as the autonomous self, central to modernity and to her growing racial consciousness that appears misplaced in the Nigerian space to which she returns in the end. I probe the conflicting constructions of home as 'the only place [Ifemelu] could sink her roots in without the constant urge to tug them out and shake off the soil' (Adichie 2014, 7), that would lift 'the cement in her soul' when she is negotiating the 'rhetorics of exclusion' (Bottomley 1992, 48), and the notion of 'home' as the 'blurred place between here and there' (Adichie 2014, 144). Foregrounding how Ifemelu's return to Nigeria is underwritten by her American passport that marks her as an 'Americanah' insured against choicelessness, despite her resistance to assimilation, I probe her doubling of the self into parallel identities in America and Nigeria, and her ability to negotiate transplantation without suffering from what Pratt describes as a permanent 'awayness' (Pratt 2008, 242). As I show, Ifemelu becomes the transnational/translocal actor, able to engage in what Aihwa Ong calls 'flexible citizenship' (quoted in Clifford 1992, 312).

In her American journey, Ifemelu meets Americans and fellow immigrants from different backgrounds, and some of them make a significant impact on her life. Among the first people she gets to know is Kimberly, who employs her to baby-sit her child. The good sister of the two she meets, Kimberly has a fairly closed-minded sister named Laura, and a close reading of the two illuminates the problematic interpenetration of the ideas of identity and difference that Ifemelu constantly has to negotiate. The sisters have a cousin named Curt whose wealth and family relations also merit a close reading for the ways Ifemelu sees and is seen in American society. Finally, Ifemelu briefly meets two interesting characters at a hair salon where she goes to get her hair braided as she prepares to return to Nigeria. Aisha's flattened Africa, where Ifemelu is expected to know every other Nigerian (Adichie 2014, 15–16) and Kelsey's equally flattened Africa (ibid., 233) would merit some discussion. For purposes of brevity discussion centres on the interconnected Kimberly, Laura and Curt meetings.

To Laura and her sister Kimberly – and to the other 'curious' Americans who engage her – Ifemelu would be the figure of the informant Clifford interrogates: made to speak for 'cultural' knowledge, but who turns out to have her own 'ethnographic proclivities and interesting histories of travel' that characterize twentieth-century anthropology (1992, 97). As he recognizes, every focus excludes, and there is no 'innocent methodology for intercultural interpretation' (ibid.). As participant observer, Ifemelu also fits in to Clifford's problematic ethnographic collecting: 'Who is localized when the ethnographer's tent is permitted in the center of the village … Who is being observed when that tent is pitched in the middle of the village?' (ibid., 98). The focal point of the village as a localized dwelling may be disappearing in modern ethnographies (ibid.), and it surely disappears from Ifemelu's world. Even though there are references to her rural 'home', it is not part of the story world. Instead, Ifemelu travels to metropolitan spaces and subjects the world of upper class Americans to a process of reverse appropriation. In her popular blog, Ifemelu dispenses with the political correctness that shrouds matters of race in America as being 'too complicated' (Adichie 2014, 404–5). She sees American 'tribalisms' – the angry black; the Mexican peril; the Asian menace, etc. – despite the political correctness, and she unpacks this 'tribalism' into its constituent parts of class, ideology, region, and race in one of her provocative blog posts (ibid., 227–8). At a store, a cashier refuses to acknowledge the raced bodies of the sales representatives who could have helped Ifemelu with her purchase (ibid., 155), while one of her early class discussions on race skirts around the politically and historically dated term for black people (ibid., 167). Obama's prospects of winning the presidency are pegged on his performance as the Magic Black person 'who is eternally wise and kind. He never reacts under great suffering, never gets angry, is never threatening' (ibid., 398).

When Ifemelu first meets Kimberly and pronounces her name, Kimberly responds: 'What a beautiful name ... Does it mean anything? I love multicultural names because they have such wonderful meanings, from wonderful rich cultures' (ibid., 180–81). But, attesting to the ways Ifemelu reverses the terms of ethnographic collecting where the native speaks while the anthropologist writes, Ifemelu describes her reaction thus: 'Kimberly was smiling the kindly smile of people who thought "culture" the unfamiliar colorful reserve of colorful people, a word that always had to be qualified with "rich." She would not think Norway had a "rich culture"' (ibid., 180). Kimberly insists that Ifemelu's name is 'is really such a beautiful name. Really beautiful', a comment Ifemelu comes to realize Kimberly only uses in relation to black people (ibid.). She interrogates Kimberly's reading of a supposedly 'stunning' black model in a magazine they are sharing by reminding Kimberly that it is okay to say black, and not all black people are beautiful. By calling attention to the ambivalence and slipperiness in Kimberly's well-meaning labels, Ifemelu resists her 'representational essentializing' and 'metonymic freezing'. In this case Ifemelu writes/inscribes, and she also travels. She is thus not localized as a 'native'. She is not a new arrival from an Africa that has not had contact with a larger world, and she problematizes Laura's flattened Africa, the stereotyped Africa of mud huts (ibid., 181) that produces doctors who do not have 'issues' (ibid., 207). She even deflates the well-meaning Kimberly's overcompensatory 'wonderful Africa'.

To Laura, it is 'horrible, what is going on in African countries' (ibid., 181). From starvation to disease and ignorance, Laura's homogenous Africa seems to have it all. Her sister Kimberly is on the other extreme. A philanthropist, Kimberly is the traditional traveller who collects cultures and romanticizes 'some of the people we met [who] had absolutely nothing, but they were so happy' (ibid., 183). Of her travel 'archive' of family photos taken in India, Ifemelu reflects:

> They were standing by an empty rickshaw, wearing T-shirts. Kimberly with her golden hair tied back, her tall and lean husband, her small blond son and older red-haired daughter, all holding water bottles and smiling. They were all smiling in the photos they took, while sailing and hiking and visiting tourist spots, holding each other, all easy limbs and white teeth. They reminded Ifemelu of television commercials, of people whose lives

were lived in flattering light, whose messes were still aesthetically pleasing. (Adichie 2014, 183)

The passage is illuminating for its presentation of Ifemelu gazing at Kimberly gazing at Indians. Kimberly and her family were consuming leisure, and thus their casual attire, easy limbs and smiles. The perceived danger of drinking contaminated water would account for the bottled water, since we are not told that they had gone mountain climbing. Kimberly and her friends compensate for Laura's 'horrible' Africa by consuming a 'wonderful Africa' peopled by beautiful people with beautiful names (ibid., 183), an Africa that gave them 'a wonderful tour guide [in Tanzania] and we're now paying for his daughter's educa-tion' (ibid., 209), where others make donations 'to a wonderful charity in Malawi that built wells, a wonderful orphanage in Botswana, a wonderful microfinance cooperative in Kenya' (ibid.). The iteration of the words 'beautiful' and 'wonderful' foregrounds the superficiality of this group's identification with others in Africa.

Kimberly and her friends seem to be of a piece with Curt's aunt, Claire. A woman who had an organic farm in Vermont and walked around barefoot because of the connection to the earth, Claire is disap-pointed to learn that her choice to walk barefoot does not align her with Africans who walk barefoot because they have no shoes (ibid., 363). When she talks about her Kenyan safari, 'about Mandela's grace, about her adoration of Harry Belafonte' (ibid.), Ifemelu problematizes Claire's need to 'overassure me that she likes black people', an assur-ance that seems to highlight her discomfort with certain differences. Others are not so subtle. Ifemelu notices that Curt's mother seems to be hoping that his phase of fascination with the 'exotic' would end quickly so that he could return to the tribe (ibid., 245). When Curt introduces Ifemelu to his white women friends, or when they hold hands on the street, the look of surprise is that of people 'confronting a great tribal loss. It was not merely because Curt was white, it was the kind of white he was, the untamed golden hair and handsome face, the athlete's body, the sunny charm and the smell, around him, of money' (ibid., 362).

Ifemelu reverses the gaze by reversing the direction of travel. She illuminates narratives that call into question the coherence of Ameri-canness. As Anne Cheng correctly argues in *The Melancholy of Race*, 'white American identity and its authority is secured through the melancholic introjections of racial others that it can neither fully relinquish nor accommodate and whose ghostly presence nonetheless guarantees its centrality' (2001, xi), leading to a situation Cheng captures in the term 'racial melancholia' (ibid.), so Ifemelu comes to understand the production of racial 'others' in American society. As Edward Said suggested in his rereading of orientalism, wherever European colonialism spread, it needed the racial other as the abnormal to its norm: the exchange between Europe and its others was always characterized by an 'us/them' binary, with the latter being the marker of negative value (1993, xxv). But the positive term was only stable in relation to its perceived difference from the negative one. In *Americanah* the stable American-ness is positive in relation to an African single story, to borrow a term Adichie popularized in her TED Talk (2009).

Adichie destabilizes the 'single story' of African poverty, disease, etc. Obinze's new-found affluence is mind-boggling to the average American student (Adichie 2014, 26); Lagos is populated by global hustlers involved in mega-deals that take them to Dubai, Miami and London and they practice their own brand of crony capitalism (ibid., 32); there is a Nigerian jet-set class that is able to finance American homes where the wives can lie-in as they prepare to deliver the now politically incorrect 'anchor babies' (ibid., 102); the choices for their children's schools range from French schools or Sidcot Hall school's British curriculum (ibid., 35); and families like Kayode's are able to spend holidays in the parents' house in England (ibid., 66). There are also families that have transnational mobility: Ginika is bi-national (ibid., 77), Kayode travels on a British passport (ibid., 79), and American college education is an affordable option. At the other extreme are families like Ifemelu's and Obinze's, occupying a marginal space in Nigeria's peripheral modernity and this exerts a 'push effect' that produces migrants relocating to escape choicelessness and uncertainty (ibid., 341). It is this pocket of migrants that goes through the 'mobility hourglass' characterized by 'masses of exploited labor at the bottom and a very narrow passage to a large, relatively affluent middle and upper class' (Clifford 1994, 311). Indeed, both Ifemelu and her Aunt Uju go through such an hourglass, the American 'nightmare' of dislocations that helps to interrogate the utopian American dream. Even though she is a practising medical doctor in Nigeria, when Uju migrates she has to work three menial jobs (Adichie 2014, 121), negotiate the urban decay and the ordinariness of the 'hood', the only place where she can afford to live (ibid., 127). When Ifemelu joins her, she has to deal with a heatwave (ibid.) and departures from the now dated utopian Cosby Show (ibid., 122, 130, 161). She has to send numerous job applications for menial jobs and is rejected by nearly all potential employers (ibid., 161). All this time she is tantalized with credit card debt-trap preapprovals (ibid., 121), and at her college the admissions staff address her in dumbed-down English (ibid., 163). She comes to read Manhattan as 'wonderful but it is not heaven' (ibid., 536).

Uju's patients withhold acceptance to her even after she gets her licence to practise medicine in the U.S., and her son Dike suffers microaggressions against him that eventually drive him to his attempted suicide (ibid., 211). Even when Uju achieves a measure of success and buys a house by the lake, the inhospitable neighbourhood calls into question the myth of America as what some have called 'humanity's second chance'. It is appropriate, then, to pay heed to Clifford's discussion of the markings of 'travel' by gender, race, and culture: '"Good travel" (heroic, educational, scientific, adventurous, ennobling) is something men (should) do. Women are impeded from serious travel. Some of them go to distant places, but largely as companions or as "exceptions"' (Clifford 1992, 105). Citing Pratt's work on discursive/imaginary topographies of Western travel being revealed as systematically gendered, Clifford shows how, in the dominant discourses of travel, 'a non-white person cannot figure as a heroic explorer, aesthetic interpreter, or scientific authority' (ibid., 106). This seems to be Aunt Uju's problem. She chooses a traditional career path and she expects that Americans will respect her for her situated authority as a medical professional. Instead, all they see is 'difference'. In addition, her experience draws focus to a key question in migration studies: does migration reinforce or loosen gender subordination? Aunt Uju wants a larger family and is willing to do anything to please Bartholomew, a fellow Nigerian and an accountant who lives in Massachusetts. Her acceptance of his very conservative views on the place of women in marital relations affirms cultural traditions that renew patriarchal structures, even as the patriarch in this case demonstrates his need for the income that his modern 'wife' brings home. Instead of using her professional standing to assert new areas of relative independence and control from the obviously dependent Bart, she submits.

Both Uju and Ifemelu enact differently gendered migration narratives. Uju relocates for Bartholomew and accepts domestication/double duty that temporarily impedes her professional advance (Adichie 2014, 270, 272, 273). In contrast, Ifemelu's self-propelled journey and refusal to quit Kimberley's employment to be with Curt, her rich boyfriend, speak to her autonomy/agency (ibid., 247). As figures from the margins, Aunt Uju and Ifemelu interrogate the gendered American dream. Because Ifemelu eventually chooses a non-traditional career path that enables her to control her labour and surplus profit, her American quest narrative turns out differently. By launching a profitable blog that enables her to support herself financially and even buy a condo in Baltimore, Maryland, Ifemelu enters the transnational space that enables the 'global assemblages' and 'reassemblages' that Aihwa Ong celebrates (2005, 697).

Ifemelu's blog provokes four questions. Is it tolerated because she is an outsider, as Shan, the sister of Blaine – Ifemelu's second American boyfriend after she breaks up with Curt – says? (Adichie 2014, 418). Is it tolerated '[b]ecause she's an African … writing from the outside [about stuff] she doesn't really feel [that is] all quaint and curious to her'? (ibid.) As Shan reckons, if she were African American like Shan, 'she'd just be labeled angry and shunned' (ibid.). Is it a lie as Blaine seems to think? (ibid., 427). A professor at Yale, Blaine blames Ifemelu for blogging about race as a game that she does not take seriously because she did not join him at a protest against the discrimination of a black staffer at the college (ibid.). To him, Ifemelu was not sufficiently furious because she was African, 'not African American' (ibid., 428). Thus, the black body is differentiated into Africans and African Americans, with Africans being accused of collecting/appropriating the racial experiences of African Americans from a privileged position simultaneously inside and outside blackness. Finally, is the blog a performance of her 'unrecognizable self' as Obinze, her former Nigerian boyfriend, thinks (ibid., 465), of a piece with the virtual 'presencing' of social media, where people 'stage' their personalities for friendly consumption? This is a thread I weave in the next section on transplantation/transnationalism/ translocality, but we may note in passing that Ifemelu creates a global public sphere that enables her to live in the disjunctive space between territory and subjectivity, in a space not defined by the territoriality of the state as Ong would say (2005, 697). Because space-compressing technology enables her to mediate between spatial and virtual neighbourhoods, she can work anywhere. This is a revisioning of Pratt's global mobilities. Aunt Uju fails to gain the requisite recognition because she tries too hard to pass as part of the host population despite her obvious marking as different. To borrow words from Steven Vertovec writing on transnationalism generally, Aunt Uju is '*in* the country, but … certainly not *of* it' (1999, 465). As participant-observer, Ifemelu comes to recognize her introjection/rejection by American society and she disarticulates her citizenship from a specific privileged territory.

The success of Ifemelu's blog premised on the idea of 'participant observer' amplifies Clifford's critique of 'the notion that certain classes of people are cosmopolitan (travelers) while the rest are local (natives) … as the ideology of one (very powerful) traveling culture' (1992, 108). As Clifford says, the important question, then, is not 'where are you from?' but 'where are you between?' (ibid., 109). Ifemelu is between places. Even when she is in the U.S., she operates in an alternative transnational public sphere characterized by 'forms of community consciousness and solidarity that maintain identifications outside the national time/space in order to live inside, with a difference' (Clifford 1994, 308). She maintains virtual ties with her family and friends in Nigeria and others in Britain, and her circle of friends in the U.S. is predominantly among equally excluded migrant or minority communities. As diaspora critics from Stuart Hall to Paul Gilroy have observed, black diaspora culture in postcolonial Britain foregrounds the 'struggle for different ways to be "British" – ways to stay and be different, to be British *and something else* complexly related to Africa and the Americas' (Clifford 1994, 308). Similarly, Ifemelu is both American and something else – Nigerian.

The metropole is the site where Ifemelu, the 'decolonized modern' negotiates her identity and representation of self through an enforced hyper-consciousness of race and her place in the world. Obinze remarks the ways Ifemelu changed in America: 'You're more self-aware … your blog also made me proud. I thought: She's gone, she's learned, and she's conquered' (Adichie 2014, 534). She is more autonomous, and she declares that '[t]he best thing about America is that it gives you space. I like that. I like that you buy into the dream, it's a lie but you buy into it and that's all that matters (ibid., 536). While Ifemelu comes to embrace Aihwa Ong's 'flexible citizenship' and thus deterritorializes her subjectivity in relation to a particular country, she also stays localized in relation to family both in the U.S. where she tries to ensure proximity to Aunt Uju, and to her immediate family when she relocates to Nigeria. She thus helps to answer Clifford's question: 'what stays the same when you travel … And how is it both maintained and transformed by the new environment? … What elements are good for traveling, what for dwelling?' (1992, 115–16). As Clifford recognizes: 'Diaspora cultures thus mediate, in a lived tension, the experiences of separation and entanglement, of living here and remembering/desiring another place' (1994: 311). Similarly, those functioning in transnational spheres include the homeland 'not as something left behind, but as a place of attachment in [what Edward Said called] a contrapuntal modernity' (ibid.). As Clifford correctly observes, 'The empowering paradox of diaspora is that dwelling *here* assumes a solidarity and connection *there*. But *there* is not necessarily a single place or an exclusivist nation' (1994, 322). Ifemelu mobilizes plurality and the translocality of the virtual space where she makes a living. She is intimately connected to others beyond the territorial state. As Pratt notes, the mass-scale reconfigurations of the human world,

> produce new forms of citizenship and belonging. Transplanted people exercise their citizenship in the form of an often permanent 'awayness' ... [that] implies dual citizenship both literally, and, in an existential sense, of a kind of doubling of the self into parallel identities in one place and the other, one language and another. This can be both a fragmenting and an empowering experience. (2008, 242)

Ifemelu undergoes this fragmenting experience, and passes through the 'subject producing discourses of the metropole' that shape her racial identity in America that turns out to be unsuitable for her Nigerian space (Adichie 2014, 586). Fundamentally, Ifemelu comes to recognize her existential being and its connection to the existence of others that might threaten one's sense of self. Having come to understand her being, she is therefore a-being-for others and she is able to explain the Other's look, as Sartre would have put it (1956, 345–6). She dates Blaine not because there is a shortage of Nigerians, as her father seems to assume, but because he seems to be suitable (Adichie 2014, 389). But she is also forced to confront her ethnicized identity in Nigeria. As her first landlord – a Yoruba – in Nigeria tells her plainly, 'I do not rent to Igbo' (ibid., 485). However, he recognizes her specialness because she is an Americanah, a member of the new ethnicities that modernity has produced. And thus Adichie seems to embrace a position that has been adopted by scholars of transnationalism as articulated by Portes, Guarnizo and Landolt: 'Transnational actors do not abandon their culture and language to embrace those of the host society. [The] emphasis [is] on preservation of original cultural endowment, while adapting instrumentally to a second' (1999, 229). This is the same notion Pratt describes as the doubling of the self into parallel identities. Ifemelu does this effectively, and her American passport is as instrumental as things could get.

Portes, Guarnizo and Landolt recognized three prospective actions by the transnational: first is the prospect of the transnational returning home; the second is seeking full admission into host society; and the third is remaining indefinitely in the transnational field (ibid.). Ifemelu returns to Nigeria, but with a mobility facilitated by her American passport. She thus remains permanently in a transnational field. As Roberts, Frank and Lozano-Ascencio noted of transnational migrant communities and Mexican migration to the U.S.: 'Minimally, a transnational field provides immigrants with opportunities and perspectives that are alternatives to committing themselves exclusively either to the new society or to the old' (1999, 239). Ifemelu maintains links with Nigerians in Nigeria and other Africans in the U.S. when she lives there. Upon her relocation back to Nigeria she links up with Nigerpolitans – fellow Nigerians who have returned from abroad – and renews her American contacts with Curt and Blaine (Adichie 2014, 586). But we also need to note the confusion surrounding Ifemelu's return: the sensory 'assault' by Lagos is described as 'falling into the strangely familiar' though the traveller is unsure whether it is Lagos that is new or something in her' (ibid., 478). She notes 'the heaps of rubbish that rose on the roadsides like a taunt … Here, she felt, anything could happen, a ripe tomato could burst out of a solid stone. And so she had the dizzying sensation of falling, falling into the new person she had become, falling into the strangely familiar' (ibid., 475). This exoticization is of a piece with the European adventure traveller, who captures the uncanny in unfamiliar places. When she is picked up from the airport by her old friend Ranyinudo, Ifemelu notices that her friend 'smelled of a floral perfume and exhaust fumes and sweat: she smelled of Nigeria' (ibid., 476). Thus, Nigeria is metonymically frozen in the otherness of Ranyinudo's body. Not surprisingly, Ranyinudo brushes aside Ifemelu's persistent complaints with the comment that Ifemelu is only seeing things 'with American eyes. But the problem is that you are not a real Americanah. At least if you had an American accent we would tolerate your complaining' (ibid.).

While the return is nostalgic and melancholic, it is underwritten by Ifemelu's American passport that acts as a shield against choicelessness (ibid., 481). But this home does not correspond to the idealized 'only place she could sink her roots in without the constant urge to tug them out and shake off the soil' that would lift 'the cement in her soul' (ibid., 7), because the real home turns out to be unhomely. 'Home' is still the 'blurred place between here and there' (ibid., 144). If 'Enlightenment travelers came home laden with curiosities and specimens' as Pratt says (2008, 241), Ifemelu returns to Nigeria with the tangible American car, and her Americanah self that positions her as outsider-insider. She doubles 'the self into parallel identities in one place and another' and thus suffers both the 'fragmenting and empowering experience' that Pratt describes (ibid., 242). She resists assimilation (thus somehow keeping alive the notion of home) as a consolidated American subject by keeping her Nigerian accent (Adichie 2014, 216, 534) and natural hair (ibid., 44), but upon her return she is labelled an Americanah/ Nigerpolitan. Is she simply seeing things through American eyes as Ranyinudo thinks and therefore finds Nigeria 'unhomely'? (ibid., 476).

If so, why does she not fit in with the Nigerpolitans, that band of 'been-to' Nigerians whose 'manic optimism' Obinze remarks (ibid.), whose constant lament is the loss of the comforts they had abroad – good customer service, 'decent' vegetarian restaurants, and whose affected mannerisms she finds off-putting? (ibid. 502). As Vertovec recognized early, transnationalism is a reconstruction of place or locality (1999, 447). It is marked by dual or multiple identifications – emphasizing individuals' 'awareness of decentered attachments, of being simultaneously "home away from home," "here and there," or ... British and something else' (ibid., 450). The transnational actor maintains several identities that link them simultaneously to more than one nation. It is 'the connection (elsewhere) that makes a difference (here)' (ibid.). The awareness of multi-locality stimulates the desire to connect oneself with others, both 'here' and 'there' who share the same 'routes' and 'roots' to borrow terms from Paul Gilroy (ibid.). As scholars (following Appadurai) now recognize, there are 'increasing difficulties of relating to, or indeed producing, "locality" ("as a structure of feeling, a property of life and ideology of situated community")' (ibid., 456). The emphasis is on Ong's reassemblages of subjectivity, citizenship and territoriality, which are mapped and remapped in a translocal virtual world. In Nigeria, Ifemelu is unable to fit yet again in a normal work environment and she once again leaves employment to set up her virtual workplace. She launches a blog that soon gains a virtual presence that enables her to reconnect with Blaine and Curt (Adichie 2014, 586).

Whereas Ifemelu felt that there was something wrong with her when she first relocated to Nigeria, she seems to find some peace after launching her blog and she begins to 'discover' Lagos again as 'she spun herself into being' (ibid.). She does this by reaching back into her Nigerian and American pasts in provocative ways. As an autonomous being who has passed through the subject-producing discourses of the metropolis – some of her meditations seem to be straight out of Sartrean existentialism, and her reading of the urban decay has overtones of a modernist angst – she dates Fred, a fellow Americanah and also engages in a sexual relationship with Obinze even while he is obviously married, although he seems to leave his wife for her in the end (ibid., 588). But she also re-activates her contacts with Blaine and Curt. She thus works in a virtual neighbourhood, lives in a local Nigerian space, but privileges her mobile American citizenship even as she identifies with others both in Nigeria and America. She is thus a trans-local/transnational/transplanted actor who has doubled the self into parallel identities able to survive in America and Nigeria, and engage in reverse appropriations in both spaces. But she, too, becomes the object of appropriation in both spaces. While she thinks that she is 'discovering' Lagos in a way that connects her to the circularity of departure and return that informs travel literature, Ifemelu's attempt to read Lagos, its traffic and decay, is interrogated by her in-dwelling Nigerian friends as the marker of her being an outsider, an Americanah. She is also appropriated and frozen metonymically as an Other in both places.

Works Cited

Adichie, Chimamanda Ngozi. *Americanah*. New York: Anchor, 2014.

—. 'The Danger of the Single Story', www.ted.com/talks/lang/english/chimamanda_adichie_the_danger_of_a_single_story.html, 2009.

Bottomley, Gillian: *From Another Place: Migration and the Politics of Culture*. Cambridge: Cambridge University Press, 1992.

Cheng, Anne. *The Melancholy of Race: Psychoanalysis, Assimilation, and Hidden Grief*. Oxford: Oxford University Press, 2001.

Clifford, James. 'Diasporas'. *Cultural Anthropology* 9.3, 1994: 302–38.

—. 'Traveling Cultures'. *Cultural Studies*. Lawrence Grosberg, Cary Nelson and Paula A. Treichler (Eds). New York: Routledge, 1992: 96–116.

Ong, Aihwa. '(Re) articulations of Citizenship'. *Political Science and Politics*. 38.4, 2005: 697–9.

Portes, Alejandro, Luis E. Guarnizo and Patricia Landolt: 'Introduction: Pitfalls and promise of an Emergent research field'. *Ethnic and Racial Studies* Special Issue on Transnational Communities 22.2, 1999: 217–37.

Pratt, M. L. *Imperial Eyes: Travel Writing and Transculturation*. London: Routledge, 2008.

Roberts, Bryan R., Reanne Frank and Fernando Lozano-Ascencio: 'Transnational migrant communities and Mexican migration to the US'. *Ethnic and Racial Studies* Special Issue on Transnational Communities 22.2, 1999: 238–66.

Said, Edward. *Culture and Imperialism*. New York: Vintage, 1993.

Sartre, Jean Paul. *Being and Nothingness*. New York: Washington Square Press, 1956 [1943].

Vertovec, Steven. 'Conceiving and researching transnationalism.' *Ethnic and Racial Studies* Special Issue on Transnational Communities 22.2, 1999: 447–62.

15

Revisiting Double Consciousness
& Relocating the Self in *Americanah*

ROSE A. SACKEYFIO

Chimamanda Ngozi Adichie has received critical acclaim for her creative artistry since her first novel *Purple Hibiscus* (2004) became an award winning bestseller, followed by *Half of a Yellow Sun* in 2006. Her collection of short stories, *The Thing Around Your Neck* (2009) and latest novel, *Americanah* (2013) unpacks contemporary themes in African literature that situate the African diaspora as a focal point of migration, transnational space(s) and diaspora identity through a gendered lens. This essay will explore Adichie's interrogation of Nigerian cultural identity within hostile environments that fracture her character's self-image, behaviours and relationships with others. All of the characters in *Americanah* are transformed by abrasive encounters and a new reality of their *blackness* that splinters their identity.

Several contemporary African writers also craft fiction about the ravages of hybridized existence in the borderless world of the twenty-first century. Writers like Sefi Atta in her collection of short stories *News from Home* (2010) and her latest novel, *A Bit of Difference* (2013), NoViolet Bulawayo's *We Need New Names* (2014), Ama Ata Aidoo's 2012 collection of short stories, *Diplomatic Pounds* and Okey Ndibe's *Foreign Gods Inc.* (2014) are significant works that represent timely and compelling themes in African literary production. These works comprise a genre of literature that mirrors the transformative nature of African experiences in the global environment of today's world.

The exploration of contemporary works by African writers that are based in the diaspora illuminates the ways in which intertextuality emerges from this growing body of works. Connecting themes within this new genre expound Adichie's insights into various forms of alienation that are expressed in *Americanah*. For example, Sefi Atta adds credence to the existence of behaviours such as double consciousness and identity conflict in her fiction. Her short stories, 'A Temporary Position', 'News From Home' and her novel, *A Bit of Difference* share similarities to *Americanah*'s Nigerian immigrant characters, whose assimilation of fake English accents, pretence and conflicting relationships to Nigeria shapes their behaviours. Children are no exception, and in *News from Home*, Atta describes how the Americanized Nigerian children that the protagonist babysits have acquired negative perceptions of Africa.

NoViolet Bulawayo's novel *We Need New Names* traces the gradual identity confusion of a transplanted adolescent from Zimbabwe whose coping mechanisms in Detroit mirror Adichie's *doubling* and estrangement from Africa. After years of assimilation, the protagonist comes to terms with her divided self through symbolism of a mask that is both and white. Ama Ata Aidoo's collection of short stories, *Diplomatic Pounds* portrays Ghanaian immigrant women in London whose lives reflect varying degrees of bifurcated existence. To illustrate, 'New Lessons' depicts a retired female professor who lives in London and thinks of her country as 'unpleasant and alien' (2012, 2) and who vows never return to Ghana. Likewise, another female character, in 'Funnyless', refers to her Ghanaian language as 'their language' (ibid., 129) that she mentally translates into English.

Foreign Gods, by Okey Ndibe vividly captures diasporic double consciousness through multiple sites of confusion in the life of the protagonist. This novel echoes themes of cultural dissonance and hybridity as the male character stumbles through a moral dilemma, resulting from his failure to succeed in America. Although he does not alter his speech patterns as a conscious act of *doubling,* he experiences a 'dreamlike state' as he observes a wealthy white woman writing a cheque for over four hundred thousand dollars. He 'imagined himself living that life, albeit on a much smaller scale' (2014, 316). His experience of marginalization and desperation propel him towards a moral corruption that is antithetical to his cultural integrity as a Nigerian, to his relationship to his people and to his cultural values. The caveat in both *Foreign Gods* and *Americanah* is the underlying theme of vulnerability of African immigrants to alter speech, behaviour, values and perceptions of themselves because of their *outsider* status within transnational spaces. The need to simply belong and to succeed is marred by the dynamics of race, class and gender and in Adichie's short story 'The Arrangers of Marriage', the female at the centre of the story narrates her new husband's attempts to mould her into a shallow replica of an American. He pressures her to change her name, behaviour, foods and speech. These works by African diaspora writers form a kaleidoscopic view of African immigrants that are enmeshed in perplexing realities and contradictions in foreign spaces.

Adichie's works add to this array of vibrant writing and draws upon her personal experiences as a Nigerian immigrant to America. *Americanah* vividly captures the challenges of hybridized existence in the alien landscapes of the West. African immigrant experiences in Western spaces confront the challenge of assimilation of incongruent lifestyles, behaviours and Western values. Adichie has skilfully woven a tapestry of familiar themes of gender dynamics, dislocation and the struggle to survive in transnational spaces. The Nigerian characters are confronted with choices that may lead to unexpected outcomes as they navigate a world that reconfigures their African identity in discomforting ways. As a consequence, *Americanah* has garnered exuberant accolades as a compelling work that uncovers the transformative aspects of diaspora life for African immigrants. The novel captures a broad range of experiences that create new forms of African identity and shed penetrating insight into what it means to be African in the twenty-first century.

Throughout history, African encounters with the West have engendered clashes of cultures, and distorted perceptions of African and African diaspora peoples, defined as the *other*. African people who live within multiple localities have experienced identity conflict through internalization of European aesthetics, behaviours and myriad cultural expressions that denote the need for acceptance by others. In the twentieth century, W.E.B. Dubois poignantly articulated transformation of self-perception among African Americans and, these changes are evident among the new African diaspora peoples in the Western spaces of the twenty-first century.

The evolution of *double consciousness* posited by W.E.B. Dubois in his classic work *The Souls of Black Folk* (1903) is a theoretical framework that elucidates the splintered psyche of African Americans that are cast as the *other* within the racially polarized environment of America. Dubois' articulation of double consciousness contextualizes the debilitating legacy of slavery borne of America's quagmire of racial oppression since the fifteenth century. In 1993, Paul Gilroy published his classic, *The Black Atlantic: Modernity and Double Consciousness* where he re-visits the concept within the spatio-temporal locus of marginalized Black immigrants in Europe. Contemporary expressions of double consciousness, hybridity and the formation of transnational identity are themes that are imperative within diaspora studies because of the didactic elements, and potential to connect the past to the present through interrogation of the new as well as the old African diaspora. In *The Making of African America* (2010: 203) Ira Berlin notes the steady stream of people into America from Africa, the Caribbean, South America and Europe from the end of the twentieth and the beginning of the twenty-first centuries. In addition, the global age has ushered a mass movement of African people across national, geographic, ethnic and racial boundaries of the nations of Europe. This growing population of immigrants in Western spaces forms a new diaspora that is vulnerable to clashes of cultures, alienation and dislocation so that double consciousness emerges as a coping mechanism with broad implications for social dynamics of identity in the global age. Thus, the psychological transformations of new African émigrés resonate with the African-American experience of the *divided self*, chronicled by W.E.B. Dubois.

Salient features that define double consciousness is the peculiar experience of *otherness* when an individual is accustomed to 'looking at oneself through the eyes of others', the 'internalization of contemptuous ideas of others', and finally, marginalized subjects in the grip of double consciousness develop 'conflicting thoughts, strivings and ideas' (Dubois 1903). Elliot P. Skinner echoes these ideas in the following assertion: 'Generations of African peoples experienced the onus of seeing themselves through the eyes of others. As "bastards" of the West, they always sensed that in many subtle and obvious ways they were illegitimate' (1999, 29). To move beyond the restrictions of a Duboisian framework among African Americans, Samir Dayal employs the term *diasporic double consciousness* to interrogate immigrant realities of cultural difference (1996, 47). In the twenty-first century, new forms of the term connote the fluidity and mobility of African immigrants' cultural positionalities, and multi-local arenas of hybridized existence.

Americanah is a masterfully crafted web of Nigerian immigrant experiences that spans Nigeria, the United States and the United Kingdom. Adichie displays penetrating insight and multiple perspectives through the skilful use of point of view to convey the complexities and contradictions in the lives of new African diaspora subjects, marginalized by their *difference*. The novel unfolds through the perceptions of Ifemelu as she narrates the evolution of her first romantic relationship in Nigeria with Obinze. They fall in love as teenagers in secondary school and when Ifemelu goes to America, their relationship falters as their lives follow different paths across transnational borders. The story moves back and forth between their points of view that connect to one of the novel's important themes, diasporic *double consciousness*. In telling the immigrant story, Adichie has interwoven the diverse, lucid and carefully nuanced perceptions of race, class and gender dynamics, and relationships among African Americans and African immigrants.

As the protagonist narrating the story, Ifemelu navigates her new life in America through uneven forms of duality that infuse her character throughout much of the novel. Her transformation begins after her first summer in America when she begins college. She recalls how she cowered and shrank from a rude encounter with a white person in response to her foreign accent. She narrates that, 'in the following weeks, as autumn's coolness descended, she began to practice an American accent' (Adichie 2013, 135). The act of speaking in a foreign voice marks the beginning of conscious *doubling* of her identity.

In the process of making sense of college life, she meets a student from Kenya, Wambui who is president of the African Students Association. She is invited to join and the experience of mingling with a diverse mix of African students provides at least some sense of release for her. However, their behaviours resonate features of Duboisian *double consciousness* wherein individuals appear to internalize the contemptuous ideas of others; Ifemelu describes how

> they mimicked what Americans told them: You speak such good English. How bad is AIDS in your country? It's so sad that people live on less than a dollar a day in Africa … And they themselves mocked Africa, trading stories of absurdity, of stupidity, and they felt safe to mock, because it was mockery born of longing, and of the heartbroken desire to see a place made whole again. Here, Ifemelu felt a gentle, sense of renewal. Here she did not have to explain herself. (Adichie 2013, 140)

One may wonder at the depth of their self-mockery and derision that is reminiscent of similar behaviours of African Americans who deride features of their own subculture in America along with perceived African cultural characteristics. At the meetings of the African students, one of the leaders gives *welcome talks* as a kind of orientation to newly arrived students from Africa. In comical terms he tells them that very soon they will adopt an American accent as a strategy to survive. These behaviours denote the commonality of alienation and hybridity among African émigrés, and suggest the pervasive nature of acquired speech patterns as a coping mechanism.

Ifemelu's most urgent concern is to find a job as worries over money begin to mount. She is frustrated and succumbs to feelings of sadness and gloom. A sense of foreboding pervades her spirit as she is rejected after many job interviews. She finds this incomprehensible and wonders what she is doing wrong. Eventually, she sinks into a depression from which she cannot escape. She stops going to class, hardly eats and becomes 'lost in a viscous haze' (ibid., 158) of hopeless inertia. She stopped writing to her boyfriend Obinze in Nigeria and they experience a period of estrangement that lasts for years. In the midst of her spiralling depression, she suddenly gets a job that temporarily eases her situation.

Ironically, Ifemelu decides to stop faking her American accent that she had perfected over time. She experiences a wake-up call when a phone conversation with a telemarketer makes her feel guilty when he remarks that she 'sounds totally American' (ibid., 177). The conversation plunges her into deep reflection and her awakening captures what is perhaps one of the novel's deepest and most compelling passages. She recounts feeling

> a burgeoning shame spreading all over her, for thanking him, for crafting his words 'You sound American' into a garland that she hung around her own neck. Why was it a compliment, an accomplishment, to sound American? ... She had won, but her victory was full of air. Her fleeting victory had left in its wake a vast, echoing space, because she had taken on, for too long, a pitch of voice and a way of being that was not totally hers. (ibid.)

Ifemelu's resolve to finally be herself represents a turning point in her splintered consciousness as she begins to reclaim her Nigerian identity. She affirms that 'the voice with which she would speak if she were woken up from a deep sleep during an earthquake' (ibid.) would be *truly her*. In becoming whole again, she opens a path to healing as she recoils from her fragmented and confused identity. She begins to map a clever strategy of mannered, over-careful pronunciations she recalled from secondary school to repel awkward response to her accent.

Narrated through flashback, Ifemelu recalls her difficult and perplexing observations of *double-ness* in other immigrants that begins when she arrives at the home of her Aunt Uju and she notices uncomfortable changes in her aunt's behaviour. Her expectation of familiarity and comfort with her relatives is shattered by the new environment and behaviours of Aunt Uju, who is very different than she remembered, and her behaviour displays the effort to adapt ungracefully to America's unwillingness to recognize her Nigerian name and identity. Ifemelu notices immediately that when her aunt's cell phone rang, she responds: '"Yes, this is Uju." She pronounced it you-joo instead of oo-joo' (Adichie 2013, 105). When Ifemelu asks about the pronunciation, her aunt says: 'It's what they call me' (ibid.), suggesting her assimilation of foreign perceptions and awkward encounters with *difference*. Name changing by African and other immigrants is one of the coping responses to the demand for names that do not jar American sensibilities. Ifemelu also notices her aunt's changed accent when they are at the grocery store.

When her aunt's son Dike takes an item from the shelf Aunty Uju warns him with a new accent:

'Dike, put it back' … with the nasal, sliding accent she put on when she spoke to white Americans, in the presence of white Americans, in the hearing of white Americans. *Pooh-reet-back*. And with the accent emerged a new persona, apologetic and self-abasing. She was overeager with the cashier. (ibid., 109)

Adichie underscores these revealing types of experiences that capture Ifemelu's aunt and her poor state of mind while observing her studying absently at the dinner table: 'Her skin dry, her eyes shadowed, her spirit bleached of color. She seemed to be staring at, rather than reading, the book' (ibid.). This description suggests the negation of her Nigerian identity, blotted by the demand to adapt and by her need for acceptance and approval in the alien environment of America. In addition, Ifemelu is shocked to learn that Aunty Uju refuses to allow her son Dike to speak Igbo: Her aunt says: 'Please don't speak Igbo to him … Two languages will confuse him.' Ifemelu asks: 'What are you talking about Aunty? We spoke two languages growing up.' Her aunt replies, 'This is America. It's different' (ibid., 110).

In contextualizing the psychological impact and historical significance of these disjointed behaviours among immigrant people, African names and languages are the strongest markers of identity. With the exception of a character called, comically, Bartholomew, Adichie's Americanized Nigerians do not actually change their names to English ones; they accept foreign versions that mutilate their African authenticity, linguistic and cultural connections to *home*.

It is no accident that when Europeans forced enslavement upon captured Africans, the first thing they did was to give them English names and to forbid African languages in a deliberate attempt to erase their identity and cultural heritage. Acquiring diaspora identities becomes a short route to confusion and raises issues of identity (re)construction within transnational spaces. In the twenty-first century, these traumatic changes reverberate in the behaviours of successive generations of African-descended peoples and new immigrants whose African identity is ravaged in the global age of social transformation, movement and flux.

Ifemelu's first summer in America firmly initiates her into more diaspora confusion when she witnesses Aunty Uju's attempts to conform to other's expectations in order to be successful. After finally passing her exams for a medical license she tells Ifemelu:

'I have to take my braids out for my interviews and relax my hair ... If you have braids, they will think you are unprofessional ... I have told you what they told me. You are in a country that is not your own. You do what you have to do if you want to succeed'. There it was again, the strange naiveté with which Aunty Uju had covered herself like a blanket. Sometimes, while having a conversation it would occur to Ifemelu that Aunty Uju had deliberately left behind something of herself, something essential, in a distant and forgotten place. (Adichie 2013: 120)

These ideas represent contemporary forms of estrangement from Africa and *forgetting* among African people enmeshed in the need to succeed at almost any cost. After years of struggle, Ifemelu's aunt has achieved measurable success in completing her medical degree. Unfortunately, she has 'made it' at the cost of eroded sense of identity, poor parenting and shallow family life and the risk of losing her son Dike. Over time, Dike is coping poorly with alienation, identity conflict and lack of self-esteem in the absence of strong cultural moorings to Nigeria as *homeland*. His mother, Aunty Uju has never told him the truth about his father, why he has her surname, and whether his father loves him. Ifemelu recalls that

since the move to Massachusetts, he was no longer transparent. Something had filmed itself around him, making him difficult to read, his head perennially bent towards his Game Boy, looking up once in a while to view his mother, and the world, with a weariness too heavy for a child. His grades were falling. Aunty Uju threatened him more often ... 'I will send you back to Nigeria if you do that again!' speaking Igbo as she did to him only when she was angry, and Ifemelu worried that it would become for him the language of strife. (ibid., 173)

To compound the problem, Ifemelu's aunt lives in an all-white neighbourhood where Dike is one of two Black children in school. Because of his *difference,* he not only stands out among his classmates but is *marked* as aggressive by his teacher. He is falsely accused of hacking into the school's computer. Dike's blackness bears the stigma of assumed criminality. Outwardly, Dike laughs it off but he is disturbed by continued racial profiling when he is asked for *weed* by his classmates.

As a teenager, Dike's alienation gradually assumes the form of *double-ness* through the attempt to become someone he is not. Ifemelu notes that with his friends, 'Dike changed; he took on a swagger in his voice and in his gait his shoulders squared, as though in a high-gear performance, and sprinkled his speech with "aint" and "y'all"' (ibid.: 334). This behaviour reflects the effort to fill up the empty space of his Nigerian-ness that is deemed unacceptable in the mainstream environment and is non-negotiable in the everyday spaces of un-belonging in America. One day, Dike attempts suicide and Ifemelu tries to unravel the events and tell-tale signs that went unnoticed. She blamed Aunty Uju and asks her 'do you remember when Dike was telling you something and he said, "we black folk" and you told him "you are not black"? You should have not done that … You told him what he wasn't but you didn't tell him what he was' (ibid.: 380). This conversation speaks volumes about the importance of identity in nurturing self-esteem, healthy psychological development and the unspoken trauma it may cause if ignored. His mother disregards the significance of an essay written by Dike where he confesses that he is conflicted about his identity, compounded by the difficult pronunciation of his name. Aunty Uju's energy is consumed by her own struggles, weak parenting skills and insensitivity to Dike's mounting alienation and depression. Fortunately, Dike survives and shows promise of healing when he agrees to the possibility of visiting Ifemelu in Nigeria.

Ifemelu narrates a vivid account of the *Americanization* of her friend Ginika whose American accented words sailed effortlessly from her mouth and who has appropriated Western perceptions of body image and the obsession to be thin. She describes to Ifemelu how she was 'close to anorexia' because she started losing weight not long after she arrived. Ifemelu observes that 'unlike Aunty Uju, Ginika had come to America with the flexibility and fluidity of youth, the cultural cues had seeped into her skin, and now she went bowling and knew what Toby Maguire was about, and found double-dipping gross' (ibid., 127). Ifemelu finds her behaviour incomprehensible and thinks to herself that Ginika is trying unsuccessfully to prove how unchanged she was.

Much of the complexity and success of *Americanah* lies in the scope of Adichie's presentation of ambiguous identities in multi-local spaces. London becomes the site of African migration into unknown waters of confusion and cultural dissonance for Obinze, the former love interest of Ifemelu. He is pushed to the periphery of Ifemelu's consciousness and is thoroughly estranged through time and distance. His story is a poignant recollection of the vulnerability as well as culpability of immigrants regarding their problematic circumstances. He is tossed about and enmeshed in a tangle of unfortunate events, betrayal and failed friendships in the hostile environment of London. He spends three years there, and all of his efforts to legalize his status lead to miserable failure. The isolation and alienation that Obinze experiences are common among newly arrived immigrants in foreign lands.

Similar to the protagonist in Adichie's memorable short story, 'The Thing Around Your Neck', Obinze avoids contacting his mother in Nigeria and, during the entire three years of his sojourn in London, he calls her only a few times. He has nothing to tell her and feels like a failure. His culture shock parallels Ifemelu's uncomfortable experiences in America as he faces a brick wall of indifference to his plight. Obinze gradually spirals into marginalization and dehumanization through his assumed identity as 'Vincent' in order to work legally in London. His job cleaning toilets makes his desperation more vivid and disturbing. He lives with his cousin Nicholas and is given advice about how to survive in London. He observes the odd, but revealing behaviours of Nicholas and other Nigerians that echo immigrant angst as diaspora subjects. Among the Nigerians he meets, dual-consciousness and distorted behaviours are the norm, conveyed through *English-only accents*, conflicted identities and obsession with fitting in. Obinze describes his cousin's speech patterns when speaking with his children: 'He spoke to them only in English, careful, English, as though he thought that the Igbo he shared with their mother would infect them, perhaps make them lose their precious British accents' (Adichie 2013, 241). In addition, the allegiance to foreign accents causes Obinze to ask whether Nna his cousin's son, would get away with disobedience if he didn't have a foreign accent. From his observations it seems that 'Nigerians here really forgive so much from their children because they have foreign accents' (ibid., 245). Nicholas's wife explains that in Nigeria people teach their children fear instead of respect.

In another account, Obinze notices that one of his cousin's friends, a woman named Chika, says that she met a man recently that she describes as really nice, 'but that he is so bush. He grew up in Onitsha and so you can imagine what kind of bush accent he has. He mixes up *ch* and *sh*. I want to go to the *chopping* center. Sit down on a *sheer*' (ibid., 246). They all laugh at this, similar to the group of African students that Ifemelu meets in America who laugh at themselves as they view African behaviours through the distorted perceptions of foreigners. One of his friends, Emenike, who is married to a British woman confided: "'I miss Naija. It's been so long but I just haven't had the time to travel back home. Besides, Georgina would not survive the visit to Nigeria!" ... He had cast home as the jungle and himself as interpreter of the jungle' (ibid., 267). During the period of slavery in America some African Americans adopted servile, demeaning and uncharacteristic behaviours as a means to survival. The best example may be the exaggerated 'Uncle Tom' figure of the fictional slave narrative, *Uncle Tom's Cabin* by Harriet Beecher Stowe. It is ironic that voluntary migration in the global age could produce outlandish behaviours among African peoples. These are self-depreciating and can never be acceptable on grounds of survival strategies.

The Nigerian immigrants that Obinze encounters in London are very shallow, and much of their time and energy is consumed by the effort to *get ahead*, so that life becomes a kind of double-edged rat race. The former classmates he encounters are self-absorbed, materialistic and completely detached from their culture and from Nigeria as their *home*. Diaspora life erodes their values and self-respect, and their efforts to gain acceptance has hardened and conditioned them to become hardly more than caricatures of Nigerian people.

Their behaviours are removed from African cultural norms that Obinze's expectations for assistance appear foolish, naïve and almost childish. Obinze thinks to himself: 'He knew of the many stories of friends and relatives who, in the harsh glare of life abroad, became unreliable, even hostile versions of their former selves' (ibid., 249). With each *friend* he contacts, he is disappointed at the vague and distracted responses to his requests for help. He fails at every attempt to settle in, including a fake marriage to a British woman that is arranged by two Angolan immigrants.

Obinze's experience with *double consciousness* takes on concrete dimensions when he actually assumes a false identity as a route to legal employment. In this context it has a different meaning from the original Duboisian framework of racial dynamics in America in the twentieth century. His false existence is abruptly shattered when he is caught just before the marriage, carted off to prison and deported, handcuffed, back to Nigeria. His life eventually changes as he becomes successful in Lagos, and settles into married life – until Ifemelu returns to Nigeria.

Americanah succeeds on multiple levels with diverse frames of reference, positionalities and insight into the world of diaspora double consciousness. The novel is peppered with social and political commentary on American and European life through the clever inclusion of a blog that is authored by Ifemelu as she gains her footing in America. The blog somehow takes on a character of its own against the backdrop of Ifemelu's intellectual and emotional transformation and eventual reclamation of her *Nigerian self*, reified through her decision to return to Nigeria. In addition, the novel is peopled by Nigerian relatives, friends and assorted immigrants whose fragmented and disjointed lives heighten the work's theme of incongruent realities within foreign spaces of the Western landscape.

Adichie explores diverse perspectives about race in America through Ifemelu's blog that is very successful. One of the most provocative postings is called: 'To My Fellow Non-American Blacks: In America, You Are Black Baby'. The articulation of this dilemma experienced by immigrants is one of the novels most compelling messages. By giving voice to these perceptions, Adichie addresses the *elephant in the room* that compounds the novel's realism. The racialized environment of America and other Western nations imposes *blackness* as an all-consuming identity without recognition of ethnicity or difference. Similarly, the book *African and American* by Marilyn Halter and Violet Showers Johnson, quotes the sentiments of the Nigerian novelist, Olúfẹ́mi Táíwò:

> All my life in Nigeria, I lived as a Yoruba, a Nigerian, an African, and human being ... As soon as I arrived in the United States of America [1990], I underwent a singular transformation, the consequences of which have circumscribed my life ever since: I BECAME BLACK! ... The difference is that as soon as I entered the United States, my otherwise complex multidimensional, and rich human identity became completely reduced to a simple, one-dimensional, and impoverished nonhuman identity. I am saying, in other words, that to become 'black' in the United States is to enter a sphere where there is no differentiation, no distinction, and no variation. It is one under which you are meant to live and one way only, regardless of what choices you wish to make. (2014: 9-10)

Ifemelu echoes the same sentiments as a form of *double-ness*, because African immigrants must grapple with a new awareness of the racialized context of their identity, mostly in uncomfortable ways. This dilemma represents a new dimension of the Duboisian framework wherein the African immigrant now views herself or himself *through the eyes of others* and through a foreign lens that demonizes *blackness*. In her blog, Ifemelu candidly speaks about African immigrants' avoidance of the stigma of *blackness* that places African Americans at bottom of the social hierarchy in America. The racial stereotypes, distorted images and low expectations of African Americans are confusing to *Non-American Blacks*. Louis Chude-Sokei supports these observations when he notes that 'African immigrants ... do not necessarily experience or respond to racism in the same way or share the same notions of affiliation as African Americans' (2014, 55). Racially charged topics like profiling, Affirmative Action, and racial slurs are uncomfortable and strange. Awakening to racial dynamics creates another layer of consciousness among immigrants through the undifferentiated lens of Black American identity as a legacy of slavery and racial oppression. Ifemelu writes in her blog:

> Dear Non-American Black, when you make the choice to come to America, you become black. Stop arguing. Stop saying I'm Jamaican or I'm Ghanaian. America doesn't care. So what if you weren't 'black' in your country? You're in America now. We all have our initiation into the society of former Negroes. (Adichie 2013, 222)

This means that, essentially, Black immigrants inhabit two worlds of difference, two layers of self-awareness and a divided sense of identity. The dichotomy among African immigrants and African Americans is the unfortunate consequence of diverse historical and cultural experiences generated by the dispersal of Africans during the Atlantic slave trade. Divisiveness, competition and ignorance fuel and stoke these tensions in contemporary settings. For African immigrants functioning within the socially constructed framework of muddled identities in the West, they must constantly manoeuver their existence and re-negotiate their place in the world beyond African borders. *Americanah* explores the complexity of contemporary life for immigrants in the multi-local environment of the new millennium.

In sum, as a theoretical framework, Dubois' articulation of *double consciousness* in the twentieth century succinctly frames the psychological impact and response to *otherness* by African immigrants in the global age. As a connecting thread from the African-American historical context to the new wave of immigrants from Africa into America and Europe, *diaspora double consciousness* reconstructs and (re)imagines the complex process of adjustment, dislocation and marginalized existence. An important and uncomfortable dimension of the African immigrant experience is the awareness of *racialized* identity of blackness as opposed to their ethnic identity from Africa. Adichie candidly expresses these rude awakenings through Ifemelu's odyssey into America's racially defined landscape.

Americanah succeeds in capturing and interpreting the African immigrant dilemma in realistic and compelling narration. The structure of the novel skilfully projects characters' point of view through gender, multi-locality, and subjectivity within foreign space(s) of the West. The demanding and alienating environments of America and London propel the acquisition of new behaviours and identities in order to survive. For Adichie's characters, immigrant life is a kind of tightrope performance where the individual must balance the dual nature of hybrid existence to achieve a sense of belonging and success.

Adichie cleverly interweaves myriad ideas about African Americans, politics and the British and American way of life through the *outsider* perspective of the protagonist and her Nigerian boyfriend, Obinze. Her rich description of Nigeria lends authenticity to the novel and conveys cultural moorings that form the core of Ifemelu's identity. Her cultural identity remains dormant, even as she struggles to cope with alienation and poverty during the early period of her stay in America. This heightens the structure of the novel and also becomes a chronicle of Ifemelu's new consciousness and eventual acceptance of herself as a Nigerian woman. Amidst the clash of cultures, transformative energies and multiple settings of the novel, an enduring love story emerges as Ifemelu comes full circle, longs for *home* and eventually returns, not as a splintered immigrant but a fully realized Nigerian woman. An important caveat in the novel is the negative consequences of identity confusion as a continuing legacy of the African encounter with the West through forced and voluntary migration from Africa. In addition, Adichie conveys, through symbolic representation of characters, the message of cultural dissonance and incompatibility of African and Western values and behaviours. More often than not, African immigrants pay a price for assimilation through a devalued and eroded sense of identity and cultural integrity that mars their happiness and success.

Works Cited

Adichie, Chimamanda Ngozi. *Purple Hibiscus*. Lagos: Farafina, 2004.
—. *Half of a Yellow Sun*. Toronto: Alfred A. Knopf, 2007.
—. *The Thing Around Your Neck*. Toronto: Alfred A. Knopf, 2009.
—. *Americanah*. Toronto: Alfred A. Knopf, 2013.
Aidoo, Ama Ata. *Diplomatic Pounds & Other Stories*. Banbury, UK: Ayebia Clarke Publishing, 2012.
Atta, Sefi. *News from Home*. Northampton, MA: Interlink Books, 2010.
—. *A Bit of Difference*. Northampton, MA: Interlink Books, 2013.
Berlin, Ira. *The Making of African America: The Four Great Migrations*. New York: Viking, 2010.
Bulawayo, NoViolet. *We Need New Names*. New York: Regan Arthur Books, 2013.
Chude-Sokei, Louis. 'What is Africa to me now?' *The Newly Black Americans*. Bloominton, MA: Indiana University Press, 2014: 52–71.

Clifford, James. 'Further Inflections Toward Ethnographies of the Future'. *Cultural Anthropology* 9.3, 1994: 302–38.

Dayal, Samir. 'Diaspora and Double Consciousness'. *Journal of the Midwest Modern Language Association* 29.1, 1996: 42–62.

Dubois, W. E. B. *The Souls of Black Folk*. New York: Barnes and Noble, 1903.

Gilroy, Paul. *The Black Atlantic: Modernity and Double Consciousness*. Cambridge, MA: Harvard University Press, 1993.

Goyal, Yogita. 'Africa and the Black Atlantic'. *Research in African Literatures* 45.3 (Africa and the Black Atlantic), 2014: v–xxv.

Hall, Stuart, Held, David, Hubert, David; Thompson, Kenneth. *Modernity: An Introduction to Modern Societies*. Oxford, UK: Blackwell, 1996: 596–632.

Halter, Marilyn and Violet Showers Johnson. *African & American: West Africans in Post-Civil Rights America*. New York and London: New York University Press. 2014: 1–33.

Ndibe, Okey. *Foreign Gods Inc.* New York: Soho Press, 2014.

Skinner, Elliot P. 'The Restoration of African Identity for a New Millennium'. *The African Diaspora: African Origins and New World Identities*. Eds Isidore Okpewho, Carol Boyce-Davies and Ali Mazrui. Bloomington, IN: Indiana University Press, 1999: 28–45.

16

Adichie's *Americanah*
A Migrant Bildungsroman

MARY JANE ANDRONE

When individuals come unstuck from their native land, they are called migrants ... we have come unstuck from more than land. We have floated upwards from history, from memory, from Time.
Salman Rushdie, *Shame* (1994)

In the final chapter of Adichie's *Purple Hibiscus* Kambili describes the letters her cousin Amaka and Aunty Ifeoma send from the United States. Amaka writes, 'There has never been a power outage and hot water runs from the tap, but we don't have time to laugh, because we never see one another' (Adichie 2003, 301). Aunty Ifeoma 'writes about the large tomatoes and the cheap bread', but Kambili adds: 'Mostly, though, she writes about the things she misses and the things she longs for' (ibid., 301). These responses to immigration to America anticipate Ifemelu's experience as a young African woman in the U.S. in Adichie's 2013 novel *Americanah*. For after 13 years as a student, a writer and a successful blogger, she acknowledges 'the cement in her soul', and decides to go home: 'Nigeria became where she was supposed to be, the only place she could sink her roots in without the constant urge to tug them out and shake off the soil' (Adichie 2013, 7).

Adichie's portrayal of Ifemelu's life in the U.S. brings to mind Carole Boyce-Davies' comment that 'Black female subjectivity asserts agency as it crosses borders, journeys, migrates and so re-claims as it reasserts' (Boyce-Davies 1994, 37). Much of what Ifemelu 're-claims' comes through her experiences as an African woman in white America which she records in her blog on race, a major text in *Americanah*; the 'agency' she asserts in these posts emerges from her statement that 'I only became black when I came to America' (Adichie 2013, 355). Boyce-Davies also sees black women writers as 'resisting subjects' and as Ifemelu writes and reflects on the diasporic reality of living in America, she begins to resist the received ideas on race, gender and nationality that she repeatedly confronts. For her immigration to the U.S. as a college student, and her promising life as a writer, blogger and girlfriend to two American men offers a coming-of-age trajectory that counters the usual bildungsroman genre as it is shaped by Western writers.

Critic Caren Kaplan employs Guatarri and Deleuze's concept of 'deterritorialization' to define the context within which migrants like Ifemelu exist and suggests that 'the moment of alienation and exile' promotes growth (Kaplan 1987, 188). She claims that 'the defamiliarization enables imagination even as it produces alienation, 'which contributes to the migrant's developing consciousness' (ibid.). The consciousness Ifemelu develops in being 'deterritorialized' is a consequence not only of observing and understanding racism in the U.S., but also coming to realize how her outsider status allows her to see that 'fitting in' would diminish who she wants to become. Rather than growing through overcoming barriers, the pattern of many bildungsromane, Ifemelu advances through her recognition that staying where she is will stunt her growth and force her to accept a place in a world which is increasingly alien.

After apparently 'assimilating' in America, Ifemelu 're-claims', as Boyce-Davies suggests, her Nigerian roots as she decides to return home acknowledging the 'layer after layer of discontent' that emerges after years in the U.S. What is evident, then, in observing Ifemelu's experiences in America is that the consciousness she develops could only come through being a migrant in an unfamiliar world where she struggles first as a student and a nanny, and later as a professional writer and a successful blogger. Her decision to leave America, though, and return to Nigeria does not come at a moment of awareness of a transition to a realized self; Ifemelu is only aware of what she is *not* and this has come through her experience as a migrant in the U.S.

The novel opens as Ifemelu travels from Princeton, where she has just finished a prestigious fellowship, to Trenton to have her hair braided for her journey home. Talking with Aisha the young Senegalese hairdresser, Ifemelu asks why she says she's from 'Africa' rather than specifying that she's from Senegal. Aisha replies, 'You don't know America. You say Senegal and American people, they say. Where is that? My friend from Burkina Faso, they ask her, your country in Latin America?' (Adichie 2013, 18). This adds to and confirms Ifemelu's dissatisfaction with being African in America because she is reminded of the ways immigrant experience robs you of some basic aspect of your self as it reshapes your identity. Ifemelu's encounter with Aisha brings to mind Adichie's anecdote in 'The Danger of A Single Story' where she narrates her experience with her first American college roommate who is 'shocked' that she speaks English so well and Adichie realizes that her roommate has a 'single story' of Africa and therefore 'there was no possibility of Africans being similar to her in any way, no possibility of feelings more complex than pity, no possibility of connections as human equals' (TED 2009). The cumulative effect of so many encounters like this with white and black Americans moti-vates Ifemelu to return to Nigeria, but Adichie does not suggest that Ifemelu's decision to emigrate to America was a mistake or even that she is diminished by the experience. As one reviewer puts it, becoming an 'Americanah' – a returnee from America to her African home – is 'an identity predicated on experience rather than nationality, trajectory rather than place' (Schultz 2013). It is the experience of being African in America and all the classes, jobs, acquaintances, friends, and lovers that determine Ifemelu's growth and offer her the insight that eventu-ally leads her to understand that she must go home. As she navigates her way back to Nigeria she is still searching for a way to reconcile what she has experienced in America with what she might discover about herself in Nigeria – a place with familiar friends and relatives, but new challenges. At the end of the novel, after confronting the obstacles the changed Nigerian environment presents, Ifemelu claims 'she was at peace: to be writing her blog, to have discovered Lagos again. She had finally spun herself into being' (Adichie 2013, 586). I would argue that the 'being' Ifemelu claims she has become results from her gradual realizations of what she does *not* want to be – which she acquires during her education, her traumatic love affairs and her various jobs and travels in America.

Among those things 'she longs for' is Obinze the boyfriend of her youth from whom she has been out of touch for many years; before leaving the U.S. she impulsively e-mails him even though she knows he's married and the father of a small daughter. One aspect of Adichie's struc-ture in *Americanah* is the juxtaposition of Ifemelu's stressful but produc-tive years in America with Obinze's disastrous experience as an illegal immigrant in London, which ends with his deportation. In narrating this novel through time shifts in both of their lives, Adichie is able to record the consciousness of both Ifemelu and Obinze at various points in their experiences as immigrants and returnees in order to suggest the tumultuous psychological shifts they both go through before going home to Nigeria, as well as when they finally are there. When Obinze fills Ifemelu in on his rougher experiences as a migrant in London he says, 'What happened was that I grew up' (Adichie 2013, 535).

What Adichie creates in these opposing narratives of Ifemelu in America and Obinze in England is a diptych where the mirrored portraits reflect the dissatisfactions both characters come to feel in foreign environments which, becomes the basis for the 'growing up' they both experience. The quest for education and work in Ifemelu's case takes her through humiliating as well as enriching encounters; she finds jobs, boyfriends and professional success, but she never adjusts to or accepts America on the terms this world demands. Obinze, on the other hand, without the credentials in London to enable him to work as anything but a menial labourer, struggles and eventually compromises and pays for a marriage which will give him the papers he needs to advance. In recording these parallel tales Adichie follows what Rosemary George labels the 'migrant genre' which might more accurately be called the 'migrant bildungsroman' since both Ifemelu and Obinze develop and grow as they struggle, learn about themselves and make choices that will determine their futures. If as Salman Rushdie claims migrants come 'unstuck from their native land' (1994, 85), they also grow because of their alienation, as Kaplan suggests, and gain agency, as Boyce-Davies asserts, because they discover deeper dimensions of their own identities.

Although both Ifemelu and Obinze observe and identify aspects of the U.S. and Britain that warn them of the limitations of existing within a foreign culture, their situations suggest the particular differences of being legal or illegal as well as being male or female. While the usual pattern of the bildungsroman as it developed in European literature centred on male experience and the process of males achieving autonomy and agency in a single, straightforward linear plot, this does not fit the experiences of female development. In his study of the African bildungsroman Walter Collins comments on the contrasting plots of male and female protagonists and cites the critiques of Susan Rosowski, Elizabeth Abel, and Marianne Hirsch who problematize this genre as it applies to women. They argue that the male pattern of this genre emphasizes individual achievement as the primary goal and affiliation with a woman as a secondary action that differs from the female bildungsroman. As Abel and Hirsch point out 'the heroine's developmental course is more conflicted, less direct: separation tugs against the longing for fusion, and the heroine encounters the conviction that identity resides in intimate relationships' (Abel, Hirsch and Langland 1983, 10–11). Rosowski sees the female bildungsroman as resulting in an 'awakening to limitations', since the growth that male characters experience is not available to her (quoted in Collins 2006, 26). I would argue, however, that the usual generalizations about male and female patterns that these critics identify – such as striving for achievement for males and yearning for affiliation in females – do not exactly match the experiences of Ifemelu or Obinze. While Ifemelu achieves professional success in America, Obinze is hindered by his illegal status and only barely manages to get by as he seeks the credentials that will give him agency and a better job in London. It is in the realm of relationships that they differ the most, since Ifemelu has two serious long-term relationships with American men, while Obinze has a one night stand which he regrets, and an aborted attempt at a marriage that he hoped would enable him to remain in London legally. It is through the failure of her relationships with men that Ifemelu learns the most; she identifies unique values and qualities in her consciousness that do not mesh with the lives of her American boyfriends. Here 'affiliation' becomes a learning experience but not a permanent reality. She does not want to be protected, she does not want to lose the intimacy with friends and family she had in Nigeria or spend her best energies competing. She remembers 'the routine of unhurried pace, friends gathered in her room past midnight and the inconsequential gossip', and she laments what she has lost (Adichie 2013, 112). Her memories of her school years in Nigeria and her relationship with Obinze express the idealism they shared and, ironically, the hopes they had for a future in America. Their opposing trajectories demonstrate Ifemelu's ability to move ahead in the U.S. while Obinze is repeatedly stifled. He does, however, achieve considerable business success and prosperity when he is forced to return to Nigeria, and marries and has a family so in his case it is only when he returns that his trajectory resembles the usual structure of the bildungsroman for males.

What is common to both plots, though, is the growing dissatisfaction both Obinze and Ifemelu experience with the people and ways of living they encounter. Through these dissatisfactions and the consequent alienation they produce that is part of the growing process, the awakening of imagination and hence self-definition, Kaplan theorizes results from characters being 'deterritorialized'.

When Ifemelu arrives in the U.S. before starting her classes in Philadelphia, she stays with Aunty Uju and the latter's son Dike in New York, and immediately notices 'there was something different about her ... her roughly braided hair, her ears bereft of earrings', as opposed to the woman who previously used bleaching creams, straightened her hair and dressed extravagantly as the well-kept mistress of a Nigerian general. While Ifemelu sees a more independent woman who does not care about her appearance, she also notices less positive changes. When she observes that Americans pronounce her name 'yoo-joo' rather than the correct 'oo-joo' and her aunt excuses it – 'It's what they call me' (Adichie 2013, 128) – she concludes that this compromise signals that 'America had subdued her' (ibid., 135). This is just the first of a series of recognitions Ifemelu comes to acknowledge that are part of the experience of being African in America. Like Obinze, she has to struggle to find employment which results in the sexual encounter with a 'corrupt eyed tennis coach' which steers her into severe depression from which she never entirely recovers. Faced with the necessity of supporting herself as a student in Philadelphia, Ifemelu goes to a job interview in suburban Ardmore only to be informed that the advertised clerical position has been filled, but that she could instead apply for a job 'to help him relax' which pays a hundred dollars. She immediately thinks: 'He was not a kind man. She did not know exactly what he meant' and she leaves and continues her job hunt (ibid., 177). Weeks later when she cannot pay her rent, she succumbs and ends up having sex for the money and falls into a deep depression. 'She felt like a small ball adrift and alone' (ibid., 190). She is unable to tell her friend Ginika what happened and she cannot 'bear to think' of Obinze, and at this point severs communication with him for years. Later she regrets not confiding in her friend: 'She wished she had told Ginika about the tennis coach, taken the train to Ginika's apartment on that day, but now it was too late, her self-loathing had hardened inside her. She would never be able to form the sentences to tell her story' (ibid., 195). Adichie's text clearly marks this event that occurs early in Ifemelu's years in America as a definitive shaping of her emotional life. Discovering what the necessity of survival in America has forced her to do shakes the very foundation of Ifemelu's sense of her identity. It is only many years later when she sees Obinze again in Nigeria that she can explain her reason for not communicating with him. When he asks 'Why did you just cut off contact? … Please tell me what happened' she tells him 'I took off my clothes and did what he asked me to do … I hated him. I hated myself. I really hated myself. I felt like I had, I don't know, betrayed myself. She paused. And you' (ibid., 542). This is a surprisingly comforting moment for Ifemelu as she belatedly weeps as she remembers, and Obinze's silent response assures her of his understanding: 'between them silence grew, an ancient silence that they both knew. She was inside this silence and she was safe' (ibid., 543).

Before returning to Nigeria both Ifemelu and Obinze grow through bumping up against, in Obinze's case, Africans in Britain and, in Ifemelu's case, against African Americans and white Americans who live on different planes of consciousness. This is where Boyce-Davies' concept of the 'resisting subject' comes into play, for both Ifemelu as a black woman in America and Obinze as an African man in Britain define themselves through a sharpened sense of their differences from others in their immediate environments. When Obinze hears Ojiugo, a former classmate from Nigeria, say 'I haven't read a book in ages' he reminds her that his professor 'mother used to say you would become a leading literary critic' (ibid., 301). But in Britain, Ojiugo is obsessed with her children's progress and she knows 'the recent test scores of all the clever children' and is an indulgent, permissive mother because 'everything is about them now' (ibid.). Later, when Ifemelu is back in Nigeria, she confides to Obinze her views on child-raising in America which echo his dissatisfactions with the way his Nigerian friends in Britain adopted new practices:

> I don't want them to have American childhoods. I don't want them to say 'Hi' to adults, I want them to say 'Good Morning' and 'Good Afternoon.' I don't want them to mumble 'Good' when somebody says 'How are you?' to them. Or to raise five fingers when somebody asked how old they are. I want them to say 'I'm fine thank you' and 'I'm five years old.' I don't want a child who feeds on praise and expects a star for effort and talks back to adults in the name of self-expression. (ibid., 564)

Both Ifemelu and Obinze begin to identify values they share from their common Nigerian childhoods they had never before realized. Obinze also reconnects with his school friend Emenike who pretended to be the son of an *igwe* (traditional ruler) in Nigeria, but who everyone referred to as 'Bush Boy' when his lie is exposed. But in Britain, Emenike reinvents himself again and thrives. Married to an English woman, a prosperous lawyer, years older than he, Emenike becomes a self-consciously fashionable anglophile who travels, hosts opulent dinners and 'assimilates' in a way that Obinze finds pretentious and offensive. He is clearly a stark example of what he never wants to become. Obinze's learning comes not only from those alienating experiences Kaplan sees as promoting growth, but which also make him critically aware of his developing values which begin to define his self. But along the way he thinks of 'his mother and of Ifemelu, and the life he had imagined for himself, and the life he now had, lacquered as it was by work and reading, by panic and hope. He had never felt so lonely' (ibid., 321).

Although Ifemelu also gains in consciousness, her trajectory does not resemble Obinze's struggles as an illegal in Britain; she lives in the U.S. many more years, has a Green Card and is well employed. Her relationships with Curt, the privileged, kind white guy, and Blaine, the liberal, intelligent and simpatico African-American professor, ensure that her years in America are comfortable and protected. But this cocoon of prosperity and companionship does not last forever, and she, too, recognizes her discomfort. Benedict Anderson speaking of 'Nationalisms and Sexualities' references the the 'proximity of politics and sexuality in nationalist novels'.[1] Claiming that '"love" in nationalist novels leaps across politically unbridgeable chasms such as caste, class and race', he suggests these relationships are ultimately 'impossible loves' given the differences they must hurdle and are therefore 'doomed to fail' (George 1996, 181). Although *Americanah* might not fit the classification 'nationalist novel', the impossibility of Ifemelu's relationships with both Curt and Blaine means they are 'doomed to fail' as Anderson theorizes, because of those 'chasms' of difference and misunderstanding that are inherent when individuals from different worlds come together. As Ifemelu tells Obinze later: 'The thing about cross-cultural relationships is that you spend so much time explaining. My ex-boyfriends and I spent a lot of time explaining' (Adichie 2013, 563).

It is through her blog on race, though, that Ifemelu achieves the 'agency' Boyce-Davies cites when black women cross borders and, through her blog, she becomes the 'resisting subject' as she articulates the challenges of being black in America, and thereby empowers her many readers who identify with her experiences. Boyce-Davies' citation of Michael Hanchard's idea of 'elsewhere' further defines the process of Ifemelu's growth for he sees 'elsewhere' in terms of 'consciousness … as a combination of knowing the condition of one's existence, imagining alternatives and striving to actualize them' (1990, 99). The 'elsewhere' for Ifemelu only begins when she names the realities she sees in her American life; she can only imagine alternatives when she moves beyond this world.

Ifemelu's blog on race reveals her growth in consciousness, since she is able to come to terms with her failed relationships with Curt and Blaine, which parallel her running commentaries. These 17 blog entries encompass her personal experience of how race operates in America and includes a litany of the most common clichés, myths and stereotypes a black person encounters on a daily basis. She covers everything from what she labels oppression Olympics: skin colour hierarchies, the politics of hair, to driving while black, as well as the notions of post-racial

[1] Rosemary Marangoly George quotes from Anderson's speech she heard at a conference on 'Nationalisms and Sexualities' at Harvard in 1989, in her chapter '"Travelling Light": Home and the Immigrant Genre' in her book *The Politics of Home*.

America and playing the race card. Making a distinction between 'AB' (American Blacks) and 'NAB' (Non-American Blacks), she offers a catalogue of typical encounters over race with the media, educators, police and co-workers and friends. Ifemelu's blog offers frank information to Africans in America (don't refer to yourself as Ghanaian or Jamaican, in America you are black) to white Americans (don't tell me about how your Irish ancestors faced discrimination in America) to Zipped Up Negroes who don't acknowledge race, to academics who insist that race is an 'invention'. She dismantles the euphemisms that equate 'urban' with poor and black, and 'mainstream' as affluent and white, as well as the nonsensical notion of 'reverse racism'. She offers praise for 'The White Friend Who Gets It' and quotes from Peggy McIntosh's 'Unpacking the Knapsack of White Privilege'.

The reason Ifemelu's blog parallels the decline in her relationships with men and ultimately explains why she chooses to return to Nigeria, is the way her observations on race reveal the tensions in her American life. Indeed, Adichie's narrative exposes how the blog and the issues in her life become one and the same. What she observes and analyses does not just have relevance for her readers, for they are a Rorschach test of everything that is wrong in her own life. Though she initially achieves intimacy through her relationships with Curt and Blaine, Ifemelu's 'loves' become 'impossible', as Anderson suggests, because they fail to bridge misunderstandings emerging not only from race and race consciousness but also differences between African Americans and Non-American Blacks. In this sense, racial and national issues foil both romances and Ifemelu is left to think about an 'elsewhere' that might redefine her life. Before she meets Curt or Blaine she repeatedly finds herself at odds with America through encounters with other Africans, with African Americans, with white Americans and even with well-meaning friends. She is constantly fielding questions from people who just 'don't get it'. When Kimberly, the woman who employs her as a nanny, includes her in a party Ifemelu hears that 'African women are gorgeous, especially Ethiopians'. Another couple tells her about their 'safari in Tanzania', and others about 'a wonderful charity in Malawi' (Adichie 2013, 209). Constantly Ifemelu interacts with Americans who are unable to relate to her except through her race and her 'Africanness', and who never have a clue how insulting this can be.

Adichie's portrayal of Ifemelu's boyfriends is the key motif in the latter half of *Americanah* that exposes Ifemelu's failed attempts to deny her unhappiness with both men. Reflecting back on her 'new American selves', Ifemelu claims that it was with Curt that 'she had first looked in the mirror and with a flush of accomplishment, seen someone else' (ibid., 235). Curt is disarmingly appealing and sensitive; he catches her off balance when he admits: 'So I'm a rich white guy from Potomac, but I'm not nearly as much of an asshole as I'm supposed to be' (ibid., 237). The time she spends with Curt hiking, kayaking, travelling to Paris or London because he's able to secure visas for her instantly, takes her away from herself as she tries 'to remember the person she was before Curt' (ibid., 370). Using his connections, he gets her a job interview in Baltimore, encourages her blog and protects her. But race issues never do get resolved: 'It was not that they avoided race, she and Curt. They talked about it in the slippery way that admitted nothing and engaged nothing and ended with the word "crazy," like a curious nugget to be examined and then put aside' (ibid., 360). They visit Curt's aunt in Vermont and 'Claire talked throughout the visit, about her Kenyan safari, about Mandela's grace, about her adoration for Harry Belafonte', so that Ifemelu complains to Curt 'I don't need her to overassure me that she likes black people' (ibid., 361). Curt's mother sees her son as an 'adventurer' who would 'bring back exotic species – he had dated a Japanese girl, a Venezuelan girl – but with time would settle down properly' (ibid., 244). Hearing this Ifemelu knows she's just another exotic trophy and not the 'proper' woman Curt will settle down with as his mother predicts. In retrieving 'the person she was before' and beginning to emerge into the person she will become, Ifemelu once again has to resist the perceptions Curt, his aunt and his mother, and other white Americans have of who she is, which is an important moment of recognition in her growing awareness not only of her impossible relationship with Curt, but also of how uncomfortable she is in America.

The reasons for the break-ups with both Curt and Blaine echo many of the race experiences Ifemelu addresses in her blog. In the autopsies of these loves and passions, Adichie reflects Ifemelu's growth as a young African woman in America and the specific ways race and nationality issues make her life in America increasingly untenable. After she, subconsciously or not, sabotages her relationship with Curt by sleeping with another man living in her building, Ifemelu records some of the cracks which begin to divide them. She acknowledges her self-consciousness when Curt introduces her as 'my girlfriend Ifemelu' and his friends look at her with surprise – Why her? ... It amused Ifemelu. 'She had seen the look before on the faces of white women ... the look of people confronting a great tribal loss' (Adichie 2013, 362). She goes on to explain that 'it did not help that although she was a pretty black girl she was not the kind of black that they could, with an effort, imagine him with: she was not light skinned, she was not bi-racial' (ibid., 362). These race and relationship issues emerge directly from Ifemelu's blog. But in her life they become personal and the looks from Curt's friends begin 'to pierce her skin', and she admits that 'she was tired even of Curt's protection, tired of needing protection' (ibid., 362).

Blaine, on the other hand, seems at first to be a potential soul mate. He is not only an intelligent, liberal, appealing young Yale professor, but they share similar tastes in culture and politics, in food and friends, even if they do not share the same national or class backgrounds. After a chance meeting on a train years before, Ifemelu encounters Blaine at a 'Blogging While Brown' conference in Washington, only to discover that he is a big fan of her blog. But her identity gets shaped under his influence, too, and she discovers that she's changing her blogs to please him. Despite their political similarities Ifemelu does not want her blog to be 'cultural commentary' as Blaine suggests, but merely 'observations' on race. Blaine's political bent comes out when he tells her that the two novels she loves and comments on by Ann Petry and Gayl Jones 'don't push the boundaries' (ibid., 387). If Ifemelu is never able to overcome the barriers between Curt and herself over race, she is unable to overcome the differences between Blaine and herself on politics in the U.S. As a 'Non-American Black' she does not always perceive America through African-American eyes and this eventually causes rifts. They are closest when they are bound by their enthusiasm for Obama and their joy at his election, but when a liberal white friend of Blaine's predicts at a dinner party that 'Obama will end racism in this country', Ifemelu is unable to be silent:

> 'When you are black in America and you fall in love with a white person, race doesn't matter when you're alone together because it's just you and your love. But the minute you step outside, race matters ... We don't even tell our white partners the small things that piss us off and the things we wish they understood better because we're worried they will say we're overreacting or we're being too sensitive. And we don't want them to say, Look how far we've come, just forty years ago it would have been illegal for us to even be a couple blah blah blah, because you know what we're thinking when they say that? We're thinking why the fuck should it ever have been illegal anyway? But we don't say any of this stuff. We let it pile up inside our heads and when we come to liberal dinners like this, we say race doesn't matter because that's what we're supposed to say to keep our nice liberal friends comfortable.' (Adichie 2013, 360)

Even Blaine is shocked at her outburst and he, too, begins to understand the gulf between them. Here the racial issues are conflated with all the political issues that separate her from Blaine. So when Ifemelu goes to a luncheon with her Senegalese friend, Boubacar, rather than joining Blaine at a demonstration at Yale protesting the unjust arrest of a black library employee who was mistaken for a drug dealer, Blaine cannot forgive her. Perhaps the definitive blow comes from Blaine's sophisticated sister, Shan, who undercuts Ifemelu by attacking her blog in front of a group of people at a party:

> You know why Ifemelu can write that blog, by the way? Because she's African. She's writing from the outside. She doesn't really feel the stuff she's writing about. It's all quaint and curious to her. So she can write it and get all these accolades and get invited to give talks. If she were African American, she'd be labeled angry and shunned. (ibid., 418)

Later when they break up Blaine repeats his sister's words 'You know it's not just about writing a blog, you have to live like you believe it' (ibid., 427). At this point Ifemelu recognizes that it is not just about her lack of political conviction 'but also about her Africanness; she was not sufficiently furious because she was African, not African American' (ibid., 428). This is the gulf that makes their love 'impossible' despite the many things they have in common. The irony underlying her break-up with Blaine is that her blog was not looking at racism in America as an outsider and seeing it as 'quaint and curious' as Shan asserts, rather it was her creative effort to understand black America – to articulate the ways systemic racism impaired human relationships, cut off opportunities and made it impossible to bridge racial and class divisions. The cruel reality Adichie underlines here is that in identifying her bonds with American blacks she ends up estranged from them. Shan resents her efforts because Ifemelu is not one of them and she sees her absorbing their reality and presenting it as her own. Shan's accusation also implies that readers will see Ifemelu's comments as valid because she is the authentic 'African', not 'African American'.

It is not until she goes home to Nigeria, and makes a new beginning that she is able to look back and find more acceptable closure with both Curt and Blaine. Even though Blaine sounds 'stilted', he is glad she calls, while Curt is upbeat and thrilled to hear from her. Ifemelu's reconnecting with both these men suggests the peace she finds in returning and her admission that 'I like America. It's really the only place else where I could live apart from here' (Adichie 2013, 563–4) suggests that her blog on race and her sense of America's flaws does not erase the gratitude and affection that rests side by side with her critique.

When Ifemelu returns to Nigeria 'she had a dizzying sensation of falling, falling into the new person she had become, falling into the strange familiar' (ibid., 475). However, this is not a final stage of growth or discovery, just a new phase in her quest for a coherent identity – an identity which includes her years in America, her disillusionment and her hope. Adichie's bildungsroman does not end with identity achieved, but rather identity building as an ongoing process. Unlike the usual bildungsroman ending, there is no resolution for Ifemelu, just a continuation of her search. It is through her new blog and more significantly her return to Obinze that Ifemelu finds a new balance. Her friend Ranyinudo accuses her of being an 'Americanah' and viewing Nigeria with American eyes. But this distancing is enabling, and Adichie's text makes it clear that Ifemelu is neither idealizing the Nigeria she returns to or is overly critical of what she observes. She is dismayed by former friends, like Ranyinudo, who juggles two relationships and is fixated on marriage, and she quickly becomes disenchanted with her new job writing for *Zoe*, a magazine devoted to insubstantial celebrity pieces which she learns her editor is paid to publish. Her co-workers have no interest in improving the integrity or content of the magazine and Ifemelu quits after a short time and devotes herself to reflecting on her new environment. Her scrutiny of prejudice is not restricted to America; her new blog, *The Small Redemptions of Lagos*, takes on returnees at the Nigerpolitan Club in Lagos, who she reminds have come home to make money or to realize dreams about changing the country, but who whine about the fact that Lagos is not New York City. She chides them for their silly complaints about their cooks not making *panini*, insisting that 'Nigeria is not a nation of sandwich-eating people' (ibid., 519–20). But she guards against some of the pitfalls of the returnees who were sanctified, 'back home with an extra gleaming layer' (ibid., 502), dropping code names of cities where they lived and studied, and yearning for American things – 'low-fat soy milk, NPR, fast internet' (ibid.).

But the most significant moment of Ifemelu's return is her reunion and rekindled romance with Obinze who by now is a 'big man' established in business and settled into the new Nigeria. Fortunately Ifemelu has none of the 'manic optimism' Obinze has observed in other returnees and he instantly connects with her as if they had never parted. Unlike her relationships with American men, Ifemelu finds with Obinze a deep bond that draws on their shared past and is free of politics and race. For the first time since his deportation from England, Obinze begins to confront his own emotions about his immigrant experience in England since 'he had never told himself his own story, never allowed himself to reflect on it, because he was too disoriented by his deportation and then by the suddenness of his new life in Lagos' (ibid., 461). When Ifemelu comes back into his life Obinze begins to face his discontent with his marriage, his disgust with his business acquaintances who flaunt their wealth as well as with the corrupt practices of the Nigerian government that accompany success in the new Nigeria. He laments:

> This was what he now was, the kind of Nigerian expected to declare a lot of cash at the airport. It brought him a disorienting strangeness, because his mind had not changed at the same pace as his life, and he felt a hollow space between himself and the person he was supposed to be. (ibid., 33)

Just as Ifemelu finds herself adjusting to the Nigeria she has returned to, so does Obinze begin to re-examine his own dissatisfactions with the hustle of the Nigerian business world that has overtaken him. Before Ifemelu returns he sends her a text confiding: 'It's strange how I felt with every major event that has occurred in my life, that you were the only person who would understand' (ibid., 460). Adichie does not offer a neat, resolved conclusion for her novel, though, since Obinze's 'marriage hung above them, unspoken, unproved' (ibid., 554). Obinze admits that when he married 'he was newly rich and newly disoriented … Kosi became a touchstone of realness' (ibid., 565). But he is shocked when their daughter Buchi is born and Kosi apologizes for not giving him a son, and he acknowledges 'the questions he asked of life were different from hers' (ibid.). As Obinze struggles with his duty – his commitment to his wife and daughter – Ifemelu retreats and despite her loss of love and Obinze she is at peace with herself, content to be at home and doing fulfilling work. It is important to note that relationship and affiliation have been conditions in Ifemelu's life in America, but here she transcends these needs and is able to live on her own and accept the loss of Obinze. In something of a surprise ending, Adichie has Obinze leave his wife to return to Ifemelu who accepts him. But this is an open-ended rather than a clichéd romantic resolution, for Adichie leaves ragged emotional issues out in the open and the reader is left wondering how these reunited lovers will embark on the joint life they planned, but gave up so many years ago.

Works Cited

Abel, Elizabeth, Marianne Hirsch and Elizabeth Langland Eds. 'Introduction'. In *The Voyage In: Fictions of Female Development*. Hanover and

London: University Press of New England, 1983.

Adichie, Chimamanda Ngozi. *Purple Hibiscus*. Chapel Hill, NC: Algonquin Books, 2003.

—. 'The Danger of A Single Story'. TED (October, 2009).

—. *Americanah*. New York: Anchor Books, 2014.

Boyce-Davies, Carole. *Black Women, Writing and Identity: Migrations of the Subject*. London and New York: Routledge, 1994.

Collins, Walter. *Tracing Personal Expansion: Reading Selected Novels as Modern African Bildungsromane*. Lanham, MD: University Press of America, 2006.

George, Rosemary Marongoly. *The Politics of Home: Postcolonial Relocations and Twentieth Century Fiction*. Cambridge, UK: Cambridge University Press, 1996.

Hanchard, Michael. 'Identity, Meaning and the African-American'. *Social Text*, 24, 1990: 83–106.

Kaplan, Caren. 'Deterritorializations: The Rewriting of Home and Exile in Western Feminist Discourse' in *Cultural Critique* 6, 'The Nature and Context of Minority Discourse', Spring 1987: 187–98.

Rosowski, Susan. 'The Novel of Awakening'. In *The Voyage In: Fictions of Female Development*, Eds Elizabeth Abel, Marianne Hirsch and Elizabeth Langland. Hanover and London: University Press of New England, 1983.

Rushdie, Salman. *Shame*. New York: Random House, 1994.

Schultz, Kathryn. 'Review of *Americanah*' in *New York Magazine*, 3 June 2013.

17

'Hairitage' Matters
Transitioning & the Third Wave Hair Movement in 'Hair', 'Imitation' & *Americanah*

CRISTINA CRUZ-GUTIERREZ

In an interview following the publication of *Americanah* (2013), Chimamanda Adichie retold some childhood memories regarding her hair story, her personal journey in relation to hair and the politics of appearance, which has undoubtedly influenced her fiction. This involved recollections of having her hair combed by her mother, as well as reflections on how, as a three-year-old, she had already internalized the predominant and pernicious idea that straight hair was beautiful and her kinky hair was ugly (Calkin 2013). The increasing attention given to such memories and experiences cannot only be found in the works of Adichie, but also in other female novelists such as Chika Unigwe, Helen Oyeyemi, Sefi Atta, Promise Okekwe, Unoma Azuah and Diana Evans, who are becoming the most representative voices in the third generation of authors writing from Nigeria and its diaspora. The blossoming of this generation around the mid-1980s (Adesanmi and Dunton 2005, 14), which coincided with the rise of the third wave of Black feminism in the 1990s, fostered the proliferation of feminist tropes and themes in their narratives, in turn offering alternative ways of imagining female characters. Discussing recent Nigerian fiction, Jane Bryce observes a 'shifting of the ground of identity-construction … away from the fully-constituted masculine self, to a notion of selfhood as split or multiple' (2008, 50), a tendency which is arguably influencing the conception and representation of female characters in Nigerian fiction and granting women more visibility.

Body politics seems to be one of the recurrent themes in the fiction of the above-mentioned authors. In the case of Adichie's work, this interest has been particularly directed to hair as a powerful signifier of ethnic and cultural difference. This article will thus offer an analysis of two of Adichie's short stories, 'Hair', published in *The Guardian* in 2007, and 'Imitation', included in her 2009 short story collection *The Thing Around Your Neck*, and of *Americanah*, described by the author as 'a novel about love, about race, and about hair' (National Public Radio 2014). I will explore the hair politics informing these works, paying specific attention to the representation of women of different ages and social contexts. The focus will be on Adichie's portrayal of the different but not unrelated forms of transitioning,[1] that is the change from relaxed to natural hair experienced by Nkem in 'Imitation', Ifemelu in *Americanah*, and the unnamed heroine of 'Hair'. In this context, transitioning will be understood in terms of the personal and socio-political implications of the process, under-lining how it changes Black women's relation to their body and iden-tity, especially after the so-called 'Big Chop', which consists of cutting the ends of relaxed, or chemically treated hair. My aim is to explore to what extent similar personal outcomes transpire for the three charac-ters in spite of the fact that they undergo the process of transitioning for different reasons and in different contexts. Additionally, I will concentrate on the interplay between modes of self-perception and personal development in the three characters as illustrative of the multifaceted values predominating in what I will call the third wave of the hair movements, following Cheryl Thompson's description of the first two 'hair movements' (2009, 843).

Although the terminology so far used to refer to the hair movements varies depending on the author, they are unanimously understood as socio-political demonstrations that originated in the United States and directed towards visibilizing the importance of Black natural hair in processes of identity formation. The emphasis is frequently put in what regards the concept(ion) of femininity as a construct. In this regard, the hair movements have directed their efforts to elaborate counter-discursive formations that undermine the pervasive impact of the Western beauty canon, which has permeated in the everyday praxis of Black women's socialization since the slavery period (Banks 2000; Byrd and Tharps 2014; Patton 2006; Rooks 2000).

Thompson refers to the first and second hair movements respec-tively taking place in the context of the Civil Rights Movements and in the late 1980s. More recently, Byrd and Tharps have noted the emergence in the late 2000s of what they refer to as the 'Natural Hair Movement', related to the popularization of social networks (2014).

---

[1] The concept(ion) and implications of transitioning described in this work have transpired from Zina Saro-Wiwa's short documentary 'Transition' (2012) for its representativeness of the third wave of hair movements.

Ellington makes echo of this term in her paper on the importance of the blogosphere in discussing hair politics (2014a, 553). Nevertheless, Byrd and Tharps do not refer to an intermediate stage between the 'Natural Hair Movement' and what they call the 'Back to Natural Movement' (2014), which took place during the Civil Rights Movements, coinciding in time with Thompson's first hair movement. Hence, I shall subsequently consider Byrd and Tharps' 'Natural Hair Movement' as a third wave of the hair movements, since it arguably continues with the legacy of the two stages described by Thompson. It seems appropriate to refer to the movements in terms of waves, since, in spite of the terminology used, they can be located in different periods, with distinctive social focuses and intensity of activity.[2] The importance of online platforms and communities, together with other features which shall be discussed below, clearly mark this period as a distinctive phase. A third wave of the hair movements, in spite of the novelties, engages with previous ones inasmuch as it rejects the dichotomist thought that labels kinky or nappy hair as 'bad hair' and juxtaposes it with 'good' straight hair, thought of as an embodiment of the hegemonic canon of beauty (Banks 2000, 51).

Although not much research has been carried out regarding the third wave, it seems to be tightly associated to the proliferation of social networks as spaces of 'participatory culture' (Jenkins et al. 2009, xi). Arguably, the deployment of Facebook (2004), YouTube (2005), Tumblr (2007) and Instagram (2010), among others, as essential platforms of diffusion and creativity, is the most significant token of the present stage of the hair movements. As alternative media, these platforms are potentially less subjected to the control of ideological state apparatuses, thus becoming inclusive spaces that challenge the beauty canon and champion self-representation (Byrd and Tharps 2014).

Another significant trait of the third wave of the hair movements is its pedagogic approach and the importance conferred to promoting self-love in children and young Black women. In this sense, hair and self are interrelated, since loving one's hair is deemed a symbol of self-acceptance and self-knowledge. In this context, the identification of hair and self stems from the intent of depoliticizing hair which comes to be seen as a reflection of individuality. As Banks remarks, 'hairstyle choice is a reflection of the person. The [ultimate] idea of choice

---

[2] Further insights into the first and second (waves of the) hair movements are found in Byrd and Tharps' *Hair Story: Untangling the Roots of Black Hair in America* (2001), and Thompson's 'Black Women, Beauty, and Hair as a Matter of Being' (2009).

remains within the individual as opposed to outside forces' (2000, 78). The willingness of sharing knowledge and teaching extends itself to adult Black women, for yet another feature of the present wave is its underscoring that a large number of Black women do not know how to take care of their natural hair. Ellington has noted the significant role of blogs and vlogs (video blogs) in creating online communities that foster self-love and dialogue among women with natural hair (2014a, 2014b). By the same token, thousands of short films and documentaries have been launched through YouTube channels and other online platforms with the aim of visibilizing the politics of Black hair and its paradigms. A significant number of those videos is directed either to teach how to take care of natural hair and to explore hair in relation to identity (see Eastside Community Heritage 2014; OkayAfrica 2015; Un'ruly 2013). Other videos describe individual experiences of transitioning from relaxed to natural hair, relating the process to a journey of self-understanding, self-discovery, and self-love (see Boyd 2013; Saro-Wiwa 2012).

In a recent interview, Adichie discussed the impact of the hair movements in Nigeria, postulating that 'the idea of wearing natural hair as a choice is still very young in Nigeria. But the natural hair movement is growing [in the country]. It started, [she] think[s], with Nigerians who had lived in the U.S. But the [hairdressers] still have no idea how to take care of natural hair' (Byrd and Tharps 2014, 203). In this respect, both *Americanah* and 'Imitation' feature Nigerian migrants who start transitioning in the U.S. and become returnees at the end of the narratives, finally adopting their natural hair. In contrast, 'Hair', entirely set in contemporary Lagos, is a feminist rewriting of a conventional fairy tale that introduces a very young heroine displaying agency and strength when her father is tricked into losing all their fortune, and poverty strikes the family. What the reader first learns of the girl's mother is that her 'greatest shame was her hair' (Adichie 2007, quoted in Mantel 2007) because 'relaxers and weaves were now unaffordable. She had been the toast of Lagos with her long and straight perm, and now she always wore a headscarf, even when alone' (ibid.). This promptly marks straight hair as a sign of their now lost high social status, an idea echoed in *Americanah*, where Ifemelu describes salons in Lagos as the places where 'ranks of imperial femaleness' (Adichie 2014, 77) are best distinguished, and the 'Lagos elite' is characterized by their just-imported Chinese weaves (ibid., 82). Concurrently, the attitude of the mother hints the legacy of the so-called 'self-hatred theory' (Grier and Cobbs 1968), which pinpoints Black women's rejection of their natural hair as an epitome of their denying their natural self. Interestingly, one of the most pressing questions in debates regarding hair politics is the impact of self-hatred, which has been widely discussed in the literature in relation to intent, agency, and the subconscious internalization of epistemological constructions of nappy hair as undesirable (Banks 2000; Byrd and Tharps 2014; hooks 1988; Rooks 2000; Thompson 2009).

By contrast, instead of dreading the loss of her relaxed hair, the heroine of 'Hair' resolves to undergo the 'Big Chop'. After cutting all her hair she 'watched in wonder as it grew back, soft and dense like wool, for she had never seen her natural hair' (Adichie 2007, quoted in Mantel 2007). This introduces the notion of perming natural hair being considered a tradition, a rite of passage for girls at a very early age (Banks 2000; Byrd and Tharps 2014; hooks 1988). The third wave's concern with adult Black women not being able to take care of their natural hair for lack of experience is brought to the forefront as the girl recognizes that 'in their old life, as soon as her hair grew out, it had been singed and straightened' (Adichie 2007, quoted in Mantel 2007). Nevertheless, the heroine instantly learns to embrace and love her natural hair, which soon becomes 'vibrant and kinky and full' (ibid.). Incidentally, a semantic field of awe, beauty and positivity associated with kinky hair runs through the story. These feelings and associations can be recalled in other compositions about natural hair directed to a young public, as it is the case of Sesame Street's song 'I Love My Hair' (2010), and Taiye Selasi's recently published poem collection for children, *Love Your Curls* (2015), where curly hair is constantly identified with freedom of movement, originality and lightness. In like manner, seeking to promote self-love in young generations, these instances emphasize the identification of 'self' and 'hair', which also characterizes personal narratives and short documentaries on transitioning published since the new wave of hair movements started.

The attitude of the girl can be contrasted with her family's defeatist standpoint. Her strongmindedness is evident in her happiness not depending on materialist prospects or external elements that might be lost, but rather on her hair – that is on herself – presented as a source of consolation and joy. In contrast, her family seems to be dominated by the Western hegemonic discourses of capitalism and beauty. This is evident in her brother asking her to imitate their mother and to cover her ugly hair with a scarf. Yet, even if undervalued by her family, in the end she proves to be more self-determined and intelligent than her brother. Nurturing and embracing her nappy hair, going against her mother's example and her brother's desires, might be conceived as a sign of her 'nego-feminist' identity, a term coined by Nnaemeka to define a branch of feminism in Africa (2004, 361) associated with negotiation and a non-egotistical attitude (ibid., 377–8). Nnaemeka defends that, inasmuch as 'in the foundation of shared values in many African cultures are the principles of negotiation, give and take, compromise, and balance... [nego-feminism] challenges [patriarchy] through negotiations and compromise' (ibid.).

'Hair' has its nego-feminist heroine striving for self-definition in refusing to cover her kinky hair, for she believes that it 'was the only beautiful thing they had left' (Adichie 2007, quoted in Mantel 2007), and 'it was her hair, untangling and twisting and glorying in it, that kept her from thinking too much of her constant hunger' (ibid.). In this manner, Adichie associates natural hair not only with embracing natural beauty and gaining confidence in the self, but also with originality, and freedom of choice. After endorsing her new identity, the girl wishes their personal situation to be reversed, and only her enchanted hair is able to grant her that wish. As a godmother figure, her hair first talks to her to offer help and consolation, manifesting magical powers and unravelling how to recover their fortune. In subsequent days, the more she nurtures and loves her hair the more information it gives her about how to solve the situation, thus passing on its knowledge and encouraging her to manifest agency, for she is finally the only one who can act to save the family.

Curiously enough, the hair's voice resembles that of the girl's late grandmother, which brings to the forefront the importance of matrilineal connections and intergenerational teaching. In the context of the story, the knowledge passed seems to be related both to taking care of natural hair, and to nego-feminist values, for the hair encourages and convinces the girl of her capacity to take responsibility for the situation. This deviates from the traditional relationship between fairy-tale characters and their godmothers, who traditionally direct female protagonists to passivity and submission in urging them to be patient in their wait for the prince. It would follow then, that this particular trait bears witness to the importance that the third wave of hair movements confers to teaching and promoting self-acceptance when writing for children.

Finally, the daughter undertakes the quest of recovering the document that will grant the family with the legal power of recovering their properties. Hence, the guidance of her magic hair allows her to succeed where her brother had many times failed. This echoes a third-wave emphasis in promoting the notion of kinky hair as interwoven with versatility and creativity, where the girl needs to pass the ordeals leading to recovering the legal document needed to regain their fortune. Following this line of thought, and recalling the identification of hair as self, it is the protagonist's hair that grants her and her family the possibility of returning to their rightful state, that of pride. She may even have prompted a change in her mother, who finally 'pulled off her scarf and touched her own hair in wonder' (Adichie 2007, quoted in Mantel 2007). In other words, it is only the main character's new alliance with her natural hair that allows them to recover their power and identity, to be themselves again, and to live happily ever after in a truly fairy-tale fashion. However, they do not completely return to their original situation, since the daughter has learned not to direct her happiness towards the recovered fortune or materialist pleasures. On the contrary, once the lesson has been learned and the deeds performed, she 'watched with joyful amusement, all the time running her fingers through her hair' (ibid.).

In 'Imitation', Adichie introduces the topic of transition by focusing on different personal circumstances affecting Nkem, the protagonist. It is Nkem's discovery that her husband has a lover in Lagos, while she is living in the U.S. with their children, that acts as a trigger for her aesthetic change (Adichie 2009, 22). Their marriage is presented as an imitation of a real marriage in the same way in which the Benin mask that hangs in their living room is an imitation of a real African mask, for they 'ha[d] settled for good imitations, although they enjoy[ed] talking about how impossible it [was] to find originals' (ibid., 23). This imitation is evident in 'Nkem pick[ing] up the mask and press[ing] her face to it; ... cold, heavy, [and] lifeless' (ibid., 25), as she reflects on her marriage. Similarly, she smiles in realizing that she has also settled for the what she calls American 'imitation yams' (ibid., 32), not like the African ones, in the same manner in which her now relaxed hair imitates that of a stereotypical American housewife of the Philadelphian suburbs she now inhabits.

Before deciding to undergo the 'Big Chop,' Nkem reflects upon the important decisions in her life having so far been made by Obiora, her husband, who systematically silences Nkem while indoctrinating her about American and Nigerian history (Adichie 2009, 23), about how things would work in America, and informing her about his decision to move to Lagos and to live apart for most of the year. Despite confessing to herself that she sometimes doubts Obiora's facts (ibid., 25), she nonetheless listens 'because she had married into the coveted league, the Rich Nigerian Men Who Sent Their Wives to America to Have Their Babies league ... She had [afterwards] become part of yet another league, the Rich Nigerian Men Who Owned Houses in America league' (ibid., 26). After recalling all the decisions Obiora took for both of them, Nkem decides to cut her permed hair, rejecting her original idea of doing a re-touch on her relaxed hair before Obiora's return.

Her 'Big Chop' is sensuously described, as she 'pulls up clumps of hair and cuts close to the scalp, leaving hair about the length of her thumbnail, just enough to tighten into curls with a texturizer' (Adichie 2009, 28). This process is followed by her watching in wonder 'the hair float down, like brown cotton wisps falling on the white sink … Tufts of hair float down, like scorched wings of moths' (ibid., 28). The description echoes the semantic field of softness and fullness used to describe natural hair in 'Hair'. Nevertheless, the process of transitioning is different in each of the stories on account of Nkem planning to apply a texturizer to her hair, showing that there is not a unique method of transitioning. Containing a certain amount of chemicals, texturizers may be applied in processes of transitioning that are to be more gradual, pointing at Nkem's identity change as more progressional and less sudden than that of the heroine in 'Hair'. Nonetheless, her decision of cutting her hair symbolizes the change of her personal situation after realizing that her marriage is an imitation of what it was supposed to be, and that her life has been planned and shaped by Obiora. Considering the external change in her hair as running parallel to her internal identity change, the identification of hair as self is once again recalled. Consequently, transitioning is ultimately associated with gaining authority and self-determination.

After cutting her hair Nkem nurtures it with curl activator (Adichie 2009, 35), and frequently caresses it, reflecting her love towards her new self. This echoes the relationship between transitioning and emancipation, as well as the celebration of Black beauty, for she does not reject her image in the mirror after cutting her hair as shall be pointed out in relation to Ifemelu in *Americanah*, and as is often the case when transitioning (Saro-Wiwa 2012). Her newly gained independence soon manifests itself when her husband arrives and enquires about her new haircut, protesting that he loved her long hair, and mocking her act, not as a representation of agency and empowerment but as a new American fashion (Adichie 2009, 40). When confronted with her indifference, Obiora suggests she should grow her hair back, arguing that 'long hair is more graceful on a Big Man's wife' (ibid.). Such an affirmation unveils the patriarchal hegemonic construction of the wife as an accessory, an object of pleasure for the husband, moulded for him and defined in relation to his needs and preferences.

Obiora's request can be read under the light of Laura Mulvey's 'male gaze', which describes how 'in a world ordered by sexual imbalance, pleasure in looking has been split between active/male and passive/female' (2009, 715). In this manner, 'the determining male gaze projects its phantasy on to the female figure which is styled accordingly … Women are simultaneously looked at and displayed, with their appearance coded for strong visual and erotic impact so that they can be said to connote *to-be-looked-at-ness*' (original emphasis, ibid.). Against this background, relaxed hair can be understood as part a performative act of submissiveness in trying to conform to the standards of femininity dictated by the patriarchal beauty canon that envisages long flowing straight hair as an epitome of beauty. Notwithstanding, Nkem's new-gained self-assurance allows her to reject the male gaze principles and to (re)define herself. Controlling her hair can thus be interpreted as metonymically being in control both of her body and her identity, which is evident in the resolution of the story, when Nkem confronts her husband in telling him that they cannot reduce their marriage to a few visits taking place whenever is convenient to him (Adichie 2009, 41). Hence, transitioning is ultimately a sign of Nkem regaining power and questioning Obiora's monolithic authority as she finally informs him that she is moving to Lagos with her children and recovering control over her life, a decision to which he does not object (ibid., 41).

To conclude my analysis of hair politics in Adichie's fiction, I will concentrate on the work in which the process of transitioning is developed in greater depth, *Americanah*. Ifemelu's transitioning in the novel is also a synonym of self-empowerment, although it cannot be contemplated as a decision inherently taken by the character as it happens in 'Imitation' and 'Hair'. Her transition comes as a result of her hair falling apart after relaxing it in order to look more professional and succeed in a job interview. Ifemelu's first days as a migrant from Nigeria in the U.S. are marked by a constant struggle to find and maintain employment – a situation that at a certain point translates into her being sexually abused, and often translates into desperation before she eventually recovers and finds a position as a babysitter. This traumatic time in her life is pivotal for Ifemelu's decision to relax her hair when seeking to take a step forward in her professional career. When her career adviser, considering her braids unprofessional (Adichie 2014, 202), recommends her to straighten her hair, she capitulates and remembers having laughed at her Aunt Uju when years ago she relaxed her hair for an interview (ibid., 119). But 'she knew enough not to laugh' at the advice anymore (ibid., 203). However, Ifemelu does not relax her hair for romantic purposes, since her decision is neither oriented to satisfy Curt, her American boyfriend at the time, nor related to issues of low self-esteem and the questioning of her own beauty. Thus, it cannot be considered an act of self-hatred. Nonetheless, she adopts what Banks calls an 'assimilationist standpoint' (2000, 8), conforming to social expectations regarding appearance, for her own experience as an unemployed migrant outweighs her previous refusal to straighten her hair. Ifemelu's situation is embedded in the psyche of many African-American women who have also internalized the idea that 'professional means straight is best but if it's going to be curly then it has to be the white kind of curly' (Adichie 2014, 204) – a fact reflected in Banks empirical study on the politics of Black hair, where she has her interviewees commenting upon 'the tension between the social world and the professional world and how such a tension is brought to bear on hairstyling practices' (2000, 39).

As already hinted, her transition comes as a result of the damaging consequences of the relaxer, since a few days after straightening her hair 'there were scabs on her scalp' (Adichie 2014, 204). Interestingly, considering that her interview turns out to be a success, pain and positive reinforcement seem to conflate, and 'she wonder[s] if the woman would have felt the same way had she walked into that office wearing her thick, kinky, God-given halo of hair, the Afro' (ibid.). Yet, her hair soon begins to fall. Her university friend, Wambui, encourages her to 'go natural', arguing that 'relaxing [natural] hair is like being in a prison', like 'battling to make [her] hair do what it [is not] meant to do' (ibid., 208). Ifemelu contrasts with Nkem and the young heroine of 'Hair' in that she does not instantly embrace her new self, but rather confesses to be scared of looking her image in the mirror after transitioning, believing that 'at best, she looked like a boy; at worst, like an insect' (ibid.).

More than Nkem and the protagonist of 'Hair', Ifemelu can be read as Adichie's autobiographical representation, inasmuch as interviews following the publication of *Americanah* reflect her hair story paralleling Ifemelu's (Calkin 2013; Channel 4 2013; National Public Radio 2013, 2014; Public Radio International 2013; Tenement Museum 2014). This can be appreciated in her retelling how, shortly after migrating to the U.S., she had a bad experience relaxing her hair which ended in having 'a scalp with really bad burns, [and] suddenly [thinking], "Why am I even doing this?" And that's when [she] stopped using relaxers. And it took a while to accept [her] hair' (National Public Radio 2014). Adichie's position towards hair politics has been repeatedly underlined as she has claimed to be 'a bit of a fundamentalist when it comes to black women's hair. Hair is hair – yet [it is] also about larger questions:

self-acceptance, insecurity and what the world tells you is beautiful' (Kellaway 2013).

Similarly, in her short documentary, *Transition*, Zina Saro-Wiwa records her 'Big Chop' and confesses perceiving her new image as non-attractive and un-sexy (Saro-Wiwa 2012). This seems to be a recurrent fear in many of the short documentaries and films published in YouTube, vlogs, and other social networks during this third wave of the hair movements. Both Saro-Wiwa's and Adichie's narratives bear witness to the extent to which the internalization of epistemological constructions of femininity provokes a number of women to partially regret at early stages of the process their decision of transitioning. The potential regret Black women may feel after transitioning runs parallel to the social punishment of being deemed less attractive, less feminine and less sociable. In this regard, Banks points out that 'when black women wear their hair close-cropped they are constructed as being unfeminine, unattractive, masculine, and lesbian' (2000, 95). These views actually affect Ifemelu, who rejects going to work after her 'Big Chop', and who is questioned about the political and sexual implications of her hairstyle when she finally decides to return (Adichie 2014, 211).

What follows is Wambui's recommendation of visiting an online natural hair community, convinced that Ifemelu would 'find inspiration' (ibid., 209). As mentioned above, the creation of online spaces where women with natural hair may share their experiences is an intrinsic part of the present stage of the hair movements. Their importance remains not only in their offering recipes for home-made products and tutorials on how to take care of natural hair, but also in the support they provide for women transitioning. In *Hair Story: Untangling the Roots of Black Hair in America* (2014), Byrd and Tharps highlight the significance of blogs and online communities, especially since 2007, and their crucial role among young generations of transitioners, inasmuch as they constitute spaces of self-expression where hair is related to creativity and freedom (2014).

Indeed, Happillyninkynappy.com opens Ifemelu's eyes into a new sphere of dialogue, understanding, and interchange of knowledge on natural hair. The members of the community claim to be 'done with pretending that their hair was what it was not … They complimented each other's photos and ended comments with "hugs." They complained about black magazines never having natural-haired women in their pages … They traded recipes … And Ifemelu fell into this world with a tumbling gratitude' (Adichie 2014, 212). In this manner, Ifemelu experiences the positive effects of participatory culture, its 'low barriers to artistic expression and civic engagement, [its] strong support for creating and sharing creations, and [its] informal mentorship' (Jenkins et al. 2009, xi). Ifemelu promptly feels a social connection with other transitioners who share similar anxieties, and their belief that all contributions are valuable in responding to each other's posts and posting thumbs-ups. It 'was like giving testimony in church; the echoing roar of approval revived her', and so Ifemelu comes to fall in love with her hair (Adichie 2014, 213).

In this context, online communities might be examined as entering the realm of what Hill Collins calls 'safe spaces' (2000, 100), described as places for Black women to resist both hegemonic patriarchal values and stereotypes of Black womanhood (ibid., 101). Such spaces foster self-definition and the generation of counter-discursive practices and images, thus being 'prime locations for resisting objectification as the Other' (ibid.). Although hair salons have traditionally been considered cultural institutions where hair care conflates with cultural interchange between Black women (Byrd and Tharps 2014; hooks 1988; Rooks 2000), it could be argued that social networks and their participatory cultural strategies have the potential to complement and even substitute hair salons in certain aspects. This would arguably be a consequence of the third-wave concern with positing empowerment-based models of self-discovery and individual self-expression for Black women to explore through social networks as spaces combining the public and private spheres.

After Ifemelu (re)embraces her natural self, Wambui is again instrumental in her deciding to start a blog to fulfill her need of sharing her thoughts on race and gender (Adichie 2014, 295). Longing for listeners and to hear other people's stories, Ifemelu resolves to create a space which follows the nurturing principles of participatory culture. Indeed, when she finally decides to close her blog upon returning to Nigeria, her followers acknowledge her as successfully having created 'a space for real conversations about an important subject [race]' (ibid., 5). Her blog discussions revolve around the many forms racial discrimination adopts in the U.S. Some of her entries are explicitly devoted to gender issues. Incidentally, Adichie introduces a blog entry after the episode in which Ifemelu painfully relaxes her hair, despite the fact that the character has not yet started her blog at that point of her history. Titled 'Understanding America for the Non-American Black: What Do WASPs Aspire To?' the entry draws her readers' attention towards 'whiteness [being] the thing to aspire to' (ibid., 205) in striving to conform to naturalized patterns of behaviour and appearance in the U.S. In her analysis of blogging in *Americanah*, Guarracino notes that the content of blog entries as introduced in the novel more or less explicitly correlates with the action taking place at that particular stage of Ifemelu's life-journey (2014, 15). In this case, blogging reveals to what extent Ifemelu will eventually be capable of reflecting upon the dialectic of racial oppression. Arguably, this allows the reader to juxtapose Ifemelu's temporary submission to the demands of dominant discourses of hair, and her future ability to criticize racial and gender inequality.

To continue the hair politics discussion, I shall now analyse the entry titled 'A Michelle Obama Shout-Out Plus Hair as Race Metaphor', where Ifemelu asserts that hair might well be 'the perfect metaphor for race in America' (Adichie 2014, 297). The post is a paradigmatic representation of 'hairitage' as a political matter during the third wave of the hair movements, for it covers candent issues and struggles inherited from the first and second waves. It first deals with the essentialist view of her white friend believing that Michelle Obama's hair naturally grows straight (ibid, 296–7), and continues criticizing mainstream media commercials historically portraying Black hair as 'bad hair' in need of being tamed and beautified (ibid., 297). It playfully unveils the problem of self-hatred which causes many Black women to prefer to 'run naked in the street [rather] than come out in public with their natural hair. Because, you see, it's not professional, sophisticated, whatever, it's just not damn normal' (ibid.). She later expands this discussion to the role of present-day Black celebrities within the hair politics landscape, later delving with the stereotypical image of Black women featuring natural hair as artistic-mother-earth people; and also denouncing the offensive popularization of Afros as Halloween costumes (ibid.). Finally, she returns to the image of Michelle Obama and invites the reader to imagine the political repercussions if Michelle Obama decided to transition: 'she would totally rock but poor Obama would certainly lose the independent vote, even the undecided Democrat vote' (ibid.).

Ifemelu's blog about race temporarily becomes with this post a space of dialogue on natural hair, especially when she updates the entry and asks her readers to contribute with information about transitioning regimes and opinions. Guarracino highlights that 'blog readers ... are always a relevant presence in Ifemelu's blogging, and allow for some interesting insights on the process of writing in the presence of immediate and continuous feedback' (2014, 16). The constant participation and instantaneous nature of blogging can at this point be associated with the potential to easily promote the teaching, creativity and self-definition fostered during the present stage of the hair movements.

Hence, transitioning constitutes the beginning of Ifemelu's journey towards self-discovery and self-understanding. Embracing her natural hair, her natural self, evokes her being in control of her own identity formation from that moment onwards, free from patriarchal epistemological discourses on gender and race. Notwithstanding, her journey differs from that of Nkem and the unnamed protagonist of 'Hair', for Ifemelu's transition leads her to become openly critical of race and gender inequality. Ifemelu's change has the potential of influencing not only her close relations but a wide range of African-American citizens, since it leads her to start blogging. In the same manner in which the magic hair in the eponymous tale encourages the girl to take responsibility and act to save her family, Ifemelu's transition and the online hair community she first explores instigate her to gain agency in order to start a blog which turns into a safe place of communication and production of counter-discursive thoughts. A blog which is not only a space of discussion in which she mediates, it is also part of herself, to the extent that she eventually realizes 'she ha[s] become the blog' (Adichie 2014, 306). In this manner, she can help others to (re)discover and come to terms with their identity, not only in the U.S. but also in Nigeria, where she eventually starts a new blog.

In light of the just revealed, Adichie's depictions of transitioning arguably underline different but complementary sides of the third wave of the hair movements. Although *Americanah* can be considered her most representative example of the revolutionary essence of hair politics, the three characters discussed represent different perspectives, personal circumstances and approaches towards transitioning, thus bearing witness to the complex nature of hair as a signifier related to identity formation. Revealing situations of gender, sexual and racial inequality, Adichie portrays transitioning as a weapon to undervalue the power of Western patriarchal constructs of femininity and beauty. Additionally, in the case of Ifemelu, discussing her transition has led to a reflection on the communicative potential of social networks within this new wave. Altogether, the notion of controlling one's hair and body as a metonymic representation of being in control of one's identity suggests that transitioning can be read as the ultimate sign of Black women rejecting previously internalized discourses of normalized femininity and appearance. Hence, not only hair but also identities can transition, from a position of controlled submissive subjects to that of empowered social agents.

Works Cited

Adesanmi, Pius and Chris Dunton. 2005. 'Nigeria's Third Generation Writing: Historiography and Preliminary Theoretical Considerations'. *English in Africa* 32(1): 7–19.

Adichie, Chimamanda Ngozi. 2007. 'Hair'. *The Guardian*, 10 November. Accessed 11 September 2015, www.theguardian.com/books/2007/nov/10/booksforchildrenandteenagers.

—. 2009. *The Thing Around Your Neck*. London: Fourth State.

—. 2014 [2013]. *Americanah*. London: Fourth State.

Banks, Ingrid. 2000. *Hair Matters: Beauty, Power, and Black Women's Consciousness*. New York: New York University Press.

Boyd C., George. 2013. 'This is Good Hair, Too: A Black Natural Hair Documentary'. YouTube video, 14:58. Accessed 3 October 2015, www.youtube.com/watch?v=mz8av9MBUok.

Byrd, Ayanna D., and Lori L. Tharps. 2014 [2001]. *Hair Story: Untangling the Roots of Black Hair in America*. New York: St Martin's Griffin. Kindle Edition.

Bryce, Jane. 2008. 'Half and Half Children': Third-Generation Women Writers and the New Nigerian Novel'. *Research in African Literatures* 39(2): 49–67.

Calkin, Jessamy. 2013. 'Love In the Time of Cornrows: Chimamanda Ngozi Adichie on Her New Novel'. *The Telegraph*, 6 April. Accessed 20 January 2016, www.telegraph.co.uk/culture/books/authorinterviews/9968921/Love-in-the-time-of-cornrows-Chimamanda-Ngozi-Adichie-on-her-new-novel.html.

Channel 4. 2013. 'Author Chimamanda Adichie: "Black women's hair is political"'. Accessed 15 December, www.channel4.com/news/chimamanda-ngozi-adichie-americanah-hair-immigration-race.

Eastside Community Heritage. 2014. 'HAIRitage, a short film exploring Black hair in Britain'. YouTube video, 15:44. Accessed 12 September 2015, www.youtube.com/watch?v=Y4fJMsI9pmc.

Ellington, Tameka N. 2014a. 'Bloggers, Vloggers, and a Virtual Sorority: A Means of Support for African American Women Wearing Natural Hair'. *Journalism and Mass* 4(9): 552–64.

—. 2014b. 'Social Networking Sites: A Support System for African-American Women Wearing Natural Hair'. *International Journal of Fashion Design, Technology and Education* 8(1): 21–29.

Guarracino, Serena. 2014. 'Writing "so raw and true": Blogging in Chimamanda Ngozi Adichie's *Americanah*'. *Between* 4(8): 1–27.

Hill Collins, Patricia. 2000[1991]. *Black Feminist Thought: Knowledge, Consciousness, and the Politics of Empowerment*. New York: Routledge.

hooks, bell. 1988. 'Straightening Our Hair'. *Zeta Magazine* 1(Sept): 33–37.

Jenkins, Henry, Ravi Purushotma, Margaret Weigel, Katie Clinton and Alice J. Robison. 2009. *Confronting the Challenges of Participatory Culture: Media Education for the 21st Century*. Massachusetts: MIT Press.

Kellaway, Kate. 2013. 'Chimamanda Ngozi Adichie: "My new novel is about love, race … and hair"'. *The Guardian*, 7 April. Accessed 11 September 2015, www.theguardian.com/theobserver/2013/apr/07/chimamanda-ngozi-adichie-americanah-interview.

Mantel, Hilary. 2007. 'Once upon a time …', *The Guardian*, Children and teenagers, 10 November. Accessed 15 November 2016, www.theguardian.com/books/2007/nov/10/booksforchildrenandteenagers.features.

Mulvey, Laura. 2009[1974]. 'Visual Pleasure and Narrative Cinema'. In *Film Theory and Criticism: Introductory Readings*, Eds Leo Braudy and Marshall Cohen (711–22). Oxford: Oxford University Press.

National Public Radio. 2013. 'A Nigerian-"*Americanah*" Novel about Love, Race and Hair'. Accessed 31 January 2016, www.npr.org/2013/05/11/181685674/a-nigerian-americanah-novel-about-love-race-and-hair.

National Public Radio. 2014. '*Americanah* Author Explains "Learning" To Be Black In the U.S.' Accessed 31 January 2016, www.npr.org/2014/03/07/286903648/americanah-author-explains-learning-to-be-black-in-the-u-s.

Nnaemeka, Obioma. 2004. 'Nego-Feminism: Theorizing, Practicing, and Pruning Africa's Way'. *Signs* 29(2): 357–85.

OkayAfrica. 2015. '"Hair Freedom" Mini-Doc Explores the Natural Hair Movement In the UK'. Accessed 12 September 2015, www.okayafrica.com/news/hair-freedom-natural-hair-movement-uk-mini-documentary-bbc-raw.

Patton, Tracey O. 2006. 'Hey Girl, Am I More than My Hair? African American Women and Their Struggles with Beauty, Body Image, and Hair'. *NWSA Journal* 18(2): 24–51.

Public Radio International. 2013. 'Race, Identity, and Good Hair: Chimamanda Ngozi Adichie on Her New Novel, *Americanah*'. Accessed 12 September 2015, www.pri.org/stories/2013-05-23/race-identity-and-good-hair-chimamanda-ngozi-adichie-her-new-novel-americanah.

Rooks, Nolike M. (1996) 2000. *Hair Raising: Beauty, Culture, and African American Women*. New Brunswick, NJ, and London: Rutgers University Press.

Saro-Wiwa, Zina. 2012. 'Transition'. Accessed 11 September 2015, www.chicagomanualofstyle.org/tools_citationguide.html.

Selasi, Taiye. 2015. *Love Your Curls: A Poetic Tribute to Curly Hair Inspired by Real Women*. New Jersey: Conopco Inc., dba Unilever.

Tenement Museum. 2014. 'Chimimanda Ngozi Adichie: On Hair.' YouTube video, 8:01. Accessed 20 October 2015, www.youtube.com/watch?v=WWuRA61N8jA.

Thompson, Cheryl. 2009. 'Black Women, Beauty, and Hair as a Matter of Being'. *Women's Studies* (38): 831–56.

Un'ruly. 2013. 'You Can Touch My Hair, a Short Film'. Accessed 11 September 2015, http://un-ruly.com/you-can-touch-my-hair-a-short-film.

Appendix
The Works of Chimamanda Ngozi Adichie

Compiled by Daria Tunca © 2004–2016 and modified from
www.cerep.ulg.ac.be/adichie/cnaprimlinks.html

Books and Key References

Decisions (Poems). Minerva Press, 1997.

For Love of Biafra (Play). Spectrum Books, 1998.

Purple Hibiscus (Novel). Algonquin Books of Chapel Hill, 2003; Fourth Estate, 2003; Farafina, 2003.

Half of a Yellow Sun (Novel). Fourth Estate, 2006; Farafina, 2006; Alfred A. Knopf, 2007. See also the film adaptation: *Half of a Yellow Sun*, written and directed by Biyi Bandele. Shareman Media and BFI, 2014.

'The Danger of a Single Story' (Address). Apr. 2009. *TED*, Oct. 2009, www.ted.com/talks/chimamanda_adichie_the_danger_of_a_single_story.

The Thing around Your Neck (Short Stories). Fourth Estate, 2009; Alfred A. Knopf, 2009; Farafina, 2009.

'We Should All Be Feminists' (Address). 1 Dec. 2012. *YouTube*, uploaded by Tedx Talks, 12 Apr. 2013, www.youtube.com/watch?v=hg3umXU_qWc.

Americanah (Novel). Fourth Estate, 2013; Alfred A. Knopf, 2013; Farafina, 2013.

We Should All Be Feminists (Essay). Vintage Shorts, 2014; Fourth Estate, 2014.

Short Stories

'You in America.' *Zoetrope: All-Story Extra*, no. 38, Winter 2001, www.all-story.com/extra/issue38/adichie.html. Later published in revised version as 'The Thing around Your Neck.'

'The Scarf.' *Wasafiri*, no. 37, Winter 2002, pp. 26–30. Later published in

263

revised version as 'A Private Experience.'

'The American Embassy.' *Prism International*, vol. 40, no. 3, Spring 2002, pp. 22–29.

'Half of a Yellow Sun.' *Literary Potpourri*, no. 12, 2002. Also published in *Zoetrope: All-Story*, vol. 7, no. 2, Summer 2003, pp. 10–17, and available online, www.all-story.com/issues.cgi?action=show_story&story_id=191.

'My Mother, the Crazy African.' *In Posse Review: Multi-Ethnic Anthology*, n.d. [c. 2002], www.webdelsol.com/InPosse/adichie_anthology.htm.

'New Husband.' *Iowa Review*, vol. 33, no. 1, Spring 2003, pp. 53–66. Later published in revised version as 'The Arrangers of Marriage.'

'Imitation.' *Other Voices*, no. 38, Spring-Summer 2003, pp. 143–53.

'Light Skin.' *Calyx*, vol. 21, no. 2, Summer 2003, pp. 49–63.

'Transition to Glory.' *One Story*, vol. 2, no. 9 (issue no. 27), 30 Sept. 2003.

'Women Here Drive Buses.' *Proverbs for the People: Contemporary African-American Fiction*, edited by Tracy Price-Thompson and TaRessa Stovall, Dafina Books, 2003, pp. 1–7.

'Lagos, Lagos.' *Discovering Home: A Selection of Writings from the 2002 Caine Prize for African Writing*, Jacana Media, 2003, pp. 76–86.

'Ghosts.' *Zoetrope: All-Story*, vol. 8., no. 4, Winter 2004, pp. 38–43, and available online, www.all-story.com/issues.cgi?action=show_story&story_id=250.

'The Grief of Strangers.' *Mothers*, issue of Granta, no. 88, Winter 2004, pp. 67–81.

'The Thing around Your Neck.' *Prospect*, no. 99, June 2004, pp. 64–68.

'A Private Experience.' *Virginia Quarterly Review*, vol. 80, no. 3, Summer 2004, pp. 170–79. Later published in the *Observer* (*Review* Supplement), 28 Dec. 2008, p. 18, and available online, www.theguardian.com/books/2008/dec/28/chimamanda-ngozi-adichie-short-story.

'Recaptured Spirits.' *Notre Dame Review*, no. 18, Summer 2004, pp. 47–58, and available online, www3.nd.edu/~ndr/issues/ebooks/NDR%2018.pdf.

'The Master.' *The View from Africa*, issue of *Granta*, no. 92, Winter 2005, pp. 19–41. The first chapter of *Half of a Yellow Sun*.

'Do Butterflies Eat Ashes?' *Fiction*, vol. 19, no. 2, 2005, pp. 3–17.

'Tomorrow Is Too Far.' *Prospect*, no. 118, Jan. 2006, pp. 56–63.

'The Time Story.' *Per Contra*, no. 2, Spring 2006, www.percontra.net/archive/2timestory.htm.

'Jumping Monkey Hill.' *Loved Ones*, issue of *Granta*, no. 95, Oct. 2006, pp. 161–76, and available online, www.granta.com/jumping-monkey-hill/.

'Cell One.' *New Yorker*, vol. 82, no. 47, 29 Jan. 2007, pp. 72–77, and available online, www.newyorker.com/magazine/2007/01/29/cell-one.

'On Monday Last Week.' *The Deep End*, issue of *Granta*, no. 98, Summer 2007, pp. 32–48.

'My American Jon.' *Me, My Writing and African Writers*, 27 Aug. 2007, thebinj.blogspot.com/2007/08/chimamanda-ngozi-adichie.html.

'Hair.' *Guardian*, 10 Nov. 2007, www.theguardian.com/books/2007/nov/10/booksforchildrenandteenagers.features.

'A Tampered Destiny.' *Financial Times*, 29 Dec. 2007, p. 1.

'Emeka.' *Four Letter Word: New Love Letters*, edited by Joshua Knelman and Rosalind Porter, Chatto and Windus, 2007.

'The Headstrong Historian.' *New Yorker*, vol. 84, no. 18, 23 June 2008, pp. 68–75, and available online, www.newyorker.com/magazine/2008/06/23/the-headstrong-historian.

'Chinasa.' *Guardian*, 27 Jan. 2009, www.theguardian.com/education/2009/jan/27/chimamanda-ngozi-adichie-chinasa.

'Sola.' *Sunday Times*, 30 Aug. 2009, p. 60.

'Do.' *Anonthology*, Fourth Estate, 2009.

'Quality Street.' *Guernica*, 1 Feb. 2010, www.guernicamag.com/fiction/quality_street/.

'Ceiling.' *Going Back*, issue of *Granta*, no. 111, Summer 2010, pp. 65–80.

'Birdsong.' *New Yorker*, 20 Sept. 2010, vol. 86, no. 28, pp. 96–103, and available online, www.newyorker.com/magazine/2010/09/20/birdsong-2.

'Miracle.' *Guardian*, 7 Nov. 2011, www.theguardian.com/books/2011/nov/07/short-story-chimamanda-ngozi-adichie.

'The Arrangers of Marriage.' *The Granta Book of the African Short Story*, edited by Helon Habila, Granta, 2011, pp. 1–17.

'Ofodile.' *Guardian* (*Weekend* Supplement), 21 Dec. 2013, p. 46, and available online, *Guardian*, 25 Dec. 2013, www.theguardian.com/books/2013/dec/25/christmas-ghost-stories-chimamanda-ngozi-adichie?CMP=twt_fd.

'Checking Out.' *New Yorker*, vol. 89, no. 5, 18 Mar. 2013, pp. 66–73, and available online, www.newyorker.com/magazine/2013/03/18/checking-out. An excerpt from *Americanah*.

'The Miraculous Deliverance of Oga Jona.' *Scoop*, 18 July 2014, www.thescoopng.com/2014/07/18/exclusive-chimamanda-adichie-miraculous-deliverance-oga-jona/.

'An Awakening, to the Sound and Dust of the Harmattan Wind' (Audio). *Soundcloud*, uploaded by Serpentine Galleries, 2014, soundcloud.com/serpentine-uk/bridge-commission-audio-wal k-4-chimamanda-ngozi-adichie.

'Olikoye.' *The Art of Saving a Life,* Jan. 2015, artofsavingalife.com/ artists/chimamanda-ngozi-adichie/.

'Apollo.' *New Yorker,* vol. 91, no. 8, 13 Apr. 2015, pp. 64–69, and available online, www.newyorker.com/magazine/2015-04-13/apollo.

'The Arrangements.' *New York Times* (*Book Review* Supplement), 3 July 2016, p. 1, and available online, *New York Times,* 28 June 2016, www.nytimes.com/2016/07/03/books/review/melania-trum p-in-chimamanda-ngozi-adichie-short-story.html.

Untitled story in the 'Tiny Stories' series. *UNICEF,* Nov. 2016, www. unicef.org/tinystories/#anchor_93182.

Essays & Lectures

'Heart is Where the Home Was.' *Topic Magazine,* no. 3, Winter 2003, www.webdelsol.com/Topic/articles/03/adichie.html.

'On Sex, We Are Just Buffoons: My Response.' *Vanguard,* 15 Aug. 2004.

'Chasing American.' *Farafina* (online version), no. 5, 21 Sept. 2004. Later published in as 'The Line of No Return.'

'The Line of No Return.' *New York Times,* 29 Nov. 2004, p. A21.

'Nsukka in the Eyes of a Novelist.' *Guardian* (Nigeria), 3 Jan. 2005. Later published as 'Tiny Wonders.'

'Blinded by God's Business.' *Guardian* (Nigeria), 19 Feb. 2005.

'Diary.' *New Statesman,* vol. 18, no. 866, 4 July 2005, p. 10, and available online, www.newstatesman.com/node/162369.

'Blissful Sloth.' *The Seven Deadly Sins,* special issue of *Johns Hopkins Magazine,* vol. 57, no. 4, Sept. 2005, and available online, pages. jh.edu/jhumag/0905web/sloth1.html.

'Tiny Wonders.' P.S. section of *Purple Hibiscus,* by Adichie, Harper Perennial, 2005, pp. 9–14.

'A Nigerian Book Tour in Australia.' *Farafina,* no. 4, Apr. 2006, pp. 3–5.

'Life During Wartime: Sierra Leone, 1997.' *New Yorker,* vol. 82, no. 17, 12 June 2006, pp. 72–73, and available online, *New Yorker,* 6 June 2006, www.newyorker.com/magazine/2006/06/12/sierra-leone-1997. Later published as 'The Little Boy Who Talked of Magic.'

'Buildings Fall Down, Pensions Aren't Paid, Politicians Are Murdered, Riots Are in the Air... and Yet I Love Nigeria.' *Guardian* (*G2* Supplement), 8 Aug. 2006, p. 5, and available online, www.theguardian. com/commentisfree/2006/aug/08/comment.features11.

'The Little Boy Who Talked of Magic.' *Times,* 19 Aug. 2006.

'Truth and Lies.' *Guardian,* 16 Sept. 2006, p. 22, and available online, www.theguardian.com/books/2006/sep/16/fiction.society.

'My College Roommate Expected Me to Be a She-Tarzan?' *Jane*, vol. 10, no. 8, Oct. 2006, pp. 126–27.

'Our 'Africa' Lenses.' *Washington Post*, 13 Nov. 2006, p. A21, and available online, www.washingtonpost.com/wp-dyn/content/article/2006/11/12/AR2006111200943.html.

'Shall I Live, Or Shall I Blog-Blah-Blah?' *Hartford Courant*, 1 Apr. 2007.

'An der Klimafront: Schwarze Weihnachten.' *Neue Zürcher Zeitung*, 11 Apr. 2007. In German. Also published in the original English version as 'Black Christmas.' *signandsight.com*, 30 May 2007, www.signandsight.com/features/1370.html.

'The Exemplary Chronicler of an African Tragedy.' *Guardian*, 13 June 2007, www.theguardian.com/books/booksblog/2007/jun/13/achebeisamodelwriterofth.

'The Writing Life.' *Washington Post*, 17 June 2007, p. BW11, and available online, www.washingtonpost.com/wp-dyn/content/article/2007/06/14/AR2007061401730.html.

'Kitchen Talk: Peppers.' *Brick*, no. 79 (Summer 2007), pp. 49–52.

'Real Food.' *New Yorker*, vol. 83, no. 26, 3–10 Sept. 2007, p. 92, and available online, www.newyorker.com/magazine/2007/09/03/real-food.

'Operation.' *What Happened Next*, issue of *Granta*, no. 99, Autumn 2007, pp. 31–37. Later published as 'To My One Love.'

'In the Shadow of Biafra.' P.S. section of *Half of a Yellow Sun*, by Adichie, Harper Perennial, 2007, pp. 9–12.

'An African Education in *No Sweetness Here.*' *All Things Considered*, NPR, 18 Jan. 2008, www.npr.org/templates/story/story.php?storyId=18142470.

'Sex in the City.' *Guardian*, 2 Feb. 2008, p. 3, and available online, www.theguardian.com/books/2008/feb/02/featuresreviews.guardianreview1.

'To My One Love.' *Utne Reader*, no. 146, Mar.-Apr. 2008, pp. 84–86, and available online, www.utne.com/arts/tomy-one-love.

'Guest Editor's Note.' *America*, special issue of *Farafina*, no. 13, Mar.–Apr. 2008, p. 3. Issue guest edited by Chimamanda Ngozi Adichie.

'Nigeria's Immorality Is about Hypocrisy, Not Miniskirts.' *Guardian*, 2 Apr. 2008, p. 32, and available online, www.theguardian.com/commentisfree/2008/apr/02/gender.equality.

'The Color of an Awkward Conversation.' *Washington Post*, 8 June 2008, p. B07, and available online, www.washingtonpost.com/wp-dyn/content/article/2008/06/06/AR2008060603141.html.

'As a Child, I Thought My Father Invincible. I Also Thought Him Remote.' *Observer*, 15 June 2008, www.theguardian.com/

books/2008/jun/15/biography.features4.

'African 'Authenticity' and the Biafran Experience.' *Transition*, no. 99, 2008, pp. 42–53.

'Strangely Personal.' *Checkpoints*, issue of *PEN America*, no. 9 (2008), pp. 34–37. Based on the speech delivered at the PEN Tribute to Chinua Achebe, New York, 26 Feb. 2008. Audio version available online, *PEN America*, 13 Dec. 2012, pen.org/book/chimamanda-ngozi-adichie-speaks-at-a-tribute-to-chinua-achebe. Transcript available as 'Strangely Personal: Growing Up in Chinua Achebe's House.' *PEN America*, 3 Apr. 2013, pen.org/transcript/strangely-personal-growing-chinua-achebes-house.

Essay in *Curse of the Black Gold: 50 Years of Oil in the Niger Delta*, photographs by Ed Kashi, edited by Michael Watts, powerHouse Books, 2008.

'Diary.' *Times*, 28 Mar. 2009, p. 2.

'Allow Hope but Also Fear.' *Kalamazoo College*, 14 June 2009, cache.kzoo.edu/bitstream/handle/10920/9000/AdichieCommencement2009.pdf?sequence=1. Video also available, 'Commencement Address at Kalamazoo College.' 14 June 2009. *YouTube*, uploaded by Kalamazoo College, 1 July 2009, www.youtube.com/watch?v=fsJoPEo142Q.

'Diary.' *Financial Times*, 11 July 2009, p. 2.

'My Hero: Muhtar Bakare.' *Guardian*, 19 Sept. 2009, p. 5.

'The Police, Our Friends.' *Next*, 30 Sept. 2009.

'Why Do South Africans Hate Nigerians?', *Guardian* (*G2* Supplement), 5 Oct. 2009, p. 2.

'Father Chinedu.' *Make Believe*, issue of *PEN America*, no. 11 (2009), pp. 91–93, and available online, pen.org/father-chinedu.

'Everywhere, Moisture Is Greedily Sucked Up.' *Guardian*, 18 Dec. 2009, p. 25.

'Letter from Lagos.' *McSweeney's Quarterly Concern*, vol. 33, *The San Francisco Panorama, Panorama Book Review*, Jan. 2010, p. 1, and available online, *McSweeney's Internet Tendency*, 5 Jan. 2010, mcsweeneys.net/articles/letter-from-lagos-from-the-panorama-book-review.

'What I See in the Mirror.' *Guardian* (*Weekend* Supplement), 23 Jan. 2010, p. 43, and available online, www.theguardian.com/lifeandstyle/2010/jan/23/chimamanda-ngozi-adichie-interview.

'The Man Who Rediscovered Africa.' *Salon*, 24 Jan. 2010, www.salon.com/2010/01/24/chinamanda_adichie_chinua_achebe/.

'Blood, Oil and the Banality of Greed.' *Next*, 4 Apr. 2010.

'A New Nigerian-ness Is Infusing the Nation.' *Globe and Mail*, 10 May 2010, p. A17.

'My Favourite Dress.' *Guardian*, 8 June 2010, p. 7, and available online, www.theguardian.com/lifeandstyle/2010/jun/08/my-favourite-dress.

'World Cup 2010: Nigeria, Ghana, Ivory Coast, Cameroon and South Africa – My Boys.' *Guardian*, 11 June 2010, p. 2, and available online, www.theguardian.com/football/2010/jun/11/chimamanda-ngozi-adichie-world-cup.

'Rereading: *To Kill a Mockingbird* by Harper Lee.' *Guardian*, 10 July 2010, p. 4, and available online, www.theguardian.com/books/2010/jul/10/kill-mockingbird-harper-lee.

'The Writer as Two Selves: Reflections on the Private Act of Writing and the Public Act of Citizenship.' Lecture delivered at Princeton University, 20 Oct. 2010.

'The Role of Literature in Modern Africa.' *New African*, no. 500 (Nov. 2010), p. 96.

'A Street of Puzzles.' *New York Times*, 5 Dec. 2010, p. WK9, and available online, *New York Times*, 4 Dec. 2010, www.nytimes.com/interactive/2010/12/04/opinion/20101205_Windows.html.

'Women of the Decade.' *Financial Times Magazine*, 10 Dec. 2010, p. 23.

'Introduction.' *The African Trilogy: Things Fall Apart, No Longer at Ease, and Arrow of God*, by Chinua Achebe, Everyman's Library, 2010, pp. vii–xiii. Also published as 'The Man Who Rediscovered Africa.'

'A Nigerian Revolution.' *Guardian*, 17 Mar. 2011, p. 38, and available online, *Guardian*, 16 Mar. 2011, www.theguardian.com/commentisfree/2011/mar/16/nigerian-revolution-young-people-democracy?CMP=twt_gu.

Lecture delivered at 'Narratives for Europe – Stories that Matter.' Amsterdam, 18 Apr. 2011. *YouTube*, uploaded by labforculture, 25 Apr. 2011, www.youtube.com/watch?v=-YEWg1vIOyw.

'No More Superpower?' *New York Times* (Opinion Pages), 24 June 2011, and available online, www.nytimes.com/interactive/2011/06/24/opinion/global/20110624_SUPERPOWER.html.

'The Year's Biggest 'He Said, She Said.'' *Newsweek*, 26 Dec. 2011 – 2 Jan. 2012, pp. 42–43.

'Why Are You Here?' *Guernica*, 15 Jan. 2012, www.guernicamag.com/features/adichie_1_15_12/.

'A Country's Frustration, Fueled Overnight.' *New York Times* (Opinion Pages), 17 Jan. 2012, p. A23, and available online, *New York Times*, 16 Jan. 2012, www.nytimes.com/2012/01/17/opinion/nigerias-latest-frustration.html?_r=2&ref=opinion.

'To Instruct and Delight: A Case for Realist Literature.' *Commonwealth Foundation*, 15 Mar. 2012, www.commonwealthfoundation.com/

commonwealth-lecture-2012.

'My Uncle Mai.' *Financial Times*, 19 May 2012, p. 26.

'Why Are We Surprised? Thoughts on Nigeria's Past, Present and Future.' Lecture delivered at Uppsala University, 15 Oct. 2012, media.medfarm.uu.se/play/kanal/90/video/2957.

'Things Left Unsaid.' Review of *There Was a Country: A Personal History of Biafra*, by Chinua Achebe. *London Review of Books*, vol. 34, no. 19, Oct. 2012, pp. 32–33, and available online, www.lrb.co.uk/v34/n19/chimamanda-adichie/things-left-unsaid.

'Chinua Achebe at 82: 'We Remember Differently.'' *Premium Times*, 23 Nov. 2012, www.premiumtimesng.com/arts-entertainment/108378-chinua-achebe-at-82-we-remember-differently-by-chimamanda-ngozi-adichie.html.

'Facts Are Stranger than Fiction.' *Guardian* (*Review* Supplement), 20 Apr. 2013, p. 15, and available online, *Guardian*, 19 Apr. 2013, www.theguardian.com/books/2013/apr/19/chimamanda-ngozi-adichie-stranger-fiction.

'#Kwaniat10 Lecture III: Chimamanda Ngozi Adichie.' University of Nairobi, 29 Nov. 2013, *YouTube*, uploaded by Kwani Trust, 10 Mar. 2014, www.youtube.com/watch?v=i0nnDkaT8aI.

'The Baby Who Never Made It to Atlanta.' *New York Times* (*Sunday Review* Supplement), 8 Dec. 2013, p. 9, and available online as 'A Flight Diversion.' *New York Times*, 6 Dec. 2013, www.nytimes.com/2013/12/07/opinion/a-flight-diversion.html.

'We Have Lost a Star.' *Premium Times*, 19 Jan. 2014, www.premiumtimesng.com/opinion/153600-komla-dumor-lost-star-chimamanda-adichie.html.

'Why Can't He Just Be like Everyone Else?' *Scoop*, 18 Feb. 2014, www.thescoopng.com/chimamanda-adichie-why-cant-he-just-be-like-everyone-else/.

'Why Can't a Smart Woman Love Fashion?' *Elle*, 20 Feb. 2014, www.elle.com/fashion/personal-style/a12670/personal-essay-on-style-by-chimamanda-ngozi-adichie/.

'Performing Gender: Sometimes I Do and Sometimes I Don't.' Lecture delivered at Gustavus Adolphus College, Saint Peter MN, 10 Mar. 2014. *YouTube*, uploaded by Gustavus Adolphus College, 10 Mar. 2014, www.youtube.com/watch?v=RhCGRwXw18o.

'Hiding from Our Past.' *New Yorker*, 1 May 2014, www.newyorker.com/culture/culture-desk/hiding-from-our-past.

'The President I Want.' *Scoop*, 4 May 2014, www.thescoopng.com/2014/05/04/exclusive-chimamanda-adichie-president-want/.

'Nigeria's Brutal Past Haunts the Present.' *Telegraph*, 31 May 2014, www.

telegraph.co.uk/culture/hay-festival/10848597/Chimamanda-Ngoz
i-Adichie-Nigerias-brutal-past-haunts-the-present.html.

'What Forms the Core of Igbo Society.' *Trent*, 25 June 2014, www.thetrentonline.com/chimamanda-adichie-forms-core-igbo-society-must-read/.

'Lights Out in Nigeria.' *New York Times* (*Sunday Review* Supplement), 1 Feb. 2015, p. 4, and available online, *New York Times*, 31 Jan. 2015, www.nytimes.com/2015/02/01/opinion/sunday/lights-out-in-nigeria.html.

'Democracy, Deferred.' *Atlantic*, 10 Feb. 2015, www.theatlantic.com/international/archive/2015/02/nigeria-election-democracy-deferred/385341/.

'On the Oba Of Lagos.' *Olisa.tv*, 10 Apr. 2015, www.olisa.tv/2015/04/chimamanda-adichieoba-lagos.

'2015 PEN World Voices Arthur Miller Freedom to Write Lecture.' Followed by an interview by Andrew Solomon. New York, 10 May 2015. C-SPAN, 10 May 2015, www.c-span.org/video/?326002-1/chimamanda-ngozi-adichie-freedom-write-lecture.

Commencement address given at Eastern Connecticut State University. 12 May 2015. *YouTube*, uploaded by Eastern Connecticut State University, 26 June 2015, www.youtube.com/watch?v=X9qJfIdMAlY.

'2015 Girls Write Now Awards Speech.' *YouTube*, uploaded by GirlsWriteNow, 20 May 2015, www.youtube.com/watch?v=3uNcvtjT8Pk.

Commencement address given at Wellesley College. 29 May 2015. *YouTube*, uploaded by WellesleyCollege, 29 May 2015, www.youtube.com/watch?v=RcehZ3CjedU. Transcript also available online, 'Chimamanda Ngozi Adichie Addressed the Class of 2015 at Wellesley's 137th Commencement Exercises.' *Wellesley College*, 2015, www.wellesley.edu/events/commencement/archives/2015/commencementaddress.

'My Father's Kidnapping.' *New York Times* (*Sunday Review* Supplement), 31 May 2015, p. 5, and available online, *New York Times*, 30 May 2015, www.nytimes.com/2015/05/31/opinion/sunday/chimamanda-ngoz i-adichie-my-fathers-kidnapping.html.

'Raised Catholic.' *Atlantic*, 14 Oct. 2015, www.theatlantic.com/international/archive/2015/10/catholic-pope-francis-chimamanda-adichie/409237/.

'Why Chimamanda Ngozi Adichie Considers Her Sister a 'Firm Cushion' at Her Back.' *Vanity Fair*, May 2016, www.vanityfair.com/culture/2016/04/chimamanda-ngozi-adichie-sisterhood.

'Chimamanda Ngozi Adichie – World Humanitarian Day 2016.' Speech delivered in New York, 19 Aug. 2016. *YouTube*, uploaded by United Nations, 22 Aug. 2016, www.youtube.com/watch?v=oj5F5XaLj2E.

'Dear Ijeawele, or a Feminist Manifesto in Fifteen Suggestions.' *Facebook*, 12 Oct. 2016, www.facebook.com/chimamandaadichie/posts/10154412708460944.

'To the First Lady, With Love.' *T: The New York Times Style Magazine*, 17 Oct. 2016, www.nytimes.com/2016/10/17/t-magazine/michelle-obama-chimamanda-ngozi-adichie-gloria-steinem-letter.html.

'Nigeria's Failed Promises.' *New York Times* (Opinion Pages), 19 Oct. 2016, p. A14, and available online, *New York Times*, 18 Oct. 2016, www.nytimes.com/2016/10/19/opinion/chimamanda-ngozi-adichie-nigerias-failed-promises.html.

'What Hillary Clinton's Fans Love About Her.' *Atlantic*, 3 Nov. 2016, www.theatlantic.com/politics/archive/2016/11/why-is-hillary-clinton-so-widely-loved/506402/.

'On the BBC *Newsnight* Interview.' *Facebook*, 25 Nov. 2016, www.facebook.com/chimamandaadichie/posts/10154547241315944.

'Now Is the Time to Talk About What We Are Actually Talking About.' *New Yorker*, 2 Dec. 2016, www.newyorker.com/culture/cultural-comment/now-is-the-time-to-talk-about-what-we-are-actually-talking-about.

Interviews

'A Q&A with Chimamanda Adichie.' By Eve Daniels. *Minnesota Public Radio*, 21 Aug. 2003, news.minnesota.publicradio.org/features/2003/08/21_newsroom_adichie/.

'Q&A.' *One Story*, 30 Sept. 2003, www.one-story.com/index.php?page=stories&pubcode=os&story_id=27.

'In the Footsteps of Achebe: Enter Chimamanda Ngozi Adichie, Nigeria's Newest Literary Voice.' Interview by Ike Anya. *Nigerians in America*, 10 Oct. 2003, www.nigeriansinamerica.com/in-the-footsteps-of-achebe-enter-chimamanda-ngozi-adichie-nigerias-newest-literary-voice-2/.

'Chimamanda Ngozi Adichie: Two-Time O. Henry Award-winning Author: 2003, 2010.' *Random House*, 2003 and 2010, www.randomhouse.com/anchor/ohenry/spotlight/adichie.html.

'Novel Approach to Nigeria.' Interview by Maria Blackburn. *Johns Hopkins Magazine*, vol. 56, no. 1, Feb. 2004, and available online, pages.jh.edu/~jhumag/0204web/wholly.html#novel.

Interview by Jenni Murray. *Woman's Hour*, BBC Radio Four, 17 Mar. 2004, www.bbc.co.uk/radio4/womanshour/2004_11_wed_02.shtml.

'Nigerian Identity Is Burdensome.' Interview by Wale Adebanwi. *Nigerian Village Square*, 12 May 2004, nigeriavillagesquare.com/bookshelf/nigerian-identity-is-burdensome-the-chimamanda-ngozi-adichie-interview.html.

'On Sex, We Are Just Buffoons.' *This Day*, 1 Aug. 2004.

Interview by Sajida Perween. *Woman's Hour*, BBC Radio Four, 27 Aug. 2004, www.bbc.co.uk/radio4/womanshour/2004_34_fri_03.shtml.

'Au Nigéria, la démocratie n'existe pas !" Interview by Pierre Cherruau. *Courier International*, no. 727, 7 Oct. 2004. In French.

'Author Explores Faith and Country in Acclaimed New Novel.' Interview by Norah Vawter. *allafrica.com*, 13 Oct. 2004, allafrica.com/stories/200410130920.html.

'Chimamanda Ngozi Adichie with Jide Salu.' 2004. *YouTube*, uploaded by Jide Salu, 10 Apr. 2014, www.youtube.com/watch?v=SWM1VRxU10I.

'*Writers Notes* Speaks with Chimamanda Ngozi Adichie, Author of *Purple Hibiscus*.' Interview by Behlor Santi. *Writers Notes Magazine*, no. 1, 2004, pp. 65–70.

'Interview.' By Daria Tunca. *The Chimamanda Ngozi Adichie Website*, 27 Jan. 2005, www.cerep.ulg.ac.be/adichie/cnainterview.html

'Off the Shelf.' Interview by Inga Gilchrist. *MX*, 24 Feb. 2005, p. 28.

'War and All in the Life of a Child.' *Sunday Telegraph*, 27 Feb. 2005, p. 98.

'I Left Home to Find Home.' Interview by Carl Wilkinson. *Observer*, 6 Mar. 2005, p. 24, and available online, www.theguardian.com/travel/2005/mar/06/observerescapesection3.

Interview by Robyn Doreian. *Sun Herald*, 20 Mar. 2005, p. 77.

'Groundnuts and Bananas: A Conversation with Chimamanda Ngozi Adichie.' Interview by A. Naomi Jackson. *Chimurenga*, Dec. 2005, www.chimurenga.co.za/archives/1399.

Interview with Chimamanda Ngozi Adichie. *African Essence*, 2005, www.african-essence.com/audio/chimamanda.rm.

'New Writing and Nigeria: Chimamanda Ngozi Adichie and Helen Oyeyemi in Conversation.' Interview by Aminatta Forna. *Wasafiri*, no. 21, Mar. 2006, pp. 50–57.

'Africa's Women Speak Out: Chimamanda Ngozi Adichie.' *BBC News*, 26 Mar. 2005, news.bbc.co.uk/2/hi/africa/4376967.stm.

'A Brief Conversation with Chimamanda Ngozi Adichie.' *World Literature Today*, vol. 80, no. 2, Mar.–Apr. 2006, p. 5.

'Reinventing Home.' Michael Ondaatje and Chimamanda Ngozi Adichie in conversation at the World Voices Festival, 22 Apr. 2005. *PEN*

America, 20 Dec. 2012, www.pen.org/book/conversation-michael-ondaatje-chimamanda-ngozi-adichie. Transcript also available, *PEN America*, 14 Mar. 2014, www.pen.org/conversation/reinventing-home.

'Miriam N. Kotzin with Chimamanda Ngozi Adichie.' *Per Contra*, no. 2, Spring 2006, www.percontra.net/archive/2adichie.htm.

Interview by Mariella Frostrup. *Open Book*, BBC Radio 4, 20 Aug. 2006, www.bbc.co.uk/radio4/arts/openbook/openbook_20060820. shtml.

'12 Questions for Chimamanda Ngozi Adichie.' Interview by Jane Ciabattari. 12 Sept. 2006. *Critical Mass*, 11 Apr. 2011, www. bookcritics.org/blog/archive/from_the_archives_12_questions_ for_chimamanda_adichie/.

'Half of a Yellow Sun.' Interview by Leonard Lopate. *Leonard Lopate Show*, WNYC, 13 Sept. 2006, www.wnyc.org/story/52648-half-of-a-yellow-sun/.

'Capturing Biafra's Brief Day in the 'Yellow Sun.' Interview by Debbie Elliott. *All Things Considered*, NPR, 17 Sept. 2006, www.npr.org/ templates/story/story.php?storyId=6088156.

'Chimamanda Ngozi Adichie: *Half of a Yellow Sun*.' Interview by Susan Page. *Diane Rehm Show*, WAMU 88.5 / NPR, 5 Oct. 2006, thedianerehmshow.org/shows/2006-10-05/chimamanda-ngoz i-adichie-half-yellow-sun-knopf.

'Young Nigerian's Powerful New Novel.' *BBC Learning English*, BBC World Service, 6 Oct. 2006, www.bbc.co.uk/worldservice/ learningenglish/radio/specials/1549_weekender_extra/page35. shtml.

'Her Stories of War Are Also Her Stories of Family.' Interview by Anna Mundow. *Boston Globe*, 8 Oct. 2006, p. E7.

'Chimamanda Ngozi Adichie.' Interview by Robert Birnbaum. *Morning News*, 23 Oct. 2006, www.themorningnews.org/article/ chimamanda-ngozi-adichie.

'Half of a Yellow Sun: An Up-and-coming Nigerian Author Revisits the War That Shaped Her Country.' Interview by Rina Palta. *Mother Jones*, 24 Oct. 2006, www.motherjones.com/politics/2006/10/ half-yellow-sun.

'Write the Power.' Interview by Meres J. Weche. *afrotoronto.com*, 25 Oct. 2006, afrotoronto.com/content/articles/43-books/537-writ e-the-power.

'Daughter of Biafra.' Interview by Dylan Foley. *Star-Ledger*, 29 Oct. 2006, p. 6.

'My Book Should Provoke A Conversation – Chimamanda Ngozi.' Interview by Wale Adebanwi. *News* (Nigeria), 9 Jan. 2007.

'Eyes on the Prize.' Interview by Davina Morris. *Voice*, no. 1270, 22 May 2007.

Interview by Sarah Crown. Podcast from the Hay Festival, *Guardian*, 6 June 2007, download.guardian.co.uk/sys-audio/Books/Books/2007/06/06/Adiche.mp3.

'Book World Live.' *Washington Post*, 19 June 2007, www.washingtonpost.com/wp-dyn/content/discussion/2007/06/15/DI2007061501485.html.

'Chimamanda Ngozi Adichie.' Interview by Gavin Esler. *Hardtalk Extra*, BBC News, 27 July 2007, news.bbc.co.uk/2/hi/programmes/hardtalk/6922214.stm.

'An Interview with Fiction Writer Chimamanda Ngozi Adichie.' By Renee H. Shea. *Poets & Writers Magazine*, 8 Aug. 2007, www.pw.org/content/interview_fiction_writer_chimamanda_ngozi_adichie.

'How Does It Feel to Be Home?' Interview by Ovo Adagha. *Vanguard*, 12 Aug. 2007.

'This is Not Just MY prize but OUR Prize.' Interview by Ahaoma Kanu. *Nigerian Village Square*, 16 Aug. 2007, www.nigeriavillagesquare.com/articles/interview-this-is-not-just-my-prize-but-our-prize-chimamanda-adichie.html.

'10 Questions with Chimamanda Ngozi Adichie.' Interview by A. Igoni Barrett. *Farafina*, no. 10, Sept. 2007, p. 67.

'Chimamanda Adichie.' Interview by Bat Segundo. *The Bat Segundo Show*, no. 141, 5 Oct. 2007, www.edrants.com/segundo/bss-141-chimamanda-adichie/.

'Excerpts from Chimamanda Ngozi Adichie Interview.' By Michael Janairo. *Times Union*, 14 Oct. 2007, blog.timesunion.com/books/excerpts-from-chimamanda-ngozi-adichie-interview/974/.

'Chapter and Verse: Chimamanda Ngozi Adichie.' *Good Housekeeping*, Oct. 2007, p. 74.

'Memory, Witness, and War: Chimamanda Ngozi Adichie Talks with *Bookforum*.' Interview by Kera Bokonik. *Bookforum*, vol. 14, no. 4 (Dec. 2007 – Jan. 2008), p. 37.

'The Stories of Africa: A Q&A with Chimamanda Ngozi Adichie.' P.S. section of *Half of a Yellow Sun*, by Adichie, Harper Perennial, 2007, pp. 2–6.

'A Writing Life.' P.S. section of *Half of a Yellow Sun*, by Adichie, Harper Perennial, 2007, pp. 6–7.

'Intervju sa Cimamandom Ngozi Adici.' Interview by Daria Tunca. *Mostovi*, no. 141–42, Jan.–June 2008, pp. 30–33. A Serbian translation of the interview found on the Chimamda Ngozi Adichie Website.

'Adichie on Knowledge Quest.' Interview by Fritz Lanham. *Houston Chronicle*, 15 Feb. 2008, p. 3, and available online, www. chron.com/life/books/article/Eggers-Adiche-pen-novels-on-plights-in-Sudan-1756203.php#page-2.

'The Sad and Amusing State of Race in America.' Interview by Anya Yurchyshyn. *Esquire*, 19 Feb. 2008, www.esquire.com/entertainment/books/a4288/lastline021908/?click=main_sr

'Ada Azodo Talks 'Creative Writing and Literary Activism' with Chimamanda Ngozi Adichie.' *JALA: Journal of the African Literature Association*, vol. 2, no. 1, Winter–Spring 2008, pp. 146–51.

'*Half Of A Yellow Sun* Chose Me.' Interview by Nehru Odeh. *News* (Nigeria), 29 Sept. 2008.

'Q&A: Chimamanda Ngozi Adichie.' Interview by Rosanna Greenstreet. *Guardian*, 25 Oct. 2008, p. 8, and available online, www. theguardian.com/lifeandstyle/2008/oct/25/chimamanda-ngozi-adiche-interview.

Interview by Hugo Pradelle. *Quinzaine Littéraire*, no. 980, 16–30 Nov. 2008. In French.

'I Am a Work in Progress.' Interview by Bunmi Akpata-Ohohe. *Africa Today*, 4 Dec. 2008.

Interview. *MADE*, vol. 1, no. 4, 2008.

'Il mondo taceva, noi morivamo.' Interview by Mario Baudino. *La Stampa*, 30 Jan. 2009. In Italian.

'Interview with Chimamanda Ngozi Adichie.' By Joshua Jelly-Schapiro. *Believer*, vol. 7, no. 1, Jan. 2009, pp. 54–61.

'Films of My Life: Chimamanda Ngozi Adichie.' Interview by Killian Fox. *Observer*, 22 Mar. 2009, Features and Interviews p. 18, and available online, www.theguardian.com/film/2009/mar/22/favourite-films-chimamanda-ngozi-adichie.

Interview by Kirsty Lang. *Front Row*, BBC Radio 4, 3 Apr. 2009, www. bbc.co.uk/programmes/b00jbs2d.

'The Interview: Chimamanda Ngozi Adichie.' By Stephanie Sadler. *Seven Magazine*, 14 Apr. 2009.

'Chimamanda Ngozi Adichie.' Interview by Renee Shea. *Kenyon Review*, Apr. 2009, www.kenyonreview.org/conversation/chimamanda-ngozi-adichie/.

'Small Talk: Chimamanda Ngozi Adichie.' Interview by Anna Metcalfe. *Financial Times*, 2 May 2009, p. 16.

'In Conversation with Chimamanda Ngozi Adichie.' Interview by Ramona Koval. *The Book Show*, ABC Australia, 26 May 2009, www. abc.net.au/radionational/programs/bookshow/in-conversation-with-chimamanda-ngozi-adichie/3147314. For a video version of this interview, see 'Chimamanda Ngozi Adichie in Conversation with Ramona Koval.' *YouTube*, uploaded by The Monthly Video, 2 May 2013, www.youtube.com/watch?v=5ZQILTkgq1U.

'Writer Chimamanda Ngozi Adichie Interview.' By Eleanor Watchel. *Writers and Company*, CBC Radio, 14 June 2009, www.cbc.ca/player/play/1503786671.

'Q&A with Chimamanda Adichie on *The Thing Around Your Neck*.' Interview by Lia Grainger. *National Post* (Canada), 17 June 2009.

'6 Questions with… Author Chimamanda Ngozi Adichie.' Interview by Eric Volmers. *Calgary Herald*, 21 June 2009, p. C4.

'Irritation And Space: A Nigerian Writer in America.' Interview by Guy Raz. *All Things Considered*, NPR, 21 June 2009, www.npr.org/templates/story/story.php?storyId=105588688.

'Chimamanda Ngozi Adichie: A Conversation with James Mustich.' *Barnes and Noble Review*, 29 June 2009, www.barnesandnoble.com/review/chimamanda-ngozi-adichie.

'How Do You Write a Love Story With Teeth? A Conversation with Novelist Chimamanda Ngozi Adichie.' Interview by Nina Shen Rastogi. *Double X*, 29 June 2009.

'Book Talk: Author Adichie Doesn't Mind Her Own Business.' Interview by Pauline Askin. *Reuters*, 1 July 2009, www.reuters.com/article/us-books-author-adichie-idUSTRE5600UP20090701?sp=true.

'Chimamanda Ngozi Adichie – *Half of a Yellow Sun*.' Interview by Harriett Gilbert. *World Book Club*, BBC, 6 June 2009, www.bbc.co.uk/programmes/p0037mh5.

'Chimamanda Ngozi Adichie: *The Thing around Your Neck* (Knopf).' Interview by Diane Rehm. *The Diane Rehm Show*, WAMU 88.5 / NPR, 6 June 2009, thedianerehmshow.org/shows/2009-07-06/chimamanda-ngozi-adichie-thing-around-your-neck-knopf.

'Chimamanda Ngozi Adichie on Her Book, *The Thing around Your Neck*.' *YouTube*, uploaded by Random House Canada, 29 June 2009, www.youtube.com/watch?v=nNXS8Zv0TKk.

'Conversation: Chimamanda Adichie, Author of *The Thing Around Your Neck*.' *Newshour*, PBS, 9 July 2009, www.pbs.org/newshour/art/conversation-chimamanda-adichie-author-of-the-thing-around-your-neck/.

'Chimamanda Adichie: Powerful Words.' *African Voices*, CNN, 13 July 2009, edition.cnn.com/2009/WORLD/africa/07/12/chimamanda.adichie/.

'I'm a Happy Feminist.' Interview by R. Krithika. *Hindu*, 9 Aug. 2009.

'An Interview with Chimamanda Ngozi Adichie.' By John Zuarino.

Bookslut, no. 87, Aug. 2009, www.bookslut.com/features/2009_08_014928.php.

'Chimamanda Ngozi Adichie, Nigerian Writer.' Interview by Carrie Gracie. *The Interview*, BBC World Service, 20 Dec. 2009, www.bbc.co.uk/programmes/p005czr3.

'Nigerian Community Struggles With Terrorist Connection.' Interview by Michel Martin. *Tell Me More*, NPR, 13 Jan. 2010, www.npr.org/templates/story/story.php?storyId=122528521.

'A Conversation with Chimamanda Ngozi Adichie.' Interview by Susan VanZanten. *Image*, no. 65, Spring 2010, pp. 86–99, and available online, imagejournal.org/article/conversation-chimamanda-ngozi-adichie/.

'20 Questions with Chimamanda Ngozi Adichie.' Interview by Melissa Hellstern. *Oprah.com*, 4 June 2010, www.oprah.com/oprahsbookclub/20-Questions-with-Author-Chimamanda-Ngozi-Adichie.

'Chimamanda Ngozi Adichie: Nigerian Author Reads at the Egyptian Theatre.' Interview by Tara Morgan. *Boise Weekly*, 9 June 2010, www.boiseweekly.com/boise/chimamanda-ngozi-adichie/Content?oid=1634755.

'Chimamanda Adichie's Stories of Africa and America.' Interview by Kate Smith. *Midmorning*, MPR, 14 June 2010, www.mprnews.org/story/2010/06/14/midmorning2.

'Chimamanda Ngozi Adichie.' Interview by Jennifer L. Knox. *New Yorker*, 14–21 June 2010, www.newyorker.com/magazine/2010/06/14/chimamanda-ngozi-adichie.

'"No puede ser que sólo se cuenten miseria y pobreza de África."' Interview by Álvaro de Cozar. *El País*, 16 June 2010, internacional.elpais.com/internacional/2010/06/16/actualidad/1276639213_850215.html. In Spanish.

'My Perfect Summer.' Interview by Victoria Maw. *Financial Times*, 3 July 2010, p. 1, and available online, *Financial Times*, 2 July 2010, www.ft.com/content/93a3f4e4-8560-11df-aa2e-00144feabdc0.

'Chimamanda Ngozi Adichie.' *Celebrating Nigeria at 50*, special issue of *Time Out*, Oct. 2010, pp. 76–77, farafinabooks.files.wordpress.com/2010/11/literature-final-71-783.pdf.

'Chimamanda Ngozi Adichie on Ama Ata Aidoo.' *Africa Report*, Oct.–Nov. 2010.

'Engaging with History Because She Doesn't Want to Forget.' Interview by Smriti Daniel. *Sunday Times Magazine* (Sri Lanka), 9 Jan. 2011, www.sundaytimes.lk/110109/Magazine/sundaytimesmagazine_01.html.

'After Shock: The Lingering Legacy of Civil War.' Interview by Bridget

Kendall. *The Forum*, BBC World Service, 14 Feb. 2011, www.bbc. co.uk/programmes/p00df8fh.

'In Conversation with Chimamanda Ngozi Adichie.' *YouTube*, uploaded by teheklatv, 4 Mar. 2011.

'Nigeria: Democracy on the Line.' Interview by Riz Khan. *Riz Khan*, Al Jazeera, 5 Apr. 2011, www.aljazeera.com/programmes/rizkhan/ 2011/04/20114595939272123.html.

"Chimamanda Ngozi Adichie with Binyavanga Wainaina.' *Lannan Foundation*, 28 Sept. 2011, podcast.lannan.org/2011/10/01/ chimamanda-ngozi-adichie-with-binyavanga-wainaina-conver sation-28-september-2011-video/.

'Nigeria's Chimamanda Ngozi Adichie's Publishing Dream.' Interview by Sharon Hemans. *Network Africa*, BBC World Service, 13 Oct. 2011, www.bbc.com/news/world-africa-15279823.

'Chimamanda Ngozi Adichie on Nigeria.' Interview by Jim Fleming. *TT Book*, 13 Nov. 2011, www.ttbook.org/book/chimamanda-ngozi-adichie.

'Chimamanda N. Adichie.' Interview by Marita Golden. *Word: Black Writers Talk about the Transformative Power of Reading and Writing*, edited by Marita Golden, Broadway Paperback, 2011, pp. 169–81.

'Chimamanda Ngozi Adichie and Michael Greenberg, 2011 Eat, Drink & Be Literary at BAM Café.' Interview by Michael Greenberg. *Soundcloud*, uploaded by National Book, 14 Apr. 2013, soundcloud. com/nationalbook/chimamanda-ngozi-adichie-and.

'Winter with the Writers: Chimamanda Adichie.' Interview by Carol Frost. Feb. 2012. *YouTube*, uploaded by Rollins College, 14 Feb. 2013, www.youtube.com/watch?v=7sMg1td3XSc.

'May Day Protests Turn Violent, Obama in Afghanistan, Novelist Chimamanda Ngozi Adichie.' Interview by Marcie Sillman. *Weekday*, KUOW, 2 May 2012, www2.kuow.org/program.php?id=26648.

'Chimamanda Ngozi Adichie.' *Literary Arts*, 3 May 2012, www. literary-arts.org/archive/chimamanda-adichie/.

'Keynote Speech by the Nigerian Author Chimamanda Ngozi Adichie, Part 2.' Short interview by Simon Stanford, and Q&A with the audience. *Uppsala Universitet*, 15 Oct. 2012, media.medfarm.uu.se/ play/kanal/90/video/2958.

'Worldwise: Arts & Humanities Dean's Lecture Series: Chimamanda Adichie.' Interview by Sheri Parks, and Q&A with the audience. 19 Feb. 2013. *Vimeo*, uploaded by UMD College of Arts & Humanities, 1 Mar. 2013, vimeo.com/60861516.

'This Week in Fiction: Chimamanda Ngozi Adichie.' Interview by Willing Davidson. *New Yorker*, 9 Mar. 2013, www.newyorker.

com/books/page-turner/this-week-in-fiction-chimamanda-ngozi-adichie.

'A Tribute to Chinua Achebe.' Interviews with Chimamanda Ngozi Adichie, Binyavanga Wainaina and Chibundu Onuzo, by Harriet Gilbert. *The Strand*, BBC World Service, 27 Mar. 2013, www.bbc.co.uk/programmes/p015zljm.

'Chimamanda Ngozi Adichie: 'My New Novel Is about Love, Race… and Hair." Interview by Kate Kellaway. *Observer*, 7 Apr. 2013, p. 5, and available online, www.theguardian.com/theobserver/2013/apr/07/chimamanda-ngozi-adichie-americanah-interview?CMP=twt_gu.

'Author Chimamanda Adichie: 'Black Women's Hair Is Political." *News*, Channel 4, 10 Apr. 2013, www.channel4.com/news/chimamanda-ngozi-adichie-americanah-hair-immigration-race.

'Humanising History – Chimamanda Ngozi Adichie.' Interview by Ellah Allfrey. Royal Society of Arts House, London, 10 Apr. 2013. *YouTube*, uploaded by The RSA, 15 May 2013, www.youtube.com/watch?v=9Lx1BDdNF4w. Longer audio version with audience Q&A also available as 'Humanising History and Connecting Cultures: The Role of Literature.' *Royal Society of Arts*, 10 Apr. 2013, www.thersa.org/discover/audio/2013/04/humanising-history-connecting-cultures-the-role-of-literature.

'Oliver Stone, Chimamanda Adichie, Web Harvesting.' Interview by Samira Ahmed. *Nightwaves*, BBC Radio 3, 10 Apr. 2013, www.bbc.co.uk/programmes/b01rr922.

'Chimamanda Ngozi Adichie on Life in US.' Interview by Matthew Bannister. *Outlook*, BBC World Service, 22 Apr. 2013, www.bbc.co.uk/programmes/p0175w3t.

'Buy Books instead of Recharge Cards – Chimamanda Ngozi Adichie.' *Sunrise*, Channels Television, 2013. *YouTube*, uploaded by Channels Television, 27 Apr. 2013, www.youtube.com/watch?v=cT8tSQdB7zE.

'Chimamanda Ngozi Adichie.' Interview by John Wilson. *Front Row*, BBC Radio 4, 3 May 2013, www.bbc.co.uk/programmes/p018l2lr.

'A Nigerian-'Americanah' Novel about Love, Race and Hair.' Interview by Scott Simon. *Weekend Edition Saturday*, NPR, 11 May 2013, www.npr.org/2013/05/11/181685674/a-nigerian-americanah-novel-about-love-race-and-hair.

'Chimamanda Ngozi Adichie's Continental Divides.' Interview by Joseph Klarl. *Interview Magazine*, 14 May 2013, www.interviewmagazine.com/culture/chimamanda-ngozi-adichie-americanah#.

'A Pioneer for Nigerian Writers.' Interview by Zain Verjee. *African Voices*, CNN, 17 May 2013, edition.cnn.com/videos/

international/2013/05/17/african-voices-chimamanda-ngozi-adichie-a.cnn.

'Race, Identity, and Good Hair: Chimamanda Ngozi Adichie on Her New Novel, *Americanah*.' Interview by Marco Werman. *The World*, PRI, 23 May 2013, www.pri.org/stories/2013-05-23/race-identity-and-good-hair-chimamanda-ngozi-adichie-her-new-novel-americanah.

'Interview with Chimamanda Ngozi Adichie.' By Anderson Tepper. *goodreads*, May 2013, www.goodreads.com/interviews/show/857. Chimamanda_Ngozi_Adichie.

'Life Across Borders: Chimamanda Ngozi Adichie Talks about *Americanah*.' Interview by John Williams. *New York Times*, 6 June 2013, artsbeat.blogs.nytimes.com/2013/06/06/life-acros s-borders-chimamanda-ngozi-adichie-talks-about-americanah/?_r=0.

'What Are the Dangers of a Single Story?' Interview by Guy Raz. *TED Radio Hour*, NPR, 7 June 2013, www.npr.org/2013/09/20/186303292/what-are-the-dangers-of-a-single-story.

'Writer Chimamanda Ngozi Adichie Discusses Her Career.' Interview by Razia Iqbal. *Talking Books*, BBC, 14 June 2013, www.bbc.com/culture/story/20130614-telling-a-new-story-of-africa.

'*Americanah* Author Explains 'Learning' to Be Black in the US' Interview by Terry Gross. *Fresh Air*, NPR, 27 June 2013, www.npr.org/2013/06/27/195598496/americanah-author-explains-learn ing-to-be-black-in-the-u-s.

'*Americanah* with Author Chimamanda Ngozi Adichie.' Interview by Kevin Sylvester. *Sunday Edition*, CBC Radio, 7 July 2013, www.cbc.ca/player/play/2395840969.

'The Varieties of Blackness.' Interview by Aaron Bady. *Boston Review*, 10 July 2013, bostonreview.net/fiction/varieties-blackness.

'Chimamanda Ngozi Adichie: *Americanah*.' Interview by Kojo Nnamdi. *The Kojo Nnamdi Show*, WAMU 88.5, 24 July 2013, thekojonnamdishow. org/shows/2013-07-24/chimamanda-ngozi-adichie-americanah.

'MacArthur-winning Author and Columbia Resident Writes Novel about Race in America.' Interview by Mary Carole McCauley. *Baltimore Sun*, 27 July 2013, articles.baltimoresun.com/2013-07-27/entertainment/bs-ae-author-adichie-20130727_1_americanah-chimamand a-ngozi-adichie-columbia-resident.

'In Conversation – Chimamanda Ngozi Adichie: Africa Needs Feminism.' Interview by Belinda Otas. *Belinda Otas*, 16 Aug. 2013, belindaotas.com/?p=12101.

'Chimamanda Ngozi Adichie i BABEL: SVT.' *YouTube*, uploaded by

SVT, 6 Nov. 2013, www.youtube.com/watch?v=KIiB5hSCfZc.

'#Kwaniat10 Book Party: Chimamanda Adichie and Yvonne Owuor.' Interview by Binyavanga Wainaina. Nairobi, 29 Nov. 2013. *YouTube*, uploaded by Kwani Trust, 21 Dec. 2013, www.youtube.com/ watch?v=IzR8nKSexP8.

'Write the Book You Want to Read: A Conversation with Chimamanda Ngozi Adichie.' Interview by Parul Sehgal. *Summer Reading*, issue of *Tin House*, vol. 14, no. 4 (issue no. 56), 2013, and available online, 'A Conversation with Chimamande [sic] Ngozi Adichie.' *Tin House*, 13 Dec. 2013, www.tinhouse.com/blog/31397/a-conversation-with-chimamande-ngozi-adichie.html.

'The Right to Tell Your Story.' Interview by Synne Rifbjerg. Louisiana Literature Festival, Humlebæk, 1–4 Sept. 2011. *Louisiana Channel*, 2013, channel.louisiana.dk/video/chimamanda-adichie-right-tell-your-story

'Storytelling, Colonial Past and the Present – A Conversation with Chimamanda Ngozi Adichie.' Interview by Jannike Åhlund. Göteborg International Film Festival, 26 Jan. 2014. *YouTube*, uploaded by gbgfilmfestival, 27 Jan. 2014, www.youtube.com/ watch?v=WCZhkweayUw.

'GIFF2014 Live: Studio Draken, Chimamanda Ngozi Adichie i Studion.' *YouTube*, uploaded by gbgfilmfestival, 27 Jan. 2014, www. youtube.com/watch?v=WJsvUXlOYvo.

'Meet Beyoncé's Favourite Novelist.' Interview by Keziah Weir. *Elle*, 15 Feb. 2014, www.elle.com/culture/celebrities/news/a18980/ chimamanda-ngozi-adichie-interview/.

'MO*lezing Chimamanda Ngozi Adichie op Mind The Book 2014.' Interview by Gie Goris. Ghent, 22 Feb. 2014. *YouTube*, uploaded by MO nieuwssite, 28 Feb. 2014, www.youtube.com/ watch?v=tEsXJv4s1HI.

'Chimamanda Ngozi Adichie.' Interview by Barbara Rottiers. *Cobra*, 28 Feb. 2014, cobra.canvas.be/cm/cobra/videozone/rubriek/ boek-videozone/1.1894014.

'Q&A: Chimamanda Ngozi Adichie Tackles Race from African Perspective in *Americanah*.' Interview by Soniah Kamal. *ArtsATL*, 4 Mar. 2014, www.artsatl.com/qa-chimamanda-ngozi-adichie-americanah/.

'Chimamanda Ngozi Adichie on the TEDx Talk Beyoncé Sampled and Why We Should Forget Feminism's 'Baggage."' Interview by Emma Gray. *Huffington Post*, 6 Mar. 2014, www. huffingtonpost.com/2014/03/06/chimamanda-ngozi-adichie-feminism_n_4907241.html.

'Hair-raising Histories.' Interview by Asha Kasbekar. *LiveMint*, 8 Mar. 2014, http://www.livemint.com/Leisure/v0hbaIky54ajloIzhoGFCP/ Chimamanda-Ngozi-Adichie--Hairraising-histories.html.

'Chimamanda Ngozi Adichie in Conversation with Damian Woetzel.' *YouTube*, uploaded by The Aspen Institute, 11 Mar. 2014, www. youtube.com/watch?v=1e0J24rTTu4.

'Chimamanda Ngozi Adichie: Tenement Talk from March 12, 2014.' New York, 12 Mar. 2014. *YouTube*, uploaded by Tenement Museum, 8 Apr. 2014, www.youtube.com/watch?v=yY1RK6aAPws.

'Tell Me More: Chimamanda Ngozi Adichie.' Interview by Maria Shriver. *NBC News*, 12 Mar. 2014, www.nbcnews.com/feature/ maria-shriver/tell-me-more-chimamanda-ngozi-adichie-n50811.

'American Africans.' Interview by Brian Lehrer. *The Brian Lehrer Show*, WNYC, 13 Mar. 2014, www.wnyc.org/story/african-america/.

'Award-winning Author Chimamanda Ngozi Adichie Part I.' Interview by Lola Ogunnaike. *YouTube*, uploaded by Arise Entertainment 360, 13 Mar. 2014, www.youtube.com/watch?v=NvHlwSp8Dfs.

'Award-winning Author Chimamanda Ngozi Adichie Part II.' Interview by Lola Ogunnaike. *YouTube*, uploaded by Arise Entertainment 360, 13 Mar. 2014, www.youtube.com/watch?v=KuCVDKR1-b8.

'Chimamanda Ngozi Adichie: 'When You're Not a White Male Writing about White Male Things Then Somehow Your Work Has to *Mean* Something.'' Interview by Anna North. *Salon*, 13 Mar. 2014, www.salon.com/2014/03/13/chimamanda_ngozi_adichie_ when_you%E2%80%99re_not_a_white_male_writing_about_ white_male_things_then_somehow_your_work_has_to_mean_ something/.

'Chimamanda Ngozi Adichie's Literary Lagos.' Interview by Henry Krempels. *Daily Beast*, 16 Mar. 2014, www.thedailybeast.com/ articles/2014/03/16/chimamanda-ngozi-adichie-s-literary-lagos. html.

'Chimamanda Adiche Speaks at the 2014 New African Film Festival.' Interview by Mwiza Munthali. Silver Spring MD, 16 Mar. 2014. *YouTube*, uploaded by Lawrence Green, 17 Mar. 2014, www.youtube. com/watch?v=hYYjeb0odqg.

'Feminism Is Fashionable for Nigerian Writer Chimamanda Ngozi Adichie.' Interview by Michel Martin. *Tell Me More*, NPR, 18 Mar. 2014, www.npr.org/2014/03/18/291133080/news-maker.

'Between the Lines: Chimamanda Ngozi Adichie with Zadie Smith.' Schomburg Center for Research in Black Culture, New York, 19 Mar. 2014. *Livestream*, uploaded by Schomburg Center, 19 Mar. 2014, livestream.com/schomburgcenter/events/2831224/videos/45613924.

'Novelicious Chats to… Chimamanda Ngozi Adichie.' *novelicious.com*, 2 May 2014, www.novelicious.com/2014/05/exclusive-novelicious-chats-tochimamanda-ngozi-adichie.html.

'Chimamanda Ngozi Adichie – *Americanah.*' Interview by Synne Rifbjerg. International Authors' Stage, Copenhagen, 19 May 2014. *YouTube*, uploaded by Det Kongelige Bibliotek, 20 May 2014, www.youtube.com/watch?v=b8r-dP9NqX8.

'Talking Children, Women and Africa with Author Chimamanda Adichie.' Interview by James Elder. *YouTube*, uploaded by UNICEF Innocenti, 30 May 2014, www.youtube.com/watch?v=8XNvQ6DXay4.

'The Rumpus Interview with Chimamanda Ngozi Adichie.' By Kima Jones. *Rumpus*, 17 June 2014, therumpus.net/2014/06/the-rumpus-interview-with-chimamanda-ngozi-adichie/.

'Chimamanda Ngozi Adichie on Her 'Flawless' Speech, Out Today as an eBook.' Interview by Alex Frank. *Vogue*, 29 July 2014, www.vogue.com/946843/chimamanda-ngozi-adicihie-feminism-beyonce-book.

'Nigerians Should Celebrate Great Writers Like Chimamanda on Independence Day.' Interview by Jessica Onah. *HuffPost Entertainment*, 1 Oct. 2014, www.huffingtonpost.co.uk/jessica-onah/nigerians-should-celebrate-chimamanda_b_5911932.html.

'Writer Chimamanda Ngozi Adichie.' Interview by Tavis Smiley. *Tavis Smiley*, PBS, 6 Oct. 2014, www.pbs.org/wnet/tavissmiley/interviews/chimamanda-ngozi-adichie/.

'Interview: Chimamanda Ngozi Adichie, Author, *Americanah.*' Interview by Michele Norris. Washington Ideas Forum, 30 Oct. 2014. *FORA.tv*, 30 Oct. 2014, library.fora.tv/2014/10/30/interview_chimamanda_ngozi_adichie_author_americanah.

'Take Note: Noted Nigerian Author Chimamanda Ngozi Adichie Talks about Her Novel *Americanah.*' Interview by Emily Reddy. *WPSU*, 14 Nov. 2014, radio.wpsu.org/post/take-note-noted-nigerian-author-chimamanda-ngozi-adichie-talks-about-her-novel-americanah.

'Chimamanda Adichie: Beauty Does Not Solve Problems.' Interview by Synne Rifbjerg. *Louisiana Channel*, 2014, channel.louisiana.dk/video/chimamanda-adichie-beauty-does-not-solve-any-problem

'Chimamanda Ngozi Adichie en 3 mots.' Interview by Catherine Simon. *Le Monde*, 5 Feb. 2015, www.lemonde.fr/livres/video/2015/02/05/chimamanda-ngozi-adichie-en-3-mots_4570655_3260.html. Video with a French audio track.

'4 Women on the Outfits They Feel Best In.' *New York Magazine*, 9 Feb. 2015, and available online, *New York Magazine*, 13 Feb. 2015, nymag.

com/thecut/2015/02/4-women-favorite-outfits.html.

'Chimamanda Ngozi Adichie: Storyteller.' Interview by Janell Hobson. *Ms. Magazine*, 6 Mar. 2015, msmagazine.com/blog/2015/03/06/chimamanda-ngozi-adichie-storyteller/.

'*Nous sommes tous des féministes*, de Chimamanda Ngozi Adichie.' Interview by Catherine Fruchon-Toussaint. RFI, 8 Mar. 2015, www.rfi.fr/emission/20150308-nous-sommes-tous-feministes-chimamanda-ngozi-adichie/. In French.

'Exclusive Interview: Chimamanda Ngozi Adichie (pt 1).' By Chiagoze Fred Nwonwu, *Olisa.tv*, 12 Mar. 2015, www.olisa.tv/2015/03/exclusive-interviewchimamanda-ngozi-adichie-pt-1.

'Exclusive Interview: Chimamanda Ngozi Adichie (pt 2).' By Chiagoze Fred Nwonwu. *Olisa.tv*, 13 Mar. 2015, www.olisa.tv/2015/03/exclusive-interview-chimamanda-ngozi-adichie-part-2.

'This Week in Fiction: Chimamanda Ngozi Adichie.' Interview by Willing Davidson. *New Yorker*, 6 Apr. 2015, www.newyorker.com/books/page-turner/fiction-this-week-chimamanda-ngozi-adichie-2015-04-13.

'Arlington Reads: Chimamanda Ngozi Adichie.' Q&A with the audience, 7 May 2015. *YouTube*, uploaded by arlingtoncounty, 19 May 2015, www.youtube.com/watch?v=BHWd65iLoUs.

'Understanding Nigeria, a Country of Pain, Promise and Complexity.' Interview by William Brangham. *NewsHour*, PBS, 4 Dec. 2015, www.pbs.org/newshour/bb/understanding-nigeria-a-country-of-pain-promise-and-complexity/.

'Chimamanda Ngozi Adichie on Race and Gender.' *Newshour*, BBC, 4 Jan. 2016, www.bbc.co.uk/programmes/p03dkgxq.

'Leçon de féminisme, par Chimamanda Ngozi Adichie.' Interview by Marc Bettinelli and Laureline Savoye. *Le Monde*, 25 Feb. 2016, www.lemonde.fr/afrique/article/2016/02/25/lecon-de-feminisme-par-chimamanda-ngozi-adichie_4871221_3212.html.

'Voices in a Promised Land with Chimamanda Ngozi Adichie, Aleksandar Hemon, and Cecilia Muñoz.' Sixth & I Historic Synagogue, New York, 7 Mar. 2016. *Vimeo*, uploaded by Sixth & I Historic Synagogue, Mar. 2016, vimeo.com/158251232.

'Marking a Decade of a Classic: Chimamanda Ngozi Adichie on the 10th Anniversary of *Half of a Yellow Sun*.' Interview by Anna Hart. *Stylist*, 22 July 2016, www.stylist.co.uk/books/chimamanda-ngozi-adichie-interview-anniversary-decade-half-of-a-yellow-sun-nigerian-author-motherhood.

'Chimamanda Ngozi Adichie – Your Questions Answered on the Obamas, Motherhood and Feminism.' *Guardian*, 3 Aug. 2016, www.

theguardian.com/books/live/2016/aug/01/chimamanda-ngoz
i-adichie-webchat-half-of-a-yellow-sun.

'Chimimndaa [*sic*] Ngozi Adichie: Black Lives Matter Is Doing Something Really Important.' *News*, Channel 4, *YouTube*, uploaded by Channel 4 News, 8 Aug. 2016, www.youtube.com/watch?v=FwQgHj8r4UU.

'The Stream – In Conversation with Chimamanda Ngozi Adichie.' Interview by Femi Oke. *The Stream*, Al Jazeera English, 2016. *YouTube*, uploaded by Al Jazeera English, 1 Sept. 2016, www.youtube.com/watch?v=Nr3goEZynho.

'Chimamanda Ngozi Adichie: Refugees, Race, and *Americanah*.' Interview by Mary Louise Kelly. Washington Ideas Forum, 28 Sept. 2016. *YouTube*, uploaded by FORA.tv, 29 Sept. 2016, www.youtube.com/watch?v=CKodkVJR8DE.

'We Should All Be Feminists | Chimamanda Ngozi Adichie – Atria.' Interview by Nancy Jouwe, and Q&A with the audience. Atria Institute on Gender Equality and Women's History, Amsterdam, 15 Oct. 2016. *YouTube*, uploaded by Atria Kennisinstituut, 15 Oct. 2016, www.youtube.com/watch?v=Ligb8wICe9w&feature=youtu.be.

'Ready To Speak Up with Chimamanda Ngozi Adichie – Presented by No7.' *YouTube*, uploaded by Boots UK, 4 Nov. 2016, www.youtube.com/watch?v=YJL4REziTvE.

'Chimamanda Ngozi Adichie and R. Emmett Tyrrell.' Interview by Emily Maitlis. *Newsnight*, BBC, 11 Nov. 2016. *YouTube*, uploaded by BBC Newsnight, 16 Nov. 2016, www.youtube.com/watch?v=_LAUgq8KX4U.

'Talking to Chimamanda Ngozi Adichie, the Beauty Brand Ambassador We All Need Right Now.' Interview by Cheryl Wischhover. *Racked*, 22 Nov. 2016, www.racked.com/2016/11/22/13714228/chimamanda-ngozi-adichie-boots-beauty.

Miscellaneous

'Sheer Beauty' (Poem). *Prime People*, date unknown.
'We Dream' (Poem). *Poetry Magazine*, vol. 3, no. 9, Sept. 1998.
Letter to the Editor, *Time*, 7 Feb. 2000.
'Visiting Nigeria' (Poem). *Poetry Magazine*, vol. 6, no. 6, June 2001.
Letter to the Editor, *Time*, 25 Mar. 2002.
'The Books Year: Who Read What in 2004.' *Irish Times*, 4 Dec. 2004, p. 11.
'Chimamanda Ngozi Adichie Recommends.' *Laila Lalami*, 4 Jan. 2005, lailalalami.com/2005/chimamanda-ngozi-adichie-recommends/.

'Hot Reads.' Compiled by Ginny Hooker, *Guardian*, 18 June 2005, p. 4, and available online, www.theguardian.com/books/2005/jun/18/summerreading2005.summerreading5. Several writers, among whom Chimamanda Ngozi Adichie, recommend works by other authors.

'Christmas Books: Speaking Volumes.' Compiled by Ginny Hooker, *Guardian*, 26 Nov. 2005, p. 4, and available online, www.theguardian.com/books/2005/nov/26/christmas.bestbooksoftheyear. Several writers, among whom Chimamanda Ngozi Adichie, recommend their favourite books of 2005.

'Best Books of 2005: Writers' Choice (2).' *Molara Wood*, 5 Jan. 2006. Several writers, among whom Chimamanda Ngozi Adichie, comment on her favourite books of the year.

'The Words That Matter.' *Age*, 16 Dec. 2006, p. 24. Several writers, among whom Chimamanda Ngozi Adichie, select the books that have made the biggest impact in 2006.

'The Great Escape.' *Guardian*, 23 June 2007, www.theguardian.com/books/2007/jun/23/fiction.travelbooks. Several writers, among whom Chimamanda Ngozi Adichie, select their best travel reading.

'Christmas Books Past, Present and Future: Part One.' *Guardian*, 24 Nov. 2007, www.theguardian.com/books/2007/nov/24/bestbooksoftheyear.bestbooks4. Several writers, among whom Chimamanda Ngozi Adichie, select their favourite seasonal reads.

'That's the Best Thing We've Read All Year – Part Two.' *Guardian*, 25 Nov. 2007, www.theguardian.com/books/2007/nov/25/bestbooksoftheyear.bestbooks1. Several writers, among whom Chimamanda Ngozi Adichie, select their favourite reads of 2007.

'Five Views of *Things Fall Apart*.' *Chronicle of Higher Education*, vol. 54, no. 22, 8 Feb. 2008, p. B7.

'Season's Readings.' *Guardian*, 29 Nov. 2008, p. 2, and available online, www.theguardian.com/books/2008/nov/29/best-books-year-2008-review. Several writers, among whom Chimamanda Ngozi Adichie, select their favourite books of 2008.

'Chimamanda Ngozi Adichie on 'Touch' by Alexi Zentner.' *The O. Henry Prize Stories*, 2008, www.randomhouse.com/anchor/ohenry/jury08.html.

'Take the Ladder Test.' *Guardian*, 9 May 2009, p. 27, and available online, www.theguardian.com/science/2009/may/09/superstitions. Chimamanda Ngozi Adichie briefly comments on superstition.

'Summer Reading: 'Coalition Books." *Guardian* (*Review* Supplement), 17 July 2010, p. 2, and available online as 'Let's Get Together: Summer Reading Recommendations.' *Guardian*, 17 July 2010, www.theguardian.

com/books/2010/jul/17/summer-reading-coalition-books

'Books of the Year.' *Guardian* (*Review* Supplement), 27 Nov. 2010, p. 2, and available online, www.theguardian.com/books/2010/nov/27/christmas-books-year-roundup. Several writers, among whom Chimamanda Ngozi Adichie, select their favourite books of 2010.

'Three-Minute Fiction Round 6: Laughing and Crying.' *All Things Considered*, NPR, 8 Jan. 2011, www.npr.org/2011/01/08/132744031/three-minute-fiction-round-6-laughing-and-crying. Includes a brief interview with Chimamanda Ngozi Adichie.

'Three-Minute Fiction Update: Good, Sad Stories.' *All Things Considered*, NPR, 26 Feb. 2011, www.npr.org/2011/02/26/134088164/three-minute-fiction-update-good-sad-stories. Chimamanda reads and comments on two of the entries received in a fiction competition.

'Three-Minute Fiction: The Winner is…' *All Things Considered*, NPR, 3 Apr. 2011, www.npr.org/2011/04/03/134982670/three-minute-fiction-the-winner-is.

'Chimamanda Adichie on 'The Garden Party' by Katherine Mansfield.' *The Center for Fiction*, June 2011, centerforfiction.org/forwriters/the-model-short-story/the-garden-party-by-katherine-mansfield/.

'Books of the Year 2011.' *Guardian* (*Review* Supplement), 26 Nov. 2011, p. 2, and available online, *Guardian*, 25 Nov. 2011, www.theguardian.com/books/2011/nov/25/books-of-the-year?newsfeed=true. Several writers, among whom Chimamanda Ngozi Adichie, select their favourite books of 2011.

'The Best Love Poems: Writers Choose Their Favourites.' Compiled by Paddy Allen, *Guardian*, 13 Feb. 2012, www.theguardian.com/books/interactive/2012/feb/13/best-love-poems-interactive. Chimamanda Ngozi Adichie selects 'Love after Love' by Derek Walcott as her favourite love poem.

'Summer Reading 2012.' *Observer* (*New Review* Supplement), 15 July 2012, p. 34, and available online, www.theguardian.com/books/2012/jul/15/summer-reading-ebooks-kindle-paper?INTCMP=SRCH. Several writers, among whom Chimamanda Ngozi Adichie, recommend books for the summer.

'Books of the Year 2012: Authors Choose Their Favourites.' *Guardian* (*Review* Supplement), 24 Nov. 2012, p. 2, and available online, *Observer*, 23 Nov. 2012, www.theguardian.com/books/2012/nov/23/books-of-the-year-2012-authors-favourites.

'An Igbo Elegy on Hearing of the Passing Away of Professor Chinua Achebe.' *Farafina Books* (and various sources), 22 Mar. 2013, farafinabooks.wordpress.com/2013/03/22/an-igbo-elegy-on-hearing-of-the-passing-away-of-professor-chinua-achebe-by-chimamanda-adichie/.

'Of Course I Never Said African Women with Brazilian Hair Have Low Self-esteem. That's Absurd.' *Fourth Estate*, Apr. 2013, www.4thestate. co.uk/2013/04/of-course-i-never-said-african-women-with-brazilian-hair-have-low-self-esteem-thats-absurd/.

'A Year in Reading: Chimamanda Ngozi Adichie.' *The Millions*, 6 Dec. 2013, www.themillions.com/2013/12/a-year-in-reading-chimamanda-ngozi-adichie.html.

Beyoncé, featuring Chimamanda Ngozi Adichie. 'Flawless' (Audio). *Beyoncé*, Parkwood and Columbia, 2013. Features excerpts from 'We Should All Be Feminists,' read by Chimamand Ngozi Adichie.

'Binyavanga Wainaina: The Memoirist with a Mission.' *Time*, 23 Apr. 2014, time.com/70795/binyavanga-wainaina-time-100/.

'Ifem & Ceiling 1.' *The Small Redemptions of Lagos*, 24 Aug. 2014, americanahblog.com/2014/08/27/ifem-ceiling/.

'Problem and Solution 1.' *The Small Redemptions of Lagos*, 27 Aug. 2014, americanahblog.com/2014/08/27/problem-and-solution-1/.

'Problem and Solution 2.' *The Small Redemptions of Lagos*, 27 Aug. 2014, americanahblog.com/2014/08/27/problem-and-solution-2/.

'Aruidimma 1.' *The Small Redemptions of Lagos*, 28 Aug. 2014, americanahblog.com/2014/08/28/aruidimma-1/.

'Problem and Solution 3.' *The Small Redemptions of Lagos*, 28 Aug. 2014, americanahblog.com/2014/08/28/problem-and-solution-3/.

'POTFRN 1.' *The Small Redemptions of Lagos*, 1 Sept. 2014, americanahblog. com/2014/09/01/potfrn-1/

'Style 1.' *The Small Redemptions of Lagos*, 1 Sept. 2014, americanahblog. com/2014/09/01/style-1/

'We Admire 1.' *The Small Redemptions of Lagos*, 1 Sept. 2014, americanahblog.com/2014/09/01/we-admire-1/.

'Ifem & Ceiling 2.' *The Small Redemptions of Lagos*, 4 Sept. 2014, americanahblog.com/2014/09/04/ifem-ceiling-2/.

'Problem and Solution 4.' *The Small Redemptions of Lagos*, 4 Sept. 2014, americanahblog.com/2014/09/04/problem-and-solution-4/.

'We Admire 2.' *The Small Redemptions of Lagos*, 5 Sept. 2014, americanahblog.com/2014/09/05/we-admire-2/

'Aruidimma 2.' *The Small Redemptions of Lagos*, 9 Sept. 2014, americanahblog.com/2014/09/09/aruidimma-2/.

'Ifem & Ceiling 3.' *The Small Redemptions of Lagos*, 10 Sept. 2014, americanahblog.com/2014/09/10/ifem-ceiling-3/.

'Aruidimma 3.' *The Small Redemptions of Lagos*, 11 Sept. 2014, americanahblog.com/2014/09/11/aruidimma-3/.

'Ifem & Ceiling 4.' *The Small Redemptions of Lagos*, 16 Sept. 2014, americanahblog.com/2014/09/16/ifem-ceiling-4/.

'Problem and Solution 5.' *The Small Redemptions of Lagos*, 17 Sept. 2014, americanahblog.com/2014/09/17/problem-and-solution-5/.

'Ifem & Ceiling 5.' *The Small Redemptions of Lagos*, 18 Sept. 2014, americanahblog.com/2014/09/18/ifem-ceiling-5/.

'Style 2.' *The Small Redemptions of Lagos*, 19 Sept. 2014, americanahblog. com/2014/09/19/style-2/

'Style 3.' *The Small Redemptions of Lagos*, 19 Sept. 2014, americanahblog. com/2014/10/31/style-3/

'Ifem & Ceiling 6.' *The Small Redemptions of Lagos*, 24 Oct. 2014, americanahblog.com/2014/10/24/ifem-ceiling-6/.

'Problem and Solution 6.' *The Small Redemptions of Lagos*, 24 Oct. 2014, americanahblog.com/2014/10/24/problem-and-solution-6/.

'Problem and Solution 7.' *The Small Redemptions of Lagos*, 24 Oct. 2014, americanahblog.com/2014/10/24/problem-and-solution-7-2/.

'Ifem & Ceiling 7.' *The Small Redemptions of Lagos*, 26 Oct. 2014, americanahblog.com/2014/10/26/ifem-ceiling-7/.

'Ifem & Ceiling 8.' *The Small Redemptions of Lagos*, 27 Oct. 2014, americanahblog.com/2014/10/27/ifem-ceiling-8/.

'Aruidimma 4.' *The Small Redemptions of Lagos*, 28 Oct. 2014, americanahblog.com/2014/10/28/aruidimma-4/.

'Problem and Solution 8.' *The Small Redemptions of Lagos*, 29 Oct. 2014, americanahblog.com/2014/10/29/problem-and-solution-8/.

'Problem and Solution 9.' *The Small Redemptions of Lagos*, 2 Nov. 2014, americanahblog.com/2014/11/02/problem-and-solution-9/.

'Chimamanda Ngozi Adichie on Winning the Best of the Best.' *YouTube*, uploaded by Women's Prize for Fiction, 4 Nov. 2015, www. youtube.com/watch?v=dZ60FcGeom4.

International Best Dressed List, *Vanity Fair*, Sept. 2016, www.vanityfair. com/international-best-dressed-list-2016/photos/women. Chima-manda Ngozi Adichie lists her favourite clothes, designers, shoes, etc.

Index

Abani, Chris, 3
Abba, 132
Abel, Elizabeth, 232
abuse, 35, 79, 82, 84, 109–10
acculturation, 102
Achebe, Chinua, 8, 15–16, 3, 90,
    139–41, 145–9, 155–6, 158, 160,
    171; works: *A Man of the People*,
    142, *Home and Exile*, 15; *Things
    Fall Apart*, 22–3
Adams, Marie Ann, 135, 137
Adesokan, Akin, 74
Adichie, Chimamanda N, 1, 7–8,
    16, 28, 31–2, 37, 40, 47, 50, 73,
    115, 119, 123, 171, 177; works:
    Americanah, 1, 10–11, 20; *Half
    of a Yellow Sun*, 7, 22; *Purple
    Hibiscus*, 20, 26, 31, 45, 57, 60,
    73; *The Danger of a Single Story*;
    2, 11–12; *The Thing Around Your
    Neck*, 9, 23
adulthood, 76, 78
Africa/African, 174, 220
    authenticity, 219
    bourgeois, 141, 148
    children, 73, 103
    civil wars, 130, 132, 137, 140
    colonialism, 21, 90, 186
    colonialist literature, 15–17, 21, 25
    contemporary, 66
    contemporary novelists, 106
    cosmology, 57, 58–9
    culture, 54

destiny, 174
diaspora, 10, 199, 213, 216
family, 69, 74, 76
francophone, 102
identity, 102, 172, 185, 203, 219
immigrants, 215, 217, 225
masks, 251; Benin masks, 177,
    251; 'mask dancing,' 103
middle class, 79; homes 73
migration, 216, 221
multiplicity, 174
people, 15–17, 220
poetic productivity, 182
politicians, 146
postcolonial identity, 102
post-independence, 129, 141
precolonial, 18
'single story', 204
stereotypes, 117, 202
women, 5, 34, 50, 58, 66–7,
    69–70, 88, 159
writers, 106, 141
African and African Diaspora
    Artists Visit Series, 3–4
African Literature, 31, 59, 70, 120,
    139, 171, 213
    African diaspora writers, 215
    fiction, 101–2; post-
    independence, 102–3
    francophone, 102
    literary discourse, 101
africanness, 240
africanization, 146

Index

Agbalajobi, Damilola T, 32
agency of voice, 105
agency, 69, 82, 177, 179, 229, 236
Aidoo, Ama Ata, 213–14
Akintola, Sardauna, 141
Akujobi, Remi, 58
alienation, 221–22, 226, 230, 232
Alkali, Zaynab, 104
Amadiume, Ifi, 115–16
America, 148; North America, 199
   African American, 215–17, 226
   Blacks (AB), 237, 239, 240
   citizenship, 210
   civil history, 154
   cultural space, 189, 191–2
   diasporic life in, 190
   dream, 194, 199, 204
   green card, 191, 194, 196
   white identity, 203
   immigration, 229
   non-American Blacks, 224, 237,
     239, 256
   preconceived notions, 194
americanization, 221
americanness, 204
Anderson, Benedict, 236–7
anti-colonial, 26. *See also*
   colonialism.
anti-essentialist, 18
anti-woman, 49
Anya, Ike, 139
Anyanwu, Chikwendu P K, 8–9
Appadurai, Arjun, 200
archaeology of space, 87, 91, 92,
   95, 98
archetype, 33, 109, 111, 129
Armah, Ayi Kwei, 142; works: *The*
   Beautyful Ones Are Not Yet Born,
   The Interpreters, 142
art, 11, 18, 31, 170
Atta, Sefi, 213–14, 245
authenticity, 172, 226
authorial sensitivity, 83
Azikwe, Nnamdi ('Zik'), 20, 143
Azuah, Unoma, 245

bad silence, 41
Balewa, Tafawa, 143, 148
beauty, western, 246
Beauvoir, De Simone, 33, 60–61
Beilke, Debra, 74
Bennett, Christopher, 74
Berlin, Ira, 216
Beti, Mongo, 101
Bhabha, Homi K., 195
Biafra, 7, 23, 91, 135, 164–5.
   'Affia attack,' 91
   ambition, 135
   birth of, 142
   children, 164
   collapse, 136
   factors, 116
   food shortage, 90–1, 133, 136
   people, 115, 133, 164; civilian
     population, 129
   post-war, 149, 164
   rebels, 132
   secession, 116, 121–2, 130, 132,
     136
   soldiers, 164
   story, 123
   territory, 131
   women, 156, 161–2, 166
   war/conflict, 90, 132–6, 142,
     164. *See also* Nigeria civil war
   war narrative, 156–7
   writers, 7
biblical dictum, 77
bildungsroman, 11, 73–4, 104, 230,
   241; migrant bildungsroman,
   232; female bildungsroman, 232;
   African bildungsroman, 232
binary opposition, 31–3, 36, 39,
   41–2, 92
binary, construction, 153–4
birth of the novel, 16
birth, 68
black body, 206
black diaspora, 103
black identity, 102
black immigrant, 215, 225

Index

black womanhood, 256
blackness, 206, 224–5
Blassingame, John, 45
blog, 224, 236, 239–40
body and city interactions, 88
body politics, 87, 245
Boehmer, Elleke, 74
Boyce-Davies, Carole, 229, 230, 232, 234, 236
brain drain, 73
Britain, 141, 143, 148
Britain, 16–17; conceptualization of literature, 19; colonial domination, 27–8
British colonization, 186
British Crown Colony, 186
British University System, 19
Brutus, Dennis, 3
Bryce, Jane, 73, 245
Bulawayo, No Violet, 213–14
Byrd, Ayanna, 246–9, 256

caged-opposition, 39
Calkin, Jessamy, 245
Caribbean, 216
Carotenuto, Silvana, 9, 177, 182
Caruth, Cathy, 121, 124
Catholic father, 60
Catholic paterfamilias, 80
Catholic rituals, 74
Catholicism, 36, 78, 82–83
censorship, 73
Cervenka, Zdenek, 131, 133, 136
Cheng, Anne, 203
child hero, 101–2, 104
child narration, 101, 105, 107–11
child narrator, 103, 108
childhood abuse, 76
childhood, 76, 101–4, 106
Chimborazo, 74
Christ, Jesus, 68, 94
Christian cosmology, 68
Christianity, 60–61, 80, 140, 147
Chude-Sokei, Louis, 224
Chukwuma, Helen, 18

citizenship, 210
Cixous, Hélène, 169–70, 172
class, 201, 240
Clifford, James, 199, 207
Cockburn, Cockburn, 134
Coetzee, J.M., 40, 125
Cohen, Carol, 154
Coker, Oluwole, 6
Collins, Hill, 256
Collins, Walter, 232
colonial rule, 24. *See also* colonialism and postcolonial studies
colonial space, 87
colonial, education, 102
colonialism, 10, 19–20, 24–5, 26, 37, 87, 89–90, 116, 125, 136, 140, 145–8, 169; European colonialism, 204
colonized consciousness, 109
colonizers, 87
coming of age, 104
communion, 74
conceptualization pattern, 47
conformism, 60
contrapuntal modernity, 207
Cooper, Brenda, 74, 80
coping mechanism, 80, 217
corporeality, 91
Cruz-Gutiérrez, Cristina 11
Culler, Jonathan, 39
cultural assimilation, 186–8, 191, 193–4, 200, 209, 215, 218
cultural behaviour, 32
cultural difference, 245
cultural expectations, 95
cultural history, 6, 98
cultural identity, 213–14, 226
cultural memory, 10, 187, 195–6
cultural space, 188–9, 191–6
culture, defined, 175,
culture, participatory, 247

Da Silva, Denise Ferreiro, 169, 178
Dawes, Kwame, 11

Index

Dayal, Samir, 216
de Pauw, Linda Grant, 153
decolonization, 19, 21, 26, 116, 187. *See also* colonialism and postcolonial studies.
deconstruction, 31, 39, 42, 105; postcolonial deconstruction, 159
deconstructionist, 122
deconstructive, 37; (reading), 159
Defoe, Daniel; works: *Robinson Crusoe*, 16
dehumanization, 69, 107, 222
deterritorialization, 230, 233
Department of Africana Studies, Flint, 3
Derrida, Jacques, 41, 122, 125, 154–5, 158
Desai, S.K., 103
diaspora identity, 213, 219
diaspora, 223
diasporic cultures, 45
dictatorship, 66, 73
difference, 170, 216, 219–20. *See also* otherness
dining room, 93–6
Diop, David, 59
dislocation, 185, 187–9, 194–6
displacement, 130, 132, 169
divided self, 216
divine responsibility, 75
Dodgson-Katiyo, Pauline, 8
domestic abuse, 75, 83. *See also* abuse
dominance, 33, 60; (oppressive) dominance, 66–7
double telling, 121
double consciousness, 10, 21, 214–17, 223–5,
doubleness, 10, 218, 221, 224
doubling, 214, 217
Du Bois, W.E.B., 21, 215–16, 225
Duboisian framework, 216–17, 223
Duran, Jane, 5
Durrant, Sam, 118, 125

Eagleton, Terry, 35
Eckstein, Harry, 158
Edgar, Nabutanyi, 6
education, 20–21
Egbunike, Louisa Uchum, 5
Ekwensi, Cyprian, 159, 165
Ellington, Tameka, 247, 248
Elshtain, Jean Bethke, 153–4
embodied subjectivity, 91
Emecheta, Buchi, 3, 50, 103, 137, 154; works: *The Joys of Motherhood*, 59, 65
Emenyonu, Ernest N., 140
Equiano, Olaudah, 26
Erickson, Eric, 129–30
essentialism, 46
ethnicity, 135, 154
eucharist, 94–5
Europe, 15, 199, 204, 216
European bourgeoisie, 141
European cultural space, 186
European Literature, 232
Europeans, 90
Evans, Diana, 245
exile, 169
exorcism, 122
Ezeigbo, Akachi Adimora, 157–60, 164

falsification, unmasking of, 180
familial intergenerational experiences, 26
family style, 51
family values, 106
family, 26, 57–8, 60, 63, 79
Fanon, Frantz, 140–1
father-figure, 105
feet washing, 76–7
female, 6, 33, 45, 92, 153
    activism, 159
    alterity, 173
    antagonism, 164
    body, 95, 97; black, 170
    characters, 54–5, 245
    difference, 170

Index

emancipation, 159
erasure, 96
heroism, 154, 165–6,
militarization, 164
misogyny, 172
radicalization, 158
space, 95
(black) subjectivity, 229
voices, 96
feminism, 2, 41, 88, 104, 111, 153,
    170, 172;
  black feminism, 245
  feminist theory, 88
  feminist, 5, 110, 159; African
  feminist, 103, 165; materialist
    feminist, 87, 92
  nego-feminist, 250; western
    feminist, 88
femininity, 78, 105, 153–4, 173,
    175, 246
fertility rites, 68
Fetterly, Judith, 154, 159
fiction, 6, 18
figurines, 35, 74, 80
first-person narrator, 83, 109
first-person perspective, 76
flexible citizenship, 207
Flint Public Library, 3
Fonchingong, Charles, 105
food, 89, 92
food knowledge, 97–8
food spaces, 95, 98
Foucault, Michel, 87
fragile negotiations, 117, 122
Frank, Reanne, 208
French policy of Assimilation,
  102
French Revolution, 19
Freud, Sigmund, 117–18, 122, 125

gender, defined, 87
  assumptions, 32
  behaviour, 32
  construct, 52, 103
  dichotomies/binaries, 32, 153

dimensions, 102
disposition, 32, 41
dynamics, 174
equality, 32
expectation, 158
fragmentation, 154
hierarchies, 32, 42
identity, 32
inequality, 163
inequity, 73
norm, 172
point of view, 225
roles, 2, 130, 134
subordination, 205
theorizing, 101
Gikandi, Simon, 140, 146
Gilroy, Paul, 207, 210, 215
God's law, 76–7
goddess, 58
good child/ good wife, 79
Gowon, Yakubu, 115, 143, 155
Green, Martin, 17
Greene, Andrée, 107, 111
Grosz, Elizabeth, 87–9, 91, 98
Guarracino, Serena, 256–7
Guarnizo, Luis E., 208
Guatarri and Deleuze, 230
Gurr, Ted R., 158

hair politics, 11, 236, 245–58,
  big chop, 246, 249, 251–2, 255
  hair, movement, 246–7; natural
  hair movement, 246–8
  black hair, 246
Hall, Stuart, 207
Halter, Marilyn, 224
Hanchard, Michael, 236
Harney, Stephano, 169–70
Harris, Wilson, 125
Hausa culture, 45; involvement in
  civil war, 187
Hausa-Fulani, 187
heathen, 76
hegemony (male-female), 163
Hewett, Heather, 74, 105, 139, 145

Index

hierarchy, 34
Hirsch, Marianne, 232
historians (European), 19
historical negation, 173
historicism (European), 19
history, 15, 17–19, 28, 92, 117, 149;
　resistance, 27
holy water, 74
home, 106, 219, 213, 226
homeland, 220
Hron, Madeleine, 73

identity, 200–1, 209–10, 225–6,
　245–6,
　African American, *see* America
　conflict, 220
　confusion, 226
　crisis, 187–8, 191–3, 214
　parallel identity, 200, 209–10
ideology, 11, 31, 33, 201
Igbo, 45–7, 146–7, 187
　Adichie and Igbo, 5, 12
　anti-Igbo, 155, 162
　English and Igbo, 82
　ethnic group in Nigeria, 187
　Catholicism and Igbo, 83
　colonialist literature, 22
　coup, 142
　culture, 25, 49, 92, 109
　epistemology, 17, 19, 28
　government, 89
　'masquerades', 147
　novel, 18–19, 146. *See also*
　　Nwana, Pita
　Oral Literature, 18
　oral narrative, 5, 16
　oral tradition, 5, 19, 140
　people, 22
　philosophy, 17–18
　society, 46, 146
　spirituality, 146
　traditional narrator, 12
　women, 45, 48, 50–2, 90–1, 93,
　　98, 130, 163, 166; (writers),
　　154

Igboland, 89; (postwar)
　Igboland, 91
Ijomah, B.I.C, 19
IMF/ World bank, 33, 107
individual effort, 32
innocence, 103
intentionality, 69
intertextuality, 74
Irele, Abiola, 18
Ironsi, Aguiyi, 142

Jaja of Opobo, 27–8
Johnson, Violet Showers, 224
Jorre, de St., 134
Jones, Gayl, 239

Kaplan, Caren, 230, 233, 235
Kehinde, Ayo, 108–8
kitchen dinner table, 89
kitchens, 94–6, 98
kleptocrats, 107
Knopf, Alfred A., 186
knowledge, 17, 21, 97
Kurtz, Roger J, 74
Kuti, Fela Ransome, 40

Landolt, Patricia, 208
Laye, Camara, 58, 101–2, 171
liberation, 26
Liberia, 132
Lindfors, Bernth, 145
Lispector, Clarice, 175
literary imagination, 101, 103–4
Lok, John, 16
low self-esteem, 59
Lozanno-Ascecio, 208
Lyons, Barry J, 74, 83

Madieba, Alexander, 141
MacIntosh, Peggy, 237
Magona, Sindiwe, 3
male, 57, 60, 62, 67, 92
　domination, 120
　heroism, 154
　sexual instinct, 68

Index

supremacy, 33
'malestream' literature, 104
man, 32, 38–9. *See also* male
marriage, 39, 58–60, 80
masculine hegemony, 158
masculinism, 70, 153–4, 156
masculinity, 97, 154, 161
materialism, 146
maternity, 57
matrilineal construction, 45
matrilineality, 54
Mbarga, Prince N, 59
Mbembe, Achille, 169, 172–3, 177, 179, 180–2
Mbiti, John S, 58
McInelly, Brett C, 16, 17
melancholia, 117–20, 125–6
melancholia, racial, 204
melancholy, 119
memory, 122, 170
Mengel, Ewald, 83
menstruation, 68, 77–8
metonymic freezing, 202
metropolitan modernity, 200
migrant, transnational, 208
migration, 9–10, 169, 205, 213
migration (immigration), 176, 187, 219, 226
migration, Mexican, 208
migration/migrant narrative, 199, 205
military dictatorship, 26, 74
Mills, Sarah, 87, 89, 92, 95, 98
mind versus body binary, 88, 92
misogynist, 78
Misra, Maitrayee, 9–10
missal, 74
Mitchell, Whitney, 41
modernist, 210
Mohammed, Murtala, 142
Mollinger, Robert, 105
moral order, 83–4
Morrison, Toni, 125
Moten, Fred, 169–70
motherhood, 57–9, 64, 66, 164

Mozambique, 132
multi-locality, 210, 225
Mulvey, Laura, 253

narrative, 121, 137
narrative of resistance, 27. *See also* Biafra, Nigerian Literature, war narrative
nature versus culture binary, 88
Ndibe, Okey, 213–14
Ndĩgĩrĩgĩ, Gĩchingiri, 10
Ndula, Janet, 5
negritude, 102
negritudists, 102
neo colony, 200
neo-liberal policies, 33
New World, 54
Ngcobo, Lauretta, 58
Ngũgĩ wa Thiong'o, 3
Nigeria
    civil war, 7–8, 90, 133, 115, 155, 157, 159–62, 164. *See also* Biafra
    contemporary, 145
    contemporary fiction, 101
    context, 105
    corruption, 149
    domestic space, 130
    Eastern Nigeria, 133
    education, 19
    elite, 131
    government, 136
    history, 137
    identity, 187, 218–19
    immigrant, 215–16, 226
    independence, 141, 148
    military rule, 27–8, 130–1
    Nigeria-Biafra, 154
    postcolonial, 60, 88, 90–91
    post-independence, 105, 107, 140, 148, 110–11
    secession in, 150 *See also* Biafra
    Southern Nigeria, 90
    upper class, 142
    women, 92, 188, 190
Nigerian Literature, 74, 103–5,

Index

139; fiction, 245
civil war novel, 7–8, 129
war narrative, 154–5, 157, 161,
165. *See also* Biafra war
narrative
Njoku, Carol I, 8
Njoku, Rose Adaure, 154
Nnaemeka, Obioma, 69, 154, 250
non-Igbo, 94
non-mothering women, 59
non-people, 94
non-women, 94
novel, 16, 22, 104
Nwana, Pita, 18, 146
Nwankwo, Reginald, 157
Nwapa, Flora, 59, 104, 120, 154,
158, 160–1, 165
Nzegwu, Nkiru N, 33
Nzeogwu, Chukwu Kaduna, 142–3

Oates, Joyce Carol, 139–40
Obama, Barrack, 202
Obama, Michelle, 257
Obiechina, Emmanuel, 19–20, 142
Odugo, Juliet, 159, 165
Ogundipe-Leslie, Molara, 31, 60
Ogunyemi, Chikwenye, 59, 65, 70
Ojukwu, Odemegwu, 115, 155
Okekwe, Promise, 245
Okigbo, Christopher, 59, 115, 117
Okolie, M, 102
Okpewho, Isidore, 155–6, 158,
163
Okri, Ben, 101, 104
Okuyade, Ogaga, 74, 110
Omotosho, Kole, 155–8, 163
Ong, Aihwa, 200, 206–7, 210
oppression, 26–7, 36, 73; (racial),
125
orality, 17–18, 19
ori-akpa festival, 147
orientalism, 204
Orwell, Goerge, 141
Osaghae, Eghosa E., 141
Osofisan, Femi, 3

Osundare, Niyi, 3
otherness, 216, 225
Oyeyemi, Helen, 245
Oyono, Ferdinand, 102

p'Bitek, Okot, 193
palm fronds, 74
participant-observer, 47, 201, 206
passivity, 37
patriarchal pride, 78
patriarchy, 103, 105, 109–10, 153,
155, 158–61, 164, 166, 169, 172,
178, 205, 252, 256, 258
perpetrator, 75
pioneer African writers, 10
Piza-Lopez, Eugenia, 42
plurality, 207
Portes, Alejandro, 208
Post Freudian Psychology, 64
postcolonial Igbo Literature, 89
postcolonial studies, 10, 15, 87–9,
175, 186; postcolonial (Africa),
73; postcolonial literature, 88,
109, 125
post-traumatic recovery, 84
power structures, 33
power, 41, 97, 172, 178
Pratt, Mary Louise, 199–200, 208
priestess, 59
psychoanalysis, 101, 117, 123
public and private spheres, 95
public versus private binaries, 8,
92
purification, 75
purple, 60

race, 201, 205
colonized consciousness, 109
glorification, 172
hyperconsciousness of, 207
racial boundaries, 216
racial consciousness, 200
racial identity, 208
racism, 224, 230, 240
Raz, Guy, 187

realism, 224
reincarnation, 25, 122
religion, 33, 39, 41, 46, 58, 67, 80, 154
religious fanaticism, 73
religious rituals, 77
representational essentializing, 202
representative of God, 59
repression, 107
resisting subject, 234
re-symbolism, 102
Rich, Adrienne, 62–3, 159
rite of passage, 67
Roberts, Bryan R., 208
romanticism, 46
Rosowki, Susan, 232
Rushdie, Salman, 229, 232
Rwanda, 132

Saadawi, El Nawal, 3, 193
Sackeyfio, Rose A, 10
Said, Edward, 169–70, 173–4, 204
Salaam, Titi, 32
Saro-Wiwa, Zina, 252, 255
Selasi, Taiye, 249
Sanchez, Sonia, 171
Sartre, Jean Paul, 208
Sartrean existentialism, 120
Schumm, Jeremiah, 76
secession, 132; secessionist, 130
self-esteem, 60
Senghor, Léopold S., 59
sex difference, 32
sexual abuse, 178
sexual freedom, 97
sexuality, 97–8, 154, 236
Shakespeare, Judith, 163
Shobat and Stam, 87, 97. See also vestigial thinking
Shrivastava, Manish, 9–10
silence, 35–8, 107; deliberate silence, 40
'single story', 172
sinners, 75
Siver, Wirngo, 194

Skinner, Elliot P., 216
Smith, Courtney, 58
Smith, Harold, 141
Smith, Tracy K., 169
social position, 97–8
social relations, 47
social value, 96
socialization, 33
Sofola, Zulu, 59
South America, 216
Soyinka, Wole, 3, 116, 122, 142
space, 97–8
speech, 37
spirituality, 82
Spivak, Gayatri C., 159, 169
Spleth, Janice, 8
storytelling, 17, 155
Stowe, Harriet Beecher, 223
Stratton, Florence, 41, 120
structuralism, 31
subjectivity, 210, 225
subjugation, 36, 41, 63, 93, 161, 163
Sundiata and Chaka; *Days of Glory* [1944 film], 129
suppression, 107
Surdakasa, Naria, 88, 92
symbolism, 58

Taiwo, Olufemi, 224
'Teaching African Literature', 4
territoriality, 210
Thiam, Awa, 159
Tharps, Lori, 246–9, 256
Thompson, Cheryl, 246
tradition/ traditional constructs, 33, 38, 39
traditional power, 41
traditionalists, 50
transcultural identity, 10, 185, 194, 187–8
transculturation, 199. *See also* migration
transgression, 78–9
translocality, 207
transnational borders, 216

transnational identity, 215. *See also* transcultural identity
transnational mobility, 204
transnational spaces, 219
transnationalism, 206, 208, 210, 215
transplantation, 200
trauma, 83–4, 107, 117, 120–6, 188
travel literature, 211
'Triumphant Entry', 94
truth, 18
Tuma, Hama, 107
Tunca, Daria, 80, 110, 263
Turshen, Meredeth, 132
Tutuola, Amos, 193
tyranny, 60, 63

Uchendu, Egodi, 157
Uko, Ini, 6
Umuahia, 133, 135–6
underdevelopment, 101
Unigwe, Chika, 245
United States Agency for International Development, 129
University of Michigan-Flint, 3–4
University of Nigeria, Nsukka, 19–20, 130–1, 143, 149, 162

Vervotec, Steven, 206, 210
vestigial thinking, 87, 97
Vickroy, Laurie, 125
victim, good, 41
victimhood, 66
violence, 35, 60, 63, 77, 83. See also *domestic abuse*
voice, 66, 106

Vranceanu, Ana M, 76

Wallace, Cynthia, 140
Walter, Bronwen, 137
war narrative, 129. *See also* Biafra, narrative of resistance, Nigerian Literature
weak binary pair, 40
West Africa, 46, 52
West African men, 88
West African tradition, 54
West African women, 53–4
Wilkinson, Carl, 187
Williams, Ruth, 60
Wilson-Tagoe, Nana, 19
womanhood, 165
womanist, 166
women, 32–3, 35, 38–9, 45, 90, 96–7; women's fiction, 41; Black women's socialization, 246; (traditional), 95; (unconventional), 48–49, 57–60, 62; women in war, 132, 137, 154, 161. *See also* female, gender
Woolf, Virginia, 163
World War II/ Second World War, 134, 154

Yoruba
gender-construct, 52
involvement in civil war, 187
precolonial, 33
women, 45

'Zik' 20, 143 *See* Azikwe, Nnamdi